# MINAS GERAIS
## in the Brazilian Federation
### 1889-1937

# MINAS GERAIS
## in the Brazilian Federation
### 1889-1937

JOHN D. WIRTH

STANFORD UNIVERSITY PRESS

Stanford, California   1977

Sources of photographs on pp. 127–32: 1. Author. 2. Casa Ruy
Barbosa, Rio de Janeiro. 3. Roberto Capri, *O Estado de Minas
Geraes* (Belo Horizonte, 1918). 4. Nelson Coelho de Senna,
*Annuario de Minas Geraes* (Belo Horizonte, 1906–18), vol. 6.
5. *Revista Industrial de Minas Geraes,* vol. 5, no. 36 (Dec. 30,
1897). 6. Biblioteca Nacional, Rio de Janeiro. 7. Nelson Coelho
de Senna, *Annuario de Minas Geraes,* vol. 5. 8. Mineiridade
Collection, Biblioteca Pública Mineira, Belo Horizonte. 9 and 10.
*O Estado de Minas* Photo Archive, Belo Horizonte.

Stanford University Press
Stanford, California
© 1977 by the Board of Trustees of the
Leland Stanford Junior University
Printed in the United States of America
ISBN 0-8047-0932-7
LC 76-23373

To Nancy

# Preface

To my colleagues, Robert M. Levine and Joseph L. Love, I am thankful for the opportunity to have worked so long and intimately with them on this collaborative research effort. We remained in frequent contact with one another from the early conversations about a joint project to the last stages of editing. The volume outlines are similar, not only from chapter to chapter but, as far as feasible, within each chapter itself. Though we attempted to keep repetition at a minimum, each book necessarily draws on a common stock of information that was freely shared throughout the research and writing. Many tasks were shared, while others were assigned individually. Love and Wirth compiled the code book for the collective biographies of the three state political elites; Levine and Love designed the SPSS program for the comparative biographical study. We spent twelve months in 1969–70 in Brazil, and met three times. Later, Love and Wirth spent a summer in Rio and Brasília, and Levine worked in the Public Record Office in London. We arranged to meet at least once a year since 1967.

Research funds for my own work on Minas Gerais were provided by the Foreign Area Fellowship Program of the Social Science Research Council and Stanford's Committee for Research in International Studies. In addition, the Center for Latin American Studies at Stanford provided small grants for a conference and photocopying. Most of this book was written at St. John's College in Santa Fe; I thank Vice President J. Burchenal Ault for his many kindnesses.

Readers will note changes in Portuguese orthography since the late nineteenth century. Conventionally, one cites author-title information as given on the title page while using modern spelling for words, proper names, and places in the text. Until 1942, the milreis was the currency of Brazil. The conto, which is one thousand milreis (written 1:000$000), was the largest monetary unit. On November 1, 1942, the milreis was replaced by the cruzeiro, one milreis (1$000) being equivalent to one cruzeiro (cr$1,00). Dollar equivalents are given in Appendix C.

I am grateful to Francisco Iglésias for his professional guidance and companionship. José Murilo de Carvalho gave the galley proofs a very thoughtful reading. Hélio Gravatá helped me in many ways. Among the researchers who assisted me, Pedro Soares, Michael Lee Conniff, Eduardo Dutra Aydos, Benício Schmidt, and Caetana de Oliveira deserve commendation. Personnel at the Biblioteca Pública Mineira were accommodating and efficient. I can say the same for employees at the other archives I consulted in Minas and Rio, including the Arquivo Público Mineiro, the Casa Ruy Barbosa, and the Arquivo Nacional. The Biblioteca Nacional in Rio provided a range of services and a good place to work.

My wife Nancy and the three boys shared this scholarly adventure, and I appreciate their companionship and patience.

JOHN D. WIRTH

*Stanford University*
*April 12, 1976*

# Contents

*Six pages of photographs follow p. 126*

# Figures and Tables

# Introduction

THIS IS ONE of three independent but coordinated studies on the regional dynamics of Brazilian federalism from the beginning of the Republic in 1889 to the establishment of the Estado Novo in 1937. The objective is to write comparative history from the regional perspective, that is, to pinpoint similarities and differences among three leading states, while identifying modes of interaction at the national level. The role of São Paulo, which is located in the Center-South, and which received the greatest benefits from export-led growth, is examined by Joseph L. Love. Politically powerful Minas Gerais, situated between the prosperous southern states and the impoverished Northeast, is analyzed by John D. Wirth. Pernambuco, the Northeast's most important state, is treated by Robert M. Levine as a case study in political and economic decline.

The period under study begins with the devolution of power from the centralized Empire to the states, and follows the course of the Union's gradual assumption of authority and responsibility over the ensuing half-century. Recentralization began well before the "Old Republic" (1889–1930) was abolished by coup d'état in 1930; it was formally and stridently proclaimed by the Estado Novo dictatorship, Getúlio Vargas's unitary regime from 1937 to 1945.

Our purpose is to bring together insights into the complex dynamics of state-level social and political structures, which have always been crucial in Brazil, but particularly during the nation's most decentralized phase, the years under study. Political events define the chronological limits of these studies, yet the coups of 1889 and 1937 and the very different constitutions that attended them are partly arbitrary benchmarks. Important political events in the states did not always mirror national events, nor did they bear the same meaning. Moreover, the neatness of this periodization is blurred by socioeconomic continuities that dilute the impact of what historians used to call "turning points." We refer both to the historic North-South shift in power and resources, which started around 1850 and rendered the Northeast an internal colony of the dynamic South, and also to the modernizing forces—social differentiation, urbanization, the growing internal market—which the political events overlay.

Though the issues of federalism are ostensibly a set of political problems, the economic, social, and cultural contexts receive extensive treatment in these books. This fact is evident from the format of the studies, which are organized on thematic rather than chronological lines. To calibrate change over time, however, each author used a chronology appropriate to his own state while relating regional events to those at the national level and those in the other states.

We also use the concept of political generations to order the several themes. Leaders born before 1869 were socialized under the Empire, with its centralized bureaucracy. Those born in the 20 years before 1889 knew the Republic as young men in the period of its greatest decentralization. Leaders in the third political generation came of age after 1910, when the impetus for a more integrated polity affected the military, fiscal, and economic policies of the nation and the states. The origins, career expectations, and experiences of these three political generations are discussed in Chapter 5. Generational analysis also informs the chapter on integration which follows it.

These volumes explore the regional dimensions of change, adaptation, and rigidities of the Old Republic and the initial phase of the Vargas government. Structural changes were extensive: in the economy, coffee and rubber exports reached their apogee and went into sharp decline; manufacturing underwent its initial surge in a complicated set of rhythms. For much of this period economic growth was largely dependent on exports and foreign capital, including investments in government bonds for infrastructural development. By the 1930's, Brazil had shifted its dependence in financial and economic affairs from Great Britain to the United States. This coincided with the acceleration of industrialization by import substitution.

Brazilian society likewise was transformed: the nation received a net inflow of between two and one-half and three million immigrants in the years 1889–1937, more than any other comparable period in its history. By the 1930's, internal migration was also greater than in any previous decade. Rapid urbanization and improvements in public health accompanied these population shifts. By 1940 the nation had two cities, Rio de Janeiro and São Paulo, with populations over one million, and 21 other cities with populations in excess of 100,000. In the cities the early labor movement was the crucible for anarchist and communist activity, only to be channeled and controlled from the top down by a government apparatus in the 1930's. In the complex interplay between federal and state units, government assumed new tasks not only in social control but also in social welfare, education at all levels (grossly neglected before 1889), and commodity marketing inside and outside the country. The period under study was also the classic age of banditry and messianism, principally but not exclusively in the Northeast, though both phenomena were vestigial by the time of the Estado Novo.

The political system established by the constitution of 1891 seemed anomalous in Latin America, even anachronistic in light of the centralizing tendencies in Mexico, Colombia, and Argentina. Yet a decentralized Republic suited the interests of powerful export-oriented groups, and the ancient patron-client system found its political expression in the *política dos governadores* by 1900. This system, directed by the president of the Republic and the governors of São Paulo and Minas Gerais, was an arrangement for the mutual support of incumbent elites at all levels of government. With a preponderantly rural population and low levels of political participation (only 1–3 percent of the population voted in federal elections before 1930), *coronelismo*—boss rule—prevailed in the countryside and made urban political groupings irrelevant until the 1920's. Without the moderating power of the Empire to remove incumbents from office, the Republic had no constitutional solution to the problem of entrenched establishments. Violence at local, state, and federal levels remained an indispensable tool in politics, sometimes involving the army, sometimes not.

In the 1930's Vargas consciously pursued a policy of deinstitutionalization of the most important state machines of the Old Republic— the Republican Parties of Minas Gerais, São Paulo, and Rio Grande do Sul. Meanwhile new antiliberal parties on right and left threatened the hybrid liberal-corporatist constitution of 1934. The Estado Novo dictatorship, outlawing all parties, was the culmination of the effort to depoliticize Brazil, as well as to centralize its government; yet success was limited, as our examination of the states reveals.

States are the units of analysis because they were the foci of political loyalty and political organization: there were no enduring national or multistate parties in the era in question. Even Pernambuco usually behaved as a politically self-centered region, despite its being the "natural" leader of the Northeast. In fact, Pernambuco's failure to marshal the Northeast as a bloc in Congress is an important theme in that state's history. Aspects of regionalism that did not follow state boundaries—markets, for example—are examined, but for the most part these books focus on the states.

We believe the three states covered were the logical choice for study, especially since Love had previously written *Rio Grande do Sul and Brazilian Regionalism*. In the era under examination, São Paulo and Minas Gerais were the economic, demographic, and political leaders, and only Rio Grande could hope to challenge their control of federal policies and institutions. Pernambuco was the most important state in Brazil's leading "problem" area—the poverty-stricken Northeast—and it provides a dramatic and, in many ways, representative case study of Brazilian regionalism from the "underside." Nonetheless, we realize that regionalism and its socioeconomic context cannot be fully understood without studies of other units, especially Bahia, Rio de Janeiro, and the old Federal District. Much remains to be done.

Region and regionalism are defined with reference to the problem at hand, which is to study politics and its social and economic bases over several decades. Thus, a region is defined as having the following characteristics:

1. It is part of a larger unit and interdependent with other regions that, together with the first, constitute the larger unit.

2. It has a definite geographic size and location, being politically bounded.

3. Each region has a set of component subregions, which are contiguous.

4. The region generates a set of loyalties on the part of its inhabitants, which vary in importance and intensity over time.

5. Loyalty to the region, however, is subordinated (nominally at

least) to loyalty to the larger unit—the nation-state—among the politically effective sectors of the region's population; this loyalty may also vary in importance and intensity.

Regionalism is here defined as political behavior characterized, on the one hand, by acceptance of the existence of a larger political unit, but, on the other hand, by the quest for favoritism and decisional autonomy from the larger unit on economic and social policies, even at the risk of jeopardizing the legitimacy of the prevailing political system. Thus the emphasis is not on regional peculiarities per se (e.g. folklore, patterns of dress and speech), but on those factors that can be demonstrated to affect the region's political, economic, and social relations with the other regions and the larger unit of government, in this case a nation-state.

Attitudes toward regionalism changed during the period under review. The hopeful modernizers of 1889 saw decentralization as a device to obtain a more efficient allocation of resources than could be achieved through the central government. By contrast, the authoritarian centralizers of 1937 blamed "selfish regionalism" for a host of social, economic, and political dislocations they vowed to set right by action at the center. Both groups thought of regionalism in policy terms, but reached radically different conclusions on its validity. Grounded in Brazilian historical experience, this prescriptive aspect of regionalism becomes part of the definition.

Regional elites believed their states were socioeconomic as well as political units which demanded allegiance. But when state was pitted against nation, their allegiances were ambivalent, as shown in the experience of São Paulo in the 1930's. Furthermore, their success in establishing the significance of the region was in doubt, or at least ambiguous. Outright failures occurred, notably in the case of Pernambuco, which could not establish political coherence. Exogenous market forces and the terrain channeled economic growth in ways the leaders of Minas did not want. Opportunities to live and work in Rio de Janeiro, the center of patronage and stylish city-state, eroded the regional ideal among Pernambucanos and Mineiros, in striking contrast to their Paulista counterparts. Above all, the interpenetration of manifold and complex structures across regional boundaries sapped regional coherence.

In holding to the regional ideal, however, the elites soon realized that regionalism was not necessarily incompatible with a strong federal government. State and nation were not necessarily antagonistic; they were part of a continuum along which the balance of forces shifted. Compartmentalized state economic policies were abandoned as early as the severe depression of the late 1890's. The elites soon came to measure and define regionalism in relation to other units and the central government. Shaping the terms of these relationships was in fact the essence of regional policymaking. Viewed this way, regionalism becomes more complex and significant than it would be if the problem were only that of nonviable states struggling against the centralizing tide.

Relationships changed as the nation became more integrated. By the time of World War I, elites were even less inclined to counterpose region to nation, although the aim of state policy was still to extract favorable terms. Thus the state elites welcomed integration when they could influence or control it, and on the whole accepted it when they had to. We devote considerable attention to the integration process, which began well before the 1930 Revolution.

In the Brazilian case, integration was the product of two congruent forces, namely, the interpenetration of social, economic, and political life across regional boundaries *and* the partial transfer of decisions and resources to a national level of political organization. We believe that the former reinforced, but did not directly cause, the latter. Thus we give attention to the interaction of congresses and meetings at state and national levels. Yet the ambiguities of the centralizing impetus are revealed in detailed case studies of state budgets and fiscal policies, and in our discussion of military forces.

Two concurrent kinds of relationships marked the integration process. One, on the horizontal dimension, occurred within and among groups based on common bonds, affinities, and shared interests. The other, structured vertically, was the process of interaction among unequals: clientelism is a prime instance. Having examined both types of social interaction, we found striking the weakness of group and interest associations and the persistence of vertical structures, though this varied by state. Furthermore, it is clear that the elites modernized selectively, minimizing social mobilization. By this yardstick Brazil was far from being a fully integrated society by 1937.

In probing the complex processes whereby the parts fit together, we also focus explicitly on the role of state policymakers—what they wanted, tried to get, and settled for. Though political integration was far from uniform or complete by 1937, we think our analysis of regional decision-makers is a way to understand what was achieved. By looking at the terms of interaction we hope to carry analysis beyond the vague proposition that the elites, in learning to cooperate, willed national integration.

Our initial hypothesis was that the states functioned as "halfway houses," pioneering in areas of social and economic legislation, and slowly ceding responsibilities to the federal government after World War I. It later became clear, however, that government responsibility at *both* state and federal levels was increasing down to 1930, and that some state responsibilities were still vigorous until 1937 and beyond. This is another way of saying that regionalism was not the antithesis of interpenetration and integration, which took place on all levels of government.

One of the most instructive aspects of the regional approach is the opportunity for comparison, and there are several topics for which comparative regional analysis is especially appropriate.

1. The political consequences of different patterns of economic growth are seen more clearly: Pernambuco in decline, Minas with a relatively weak economy, and São Paulo in rapid expansion developed different political strategies at the state and national levels.

2. The alleged causal links between the level of socioeconomic development and types of political organization are brought under triangulation, allowing for a better view of other factors affecting leadership and organizations.

3. Different center-periphery relationships are highlighted in these studies. Pernambuco tended to predominate among the Northeastern states, but was itself a satellite of the central government; Minas was on the margins of the Center-South; São Paulo enjoyed a rapidly expanding domestic market; all had their export links and contrasting patterns of international financial obligations.

4. Similarities and differences in identically defined political elites are thrown into relief by the comparative analysis of computerized biographical data.

5. The role of the states in fostering or impeding political and economic integration emerges from the comparative study of state militias, budgets, specialized congresses, and associational activity.

As histories of Pernambuco, Minas, and São Paulo, these studies are schematic, not exhaustive. The stress is on structures, parallels, and linkages, rather than on detailed narrative exposition, for which there is still need. We hope that some of the richness of a unique regional society emerges in each volume. Inevitably, each study reflects the type, amount, and quality of source materials and previous studies available to the individual authors, who are responsible for their own volumes. In sum, each study stands alone; but all three follow the same design, which is the product of collaborative effort.

It was our intention not only to illuminate the Brazilian past but also to make a contribution to the literature on social and political change. The three works are case studies of major subnational units during the early phases of modernization. In charting the strategies of the elites to promote or retard change and the political consequences of shifts in the economic base, we hope these volumes will be read by students of the processes of capitalist modernization as well as by those interested in the unique features of Brazilian history.

We also hope to contribute to the comparative literature on regionalism and federalism. The problems and perspectives of regionalism are far from dead in the United States, where such issues as revenue sharing and state vs. federal control of energy resources are widely debated. Furthermore, it seems clear that many of the world's underdeveloped countries are experiencing profound currents of regionalism (often reinforcing ethnic cleavages), as social mobilization brings new groups into the political process. One form this can take is separatism and civil war, as the recent tragedies of Bangladesh and Nigeria illustrate. There is also a possibility that regionalism will lead to a more creative definition of the nation, as may be occurring in parts of Western Europe. Finally, in Brazil itself the issues of federalism are by no means dead, and it has yet to be demonstrated that the allegiance of the masses to the nation-state of Brazil parallels those of political and economic elites.

R.M.L.

J.L.L.

J.D.W.

# MINAS GERAIS
in the Brazilian Federation
1889-1937

## CHAPTER ONE

# The Minas Mosaic

MINEIROS LIVING in their landlocked, France-sized state are known as the "mountain people," with a distinct regional identity that taps back to eighteenth-century roots. Yet recently, the traits for which Mineiros were famous seemed old-fashioned, especially to Brazilians from the Rio and São Paulo urban centers. Mineiros' conservatism strong sense of place were increasingly out of step with the new values of an industrializing Brazil. Minas played a central role in national politics after the Empire collapsed in 1889, but the limited results were viewed critically by many (including Mineiros) to whom economic development was becoming the criterion of success. That Minas Gerais did not participate fully in the modernizing trends sweeping southern Brazil after 1890 is a central dynamic of this region's recent history.

Neighboring São Paulo pulled ahead of Minas in the 1890's, after which the gap between their two economies widened. By 1920, São Paulo's gross agricultural and industrial output was double that of Minas. A neo-colonial relationship developed that Mineiros were unable to reverse: Minas sent out people and raw materials, São Paulo shipped back manufactures and processed food. By 1940, almost one-fifth of all native-born Mineiros had emigrated to greener pastures in São Paulo or Rio de Janeiro, and increasingly to the Paraná frontier.

The 6.7 million Mineiros who stayed behind in 1940 lived mostly in the vast countryside, or else in small cities, towns, and hamlets. And whereas the pace of urbanization quickened after 1920—notably in the new state capital at Belo Horizonte—the majority still timed their lives to preindustrial rhythms. Into recent years, there was an untouched quality to Minas life, emotive, marked by spontaneity across the highly developed, well-defined social hierarchy. The elite who were the visible history-makers in this period never repudiated their past. Yet they were also heavily influenced by Rio de Janeiro, the federal capital, to which they looked for education, imported culture, political and economic opportunities.

Minas Gerais was a region complexly related to wealthier and more dynamic units lying to its south. Viewed from the perspective of Brazil's impoverished Northeast, however, Minas was not only well endowed in power and resources but also viable as a region. In fact, it ranked in the upper third of Brazilian states in industrial product, transportation, and state income. Other indicators were grim: in literacy, per capita income, and public health Mineiros had more in common with Northeasterners than they had with compatriots in the South.[1] Second to none in political power, Minas dominated the federation in the Old Republic (1889–1930) along with São Paulo and Rio Grande do Sul. This state was not marginal. It was transitional, a heartland region fronting on and in part belonging to the dynamic South, but also lying next to vast, dependent regions to the north. Political strength mixed with relative economic and social weakness is the essence of Minas Gerais during this period of Brazilian history.

*The Land*

All Brazilian states are political creations, but none claim the variety of landscapes that is the peculiar patrimony of Minas. The state's frontiers do not define a coherent geographical region. They do reflect Portuguese colonial convenience, which was to isolate the modern world's first gold rush at General Mines (1690–1740) from other European powers and to frustrate smuggling and tax evasion in the gold fields. Communications were restricted to easily guarded land routes, principally north to Bahia, west to Cuiabá, and south to the capital at Rio. The route to Vitória port on the Espírito Santo coast was kept closed and remained undeveloped into this century. Consequently, Minas had no seaport of its own during the age of export-led growth lasting from 1850 to 1930. Poor transportation hindered the internal circulation of goods. Modern highways and plentiful electric power were introduced in the 1950's, but old obstacles to integration continued even then. Thus colonial policy bent geography to its ends—in the Mineiro case, outrageously so.

That Minas is not one region but rather a mosaic of seven different zones or subregions is fundamental. See Figure 1. For one thing, this heterogeneous state, which is 7 percent of Brazil, reflected the historical pull of other units beyond the political boundaries of the region. Also, each zone developed on a different time line, giving the state a long history of disarticulated and discontinuous growth.[2] In sum, these seven zones into which the state is customarily divided all have particular histories and special problems that challenge common solutions.*

West and southwest, the Triângulo and the Sul are logical extensions of the São Paulo hinterland, to which the former was linked juridically until 1816, and to which economically and culturally they still are drawn. Most of the vast São Francisco River Valley is geographically part of the Brazilian *sertão*, which stretches beyond Bahia and Pernambuco into Ceará. In fact, northern Minas was administered from Salvador, Bahia, until 1750; almost all its exports went through Salvador until this century. The West belonged to the colonial cattle frontier, extending from Bahia to Goiás. Southeast, the Mata zone gravitated toward the port city of Rio de Janeiro, forming part of Rio's hinterland since the coffee boom began in 1830. And beyond the frontier East zone, tiny Espírito Santo isolated Mineiros from the sea as Portugal had intended.

From the Center, seat of provincial and later state government, officials into the 1930's saw their authority over other zones attenuated by poor communications and a lack of economic influence. Isolated from the rest of Minas, the Center with its eighteenth-century baroque cities developed traditions that came to typify Mineiro culture. But this re-

---

* Unfortunately, there is no generally agreed upon definition of the zones that historians can use. Brazilian geographers recently specified 17 physiographic subregions to suit their purposes; these appear on most maps and reports, but their scheme is not very useful for tracing historical trends. Regrettably, the old electoral districts in use up to 1930 did not conform to zonal boundaries and were different for state and federal posts. So I decided to retain the seven traditional zones, which reflect different patterns of settlement as well as political, social, and economic changes better than any other format. The map shows zonal boundaries that are approximate, but that are also sanctioned by custom. This seven-unit division was used throughout the book.

Fig. 1. Mineiro zones, according to customary usage.

gional culture at the Center must be seen in the context of influences
from other units with their hinterlands extending into Minas Gerais.
The more developed subregions south of the 19th parallel, that is, the
Mata, Sul, and Triângulo, were linked historically to the Rio and São
Paulo growth poles. The less developed North and West were back-
waters of Bahia.

Thus the landscapes of Minas Gerais give different readings on the
historian's geiger counter. The Triângulo took shape as a modern agro-
pastoral economy from the 1880's. Culturally and economically it was
a new zone. The North, by contrast, followed in the traces of a seventeenth-century ranching economy, a diamond rush (over by 1830)
excepted. Its old cities stagnated on the margins of vast latifundia until the railroad arrived in the late 1920's. The West exported cattle
south, its towns having been linked by ancient cattle trails and then by
rail and highways in this century. Coffee financed the mid-nineteenth-
century rise of the Mata and the Sul. As for the Mata, it had been Indian land until 1830, when the coffee frontier began to move eastward

through the virgin forest. The Sul also developed a coffee-based agriculture, its economy having been centered on gold mining in the eighteenth century. During the Old Republic, these two zones led the others in wealth, population, and political power.

The Center zone lost ground to the Mata and the Sul throughout the nineteenth century, where many elite families established themselves in agriculture after migrating from the decadent mining area. There they mixed with other migrants from the Paraíba Valley to form a new elite. Thus the state's lines of force bent southward during the period under review. The Center's long decline was arrested after 1920, however, when the growth of consumer industries, banks, and commerce gave the new political capital at Belo Horizonte an economic base. This restored the administrative Center to its old preeminence, especially after 1930.

The givens of geography also determined this pattern of disarticulated growth and stagnation. Minas is not a natural economic unit. The river basins flow outward, forming several disconnected systems. For example, the one river suitable for navigation in Minas, the São Francisco, flows north into Bahia and on to Pernambuco. It does not connect to the partially navigable Rio Doce, which flows east to the sea. Attempts to establish regular steamship service in Central Minas failed because the Rio das Velhas, a tributary of the São Francisco, has a shallow bed and irregular flow. On the border with São Paulo, the Rio Grande and its tributaries flow west to the Paraná Basin, away from population centers and markets. The Paraíba River running east captures the Mata system, while northeast the Jequitinhonha and Mucuri rivers tie remote valleys to an isolated section of the Bahian coast.

Several mountain ranges split up the subregions and impose communications barriers that a modern highway system has only recently overcome. Running north-south through the Center zone, the Serra do Espinhaço, or Backbone Range, isolates the Northeast and upper Rio Doce Valley from the São Francisco River and the West. A less formidable barrier, the Brazilian Plateau, defines the border with Espírito Santo, which until recently was isolated because of other factors. Girdling Minas from west to east, the Canastra and Mantiqueira ranges define the Sul and the Mata. Mountainous highlands separate these two zones, yet both have access to the Paraíba Valley, a natural

corridor on Minas's southern border that since colonial times has linked
Rio with São Paulo. This terrain was part of the colonial legacy, creating what a leader in the 1930's called "our economic dissociation," and
complicating "the administrative, political, and social articulation of
our state."[3]

The image of Minas as a mountain state derives from the gold and
diamond rushes, when the eighteenth-century cities were clustered far
from the coast in rough terrain. Some 16 percent of the state's approximately 587,000 square kilometers is above 900 meters, but the relief is
far from uniform. Thus the hilly Sul and Mata zones, taken together
with the rugged Center, offer sharply contrasting landscapes to the
northern *chapadas* (plateau country), or to the rolling *campo cerrado*
scrub plains in the West and the Triângulo. Thanks to abundant rain,
dense tropical forests once covered the Sul, Mata, and East zones.
Deforestation was caused by burning, by population growth, and,
starting in the 1920's, by the charcoal-fueled steel industry. The North,
while hot and humid, is subject to periodic droughts that mark it as
the southernmost extension of the sertão. Dams and irrigation works to
harness these water resources were initiated only in the 1950's, 20 years
after northern Minas was officially included in the famous "drought
polygon" of Brazil's Northeast.

Not scenic in an obvious way, Minas landscapes inspire a sense of
space and power and, at times, of intimacy as seen in the vestiges of
the old high forests that nestle in the contours of the eroded southern
hills. "As throughout the tropics," a French geographer observed, "nature in Minas Gerais is monotonous, seductive, and brutal."[4] This iso-
lating landscape has left its mark on the regional character. On meeting
casually in the street Mineiros will often remark, "Voce sumiu,"
"You've dropped out of sight."

The tropicality of Minas, combined with the varied terrain and
difficult communications, conditioned the agricultural development of
what was still predominantly an agro-pastoral economy in 1937. It was
customary for political orators to extol the "most fertile" (*uberíssimo*)
soils of Minas, as if the state's agricultural potential was limited only
by human effort and imagination. Using predatory slash-and-burn
techniques learned from the aborigines, many families did make fortunes by exploiting the humus-bearing, lateritic soils of the Sul and
Mata zones for coffee production. But the results—erosion, leaching,

and soil exhaustion—throughout the agricultural southern zones produced a deteriorating environment. Smoke rising hundreds of feet
from burning woods and grasslands dimmed the sky; at night the
clouds glowed pink.[5]

By 1930, good soil conditions were limited mostly to the Triângulo,
the East, and southern parts of the West, where the gentle terrain also
lent itself to mechanization. Starting in 1900, the Triângulo began to
produce abundant crops of rice, corn, and beans, as well as more
specialized products. The old coffee areas, by contrast, switched gradually into dairying, tobacco, and some cane sugar, not to mention the
subsistence farming that was known throughout Minas. After 1900,
with coffee in decline, their agricultural future was saved by the
rapidly growing urban markets for cereals, poultry products, butter,
milk, and cheese in São Paulo and the Federal District. Meanwhile,
the coffee frontier shifted northeast, beyond Muriaé and Carangola in
the Mata to the pioneer East zone, with its virgin forest land. Subsistence farming and large ranches dominated northern Minas. For
lack of transport, crops could not be shipped south to the growing
Belo Horizonte market until the 1930's. Cotton, a traditional northern
product, never lived up to expectations because of poor quality control.

Wasteful, backward, and predatory are words that appear all too
frequently in the literature on Mineiro agriculture. On the other hand,
Mineiro farmers living on the São Paulo and Paraná frontiers were
famous for their hard work and skill at opening up new ranches and
fazendas.[6] Whether the agricultural sector performed as badly as
many observers thought is questionable (see Chapter 2). The basic
staples—feijão (black beans), rice, and corn—were grown locally.
Except for a brief period during the coffee boom of the 1890's, the
state fed itself; it was not until the 1930's that state authorities began
to deny that Minas was importing feijão.

In 1920, Minas ranked third behind São Paulo and Rio Grande do
Sul in the value of rural properties. Almost all these holdings were
owner-operated, which was a source of social stability. Almost none of
the individually owned farms were held by foreigners or naturalized
Brazilians (only 4 percent in 1920, 2 percent in 1940), a source of
social cohesion. But land values were low, the result of low productivity and poor communications. São Paulo's 80,000 properties were

## TABLE 1.1

### Land Tenure in Minas Gerais, 1920 *and* 1940

| Size in hectares | Number | | Percent | | Area | | Percent | |
|---|---|---|---|---|---|---|---|---|
| | 1920 | 1940 | 1920 | 1940 | 1920 | 1940 | 1920 | 1940 |
| Small (1–40) | 37,375 | 177,893 | 32.3% | 62.5% | 790,151 | 3,460,277 | 2.8% | 10.3% |
| Medium (41–100) | 32,650 | 44,808 | 28.2 | 15.7 | 2,247,844 | 3,229,596 | 8.2 | 9.6 |
| SUBTOTAL | 70,025 | 222,701 | 60.5 | 78.2 | 3,037,995 | 6,689,873 | 11.0 | 19.9 |
| Fazendas (101–1,000) | 41,622 | 57,572 | 35.9 | 20.2 | 12,227,631 | 15,385,416 | 44.6 | 45.9 |
| Latifundia (1,001 & over) | 4,008 | 4,282 | 3.4 | 1.5 | 12,124,910 | 11,400,592 | 44.2 | 34.0 |
| TOTAL | 115,655 | 284,555 | 99.8% | 99.0% | 27,390,536 | 33,475,881 | 99.8% | 99.8% |

SOURCE: Based on data in Brazil, *Recenseamento geral, 1940*, Parte XIII, Minas Gerais, tomo 3, p. 1. Of an estimated 60 million hectares in Minas, only 27 million were enumerated in the 1920 census, and of the lands surveyed, 5.4 million were in forests, 1.5 were under cultivation, and 20.4 were listed under "use unknown"! See Minas, *Annuario estatistico, 1921*, Anno I, p. 9.

NOTE: 1940 small holdings are 1–50 hectares, medium holdings 51–100 hectares.

evaluated one-third higher than Minas's 115,000 rural holdings. In 1935, a state official said Paulista land prices "are much higher than in Minas, and 10 to 15 times higher than in north Minas."[7] Large tracts were held for speculation, and much of the East was still public land. In comparison with São Paulo, moreover, real estate in Minas did not fuel the engine of social and economic progress with sustained booms.

Four out of five Mineiros worked in the countryside, but for lack of a cadastral survey, estimates of land ownership and size were very crude. From the census, one cannot determine multiple ownership or get at interlocking family holdings. Land ownership was concentrated, as is clear in Table 1.1. In 1940, nearly 80 percent of all establishments occupied only 20 percent of the land. These were small holdings of up to 50 hectares, and intermediate establishments of up to 100 hectares. Large fazendas and latifundia accounted for four-fifths of the total enumerated area. According to Table 1.1, there was a shift by 1940 toward smaller units, while latifundia declined. Probably the 1920 census underestimated the smaller holdings, but it also seems likely that the ranks of small holders swelled because the area under cultivation in small plots expanded. What I call "fazendas" maintained their ranking, perhaps because they were the most profitable and productive units.

Size also depended upon crop requirements and the terrain. Nelson de Sena, the geographer and state deputy, estimated that few Mata fazendeiros held 300 alqueires of land in 1919, or 750 hectares, the mean being from 250 to 500 hectares. Spreads of 125 to 500 hectares were common in the East. Huge holdings were concentrated only in the less developed ranching zones, which led Sena to conclude that "Minas is not a state dominated by latifundia." Based on the 1940 census, which had more complete and reliable data, Coelho de Souza devised an explicit profile of average holdings by zone. Accordingly, the upper limit for predominantly agricultural areas was 60 hectares. These small farms were located mostly in mountainous areas of the Sul, Mata, the East, and in several subsistence-oriented municípios in the North. Ranches in the Triângulo, the North, Jequitinhonha Valley, and the West accounted for the large holdings.[8] Noteworthy in the 1940 profile of rural properties was the large number of intermediate units (60–141 hectares) found in agricultural regions where mixed agro-pastoral production took place. In this group, 70 percent of the land was likely to be used for pasturage, with 10 to 15 percent reserved for agriculture. As expected, the rural population was concentrated in the agricultural zones with 34 inhabitants per square kilometer, and sparse in the pastoral regions where the corresponding figure was 12.

Stock raising was the second traditional pillar of the economy. With two-thirds of the state in grasslands, Minas is ecologically well adapted to extensive ranching, notably above the 19th parallel and in the Triângulo. Bahians pushing down the São Francisco River Valley in the seventeenth century brought the techniques and the social organization for ranching, which later changed but little. Range management consisted of firing the grasslands once a year to produce good pasturage in the rainy season while abating snakes and insect pests. Pasturage during the dry season (May–August) was sparse and livestock losses were very heavy in bad drought years. However rudimentary, these techniques and a favorable environment produced Brazil's largest herd of beef cattle.

Northern stock were driven over the old colonial road to Bahian markets. Cattle from the West, the Triângulo, and Goiás moved southeast on old trails to the cattle fairs in the Sul, where they were sold to Carioca buyers. The cattle economy changed rapidly after 1880, thanks to railroads and to a burgeoning demand for beef in Rio de Janeiro, which almost tripled in population between 1872 and 1900. Cattle still moved overland to the Sul and the Triângulo, but the routes now usually included an intermediate pasturage, followed by fattening at winter grasslands (*invernadas*) near the railroads servicing cattle fairs in the Sul de Minas. Northern centers developed as the Central do Brasil Railroad reached Curvelo (1905) and Montes Claros (1926). Eastward, the cattle economy grew rapidly, starting in the 1920's. Meanwhile, Mineiros specializing in the opening of new ranches became very active in São Paulo, and by 1900 they dominated ranching in the contiguous zones of neighboring Goiás.

Starting in 1891, progressive ranchers in the Triângulo imported Zebu cattle from India and became breeding specialists who sold select stock throughout the Center-South. In Minas, the native Curraleiro or Pé-douro cattle began to be replaced by larger and more profitable mixed breeds (*azebuado*). By the late 1930's, Mineiro ranching entered a phase of speculative euphoria. The Zebu's promise was limited, however, by transportation problems and by the fact that Mineiros, with their low purchasing power, could not add much beef to their traditional diet of pork, corn mush, manioc, rice, and beans.

"A heart of gold jacketed with iron" is how the French engineer Henri Gorceix described Minas Gerais. Although the gold-mining boom was over generations ago, hopes for a new strike lingered on. It could happen anywhere, any time, in the popular imagination. In 1852, the fabulous "Southern Star" diamond weighing 254 carats was found near the Triângulo town of Bagagem (meaning "baggage"); a maharaja bought it and the city proudly renamed itself Estrela do Sul. Prospecting for diamonds and semiprecious stones still provided a precarious livelihood for thousands whose dogged persistence helped to keep alive the historic image of a Minas fabulously endowed with minerals and gems. Well into the 1930's, the British-owned Saint John Del Rey Company's gold mine at Morro Velho was the state's largest single industrial employer. But of the nine Brazilian and foreign-owned gold-mining companies active in 1900, it alone survived. The great expectations of this century were aroused by iron ore, of which one-fifth of the world's known deposits are located in the so-called Iron Quadrangle of Central Minas. Engineers trained by Gorceix at the Ouro Preto Mining School founded several small steel plants.

Having discussed the land and patterns of resource use, I want to look at general demographic trends and race before moving on to discuss the seven zones of Minas in greater detail.

## The People

Minas Gerais led the federation in population until the 1920's, when São Paulo thrust ahead. Having experienced rapid demographic growth throughout the nineteenth century, Minas slowed to less than half the national average between the wars, while São Paulo and Rio Grande continued to expand at rates well above the mean. That this decline was chronic is revealed by comparing Minas, growing at 1.6 percent a year between 1920 and 1960, with the nation, which grew annually at a rate of 3.2 percent.[9] Faced with a high birthrate and a sluggish economy, Minas was the leading state for emigration: it "lost" perhaps three million native sons to other units. On the basis of calculations by the French geographer Yves Leloup, it appears that almost one in five Mineiros lived out of state by 1940. Demographic

TABLE 1.2

*Population Growth, Minas Gerais and the Nation, 1872–1940*

(Thousands)

| Census year | Minas Gerais | | Brazil | |
| --- | --- | --- | --- | --- |
| | Population | Intercensal growth rate | Population | Intercensal growth rate |
| 1872 | 2,103 | 2.3% | 10,112 | 2.0% |
| 1890 | 3,184 | 1.2 | 14,334 | 1.9 |
| 1900 | 3,594 | 2.5 | 17,319 | 2.9 |
| 1920 | 5,888 | 0.7 | 30,636 | 1.5 |
| 1940 | 6,736 | 0.7 | 41,236 | 1.5 |

SOURCE: Brazilian published census data.

TABLE 1.3

*Projected Population Loss, Minas Gerais and the Nation, 1900–1960*

| Time period | Loss | Total growth | |
| --- | --- | --- | --- |
| | | Minas Gerais | Brazil |
| 1900–1920 | 426,233 | 31.9% | 37.8% |
| 1920–40 | 1,189,066 | 7.2 | 17.3 |
| 1940–50 | 763,345 | 14.5 | 25.9 |
| 1950–60 | 712,345 | 26.9 | 36.2 |
| TOTAL | 3,090,989 | | |

SOURCE: Yves Leloup in *Les villes du Minas Gerais* (Paris, 1970), pp. 16–17, bases his loss projections on the difference between the Minas rate of increase and the national rate. Thus, if Minas had grown at the national rate of increase, it would not have lost three million people.

shifts on such a scale can only mean that Minas, renowned for its conservatism and social stability, paid a high price in human capital. See Tables 1.2 and 1.3.

Negroes appear in every population census since the eighteenth century, when over one-third of Mineiros were enumerated as black. Of an estimated 723,000 Brazilian slaves freed in 1888, some 192,000 or nearly 27 percent were from Minas, more than any other province. And in 1940, the colored population still numbered, in equal parts, almost 40 percent Negro and mulatto. After abolition, mobility channels remained few and difficult for men of color; whites continued to hold the high-status positions in a hierarchical, agrarian-based society. Although the elite prided themselves on a tolerant, even-handed attitude toward race, they had a low estimate of the black man and expected him to disappear through miscegenation, which Nelson de Sena, among others, called the Mineiro way in race relations.[10]

Race data from the 1890 and 1940 censuses do not support this self-image of a whitening population. To be sure, mixed bloods did decline from 38 to 19 percent, whereas the whites increased from roughly 41 to 61 percent. Miscegenation at such a rate would confirm the fondest hopes of Mineiro boosters, were it not for the notorious unreliability of Brazilian racial data and the fact that those listed as *mestiços* in 1890 may not correspond neatly with their grandchildren listed as *pardos* in 1940. Less ambiguity probably attaches to the black population, known as *pretos* in both censuses. Turning to the blacks, one finds a significant percentage shift, from 15.2 to 19.4, for a net increase of 12.8 percent! Whitening, thus, was not so much demographic fact as it was a cultural norm.[11]

Where this increasing black population lived is revealed by identifying the percent of Negroes in the total population of each zone. See Table 1.4. Excepting the North and the pioneer East, all the subregions were remarkably consistent. The Sul diverged somewhat—was this due to enumerating errors or migration?—but percentage increases in the two zones bordering Bahia more than offset it. In part, this "blackening" of the North and the East may have resulted from an in-migration of Bahians fleeing the droughts (discussed below) or seeking open land. In part, it may be that the blacks of North Minas were left behind in the general exodus to São Paulo after 1930 (also discussed below). That several towns on the São Francisco River were almost completely black is a fact often noted in the contemporary travel literature. Although this evidence is not conclusive, the heavy black population of these towns including North Minas was probably

TABLE 1.4

*Proportion of Negroes in the Population, 1890 and 1940*

| Zone | 1890 | 1940 | Zone | 1890 | 1940 |
|------|------|------|------|------|------|
| North | 15.72 | 24.10 | Center | 19.15 | 21.25 |
| East | 12.93 | 22.02 | Sul | 18.03 | 14.04 |
| West | 14.56 | 13.06 | Mata | 24.18 | 23.67 |
| Triângulo | 13.84 | 11.77 | | | |

SOURCE: Compiled from 1890 and 1940 census data on race by município, and aggregated by zones.

symptomatic of extreme poverty in the sertão. By contrast, one notes that the Triângulo, the state's most prosperous zone, also had the lowest Negro population in 1940.

Of the Indians, most surviving tribes had long since migrated into Goiás, the one alternative to being hunted and enslaved by settlers or catechized by missionaries. Indian removal by these ancient methods proved effective; few pure bloods survived by the 1890's. Those who remained, mostly Aimorés in the undeveloped East zone, faced extinction at the hands of settlers, or mestization in missionary villages. A few hostiles, the so-called *bugres* (savages), raided Rio Doce Valley settlements into the 1900's, to be pacified at last in army camps. Their passing was lamented after the fact by journalists and cultural leaders who realized, sadly, they "knew all about the Esquimo, but nothing of our own Indians."[12] And although the Indian's ethnic contribution was slight, his agricultural methods and foodstuffs had long since passed into the dominant society along with many hundreds of place names, haunting reminders of a doomed race.

Choosing to ignore the Negro and the pardo, tending to sentimentalize the vanished Indian, Mineiros directed their attention toward the European immigrant, who, in turn, preferred São Paulo and the southern states to Minas. It was not that foreigners, as individuals, made no impact. The French missionary-teacher, the German mechanic, the Italian stone mason and baker, the British mining engineer, and the Syrian peddler all touched the fabric of Mineiro life. It was that foreigners, in the mass, were relatively unimportant. To be sure, German colonists turned artisans were the original talent pool for Juiz de Fora's entrepreneurial class, starting in the 1860's.[13] Less dramatically, Italian field hands turned craftsmen and merchants provided urban services for the Sul's small cities, that zone being the major area of Italian immigration in the late nineteenth century. Juiz de Fora, São João del Rei, and Barbacena likewise benefited. Several of the Italian, Spanish, and Portuguese laborers who constructed Belo Horizonte stayed on to grow fresh vegetables or found small businesses. In retrospect, however, immigration was a failure. There was a net out-migration of foreigners from Minas between 1900 and 1920, and by that base year Minas, with only 14.9 foreigners per 1,000 people, ranked much closer to Pernambuco (5.8) than to São Paulo

TABLE 1.5

*The Foreign-Born in Minas Gerais, 1872–1920*

| Year | Total population | Native-born | Foreign-born | Percent foreign-born |
|------|------------------|-------------|--------------|----------------------|
| 1872 | 2,102,689 | 2,055,789 | 46,900 | 2.23 |
| 1890 | 3,184,099 | 3,137,312 | 46,787 | 1.47 |
| 1900 | 3,594,471 | 3,452,824 | 141,647 | 3.94 |
| 1920 | 5,888,174 | 5,800,161 | 88,013 | 1.49 |

SOURCE: Brazil, *Anuário estatístico, ano* V, p. 1302, and Brazil, *Boletim commemorativo da Exposição Nacional de 1908*, p. xxi.

(181.5). See Table 1.5. The conclusion must be that traditional society was not much altered by foreign blood and talent.

Despite concerted efforts that included state-subsidized passages (1894–97) and agricultural colonies, Minas could neither attract nor hold immigrants during 1880–1920, the phase of major population transfers from the Old World to the New. The high point came after abolition (1888), until the coffee price fall of 1897: some 69,500 Europeans came to Minas at state expense but soon left the coffee fazendas for rural São Paulo or the cities. When coffee prices recovered after 1907, Minas attracted a mere 6,600 immigrants between 1908 and 1914, while magnetic São Paulo drew 363,000 from 1910 to World War I.[14]

Opportunity beckoned in the diversifying Paulista economy, whereas all too often upon arrival in Minas the immigrant found himself welcomed not as a colonist willing to set down roots in the Mineiro soil but as a source of cheap labor. He could not clear title to his land without lengthy litigation; he sharecropped and bought in the company store; he suffered status anxiety; in short, he faced the usual obstacles of traditional society—so he left.[15] In turn, many planters who were pressed by declining coffee prices after 1897 and falling yields from old plantations discharged their labor and moved into dairying. On balance, immigration failed because the coffee planters, for whom it was in large part intended, were both unwilling and unable to hold foreign labor. Nor did the state colonies, designed to promote new crops and new agricultural techniques, convince enough foreigners by example that the freewheeling ways in which public lands were alienated for private use would benefit them.

The wishful image of Minas as "a state in immigration, short on labor and long on land," persisted into the 1920's. In saying this, however, Governor Artur Bernardes hoped to associate native-born Mineiros with immigrants on state colonies in order to upgrade the general labor pool.[16] Thus the failure to attract Europeans drew attention to the residual labor force, the ex-slaves and mixed-blood *caboclos*, who traditionally were thought to lack motivation, loyalty, and skill. Poor but happy, the guitar-strumming caboclo had long been thought to live carefree and easy off the land. His image improved with the need for his labor. But this appreciation of the native-born Mineiro also owed much to a new awareness of social conditions, including the recently discovered poor state of public health in Minas.

By tradition, certain places in Minas were known to be unhealthy. One was the Rio Doce Valley pioneer zone with its malaria. Another was Caraça, the elite secondary school where generations endured beriberi, the worst outbreak of which forced students to evacuate the school in 1910. Lost in the mountain fastness of Central Minas, Caraça under the French Redemptionist Fathers was famous for rigid discipline and very bad food. Contemporaries blamed beriberi on the mountain air, but the penny-pinching padres caused the problem by serving bug-ridden beans and old rice deficient in vitamin B1.[17] Opponents of Belo Horizonte drew attention to the site's unhealthy reputation by calling it Goiterville (*papudópolis*) in honor of the bulbiferous caboclos living there when construction on the new capital began. Fatalism, often levity, sparked discussions about health in the lively small-town society of rural Minas. Consider the plight of Colonel Américo Pio Dantas, who boasted that his cistern gave the best-tasting water in Montes Claros. This cistern became even more famous when engineers traced the thin greasy film on his water to the town cemetery.[18]

Disease and death stalked all classes in Minas. Yet few realized the extent to which sickness was endemic in their rural, dispersed society until 1912, when the first medical surveys of the interior were conducted out of Rio's Oswaldo Cruz Institute. To face catastrophes such as the cholera epidemic of 1894–95 or the influenza epidemic of 1918 was one thing. Luck in avoiding such disasters is often cited in the memoirs, as for example by Belmiro Braga who, as a young sales clerk in Carangola in 1894, fled when yellow fever struck the Mata for the third time, killing (he recalled) 30 percent of the town's inhabitants.[19] But to realize that the general population as a whole was sick or threatened with malaria, tuberculosis, syphilis, and hookworm was quite another. Infant death rates of 50 percent and higher were shown to be not acts of God but caused by malaria and intestinal dysentery. In short, to paraphrase Dr. Miguel Pereira's famous aphorism: "Minas was a vast hospital."

The discovery of Chagas disease by Carlos Chagas, a medical research pioneer, helped to publicize the *barbeiro,* a blood-sucking carrier bug that infested the thatched huts of central Brazil, including Minas. Having raised the alarm at a 1912 medical congress in Belo Horizonte, Carlos Chagas joined a running polemic in the press with conservative physicians who questioned his results. Alarmists at the other extreme said that a fantastic 4,500,000 Mineiros had been "cretinized" by Chagas disease. But the infestation was real enough.[20]

The dimensions of the public health problem staggered a generation that had enjoyed the illusion of progress based on the successful yellow fever abatement program in Rio de Janeiro. Facing inward, to the interior of Minas, Bahia, and Goiás, the view was somber. What these desperate conditions meant for Minas was clear in a famous report by doctors Belisário Pena and Artur Neiva of their trip through the Sertão in 1912. They saw not the poetic landscape imagined from the cities but "bits of purgatory" peopled with sick human beings. The sertanejo, they concluded, was not by nature lazy and unreliable. Rather he was pitiable in his abandonment and neglect by the national society.[21] The doctors did not once mention Negro blood as the causal factor; they did point out that disease, poverty, and illiteracy— "abandonment," in short—were urgent problems that demanded government action.

Town life became healthier in Minas after 1910, notably in the more developed zones where municipal sewage systems were installed at an accelerating rate (21 alone between 1910 and 1920), with the Sul (12) and the Mata (10) taking the lead in this key index of urban progress. By 1923, 40 of the state's 178 municipal seats had sewage systems, 149 had water systems of one kind or another.[22] Death rates fell with the improving quality of life in Brazil's capital cities, and Belo Horizonte was happily no exception. See Table 1.6.

Tuberculosis and other diseases of the lung were the most important

TABLE 1.6

Death Rates per Thousand, 1939

| City | General population | Deaths of live-born infants in the first year of life |
|------|------|------|
| Federal District | 16.1 | 159.3 |
| São Paulo | 13.3 | 137.8 |
| Belo Horizonte | 17.9 | 160.9 |
| Recife | 17.5 | 272.3 |

SOURCE: General death rates are from Brazil, *Anuário estatístico*, Ano V, pp. 111–20; infant mortality figures, which are for 1939–41, are found in Barretto, *Povoamento e população*, 1:196, who cites IBGE statistics.

causes of adult death in Belo, undoubtedly because the city became a national center for treatment of these ailments. A parody on "Cidade Maravilhosa," the samba glorifying Rio de Janeiro, made light of a grim subject.

> Cidade tuberculosa
> Cheia de microbios mil
> Cidade tuberculosa
> O sanatório do Brasil!*

If the towns were safer, the countryside was still burdened by disease and malnutrition, so that by 1950, as can be seen from Table 1.7, a Mineiro's life expectancy was among the lowest in the nation. These statistics for the census decade 1940–50 revealed what many had known for years, namely, that the Mineiro reduced his life chances if he stayed in Minas. In fact, the mountain people did leave in large numbers, so that by the 1920's out-migration was manifest even to the most optimistic state booster.

Migration is as Brazilian as rice and beans, and the Mineiros were no exception. When the gold rush ended, Sul Mineiros washed back into eastern São Paulo, whence many of their families had come, and later in the mid-nineteenth century opened up fazendas in North São Paulo, followed by the West, Paraná, and Mato Grosso coffee frontiers.[23] By the time of the Republic, the scrupulous Mineiro with his small nest egg and capacity for work was a familiar figure in the São Paulo countryside. With the Mata soils in decline by 1900, many

* "O city of tuberculosis/Microbes the air do fill/O city of tuberculosis/ The sanatorium of Brazil!" Anecdote courtesy of Hélio Gravatá.

TABLE 1.7

*Average Life Expectancy*, 1950

| State | Men | Women | Both |
|-------|-----|-------|------|
| Rio Grande do Sul | 51.2 | 59.4 | 55.2 |
| São Paulo | 46.1 | 53.3 | 49.8 |
| Pernambuco | 39.0 | 47.8 | 43.3 |
| Bahia | 37.9 | 44.9 | 41.4 |
| Minas Gerais | 37.6 | 42.3 | 39.9 |
| Rio de Janeiro | 36.9 | 42.3 | 39.5 |
| Brazil | 39.3 | 45.5 | 42.3 |

SOURCE: Barretto, *Povoamento e população; política popula-cional brasileira*, 2:502.

fazendeiros moved to São Paulo, opening up fazendas there or dairy farms in the Paraíba Valley, where land values after abolition were low. And in the 1930's Goiânia, the new, planned capital of Goiás state, became the emporium for a ranching economy that since the 1890's and perhaps earlier had owed much to Mineiro pioneers.[24]

The migration was by no means limited to those with capital and skills. Field hands by the tens of thousands were attracted to São Paulo by the promise of wage labor, and over the years many former seasonals took up residence. Contractors hired Mineiro track hands to work on Paulista railroads. And after World War I slowed European immigration to São Paulo, Mineiros and Bahians migrated there in very large numbers. Still others went to the Federal District, lured by employment on public works projects in the Rodrigues Alves administration (1902–6) and later. Why Minas could not hold its labor force was frequently debated among the political elite. The shifting of this countryside migration to a rural-urban focus in the 1930's only confirmed the fears of physiocratically inclined conservatives who felt big cities were corrupt.[25]

Of the push factors in migration, none was more obvious to contemporaries than the severe *sêcas* (droughts) that devastated the Minas sertão in near-decennial intervals. In fact the Republic arrived with the great 1888–89 drought, followed by the 1899 disaster, which north Mineiros dubbed "*a fome dos nove*." Sêcas in 1913, 1927, and 1937 forced sertanejos south, and often over the São Paulo frontier, accompanied by equally driven Bahians. Tremendal (later Monte Azul) lost an estimated 60 percent of its population in the 11 years

TABLE 1.8

Growth of Minas Population by Zone and Census Year, 1872–1940

(Thousands)

| Zone | 1872 | Growth rate | 1890 | Growth rate | 1900 | Growth rate | 1920 | Growth rate | 1940 |
|---|---|---|---|---|---|---|---|---|---|
| North | 354 | 1.9% | 501 | 1.4% | 575 | 2.1% | 864 | — | 865 |
| East | | | 138 | 1.4 | 158 | 7.4 | 654 | 2.1 | 989 |
| Center | 538 | 2.3 | 808 | 1.0 | 889 | 0.2 | 933 | 1.2 | 1,185 |
| Triângulo | 146 | 1.6 | 193 | 1.1 | 215 | 2.9 | 380 | 1.3 | 488 |
| West | 260 | 2.1 | 379 | 0.9 | 413 | 2.6 | 692 | 0.9 | 828 |
| Sul | 395 | 2.5 | 617 | 1.6 | 724 | 2.7 | 1,242 | — | 1,240 |
| Mata | 348 | 2.6 | 548 | 1.6 | 641 | 2.6 | 1,075 | 0.3 | 1,140 |

SOURCES AND METHODS: Intercensal growth rates are annual average cumulative, using compound interest tables. Zonal figures are based on published data by município in the standard census materials, and reworked into the zonal format. The dash indicates a growth rate of less than 0.1 percent.

after 1888. Jails filled with thieves and rustlers; the weak perished; whole families fled to the East zone or to São Paulo—many to return with the heavy rains (1900) that usually followed every drought. By 1908 almost two-fifths of the remaining population in Tremendal had visited São Paulo or other parts of Minas.[26] Sudden and terrifying as these sêcas were, they cannot be the main reason for the statewide out-migration. Moreover, the other zones were affected only indirectly by the hungry and sometimes armed hoards. Overpopulation, low wages, and low productivity were the continuing and underlying causes. In fact, a large part of the Minas countryside may have reached its carrying capacity by 1920.

To be sure, leaving the North was customary since the mid-nineteenth century. By the 1870's, slave convoys were moving south to the coffee zones, sold down the São Francisco River by their debt-ridden owners. Seasonals departing for São Paulo were waved off by the old folk, women, and children in a determinedly gay fiesta. Others marshaled outside Juiz de Fora with their goods—hammocks, knives, leatherware, and straw hats—before splitting off in groups of ten, 20, and 50 to work on the coffee plantations in Rio de Janeiro Province during the late Empire. With the harvest in, they returned via Juiz de Fora to purchase goods on their way back north.[27]

Laborers from the more developed southern zones were no less willing to seek employment out of state. It was not the lack of people, but rather the shortage of field hands that led farmers in the Mata and the Sul to bemoan their inability to obtain steady labor after 1910.

Triângulo farmers paid the best rural wages, but they, too, lamented the "fickleness" of labor while noting the migration trend. With whole municípios losing people to São Paulo and Paraná by the 1920's, the elite became alarmed. Too many Mineiros were outward-bound. The migration reached flood tide by the 1930's. In Rio, Mineiros entered the building trades as the capital and its bureaucracy grew rapidly under Vargas. This was rural-to-urban migration, but in São Paulo they took the place of native and foreign-born field hands who had themselves migrated to the city. By 1940, large numbers were settling in Paraná.[28]

Except for the Triângulo, the Center, and the East, all the other zones had almost ceased to grow. See Tables 1.8 and 1.9.

Averaging 36 percent of the state's population between them, the Mata and the Sul retained the commanding lead that the nineteenth-century coffee boom had given them. Yet their decline in total state population after 1920 reflected near-stagnation. The North declined at an accelerating rate. Of these three zones, only the Mata grew at all after 1920, and this by only .3 percent. It was one thing for the backward North to decline, quite another for the coffee regions, which belonged to the Brazilian south, to lose their demographic dynamism. For Juiz de Fora, the future was not bright. Known as the "Brazilian Manchester" for its textiles and light industry, Juiz de Fora had grown from a nineteenth-century commercial and communications center servicing the Mata coffee frontier. In fact, the more prosperous southern half of Minas lost momentum to the Center, reversing the historic flow out from the old mining zone.

Sparked by ranching and agriculture, the Triângulo retained its

TABLE 1.9

*Percent of Population in Major Regions of Minas Gerais, 1872–1940*

| Zone | 1872 | 1890 | 1900 | 1920 | 1940 |
|---|---|---|---|---|---|
| North | 17% | 16% | 16% | 15% | 13% |
| East | | 4 | 4 | 11 | 15 |
| Center | 26 | 25 | 25 | 16 | 18 |
| Triângulo | 7 | 6 | 6 | 6 | 7 |
| West | 12 | 12 | 11 | 12 | 12 |
| Sul | 19 | 19 | 20 | 21 | 18 |
| Mata | 17 | 17 | 18 | 18 | 17 |

SOURCE: Same as Table 1.8. Figures may not add to 100 percent because of rounding.

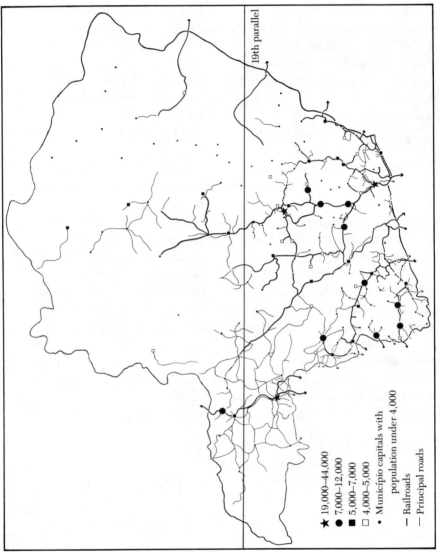

★ 19,000–44,000
● 7,000–12,000
■ 5,000–7,000
□ 4,000–5,000
• Município capitals with
  population under 4,000
— Railroads
— Principal roads

Fig. 2. Minas Gerais in 1920. Adapted with minor modifications from Yves Leloup,

share of population, as did the West. The Triângulo was one of two new zones, and the city of Uberaba served it as a commercial and banking center. The other was the frontier East, which despite malaria and poor transportation led the state in population growth. Initially, the East grew at the Center's expense. Migrating northerners and Capixabas (from Espírito Santo) contributed, as well. These data show that the Center almost ceased to grow between 1890 and 1920, but then the historic movement outward reversed itself. Families spilled back into the city and its heartland. Belo Horizonte developed an economic base; the small bureaucratic capital quadrupled in just 20 years, reaching over 200,000 people by 1940.[29]

A glance at Figure 2 shows that Minas Gerais was still sharply divided between the backward North and the developed South at roughly the 19th parallel. Excepting the Triângulo, all but six of the county seats north of the parallel had fewer than 4,000 inhabitants. By 1937, two of these were leading regional centers: the North's Montes Claros and the East's Teófilo Otoni. Transportation, giving access to urban markets, was the key to growth. The more developed southern half of Minas, by contrast, exhibited a well-articulated network of towns and transport routes in 1920. These had taken their modern functions during the great coffee boom and railroad construction phase between 1850 and 1900, discussed in the next chapter. Marshaling the lion's share of population, productivity, and transportation routes between them, the Mata and the Sul were the most urbanized zones of Minas. And whereas the Triângulo consolidated its late-nineteenth-century growth pattern, the major changes in this map by 1940 occurred in the Center and the East, with the North and West still lagging in towns and transportation.

This having been said, it bears repeating that most Mineiros lived isolated, rural lives. In 1920, with only 11 percent living in municipal seats and the rest considered rural, Nelson Sena called Minas "the state where urbanism is least conspicuous." And if cities smaller than 5,000 are left out, the urban population falls to 5 percent. In 1940, 25 percent lived in cities, but 13 percent were in cities under 5,000, the dividing line between what Leloup considers urban and "concentrated rural" populations.[30] The small cities cherished their identities, many of which went back to eighteenth- or early nineteenth-century origins. However, most of the cities under 5,000 probably were not sufficiently differentiated in function from their countrysides to support a truly urban life-style. For the most part, they appended from the rural society that they provided with weekend markets, minimal services, and the traditional religious and secular functions including elections.

Urbanization can be measured roughly by charting the growing number of municipal governments that proliferated from 91 in 1888 to 288 in 1938, often for political and prestige reasons. Using non-political standards, one may differentiate cities with agro-pastoral economies from other cities that were organized around more typically urban activities, such as manufacturing, merchandising, and transportation. However, it should be emphasized that real urban environments were found only in the few cities over 10,000. These true cities grew rapidly after 1920. Thus, between the three census periods 1920, 1940, and 1950, the number of larger cities grew from five to 22 to 36, and attracted first 2, then 8, and finally 13 percent of the state's population.[31]

However small and isolated most of the cities were by contrast to the true urban centers, this did not imply a flagging of the elite's respect for urban values and institutions, as will be discussed in Chapter 3. And Minas, a society in migration, did participate in the national urbanizing trend, especially after 1930. As elsewhere in Brazil, the towns appealed to countrymen with their *movimento* (hustle and bustle), their cinemas and pharmacies, their schools and health care centers, and above all by offering the hope of work. Change there was, if on a scale still modest by post–World War II standards.

Ranking the leading municipalities by income is another way to measure change, as a glance at Table 1.10 suggests.

One trend is the rapid rise of Belo Horizonte and, by contrast, the relative decline of Juiz de Fora. Note that in 1889 Juiz de Fora led the old capital at Ouro Preto by more than 2:1 in revenue. Yet by 1910 it trailed Belo Horizonte by 3:2, then 2:1, and, finally, with its industries in depression and its coffee trade paralyzed, the once dominant Mata city had slipped in 1937 to 10:1. By the 1920's, Belo Horizonte was differentiating beyond its primary bureaucratic function to command substantial commercial and industrial resources in its own right. To be sure, Juiz de Fora did not stagnate; rather, it held a constant 2:1 lead over dynamic Uberaba, the ranching, rice-milling, and commercial center for the Triângulo. Note also the stable positioning of

TABLE 1.10

Municipalities, Ranked by Income, 1889–1937

(In round contos)

| Municipality | Income | Municipality | Income |
|---|---|---|---|
| **1889** | | **1910** | |
| Juiz de Fora (M) | 88 | Belo Horizonte (C) | 945 |
| Além-Paraíba (M) | 46 | Juiz de Fora (M) | 630 |
| Ouro Preto (C) | 38 | Uberaba (T) | 376 |
| Leopoldina (M) | 37 | Barbacena (C) | 212 |
| São João del Rei (C) | 29 | Ponte Nova (M) | 168 |
| Mar de Espanha (M) | 28 | Carangola (M) | 142 |
| Uberaba (T) | 20 | Poços de Caldas (S) | 128 |
| Barbacena (C) | 20 | Além Paraíba (M) | 128 |
| Muriaé (M) | 20 | Itajubá (S) | 126 |
| Diamantina (N) | 17 | São João del Rei (C) | 120 |
| Pomba (M) | 15 | Cataguases (M) | 111 |
| Ponte Nova (M) | 14 | Leopoldina (M) | 107 |
| **1923** | | **1937** | |
| Belo Horizonte (C) | 2,575 | Belo Horizonte (C) | 33,407 |
| Juiz de Fora (M) | 1,269 | Juiz de Fora (M) | 3,687 |
| Uberaba (T) | 660 | Uberaba (T) | 1,762 |
| São João del Rei (C) | 515 | Uberlândia (T) | 1,137 |
| Barbacena (C) | 507 | Poços de Caldas (S) | 1,097 |
| Carangola (M) | 496 | Barbacena (C) | 1,093 |
| Poços de Caldas (S) | 360 | São João del Rei (C) | 1,085 |
| Ouro Fino (S) | 342 | Araguari (T) | 835 |
| Ponte Nova (M) | 301 | Pouso Alegre (S) | 739 |
| Manhuaçu (M) | 300 | Itajubá (S) | 718 |
| Ubá (M) | 282 | Caxambu (S) | 707 |
| Uberlândia (T) | 281 | Teófilo Otoni (E) | 683 |

SOURCE: Municipal income from the following: 1889: Senna, *A terra mineira*, 2:276. 1910: Brazil, *Anuário estatístico*, ano I, vol. 2, pp. 350–61. 1923: Brazil, *Estatística das finanças*, Table XXIX. pp. 110–20. 1937: Menelíck de Carvalho, *A revolução de 30 e o município* (Quadros demonstrativos da arrecadação efetuada pelos municípios mineiros no período de 1931 a 1938), n.p.

NOTE: Subregions are indicated in parentheses: Center, East, Mata, North, Sul, Triângulo, West.

São João del Rei and Barbacena, two small manufacturing cities that prospered throughout the period under review.

Another trend is the shift in Mata coffee wealth from the old Imperial bastions of Leopoldina and the south Mata cities, out beyond Carangola and toward the frontier East, where by 1937 Caratinga ranked fifteenth in municipal income. Juiz de Fora excepted, the Mata towns were relatively less affluent by the 1930's, with Ponte Nova, the railroad division point and sugar-refining center, having slipped from fifth place in 1910 to ninth in 1923 and fourteenth in 1937. For its part, the Sul was buoyed first by the popular watering spots at Poços de

Caldas and Caxambu—which attracted wealthy Paulistas—and second by the distribution and food-processing centers at Ouro Fino, Pouso Alegre, Itajubá, and Lavras. Also noteworthy was the Triângulo's growth sparked by the uplands rice boom after 1910 and by integration into the São Paulo market. Joining Uberaba on the index were Uberlândia (1923) and Araguari (1937), the latter a railroad supply point for southern Goiás and the new capital at Goiânia.

Finally, the emergence of Teófilo Otoni on this ranking draws attention to the East, a zone that later took a great leap forward with the construction of a World War II strategic highway from Rio to Salvador, Bahia. Drawing Mata commerce away from Juiz de Fora, the new Rio–Bahia highway would do to that leading Mata city in the 1940's what Belo Horizonte had done since 1910.[32] Although North and West regional cities scarcely appear on this ranking, municipal income figures for the 1930's mark the rapid ascendency of Montes Claros, where revenues increased from 200 contos in 1934 to 685 contos in 1938, clear evidence of its emergent role as the North's commercial center.[33]

This was a mosaic of regions, some facing toward São Paulo, others toward Rio, still others toward Bahia; each zone with its discrete history, yet still a distinct unit with a definable identity: what historical experiences did the Mineiros share, and how did their mosaic hold together?

## Regional Dynamics

Unity, although fractured along several lines, was the ideal of a political elite for whom dismemberment of the territorial unit was a possible consequence of weakness. Fired with regional patriotism, Mineiros in the 1890's used the decentralized Republic to make their old province more viable. Their guidelines were drawn from two centuries of experience as an isolated, interior province, a legacy that was highlighted by the Inconfidência Mineira, an abortive revolt for autonomy led by Joaquim José da Silva Xavier, called Tiradentes, against the Portuguese in 1789.

A central tenet of what can be called the "symbol pool" of ideas from the Inconfidência was the establishment of a new capital city to replace Ouro Preto, an isolated, bureaucratic city in decline with the gold mines. "The sooner another site for the capital is found the better," reported Richard Burton, the nineteenth-century British traveler who agreed with those Mineiros who saw great benefits accruing from a better-located capital.[34] Tiradentes himself wanted São João del Rei in the Center zone. By the 1890's, several other cities were in self-proclaimed contention, from isolated Minas Novas in the North, which actually constructed a "governor's palace," to Juiz de Fora in the Mata, with its good communications to Rio and commercial importance. After considerable debate among regional political groups, the entirely new city of Belo Horizonte was selected in 1893 and inaugurated in 1897. And whereas the slowness with which Belo Horizonte became an economic and communications center was disappointing to many who had expected quick results, the graceful new capital symbolized Tiradente's legacy for a more perfect union.

Having agreed to a new, centralizing capital, the Mineiros abandoned separatism, an idea recently popular among the zones as a solution to their different problems. In 1873 the Emperor himself endorsed a bill to create a new province in the São Francisco Valley corridor from Montes Claros in Minas to southern Pernambuco, thus strengthening the Empire's riverine communications between north and south Brazil. This bill foundered on provincial rivalries, even as northern Mineiros imagined a different future for themselves.[35] In an 1888 anecdote a young northerner dreamed that he awoke in the progressive Montes Claros of 1938, where newspapers fat with advertisements for railroad stocks and diamond mines were hawked in bustling streets through which the coach and escort of the governor of Minas do Norte clattered past.

The Triângulo was also swept by talk of separation. Neglect by the distant capital at Ouro Preto, high taxes, and the fact that commerce moved through Santos were the reasons why Uberaba and neighboring towns wanted to join São Paulo or to form a separate province of their own in the 1870's. Consider, also, the many bills to establish an independent Minas do Sul—denied by the Provincial Assembly in 1862, 1868, and 1884—or the plan to join the Sul with northern São Paulo. These two contiguous zones claimed they were being "asphyxiated" by the newer, richer units on the coffee frontier, which got most of the railroad projects.[36] After the Empire collapsed, however, Mineiros closed ranks to fortify the new state.

It is true that separatist sentiment persisted, along with poor internal communications and power inequalities among zones. Separatist rhetoric helped politicians to extract resources and concessions from the governor. Yet these zonal demands occurred in a Republic whose ideological center of gravity was the statehouse, and in a state whose existence was predicated on a unique type of regional solidarity.

Politically, Minas evolved into a mini-federal system. This allowed regional interests to be juggled and balanced off within some reasonable conception of the whole. After the state constitution was promulgated in 1891, separatism, by whatever pretext, was considered unpatriotic and subversive. This the city of Campanha discovered when it raised the standard of revolt in January 1892 for an independent state of Minas do Sul, thereby inviting federal intervention.[37] Once the Mineiros were freed of central government tutelage, redrawing the old colonial boundaries seemed as dangerous and undesirable to them as it did to decolonized Africans in the 1950's, who faced the much more serious problem of tribalism.

The drive for unity that shaped Mineiro patriotism also contained another imperative from the eighteenth-century symbol pool: to stem the "loss" of resources with which a more viable economic system could be built. The *inconfidentes* resented Portugal's taxing of their gold exports while prohibiting manufacturing and the development of provincial institutions, such as a university, with which to transform the wealth at home. After this colonial experience, it was inevitable that a landlocked exporting unit like Minas would resent its neo-colonial economic role vis-à-vis Rio and São Paulo, which, with their seaports, controlled the export-import trade and communications. Over the years, Mineiros decried what they called "the loss of their substance" to other units.[38]

Attempts to obtain better terms for exports, thus alleviating their historic role as exporters of low-value foodstuffs and raw materials in exchange for high-priced goods and services, were attempted from 1890 to 1937. Even with the best of intentions, however, it was difficult to break this structure of dependency. Economically, the results were disappointing, despite some short-term success. Psychologically, fears for this "loss of substance" were an important part of the political culture.

To Senator Teófilo Otoni, the nineteenth-century Liberal statesman, obtaining a seaport was the key solution to this problem as landlocked Minas entered the age of exports in the 1850's. For lack of a port, Mineiro traders could not compete on equal terms with their Carioca and Paulista counterparts. Foreign middlemen in Rio and Santos also reaped profits on coffee, the main state export, before it left Brazil. Illogically, the ocean port at Vitória belonged to another unit, a legacy of Portuguese colonial policy. To facilitate a political union with Espírito Santo, some delegates to the 1891 state constitutional convention wanted to decentralize Minas into several autonomous cantons on the Swiss model. But this unionist proposal (with or without the cantons) dissolved in a flourish of federalism as political groups from Vitória claimed they would lose their *own* cultural identity, not to mention their right to an independent judiciary and separate patronage.[39] A long-standing border dispute then helped to delay the economic integration of these two units for many years. This most direct route to the sea was not opened by rail until 1935, and not fully accessible by road until the trans-Minas highway from Uberaba to Vitória was completed in late 1969. Meanwhile, the port solution to Minas's "loss of substance" was fading by the 1930's, overshadowed by the realization that Minas faced certain structural problems of underdevelopment that a seaport might alleviate but could not resolve.

Regional solutions to Minas's economic problems were never popular in Rio and São Paulo, where state policies along these lines were viewed as "narrow regionalism," as artifacts of the Mineiro's innate conservatism, as awkward and absurd. Speaking only from the economic point of view, it is true that the state's "natural" role was to be someone else's hinterland. Mineiros could do little to reverse the disaggregating effects of the export economy, in which, to be sure, many of them profited. After 1930, the growing national market for domestic manufactures reinforced links to São Paulo, while the Mata and the East remained in Rio de Janeiro's commercial orbit. At the same time, however, Belo Horizonte began to integrate its own hinterland. For the first time since the mining boom, political power at the capital was equivalent to economic power.

As a region, Minas was defined not only by its diffuse economic base but also by cultural and political values. Mineiro regionalism was primarily a political-cultural conception, which did not mesh easily with economic factors. Regional coherence was thus powerfully determined by the existence of political boundaries. That Minas was not a coherent economic unit derived from its eighteenth-century origins as an administrative convenience of the mother country. Since Tiradentes, however, the ideal of unity and of trying to make the political unit more viable economically was an important legacy of this state's political culture. This ideal sparked the founding of Belo Horizonte in 1897. Later, a Mineiro president of Brazil (Juscelino Kubitschek) moved the federal capital to Brasília in 1960 for much the same reasons.

The thrust of Mineiro regionalism was to provide an economy for the fortifying of provincial power. Two American geographers, Howard Odum and Harry Moore, called this the essence of regionalism in their study of ways to improve the American federal system in the 1930's. Because their own regional development plan depended upon the creation of new political units, it was ignored by federal and state officials.[40] Mineiros did not have this problem: their region coincided with the existing political frontiers. Thus they enjoyed a political base. But the results of regional policy were disappointing, in part due to political defects; in part because the regional prescription was ambiguous owing to the state's peculiar location and mosaical pattern of development. This theme runs throughout the book.

Reshaped, but still rooted in eighteenth-century origins, Mineiro regionalism differed significantly from that of São Paulo and Pernambuco. The expanding frontier, the boom in export agriculture, and the rise of São Paulo city created a new Paulista elite in the nineteenth century whose politics and values were shaped by the growing economy. In the case of São Paulo, economic power led the growth of political power. By contrast, Pernambuco began as a seventeenth-century plantation society whose elite developed neither the values nor the economic base for an effective regionalism after 1890. Having been an important unit during the Empire, Pernambuco's complex decline is chronicled in a companion volume to this study. In sum, Minas did relatively less well than São Paulo, and much better than Pernambuco. To explain why is the challenge of comparative history, and this points up the need to reexamine Minas and its regionalism in the light of old problems and new questions.

## CHAPTER TWO

# The Economy

UNEVEN, MODERATE GROWTH—but not stagnation—describes the Mineiro economy from 1889 to 1937.[1] Moderate growth, however, was not commensurate with the state's political power and large population. Whereas other large states in the Center-South underwent structural transformations, the rate and direction of economic change in Minas was less profound, less supportive of modernization based on capitalist techniques and aspirations. A landlocked state with difficult internal communications, Minas did not derive enough benefits from, or participate fully in, the growing national internal market that accompanied export-led growth. If falling behind was to be the long-term fate of Minas, falling into a dependency relationship with the Federal District and São Paulo was the fear imbedded in the "loss of substance" theme. In sum, the economy expanded but not fast enough, so that Mineiros had to live with a situation of relative decline.

In 1939, Minas ranked second to São Paulo in gross agricultural and industrial production, with Rio Grande third. To be sure, the Paulistas were widening the lead they had held since the late Empire, and the Gaúchos pulled even with Minas in the 1930's. Allowing for cyclical trends, however, the production of basic food grains, beef cattle, and dairy products expanded throughout this period. Coffee, of which Minas was the second producer, was the most valuable export crop. The share of manufacturing in the state product was small but growing, sparked first by textiles in the 1870's, food products in the 1900's,

TABLE 2.1

Exports per Capita, 1890–1940, Based on Official Values

| Date | Population | Exports | Exports per capita | In 1912 milreis | In current dollars |
|---|---|---|---|---|---|
| 1890 | 3,184,099 | 60,005:984$ | 18$846 | 29$3 | $8.67 |
| 1900 | 3,594,471 | 151,386:925$ | 42$116 | 38$7 | $7.84 |
| 1906–8 | 3,960,000 | 142,684:843$ | 36$031 | 38$2 | $11.16 |
| 1920 | 5,888,174 | 455,052:203$ | 77$282 | 40$9 | $17.40 |
| 1921 | 5,888,174 | 524,544:492$ | 89$084 | 65$0 | $11.69 |
| 1930 | 6,312,295[a] | 687,563:452$ | 108$924 | 76$2 | $11.67 |
| 1938 | 6,736,416[b] | cr$1,408,122,000 | cr$209.03 | cr$86.7 | $12.21 |
| 1940 | 6,736,416 | cr$1,654,102,000 | cr$245.54 | cr$98.2[c] | $14.88 |

SOURCE: Based on official state export values cited in Jacob, *Minas Gerais no xx° seculo*, p. 365; Governor Bernardes, Mensagem, in Minas, *Annaes da Camara, 1922*, p. 42, and Governor Valladares, Mensagem, in *1937*, p. 59; and state figures cited by Daniel de Carvalho, *Estudos de economia e finanças*, p. 180. The price index for 1912 contos is a splice of a foodstuffs price index through 1929, compiled by Lobo et al., "Evolução," and a general cost-of-living index from 1921 to 1939 in Brazil, *Anuário estatístico, 1939/40*, p. 1384; Michael L. Conniff amalgamated the two series to produce the overall index used here. He also prepared the series on U.S. dollar equivalents, 1892–1940.
   [a] Arbitrary estimate.   [b] 1940 population.   [c] 1939 index figure.

then iron and steel in the 1930's. Gold mining continued; and although some manganese and iron ore were exported, Minas had in fact ceased to be a mining economy in the early nineteenth century. By 1937, the state product was still based largely upon agriculture and stock raising.

The available indicators, however crude, show the effects of uneven growth. Export values per capita increased threefold overall. See Table 2.1. The share of manufacturing in gross agricultural and industrial production climbed from 17 percent in 1920 (the first year such figures are available) to 26 percent in 1939.[2] According to data in Table 2.2, Mineiro manufacturing increased from 19 percent of Paulista output by value to roughly 22 percent. In sorry contrast, agriculture declined from 72 to 62 percent of São Paulo's production by 1939. Out-migration accelerated, and the state's population almost ceased to grow between the wars.

Several long-term factors helped to dull the stimulus of market forces. These included a low per capita income, low productivity, and lack of credit, coupled with overdependence on coffee and an inadequate transportation system. Above all, there was the basic fact that Minas, with its mosaic of different subregions, was not a coherent economic unit. Furthermore, in contrast to the other two leaders, Minas tended increasingly to become a marginal producer of all items in its primary export sector, including dairy products. Rio Grande and

São Paulo produced more efficiently for the Brazilian domestic market; São Paulo reaped the lion's share of profits from the foreign market and of the benefits, such as immigrants, loans, and investment capital; Minas Gerais did relatively less well in both markets. This was not stagnation, of which Pernambuco is the example in our tristate comparison. It was a situation of *relative* decline, as is clear in Table 2.2.

Minas was pulled toward the São Paulo and Rio growth poles, shipping low-priced raw materials, buying back high-value industrial goods and processed foodstuffs.[3] This had the effect of a neo-colonial relationship of dependence, or at least of regional disequilibrium. Market integration on these terms was galling to Mineiros, who saw it as a disaggregating influence, running counter to regionalist ideology. Few, if any, then thought in terms of the São Paulo–Belo Horizonte–Rio de Janeiro industrial triangle, a new productive unit that emerged clearly for the first time during World War II.

Dependency was dramatized by the patronizing attitudes of wealthy Paulistas on vacation at the fashionable spas of southern Minas. Their saying "Where the Mineiro goes, progress stops" was a smug certitude. Another remark (still heard in São Paulo), "Where the road stops,

TABLE 2.2

*Gross Agricultural and Industrial Production, 1920 and 1939*

(1920 values in current contos; 1939 values in 1969 million cruzeiros)

| State | Agriculture | Industry | Agriculture and industry | Agriculture and industry as percent of São Paulo |
|---|---|---|---|---|
| São Paulo | | | | |
| 1920 | 1,210.7 | 914.9 | 2,125.5 | |
| 1939 | 2,893.9 | 2,810.4 | 5,704.3 | |
| Minas Gerais | | | | |
| 1920 | 872.4 | 174.2 | 1,046.6 | 49.23 |
| 1939 | 1,789.4 | 621.7 | 2,411.1 | 42.26 |
| Rio Grande | | | | |
| 1920 | 465.8 | 353.7 | 819.6 | 38.55 |
| 1939 | 1,590.8 | 670.2 | 2,261.0 | 39.63 |
| Pernambuco | | | | |
| 1920 | 302.9 | 138.4 | 441.3 | 20.76 |
| 1939 | 525.8 | 359.4 | 885.2 | 15.51 |

SOURCE: Data from the 1920 census are in João Lyra, *Cifras e notas*, pp. 44–45; 1939 data are from Brazilian National Accounts, in *Conjuntura Econômica*, June 1970, p. 55. I have not included the tertiary sector in these comparisons because Lyra does not list it. In 1939, however, the total products of Minas, Rio Grande, and Pernambuco were 32.1, 32.7, and 14.2 percent, respectively, of São Paulo's total product.

Minas begins," pointed up the growing gap in economic performance between the two states. After 1930, São Paulo became a net exporter to the rest of Brazil, and Minas's trade balance with its neighbor worsened.[4]

Mineiros preferred to blame their less impressive performance not on cultural values, such as conservatism and the avoidance of risk-taking, but on markets and the accidents of geography. The Triângulo and large parts of the Sul were a natural part of the Paulista market, to which they were linked by good road and rail communication. Commercial guides to São Paulo included the Triângulo municípios, at the back, in small print. The Mata was integrated commercially with the Federal District. The North, a backward ranching zone, slowly integrated with the capital, which became a growth pole in the 1920's, but only matured in this role by the late 1950's, when Minas finally developed an extensive statewide transportation system.

Landlocked Minas depended upon Rio and Santos for export services, which favored the export-import houses there, drained off talented native sons, and attracted capital to out-of-state banks. "We lack railroads to carry progress and prosperity toward the Center [of Minas]," wrote Afonso Pena, the future governor and president, in 1890. Thus "the human and material capital emigrates, contributing a great deal to our backwardness."[5] Stimulating the internal market, generating more revenues in the heartland, and ending Minas's "colonial" dependence on the coast were very old aspirations.

All the same, Rio de Janeiro—the center of politics, literary culture, and imported fashions—fascinated the Minas elite. Commercial ties reinforced and deepened this attraction. Money deposited in Rio banks weighted investment opportunities toward federal bonds, commerce, real estate, and industry in the Federal District. Cariocas lampooned the outlanders for their country ways, and their saying about Mineiros was "The best ones always leave." Mineiros, for their part, developed a love-hate relationship with the national capital while promoting policies of regional self-assertion and analysis, including the oft-repeated "loss of substance" theme.

### Rural Labor

The impact of abolition was at first severe, although in retrospect it was more a political turning point than the socioeconomic upheaval

Mineiros feared at first. Having made few preparations to attract immigrant labor (unlike São Paulo), most planters saw no alternative to gradual abolition. The author of a report on São Paulo labor policies predicted that the transition would be more difficult for Minas.[6] Production slumped throughout the province: coffee exports declined 28 percent in 1889; cereals rotted uncollected in the fields while *libertos* (freedmen) moved into the towns; ranchers in the West and the Triângulo complained they could not get help. Consequently, several fazendas failed, land values fell, and the Banco Territorial, one of two new commercial banks, collapsed.[7] Conditions, while uncertain, were hardly catastrophic. By 1891, inflation eased planter debts and the planters met wage costs in a depreciating currency while coffee prices rose. That the first state budget was $1.3 million in surplus eased the political transition (see Chapter 4) as well.

Paying wages was a painful experience for many fazendeiros, who were at first nostalgic for the days of "supervised" (lash-driven) labor, and complained about the lack of a steady, reliable, and above all cheap labor force. A number of ex-slaves seem to have stayed in the towns, while others went into subsistence; libertos who wanted to work accepted sharecropping, contract labor, and partial wage systems in addition to the daily cash payment, which cushioned the impact of abolition.[8] Immigrants began arriving in modest numbers. That the planters were unable, and in many cases unwilling, to pay good wages was probably the major cause for labor shortages in the coffee areas.

Fazendeiros elsewhere complained that high coffee prices were driving wages up, attracting labor away from the small farms where basic staples were raised. The planters also drew on seasonal labor from the North and West zones, something the poorer regions could protest but not prevent. And meanwhile, the shift of exhausted coffee lands in the Mata and the Sul to ranching and dairy farming actually displaced labor to the newer coffee zones. Concurrently, inflation in the 1890's eroded the wage earners' purchasing power, encouraging migration or a move into subsistence farming.

These adjustments, the regional competition for labor, and in fact the entire labor shortage was seen by agriculturalists everywhere as a question of labor discipline. To men dependent on cheap agricultural labor for their profit margin, the so-called "vagrancy problem" was an obsession. Responding to a state questionnaire in 1894, several fazendeiros said transportation and vagrancy were the two main obstacles facing Mineiro agriculture. Labor they regarded as fickle, unreliable, and disloyal, as all too willing to live off the land in idleness—in short, as a social problem for the authorities. In the words of one fazendeiro, "It is society's duty to put these miserable sons of the forest under a regime of steady work, thus modifying their grosser habits."[9]

The congressional delegation voted for a labor contract law in 1896, but the Supreme Court ruled that certain provisions to force fulfillment of work contracts were incompatible with a free society, and President Prudente de Morais vetoed it. Unable to secure restrictive labor legislation, or to attract immigrant labor, fazendeiros asked the state police to round up vagrants at harvest time. "What must be done first of all is to employ our own large native Brazilian working population," a fazendeiro leader said. "Instead of working with the implements of agriculture, these men—a floating population—carry firearms and knives, terrorizing fazendas, alarming the countryside, brawling and robbing as they go."[10] Police activities were stepped up after 1900. Supplementary measures, such as municipal labor registries, work cards, and state penal farms, were often suggested but never implemented, largely because the police and the state forces would have been given a broader mandate to meddle in local politics. By the 1920's, urbanization and the blandishments of Paulista labor contractors replaced vagrancy as the causes most frequently cited by fazendeiros for their labor problems.[11]

Hoping to attract and fix native Brazilian field hands on their land, many fazendeiros by 1900 were turning to the *meiação*, a shares system widely used in the Paraíba Valley coffee region to attract libertos. The meiação became the dominant labor system in the Mata, but fazendeiros were very reluctant to subdivide their lands outright so that small farmers could take title.[12] The meiação and other forms of sharecropping (*parceria*) cushioned the impact of depression during 1897–1909, but restrained purchasing power and productivity in good times. Rice farmers in the Triângulo used it often, but it was less frequent on coffee plantations in the Sul. Wage labor predominated in the Center, stimulating commerce and manufacturing in the capital with its growing hinterland. Sharecropping appears to have leveled off by World War I, being closely tied to the fortunes of coffee. The 1940 census data show that parceria accounted for only one-fifth of the value of agro-pastoral production, while salaried labor was responsible for two-thirds.[13] In retrospect, there was a labor shortage—because of low wages—but no shortage of Mineiros.

## Coffee

Coffee was the state's most valuable export, its budgetary mainstay, the reason why two of its regions—the Mata and Sul—dominated state politics for most of the Old Republic. Starting in 1900, Minas averaged about one-third of São Paulo's output, making it Brazil's second producer. (Nine Mineiro municípios ranked among the 20 top coffee producers in 1920.) Yet Minas is treated as a peripheral area in the abundant literature on Brazilian coffee. São Paulo had a large comparative advantage in coffee growing: better, more abundant land, plentiful immigrant labor, and excellent rail service from the coffee frontier to Santos. Minas coffee lands were less productive, the growers paid lower wages when they did not use sharecropping, and coffee generated less revenue for the state—all this despite having good rail service in the Mineiro coffee zones. Thus Minas Gerais was an important but nonetheless marginal producer of Brazil's prime export.

The Sul produced one-third of the coffee, exporting via Santos; the rest came mostly from the Mata and was shipped through Rio. Because of different soil conditions, the Mata grew an abundance of lower grades, 7 through 9, whereas the Sul specialized in the better-quality fines, for which there was a stronger market. Mata fazendeiros were concerned primarily with shoring up the price of low-grade types, which suffered severely during market slumps. The Sulista growers shared São Paulo's interest in improving the overall marketing position of the industry, which meant limiting low-grade types if necessary. To complicate things further, Mata planters exporting through Rio bore the full burden of Minas state export taxes; Sulistas using the port of Santos received a partial tax rebate from the exporters and paid lower freight rates as well.[14] Given these regional differences, the coffee growers rarely spoke with one voice. Unlike their Paulista counterparts, they had difficulty organizing an effective pressure group. Economic and political factors produced a different environment in Minas, which was not, therefore, a mere replica of the Paulista coffee sector.

Minas relied heavily upon coffee while lamenting overdependence on this one major export. See Figure 3. In good years—1891–96, 1911–12, 1920–27—the state prospered, but efforts to diversify the agricultural economy faltered.* In bad years—1897–1909, 1929–37—the entire economy suffered because of low coffee prices, but diversification was encouraged. To a state reaching both foreign and domestic markets, coffee presented a dilemma. Getting out of coffee was unthinkable, although in terms of world marketing conditions this would have made economic sense.

Starting in 1896, huge Brazilian coffee crops caused a marked excess of supply over world demand, which Mineiro growers blamed on São Paulo for overplanting virgin frontier lands. Correctly, they also linked falling prices to the manipulations of foreign middlemen, who speculated with warehoused stocks abroad. What to do about the crisis of overproduction was the subject of intense debate at the state, interstate, and national levels. Promoting more coffee sales abroad, which was the remedy preferred by the Mineiro planters, was impractical both because of excess stocks and because of the coffee's relative price inelasticity of demand. Limiting their own plantings, combined with a ban on the export of low-grade types were policies of market discipline that some officials in the state government advocated but the planters opposed. The planters faced ruin, especially with the federal treasury's tight money policy, which was designed in part by Finance Minister Murtinho to force marginal coffee producers out.[15]

To discuss the agricultural crisis, producers, politicians, and bureaucrats convened an Industrial, Agricultural, and Commercial Congress at Belo Horizonte during the week of May 13–19, 1903. Discussion ranged over many issues, but the main purpose of this elaborate congress was to reach a consensus on coffee. Ranchers, merchants, and industrialists were content to use the congress as a forum to air their problems and suggest solutions. But the restive planters wanted nothing less than to take control of coffee policy, while the state, in turn, sought to keep them under political control, as will be discussed in

---

* During the earlier coffee boom, basic food staples had to be imported in Minas. Export-led prosperity in the 1920's financed foreign food imports, which cut into Mineiro markets.

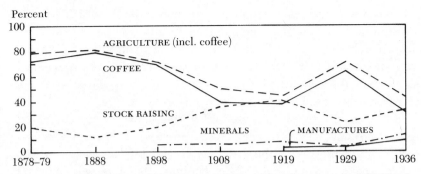

Percent

Fig. 3. Value of Minas exports, 1878–1936. Based on data from Rodolfo Jacob, *Minas Geraes no xx° seculo* (Rio, 1911), pp. 411–12; Bernardes, Mensagem, in Minas, *Annaes da Camara*, 1920, p. 311; Valadares, Mensagem, in *Annaes da Camara*, 1937, pp. 62–63.

Chapter 4. Proceedings of the 1903 congress reveal just how far apart the two sides were.

Chaired by João Pinheiro da Silva, an industrialist who would soon be governor, the Preparatory Committee drew up propositions that several study committees then elaborated upon before discussion was opened to the floor. Pinheiro's official group came out strongly for market discipline, based on differential freight and tax rates to penalize the poorer coffee types below grade 7. The Coffee Committee accepted this and suggested also that valorization, a marketing policy based on minimum price supports, be worked out with the other coffee states and the Union. These ideas were consistent with current Paulista thinking, but none of them were adopted by delegates on the floor.

Instead, the congress voted to set up an agricultural association in Juiz de Fora, with *indirect* state support. The association would promote, and perhaps market Mineiro coffee abroad, thus bypassing the foreign middleman. Located away from the new capital, the new interest association would be dominated by Mata planters, who refused to limit plantings of low grades. The planters did not reject valorization, but they clearly wanted to speak with a strong independent voice in any negotiations with other states.[16] Such an interest association would also have had political power, something the state authorities wanted none of.

Starting in 1904, São Paulo led the fight in congress for federally financed price supports. When President Rodrigues Alves refused to compromise his tight money policies for valorization, Minas, São Paulo, and Rio de Janeiro state negotiated the Taubaté agreement on their own in February 1906. These states planned to negotiate a foreign loan themselves, with federal participation. The tri-state agreement also provided for a surtax of three gold francs on each 60 kilo sack exported, to be used as security for a foreign loan.

In August, the state legislature ratified the Taubaté Convention, but refused to limit new plantings—a key provision of the agreement— and was unhappy with the gold surtax and the agreement not to valorize coffee below grade 7. Furthermore, the state was reluctant to take on more foreign indebtedness during the depression. Planter opposition, combined with the state's own fiscal conservatism, led Minas to back away. São Paulo moved ahead alone, financing the first coffee retention plan with loans from the foreign coffee commission houses and with state loans. Minas and Rio de Janeiro also withdrew their pledge to support the tri-state surtax fund. In effect, the two marginal producer states scuttled the Taubaté Convention while supporting the concept of a valorization plan.

São Paulo always maintained that coffee was a national resource, not a regional problem. Minas helped to sell this idea to the other states, and pressed for the ratification of Taubaté in congress, although by now the convention was nothing more than a statement of intent. Two of the three states were not participating financially, nor was the treasury. At this juncture the Mineiro delegation swung the congress behind companion legislation on the exchange to make valorization work.

David Campista, a very able deputy from the Mata who would soon become Minister of Finance, led the floor fight for a controversial Exchange Bank scheme to stabilize the national currency at relatively low levels.[17] Without such a mechanism, the exchange rate would have risen because of the favorable balance of payments due to stronger coffee prices. The planters preferred a falling exchange to raise their domestic profits; they settled for stable rates when they felt pressure from the treasury, which had to meet foreign payments; Campista's bill conciliated the two positions. Furthermore, stabilizing the exchange at lower levels was also consistent with the protectionist thrust of Mineiro economic policy, discussed below. Under the Exchange Bank scheme, products such as butter, rice, and meat would be sheltered from foreign imports.

Minas also agreed to collect the 3 franc surtax, and pressed congress to guarantee the São Paulo state loan, which it did in 1908. In return, São Paulo agreed to lower support coverage through grade 9—this was financed by a small federal loan in 1907—thus mollifying producers of low grades in the Mata and Rio de Janeiro.[18] Minas huddled under the umbrella of this, the first of four price support plans that São Paulo sponsored and in large part financed over the next 25 years until the federal government took charge. São Paulo followed an internationalist solution to overproduction, which was "respectable." Financing the retention plans with foreign loans was also something a wealthy state could afford. The Minas approach to coffee policy was a less affluent state's solution, consistent with its economic conditions and traditions, but less "respectable." This is perhaps another reason why Minas was ignored in much of the contemporary literature on coffee. In fact, the state made several attempts to modernize this and other sectors of Mineiro agriculture.

Governor João Pinheiro (1906–8) was a forceful advocate of cooperatives, through which the planters would sell directly to consumers and receive low-interest loans from the state's Banco de Crédito Real. At São Paulo's insistence, Pinheiro imposed the unpopular gold franc surcharge, and then tapped this new revenue (which in 1907 brought in $1.5 million dollars) to fund cooperatives. Upgrading production, improving methods of cultivation, and diversifying into new crops were also goals of Pinheiro's co-op program. Such a program under state direction also had political advantages for a man who wanted to be a strong governor. Growers in each coffee município were encouraged to organize cooperatives. For its part the state would advertise Mineiro coffee abroad and establish warehouses in Rio, Santos, and European ports. "Cooperatives are the main solution" for Minas, a prominent state economist wrote. Yet, to be sure, the state was also joining "other support measures," including the Paulista plan.[19]

The cooperatives were based on the idea that protectionism, better techniques, and new technology would do for Mineiro agriculture what they had accomplished for the United States. This had been

Pinheiro's dream since the Republic began. To the state, better revenues would accrue; to the fazendeiros, better prices and credit; to the
society as a whole, the many benefits of modernization. Nineteen
cooperatives were active by 1909, and 36 were functioning just four
years after Pinheiro's untimely death in 1908.

João Pinheiro expected the cooperative movement to spread into
dairy farming, cotton, tobacco, and ranching. Without having been
given a real test, the cooperatives foundered when several societies
failed to meet sales contracts and their obligations to the banks.[20]
Furthermore, the state began diverting surtax funds to general revenues to pay salaries of bureaucrats and the judiciary. For the planters,
who all along suspected that their taxes would be earmarked for
general revenues, this dampened the spirit of cooperation. Budgetary
data show that the largest disbursement of coffee support funds
occurred in 1909, on the eve of a disputed presidential election.[21] This
was followed by a scandal in the Secretariat of Agriculture over mis-
use of the surtax funds. Moreover, with São Paulo and the exporters
funding valorization, and with the United States continuing to be the
main purchaser of Mineiro coffee, schemes to increase European coffee
sales were quixotic. The higher coffee prices obtaining during 1911–
13 must have been another disincentive to cooperation, for by World
War I the co-op movement was discredited and all but forgotten.

The second coffee valorization began in 1917 to counteract the
bumper 1917–18 crop, which again threatened prices. Minas again
backed São Paulo, and helped to make valorization a national institution.* A third intervention followed in 1921, based on a federal loan,
and the Institute for the Permanent Defense of Coffee was established.
This federal program was abolished when President Artur Bernardes,
a Mineiro, took the Union out of price supports in 1923 to economize.
São Paulo again stepped in unilaterally. And in 1927 the producing

---

* Congress and the public considered valorization a success. Whether it was
advisable to concentrate so much of the nation's resources on this luxury product
is questionable, given distortions in the growth process and the fact that coffee
was favored over the rest of agriculture. Consult Delfim Netto, *O problema*, and
Peláez, "Análise econômico." Taking a different perspective, Krasner points out
that Brazil, an underdeveloped country, succeeded in actively influencing the
world coffee market, obtaining higher and more stable prices, which consumers
could not prevent. The 1906 valorization "was the first major attempt by any
Latin American exporting country to influence the market on which its earnings
depended" (p. 499).

states, including Minas, signed the so-called Second Coffee Convention, the key provision of which was to regulate exports on a monthly basis, thus bypassing the exporters, who could not speculate on warehoused stocks.[22] Overplanting undermined this scheme, which collapsed in 1930. In early 1931, the states met again to establish a united coffee policy, this time to destroy excess stocks. But the problems of overproduction, eliminating low grades, and upgrading quality controls were now considered a federal responsibility, and in May of 1931 the Union stepped in for good.[23]

In Minas, relations between the growers and the state improved because of valorization. As governor in 1919 Bernardes lowered the state export tax on coffee. Nonetheless, the planters continued to complain about the lack of credit and the diversion of their surtax funds to other uses. In 1925, they attended a large coffee congress in the capital, following which the state pledged to channel the surtax through its Banco de Crédito Real for loans to fazendeiros.[24] The Mineiro Institute for Coffee Defense (IMC) was established to coordinate defense measures with the São Paulo state institute while bringing the growers directly into policymaking as elected members. In return for access, the growers were called upon to legitimize state coffee policy, a tactic of corporatist control often used by Vargas in the 1930's.

The planters were mollified at first by a flow of credits. Starting in mid-1929, however, they organized themselves into a new pressure group called the Centro dos Lavradores Mineiros at Juiz de Fora. A combination of weak coffee prices and political instability favored this maneuver, which had been attempted a generation earlier at the 1903 Congress, and again at Cataguazes (1916) and Juiz de Fora (1917), when the short-lived Confederação Mineira de Agricultura was established. Following the 1930 Revolution, the Centro dos Lavradores took control of the IMC without, however, abandoning the advantages of close association with the state.

The Centro's links to Belo Horizonte flowed through Jacques Maciel, the governor's nephew, who headed the IMC during 1930–34. Pressure on the state for better credit services led to the founding in 1933 of the Mineiro Coffee Bank, a mixed corporation of state and private capital also directed by Maciel. This bank was controlled by private coffee groups, exactly the opposite of what occurred in the Vargas government's mixed enterprises. The Centro's solution to the coffee crisis was that of the Paulista Society of Agriculture: return to free market policies and get the federal government out of marketing except to guarantee minimum prices.

Such independence ran counter to the centralizing politics of Vargas, who had reorganized the federal coffee service in 1933. Following the death of Governor Olegário Maciel, Vargas appointed his own man, Benedito Valadares, the new interventor of Minas Gerais. In March 1934, a platoon of state police seized the IMC headquarters in Rio and Jacques Maciel was fired. From then on the coffee bureau was run by a functionary loyal to the new chief executive in Belo Horizonte, who in turn took his orders from Rio.[25]

The reestablishment of state control over coffee policy coincided with a drastic decline in coffee receipts, from over half the value of all state exports in 1932 to only 31 percent two years later. Federal credits from the National Coffee Department helped to keep the industry alive. Although phasing out coffee altogether was still unthinkable, its collapse encouraged diversification into other crops, including sugar and cotton in the North. By 1937 Valadares said the state was "definitely shifting into polyculture, which suits the Mineiro economy better."[26] This rhetoric had been heard before.

In the late 1890's, with coffee prices falling, it became intolerable to import basic staples of which Minas, because of monoculture, had ceased to produce enough for its own needs. Developing the national internal market was considered the best way out of depression. The means were lower freight rates, protective tariffs, and the establishment of producers' cartels and cooperatives.

Lower, uniform freight rates on cereals after 1898 allowed Mineiro corn, beans, and rice to compete with and displace foreign imports in the Rio market. Between 1900 and 1910, corn exports increased by a factor of 2.7, feijão (black beans) by 5, and rice exports 28-fold.[27] "Protective tariffs are the economic salvation of Brazil," Pinheiro told the 1903 Congress. Deputy João Luís Alves managed the protectionist bills through congress, where vigorous bargaining with other states took place (see Chapter 6). Tariffs on rice, lard, potatoes, charque (beef jerky), beef cattle, and butter all went up between 1903 and 1906, the high tide of protectionism. Modeled after German cartels, the Syndicate of Mineiro Dairy Products Producers cornered the domestic butter market behind a tariff wall. Pinheiro also expected the coffee cooperatives to carry out aggressive sales abroad.[28]

Poor transportation and low productivity limited the extent to which Mineiro products could expand into the domestic market. Being dependent on customs receipts to cover foreign obligations, the treasury opposed further tariff hikes, and the Paulistas, who courted immigrants and foreign investments, were not enthusiastic about protectionism. Rising coffee prices encouraged foreign imports, which, despite temporary disruption during World War I, resumed again in the 1920's as the competitive position of Mineiro agriculture declined.[29]

Whereas João Pinheiro's generation responded imaginatively to the depression crisis, the Valadares group seemed unwilling or unable to act decisively. Correia Dias, a Mineiro sociologist, suggested that the Valadares government did little because it was passively subject to the central power.[30] That Minas became a political client of Vargas is of course true (see Chapter 4). But the state also faced a systemic crisis of underdevelopment in agriculture that was both more complex and more severe than in the previous depression.

Diversification failed on the whole. Cotton, which attracted many former coffee planters in São Paulo, did not meet expectations in the North because of poor quality control. Paraíba Valley dairies south of Minas captured an ever larger share of the Rio and São Paulo markets, while the famous Minas cheese met with consumer resistance, and Mata milk was occasionally contaminated. The familiar obstacles to modernization were still there: poor transportation, low productivity, low wages, lack of agricultural credit. Newer factors included soil exhaustion near the main consumer centers in the Mata and the Sul, and tougher competition from other states in the Center-South. The rate of growth slowed alarmingly in the 1930s' as agriculture stagnated.

*Stock Raising*

Beef on the hoof, meat, and animal products were the second export sector after agriculture. With the largest herd in Brazil, Mineiro ranchers improved their breeding stock with the Zebu and pushed the cattle frontier westward into Goiás and Mato Grosso. Cattle exports increased sixfold. See Table 2.3. Yet the state lost many opportunities to expand, upgrade, or even hold onto its share of the national market for animal products. Stock raising tended to follow coffee's

TABLE 2.3

Exports of Live Animals, 1895–1936

| Year | Number | Year | Number |
|------|--------|------|--------|
| 1895 | 101,425 | 1920 | 385,165 |
| 1900 | 172,545 | 1927 | 520,296 |
| 1905 | 273,495 | 1934 | 412,439 |
| 1910 | 297,548 | 1936 | 598,117 |
| 1915 | 347,478 | | |

SOURCE: Singer, Desenvolvimento econômico e evolução urbana, pp. 220, 252.

fortunes. Imports rose when coffee prices were good, depressing cattle prices and also making less urgent schemes to modernize the industry. Also Mineiro ranchers failed to master changes in interregional patterns of production and marketing. The usual pattern was for cattle to reach the large urban markets via winter pasturage centers and fairs in the Sul, where they were purchased by Paulista and Carioca dealers. After 1900 this system bifurcated into Rio and São Paulo sectors. Mineiros neither shaped this development nor reaped the benefits.

Responding to the growing urban market for Mineiro beef, and also to the beginnings of an export trade, Paulista buyers led by the British-owned Anglo Frigorífico Co. captured the cattle trade in western Minas, the Triângulo, Goiás, and Mato Grosso. Range cattle now moved by rail over newly constructed branch lines to the São Paulo pasturage, and by 1910 the Sulista fattening centers at Passos and Santa Rita de Cassia were in decline.[31] Most of this beef was processed at Barretos by Anglo. In addition to supplying São Paulo, Anglo began shipping meat products abroad and to the Federal District.

Pork products followed close behind. By World War I, traditional Mineiro exports to Rio of salted pork, bacon, and sausage—still "packed in baskets and hampers"—were being displaced by modern packaged goods from São Paulo. Things had reached the point where "to buy a slice of bacon in Belo, one now must purchase the Paulista product," a businessman lamented in 1923.[32]

Traditionally, cattle for Rio de Janeiro were fattened near market fairs run by concessionaires in the Sul and Mata. Cattlemen either drove their herds to the slaughterhouse outside Rio, where their emaciated animals brought low prices, or sold to traders through the concessionaires, who raked off commission fees at the cattle fairs. To pacify middle- and lower-class consumers who were hit by inflation, President Floriano Peixoto granted a monopoly contract to the Rio slaughterhouse at Santa Cruz in 1891. Stockmen also had to compete with better-quality Platine beef that the Santa Cruz monopoly imported to depress domestic prices. Starting in 1898, three fairs were put under state regulation: Sítio and Bemfica in the Mata, and Três Corações (the largest) in the Sul. The objective was to concentrate sales at a few points where the ranchers could hold their cattle while awaiting good prices. Regulated trading, it was hoped, would prevent Carioca buyers from dictating prices.[33]

Falling exchange values, which raised the price of Platine beef, and better rail links to the Federal District made this scheme possible. The Santa Cruz monopoly was abolished and a tariff placed on imports, both owing to action by the Mineiro congressional delegation. By 1902, almost 150,000 animals were registered at the three cattle fairs. But the price advantage did not shift to producers, as is clear from debates at the 1903 congress. Retailers and middlemen still bought cheap, at 300–350 reis per kilo, and sold dear to the Rio consumer, who paid anywhere from 900 to 1$200 reis for his kilo of fresh beef.[34] For purposes of keeping prices up, three fairs were too many. The state never intended to intervene directly in cattle sales: a domestic "valorization" plan for beef would not have been politically possible. Instead, cattlemen were encouraged to conduct their own sales through cooperatives.

Defeat was snatched from the jaws of victory, or so a former officer of the Sul-Mineira Pastoral Cooperative recalled years later. Organized in 1914, this co-op embraced fatteners throughout the Sul, including those who traded through Três Corações. They patterned the cooperative after a similar organization in the West, where cattlemen banded together to combat low prices paid by Paulista dealers. For his one conto entrance fee (about $318), a rancher gained access to collective marketing by co-op agents in Rio. This group turned a profit on its first shipment of chilled beef to Europe. But just as it was well positioned to put pressure on the Rio dealers, a large rancher bolted and the organization faltered. The original officers resigned under recriminations, to be followed by others who took a commission on sales before the co-op collapsed in early 1915. "What could one expect?" said one of the organizers; "Among Brazilians the associational instinct is rudimentary, and when we do associate someone always breaks off yelling."[35] Carioca buyers also broke the co-op's united front by successfully manipulating their old trading connections with the ranchers.

Because of the cattle cycle, it is doubtful that stockmen with live animals to sell could have obtained stronger prices unless a significant part of their herd were processed at cold storage plants in Minas. Shipping cattle on the hoof to slaughterhouses and *frigoríficos* out of state resulted in higher transport costs, weight loss, and profits deferred to other units. The drawbacks of this neo-colonial situation were well known, but the solutions were illusive.

Governor Silviano Brandão urged American investors to set up a packing plant in the late 1890's to serve the Rio and São Paulo market for processed meats.[36] This was unrealistic, because the Americans did not move into Rio Grande, with its better business climate, until 1917, preferring until then to invest in Argentina. Frigorífico Anglo's extensive operations, coupled with Brazilian-owned slaughterhouses near the large urban markets, made it all the more difficult for Mineiros to get started in the processing business after 1918. The British integrated their Barretos plant with large ranching properties in western Minas and sent out purchasing agents. Their slaughtering operations for the Rio market were concentrated at Mendes, just outside the city and linked by rail to pastures in north and central Minas. When the Central do Brasil Railroad reached Montes Claros in the 1920's, an Anglo company agent took up residence. Young, attractive, and single, he received the attention and prestige accorded someone serving a powerful organization.[37] The presence of capable foreigners, who sold reliable products and offered good service to urbanites, was doubtless intimidating to would-be national entrepreneurs in Minas.

In 1928, the state offered tax incentives to investors (hopefully including foreign firms) to establish five slaughterhouses, which, when expanded, would provide one modern packing plant each to the Mata, West, Sul, Triângulo, and North zones. This scheme died in the depression, if indeed it was ever viable in the face of established operations near the Rio and São Paulo markets. The arguments for establishing a network of regional plants to process Mineiro beef were still compelling to the postwar generation.[38] By 1960, state, privately owned, and mixed packing plants were operating in the capital, Montes Claros, and the East. Yet the best beef still went to Rio; the tough, low-grade "Belo Horizonte type" stayed for consumption in the region.

## Industry

Almost all the plants, small factories, and artisan shops existing by 1920 had been founded after 1889. Classically, textiles and food products led this early import substitution phase, contributing 82 percent of the value of industrial production in 1920 and employing four-fifths of the industrial labor force. By 1939, these two consumer-based industries between them accounted for half of the state's industrial production. However, iron and steel now comprised the state's second industry (ahead of textiles), having expanded tenfold—to 20 percent of production—from its humble origins in the late nineteenth century. Labor also changed: the two pioneer sectors between them employed just over one-third of all industrial workers in 1939, and one-fifth were now working in metallurgy.[39]

Almost all of the capital, labor force, and industrial establishments (from artisan shops to factories) was concentrated in the developed southern half of Minas. See Table 2.4.

Gold, iron, and manganese mining was concentrated in the Center, the home also of the iron and steel industry and of textile plants both in the capital and north along the Central do Brasil mainline. Mining accounted for 22 percent of the state's total capitalization but only 5 percent of its industrial product. All but 3 percent of mining capital

TABLE 2.4

*Minas Industry, 1937*

| Region | Capital (880,268 contos, or $76 million) | Labor (77,821) | Establishments (9,237) |
|--------|------|------|------|
| Center | 68% | 43% | 19% |
| Mata | 16 | 26 | 28 |
| Sul | 9 | 17 | 31 |
| TOTAL | 93% | 86% | 78% |

SOURCE: Based on state data in Minas, *Annuario industrial, 1937*, p. 258.

was in the British-owned Morro Velho gold mine, the state's largest employer. Iron ore exports were insignificant until World War II; German and American companies exported some manganese. Twenty-nine percent of all industrial assets was invested in metallurgy, of which three-fifths was held by Belgian-controlled plants.[40]

Although the state industrial plant was still small in 1939—with 13 percent of the nation's factories, Minas accounted for only 7 percent of its industrial product—Belo Horizonte rapidly increased its share within Minas. Three of every four plants existing there in 1936 were founded after 1925.[41] Only Juiz de Fora, which liked to be called "the Manchester of Minas," and the capital were true industrial centers. Industrial establishments were mostly small, oriented to local markets, and employed few people. Rio's industrial wages for adult males in 1920 were 17 percent higher than those in São Paulo, and 63 percent more than in Minas. Other salaries showed comparable differentials.[42]

Conditions, while not unfavorable to industry, channeled investments into small, compartmentalized markets based on coffee and ranching. A combination of tariffs, exchange devaluations, and high railroad freight rates to the coast produced the first industrial boom in the 1890's. Foreign textiles were kept out, and although freight rates on agricultural exports went down at Minas's insistence, manufactured goods from Rio and São Paulo were not so favored. In fact, Mineiro food products and textiles had a competitive edge until highways began to lace together the countryside in the 1930's, letting Paulista products flood the Sul and Mata.

The textile industry grew rapidly until the late 1920's, based largely on the production of coarse cloth as in Pernambuco. In the early days, local transit taxes between municipalities constrained the market, while interstate tariffs drove up the price of Bahian cotton. Like their competitors in Rio and Sao Pãulo, Minas mill owners could not import replacement parts and new equipment in the 1930's. But the biggest obstacle to expanding nationally was the fractured home market that originally shaped this industry. Too many plants, many with outmoded equipment, were small and inefficient. Bernardo Mascarenhas, who pioneered with modern packaging and marketing techniques at his large Juiz de Fora plant in the 1920's, was exceptional.[43]

Iron and steel products led the second industrial boom, in the 1930's.

Several charcoal-based steel plants began production, including the 100,000-ton-capacity mill at Monlevade owned by Belgian interests. Concurrently, small blast furnaces smelted pig iron for rolling mills and machine shops located outside Minas near the nation's large consumer centers. With large reserves of iron ore and manganese, the potential for large-scale steelmaking existed in Minas. For a time it seemed that Minas Gerais could become the Brazilian Ruhr, to have at last the dynamic economic base that neither coffee in its heyday, ranching at its most profitable, nor the consumer-products industry could provide. Unfortunately for Minas, its role by 1945 was still, and more than ever before, that of a specialized supplier of raw materials and foodstuffs to cities and factories out of state.

Abundant, proved reserves of high-grade iron and manganese ores existed near Belo Horizonte. Yet the obstacles to transforming this potential wealth into an economically expoitable resource were severe. Major development of these mineral deposits was delayed until the 1950's by such factors as bad railroad service, long distances to embarcation ports, capital shortages, and uncertain legal titles—all of which Mineiro policymakers did not adequately assess in their ambiguous, at times hostile attitude toward exporting this patrimony. Having shipped their gold to Portugal in the eighteenth century, the Mineiros were determined not to let the rising demand for iron ore in Europe and the United States create the conditions for a new colonial experience in the twentieth. Their desire to promote steelmaking was hampered by yet another factor, the lack of fossil fuels, although several small plants based on charcoal fuel were established. Of these, only the Monlevade works was large enough to offer economies of scale, partially offsetting the obstacles of distance from consumer markets and poor transportation. All of these factors pointed up the advantages of a coastal location, where foreign coking coal could be easily exchanged for ore.

The story of Percival Farquhar and Itabira Iron Ore Company is well known.[44] From 1910 into the 1930's, the most promising solution to the ore-steel-transport-market puzzle was Farquhar's scheme to export ore over a private industrial railroad through Vitória port in Espírito Santo; to import high-grade coal in the returning ore ships; and, under pressure, to construct a large (250,000 ton capacity) steel mill on the seacoast or within the Minas frontier. Itabira, as well as

the other foreign owners of mineral holdings in Minas, was interested
primarily in the iron ore trade. But Farquhar might have built the
steel plant, for which there was a domestic market. Why Itabira was
rejected for less adequate solutions is still controversial.

The Minas case is an early example of an underdeveloped region
trying, and failing, to maximize the benefits from its large holdings of
raw materials. This worked for coffee but not for iron ore. Using the
carrot-and-stick approach, the Mineiros attempted to encourage steel
production by a differential ore export tax by which exporters who
used up to 5 percent of their ore in steelmaking would receive a 99
percent tax reduction. This strategy grew out of their favorable experience with protectionism and reduced freight rates in the early
1900's, and was promoted vigorously by Governor Artur Bernardes,
Clodomiro de Oliveira, the metallurgical expert, and João Luís Alves,
his Secretary of Finance, in 1919. When, to their surprise, Farquhar actually agreed to build the plant in exchange for very low ore taxes,
Bernardes realized this would give Itabira a monopoly over all sectors
of the business.

Bernardes backed off in favor of small, charcoal-based plants near
the ore deposits. He preferred the French-speaking Belgians, who
began producing at Sabará and were careful to accept local equity
capital while cooperating with the other small concerns, to the
English-speaking Farquhar, who was patronizing. The other small
producers attacked Itabira as colonial, knowing they could not survive
existing foreign competition—let alone Itabira—without tariffs and
state subsidies. Leading public figures and industrialists, men like
Euvaldo Lodi, Ribeiro Junqueira, and Américo Gianetti, had invested
heavily in the existing small industry. Gianetti spoke for the producers
against Farquhar at a state steel congress in 1925.[45] (Twenty years
later, however, he worked very hard to attract modern heavy industry
to Minas.) The upshot was to encourage high-cost production in the
name of saving the nation from Farquhar.

However understandable, the decision to block Farquhar was short-
sighted. Opening up the Rio Doce Valley would have shifted the
industrial-development axis toward the pioneer East zone and Vitória
with its excellent port. In turn, the Mineiros were ridiculed for insisting on a narrow regionalist solution to heavy industry while their ore
deposits stayed unmined. Bernardes' poorly conceived steel plan

channeled development toward small-scale plants. The industry expanded rapidly during the depression, but its main product was raw steel and pig iron shipped to out-of-state plants, where most of the value-added operations took place. In 1942, the Vargas government began the Volta Redonda works outside Minas and close to the two big consumer markets. The role assigned to Minas in the interregional solution was once again to supply the raw materials.

## Commerce and Banking

Economic growth was also hampered by another set of factors, namely, the existence of small disarticulated consumer markets and low purchasing power. Large parts of the Sul and the Triângulo were linked to the Paulista market; the Mata and the East were traditional clients of the Rio merchant houses; and the North traded through Bahia until the 1930's. Wholesaling was concentrated in Uberaba, Juiz de Fora, and (after 1910) in Belo Horizonte. Goods imported through Rio and Santos were distributed from these cities to merchants in the many small towns that made up the fragmented Minas market. If anything, these traditional patterns of trade were reinforced by the growing internal trade in national industrial products after 1930.[46] Concurrently, Belo Horizonte was becoming the commercial and transportation hub for the northern half of Minas, finally fulfilling one of the arguments for moving the capital.

The ethos of merchant capitalism was well developed in Minas, where the buying and selling of goods was a respected occupation. Merchants frequently served their apprenticeships in Rio commercial houses. They often stayed in lodgings provided by their commercial correspondents when they were in the capital on buying trips. Several Rio houses in turn dispatched *cometas* (traveling salesmen) to the interior with goods, lines of credit, and advice on the latest fashions. Thus Minas, particularly the southern half, was integrated to the coast through well-established commercial ties.

Historically, Mineiros had been doubtful about the benefits of this relationship. The sense of being exploited by the port merchants and overcharged by middlemen was articulated by the Inconfidentes, with echoes into the Republic. The ports raked off perhaps as much as one-fifth of the value of Mineiro trade, an economist estimated in 1929.[47] Twice the state authorities and commercial groups tried to redirect the import-export trade directly into Minas via an *alfândega sêca,* or inland customs house. Construction on a customs warehouse began in Juiz de Fora in 1894; a customs administration building was erected at state expense in Belo Horizonte after 1925. Neither edifice was ever staffed with federal customs officials, which says much about the commercial and political obstacles to this unconventional solution.

Juiz de Fora received federal and state approval for the first customs house in 1893, shortly after this commercial center lost its bid to become the new state's capital. Something of an interstate trade-off was also involved, for the city of São Paulo was authorized to establish its own inland customs house. In "The Commercial Emancipation of Minas" a prominent Mata writer justified the project with references to Tiradentes. Too much capital was being drained off to Rio. The new entrepôt would encourage railroad building and promote the economic integration of remoter zones, he added.[48] Linking it to Angra dos Reis on the coast would give Minas another ocean outlet, others argued. In addition to customs personnel, the Union was to provide sealed customs trains to run between Juiz de Fora and the coast.

Critics charged that such a customs house based on elaborate marshaling yards and federal rolling stock would be costly to implement and operate. Furthermore, the feeder lines to carry goods into southern Minas and beyond were not yet built. By 1898, with the nation in depression, sentiment in congress turned against the concept of decentralized customs houses and Minas was left with a half-completed, empty warehouse.[49] Juiz de Fora wanted to revive the project, but by 1920 the initiative passed to merchants in the capital.

Groundbreaking took place in September 1925, and the Belo Horizonte customs building was handed over to federal officials four years later. The arguments and rhetoric were familiar. Governor Melo Viana called this "the first step toward emancipating the Mineiro economy from an almost colonial situation, looking to the day when we can send the greater part of our products directly to customers here and abroad, and receive the goods we need at lower cost." This scheme also depended on rail service, but this time the customs house was tied into a state transportation plan in which Belo Horizonte was the hub of new or projected lines fanning off to the West, the Triângulo, and the North. A good part of this railroad construction was under way or finished, making this plan less quixotic than the earlier one. Furthermore, the capital was much better located to integrate the state commercially. Whether Minas could in fact redirect commercial patterns by this means was debated in the press. Given the capital's rapid growth, it might have worked. But the onset of depression, coupled with political tension with the central government, led to abandonment. The new Vargas government did not favor state initiatives of this kind, and the new customs building reverted to the Secretariat of Agriculture.[50]

More practical if less dramatic means to stimulate commerce were discussed at the 1903 Congress, including the establishment of better roads, a banking system, statistical services, and yearly trade fairs in the capital and the municípios to show local and regional products. Promoting closer commercial ties between the subregions was still a major theme at the 1923 Municipal Congress.[51] But throughout this whole period transportation was seen as the key to commercial growth.

Trade increased despite persistent obstacles, and changes in the import list reflected a developing economy. Foodstuffs, including sugar, flour, and salt for the cattle industry, led the list in 1908, followed by tools, wood, building materials (including cement), kerosene, and agricultural machinery. By 1929, machinery of all kinds was first in value, followed by automobiles, fuel, and cement, then flour and salt. Chemical products and pharmaceuticals were also among the leading imports. Textiles declined by the early 1900's, although shoes and hats were still coming in large quantities by 1929. Alcoholic beverages were a minor import item throughout this period.[52] As for the basic staples —rice, beans, and corn—the state fed itself except during the first coffee boom.

Banks were attracted by the quickening pace of trade and commerce, but belatedly, for Mineiros traditionally did their banking on the coast. The isolation between trading centers, the lack of a port city, and the fact that the coffee zones were tied into the Rio banking network reinforced this pattern. There was no lack of speculators ready to lend at high interest in the nineteenth century; often their operations carried into other provinces. Merchants in the remoter zones kept a strongbox to hold accounts of commercial houses in Rio and Ouro Preto, and handled payments to their agents.[53] Until the

1930 Revolution, moreover, Mineiros preferred to invest in federal bonds. Thus the growth of banking after World War I was a notable departure from old patterns.

The first commercial banks were founded in Juiz de Fora in the late 1880's. One, the Territorial, soon collapsed and the other, the Crédito Real—a semiofficial institution to make agricultural loans—limped along by handling state accounts. Of seven banks active by 1895, all but one were located in Mata coffee towns. The Bank of Brazil's failure wiped out several accounts and hurt Mineiro banking, which then atrophied during the long depression. By 1921, there were 63 banks, agencies, and branches in over 40 towns—all but four of them, to be sure, in the southern half of Minas. Buoyed by coffee, ranching, and small industries, the Sul led with 25, followed by the Mata with 20, the Center with seven of the largest institutions, and the Triângulo which now had five.[54] Minas ranked third in the number of banking institutions, but it was a distant third. The Federal District and São Paulo between them held nearly three-quarters of all bank deposits between 1921 and 1936. The Minas share rose from 2.5 to 5.9 percent, whereas Pernambuco's declined. The share of foreign banks in current accounts was insignificant, compared with Pernambuco and São Paulo.[55]

Credit operations by Mineiro banks lagged behind demand, leading to the conclusion that they followed opportunities more than they promoted economic growth. Thus an industrialist struggling to start a steel plant complained in 1899: "However well conceived, an iron and steel project cannot get finance from the banks, which consider these companies dangerous. Private capital is interested only in public debt titles, or goes into short-term mortgages. And foreigners will only finance their own operations.[56] The need for more banks and lending capital was reiterated over the years. There was room for another dozen banks, a leading political economist advised after World War I.[57]

The lack of agricultural credit was a constant lament of the planters, who paid the bulk of state taxes. Their plight worsened when the coffee commission agents, who had advanced them credit, declined by 1900. Rerouting the coffee surtax funds back to them in the form of credit did not go far enough, when these funds were so applied. Mortgage funds were in short supply: the state's Crédito Real was bogged down in bureaucratic routine, and the Banco Hipotecário, the other semiofficial institution founded in 1911 with French capital, did not meet expectations. Commercial banks preferred to operate in the larger population centers: "They don't like to make long-term, low-interest loans and small loans to agriculture," a banker commented in 1927. Rice growers in the Triângulo could not get bank credit to expand, and when they did, it was at 12 percent, repayable in four months. "In truth, we have only commercial credit, on short terms and high interest," another expert said.[58]

The entrance of official lending agencies changed the credit situation somewhat in the 1930's without granting much relief. The Union dominated credit and controlled large reserves through the Bank of Brazil and its savings banks and pension plans. The state Coffee Bank (later the Mineiro Bank of Production) began making loans in 1934 and expanded into other sectors. The federal government reduced agriculture mortgage debts by half in the Economic Readjustment Act of 1933. But this relief plan helped the large Paulista planters, who received half the national total, more than the Mineiro smallholders, whose problem was credit rather than a heavy burden of indebtedness.[59] Bank of Brazil loans continued to be hard to get outside Rio and São Paulo, where three-quarters of the outstanding loans to farmers, industrialists, commercial firms, and individuals were concentrated in 1937. Mineiros held only 6 percent of the national total (about $60 million) outstanding in 1937. Only in the mid-1940's did large amounts of federal loan money filter into Minas agriculture, probably owing to politics at the end of Getúlio Vargas's dictatorship in 1945.[60]

## Transportation

Minas led the nation with one-quarter of all railroad trackage in 1938 (8,160 kilometers), ahead of São Paulo—which had only half the area—with 22 percent, and far outclassing Pernambuco's 3 percent of the nation's track. The first phase of railroading (1870–1900) began in the Mata, where several small, speculative lines were built starting in the mid-1870's. Construction in the Sul and the Triângulo began for the most part after 1890. These two zones, being close to São Paulo, were tied into the Mogiana Railroad system and the port of Santos. In the meantime, the federal Central do Brasil (EFCB) reached the highlands in time to link the new state capital with Rio de Janeiro. Almost all these early railroads received liberal concessions, based on subventions by the kilometer and/or guaranteed gold interest payments on invested capital from the provincial and Imperial governments. Logrolling and localism also counted, as an English engineer observed in 1873 while traveling the Pedro Segundo Railroad (later the EFCB) near Minas: "The whole of this [Paraíba] valley belongs to a comparatively few wealthy and important Brazilians, Viscondes and Barões, of such influence that the railway has had to cross the river five times between Pirahy and Porto Novo da Cunha by long and expensive bridges to serve the interests of a Barão this side, or a Visconde on the other." Several lines were constructed by the coffee planters themselves in conjunction with British capitalists.[61] The combination of booming coffee sales and pork barrel concessions produced results: over 3,500 kilometers of track was laid in Minas alone between 1875 and 1899, half of it in the 1890's.

Uncoordinated and undercapitalized as many of these early railroads in Minas were, they functioned reasonably well as long as coffee —a high-value, low-weight crop—could support the high freight rates needed to turn a profit. All of Minas caught railroad fever in the 1890's. Excepting the Bahia and Minas Railroad, however, an inefficient line from Teófilo Otoni to the Bahian coast, very few private companies actually laid track outside the southern zones. By the late 1890's, with coffee in decline, many private ventures passed into government ownership, and some 21 Mata roads were incorporated into the British-owned Leopoldina system.

In phase two (1900–1930), the federal government rescinded most of the remaining private concessions and dominated railroad construction until the state government became actively involved in the 1920's. Federal engineers completed the west Minas line after 1910, so that travelers could now reach Uberaba from the state capital, albeit by a still circuitous route. They also pushed the long-delayed EFCB tracks into north Minas, reaching Pirapora on the São Francisco River in 1922, and Montes Claros in 1926. An exception to government initiative was the French-financed Vitória a Minas Railway. This narrow-gauge line opened the Rio Doce to settlement, although under Percival Farquhar's control after 1909 it was redesigned to haul iron ore rather than to serve as a pioneer trunk line. In taking control of the floundering Paracatú Railroad in the West, and the Goías Railroad leading from the Triângulo into Goías, the Bernardes state administration (1918–22) assumed a large, direct role in railroad ownership and management. In 1920 it rented what became the Rêde Sul Mineira (joining several small lines in the Sul and Rio de Janeiro state) from the federal government. And with the renting of the federal west Minas line in 1931, the state's entire system was renamed the Rêde Mineira da Viação. In line with this policy, responsibility for coordinating all existing and projected rail routes in Minas was shouldered by the state in 1924, when it drew up a master railroad development plan. Despite large expenditures, however, the Mineiro state system was still undercapitalized and incomplete when the depression curtailed further state efforts to create an integrated rail net.

Whether in retrospect Minas derived the full benefit from this Brazilian railroad age is a matter of some doubt. For one thing, much of Minas with its mountainous terrain was not good railroad country. The steep grades, many curves, different gauges, and uncoordinated systems pushed costs up and efficiency down. For another, the railroad was a system that reinforced the historic outward reach of subregions to export markets, while at the same time it could not respond flexibly, as for example truck transportation could, to changing conditions in each zone.[62] Substantial sections of the state's Rêde Mineira da Viação and the British-owned Leopoldina system ran through old, unproductive coffee lands. Because of high construction costs, the rails tended to follow economic opportunities rather than to pioneer them. Moreover, the episodic and uncoordinated construction programs did not produce the massive impact on production factors (as in the United States) that might have worked to integrate the Minas mosaic. Ironically, the railroad technology that served São Paulo so well after the 1880's helped to assure that one of the 20 empty boxcars pulled by the Paulista locomotive would be Minas Gerais.

At first, railroads appeared to offer nothing but advantages to landlocked Minas. Those who wanted to relocate the capital claimed that Belo Horizonte would become a rail hub for lines radiating north to the São Francisco River, east to Vitória with its deep-water seaport, southwest to the Triângulo and Central Brazil, and down to the Federal District on the EFCB mainline. Even opponents of the new capital, such as Cesário Alvim, the first governor after 1889, called for a

state-wide rail net to tie the regions together with bands of steel as
Tiradentes would have wished.[63] In fact, the Republican experiment in
Minas was predicated upon integration by railroad. Fanning out to
the compass points, the new and projected trunk lines were supposed
to valorize land, attract immigrants, stimulate local economies, and
accelerate the circulation of goods; in short, to repeat the North American success story now hopefully facilitated by the new federal institutions.

Mule troops and oxcarts nonetheless fed the new railheads far longer
than the early modernizers would have wished. Indeed, many of the
projected trunk lines still were not built by 1920. Beaumont joined a
mule train in the late 1890's making the six-day journey north to
Diamantina from the EFCB railhead at Sete Lagoas, near Belo Horizonte. The Britisher noted that the mules, carrying 120 kilos each,
often traveled 400 to 500 miles from the sertão to the railhead, where
hides, sugar, or coffee were exchanged for cotton textiles, canned provisions, hardware, crockery, and salt.[64] These old colonial trails to
Bahia and Goías were used into the 1930's. Cities north of Belo
Horizonte grew rapidly when the Central arrived, stimulating the
textile industry at Sete Lagoas and Curvelo, which used cotton from
north Minas, and promoting agriculture and especially ranching in
the Montes Claros area.[65] But towns in the extreme North were not
linked to the mainline Central until 1947, more than 80 years after
this line first reached the Mata. For lack of a rail link to the Central
system, heavy industry was delayed until the late 1930's in the upper
Rio Doce Valley. Well served by the mule but disillusioned with railroads, Mineiros turned enthusiastically to the motor vehicle.

The truck arrived too late to spare Minas a long and expensive in-
fatuation with the iron horse. By 1920 one subregion, the Triângulo,
had already developed an extensive highway net to serve its railroads.
In fact, this was a harbinger of the system that was best adapted to
Mineiro conditions. British companies pointed the way. Cattle on the
huge British-owned Brazil Land and Packing Company holdings in
west Minas were trucked to the railroad, and the São João del Rei
Company used trucks on its extensive properties near Belo Horizonte.
To be sure, most of Minas north of the 19th parallel still had no
modern transportation in 1920. But it was generally agreed that trucks
were the inexpensive alternative to railroads in remote and rugged

TABLE 2.5

Roads and Trucks in Minas and São Paulo, 1920–1942

| | Roads (km) | | Trucks | |
|---|---|---|---|---|
| | Minas Gerais | São Paulo | Minas Gerais | São Paulo |
| 1920 | | 9,000[a] | | 220 |
| 1925 | 7,165 | | 1,718 | 4,395[b] |
| 1928 | 12,409 | 28,062 | 5,747 | 26,000 |
| 1930 | 20,970 | 28,062 | 5,218 | |
| 1937 | 36,829 | 48,059 | | |
| 1939 | 42,410 | 51,705 | | |
| 1942 | | | 6,229 | 29,013 |

SOURCE: Compiled from Pereira Brasil, Minas na grandeza, pp. 512–13; Gordilho, Os transportes; Moacir M. F. Silva, Geografia dos transportes, pp. 129, 136.
    [a] 1921.   [b] 1924.

areas, such as the Jequitinhonha and Mucuri valleys in the northeast. Rapid was the conquest of time and space, thanks to the internal combustion engine. By 1935, only nine municípios in Minas were without motor vehicles, six of them in the isolated eastern frontier zone.[66] The rapid growth of motor vehicles and roads in Minas after 1917 was surpassed only in São Paulo. See Table 2.5.

Once begun, the motor age was limited mainly by the capacity to import vehicles, by the high cost of gasoline outside the port cities and of imported asphalt, and by the availability of municipal and state funds for roads. Until 1940, almost no federal money was allocated for road construction. São Paulo in 1921 and Minas in 1924 had road development plans long before the central government set up an effective road-building agency in 1945.[67]

Almost all of the first roads were built by municipal governments and by private initiative, as typified in the Triângulo. These inter-municipal routes also gave better access to railroad stations. Heavily committed to railroads, the state was at first unwilling to allocate money for highway construction. Many of the old provincial roads and bridges had been neglected since 1870, and an excellent macadamized post road from Juiz de Fora to Petrópolis was abandoned when the EFCB reached the Mata. As a convinced railroad man, Governor Barnardes felt that highways would inevitably be supplanted by good railroads; hence the state should open oxcart trails to the railroads by means of private concessions.[68] However, at the urging of Juiz de Fora and other municípios along the old highway to Petrópolis, this route was reopened and extended on to Belo Horizonte, which until 1924 could only be reached by train, horseback, and airplane, but not by car. In 1929 the capital was finally linked to São Paulo by dirt road. Road mileage almost doubled in the 1930's, testament to the very great demand for convenient, cheap transportation.

Impressive as this Mineiro road-building program was, it still did not integrate the state. Remote areas in the North, the Center, and the East pressed for roads as they had for railroads a generation before. Unable to sell out of state, the elite from these areas called for a larger state market based on good roads.[69] The Triângulo, by contrast, was all too well integrated with the Paulista market. For lack of transportation to Belo Horizonte, that "extensive and rich region behaves as if it belongs to São Paulo more than to Minas; the exchange of products is hindered, commercial relations and even the routine administrative and police ties are attenuated." An estimated 95 percent of all goods sold in the Triângulo in 1935 were from São Paulo, just as 95 percent of its products went to the Paulista market.[70] But with state funds limited, only the federal government had the resources to build modern, all-weather highways on the scale required by Minas, which it did starting in the 1950's, when large gasoline tax funds became available. And when modern highways did crisscross Minas, a boon for agriculture, Paulista industry was even better positioned than before to penetrate beyond its traditional hinterland in the Triângulo and the Sul.

The impact of fast, cheap transportation on the isolated small-town society of Minas was profound. Millions in rural areas who had never heard a steam engine's shrill whistle in their lonely valleys and isolated plains were suddenly only hours away from the commercial centers. Truck drivers, like muleteers before them, carried news and gossip between town and countryside. One Mata historian claims that railroads as mere economic systems had no "civic content." Roads, by contrast, reinforced the sense of collectivity such as the Mata's small towns had not enjoyed since the days of Republican agitation in the late 1880's.[71]

*Politics, Economics, and Modernization*

Inadequate growth affected politics, but the causal linkages between economic power and political power are complex. That economic difficulties did not automatically trigger political decline is a finding of this study. To argue otherwise (as many have) is to misinterpret a prime dynamic of Minas in the Republic. The age of greatest national power began at the outset of a 13-year depression and lasted 30 years, until 1929. Why did political power persist for over a generation after it became clear that the Minas economy was in trouble?

In part, the answer lies in assessing correctly the nature of that economic decline, which I have called relative. Inadequate growth is after all much better than stagnation, such as Pernambuco faced. Economically, Minas was still the federation's second power in 1937. The state machine had access to economic resources at home. It was also powerful enough to extract resources out of the federal system: railroad equipment, freight rate reductions, and tariff relief.

That each zone had a different economic base was a disunifying force in politics, yet the state government was strong enough to offer something to each zone. If the pie was not cut evenly, collective action at the state and federal levels could and did bring results. The backward North wanted railroads and markets. Producers throughout Minas sought better prices and access to credit and transportation, although they often had different interests—the two coffee zones come to mind. Towns wanted urban services, including schools. The political system could satisfy some of these demands; the economy did not stagnate.

Retrospectively, it seems that periods of economic crisis were times of political opportunity. With municipal bosses short of revenue, producers' groups looking for relief, and job aspirants seeking patronage, the state machine fortified itself. Two of the ablest governors consolidated their power bases during depressions: Francisco de Almeida Brandão (1898–1902) projected Minas into national leadership, and Benedito Valadares (1933–45) became a pillar of the emergent Vargas system. Without doing too much violence to this history, the opposite was also true. Interest groups and dissidents aspired to more freedom of maneuver in periods of prosperity, as in the 1890's and the 1920's. The coffee producers association, abortive under João Pinheiro but temporarily successful later on, is a case in point. Even so, the politics of co-optation eroded independent action, as will be shown below.

Despite several plans and programs, the performance in economic policymaking was unimpressive overall. Probably this says as much about the inadequacies of the Minas political system as it does about the persistent obstacles to growth and development. Even in that age of relative laissez-faire, the Mineiros' inability to marshal available and potential resources was a deficiency of government. Mineiros could have done more to restructure (but not eliminate) this region's dependency on the coast. Just as the economy grew, but not enough, they tried, but more might have been expected. In the interregional division of labor in the Center-South, Minas played a neo-colonial role. Partly for this reason the society seemed old-fashioned in 1937, picturesque, the subject of caricature, perhaps not to be taken all that seriously. But part of the answer lies in the fabric, shape, and aspirations of Mineiro culture, the subject of the next chapter.

## CHAPTER THREE

# Society and Culture

ALBERTO SANTOS DUMONT: who was he, this "inventor of the aeroship who, like a victorious eagle, circled the Eiffel Tower three times in triumph to the frenetic acclaim of Parisians"? Of Henrique Dumont, the father, much was known, remarked *O Diário de Minas* in 1901. Diamantina-born of French parents, Paris-trained in engineering, well-married into the Paula Santos clan whose gold mine he had managed, Henrique, on his death in 1893, owned the largest coffee fazenda in São Paulo, where he raised three sons. One was a fazendeiro, another a banker, and then came the pioneer aviator about whom the Belo Horizonte daily knew little, not even his birthdate in Minas. Of the flight itself, the technology employed, the implications for Brazil, very little was said. That the event was important seemed not to need explaining, perhaps because it was recognized internationally. What mattered to the editors was to identify the inventor's Mineiro family roots. Having done so, *O Diário* closed on a note of regional pride.[1]

Pride of family and of origin gave the Mineiro elite a strong sense of place. Their belief in a satisfying local world was more than a politician's delight, a journalist's feel for hyperbole. The extent to which this theme appears in their memoirs and creative literature shows it was a hallmark of Mineiro regionalism.

This grounding in origins and roots connotes stability, a longing for order in a changing environment. Yet the modernizing currents that were eroding localism by the 1880's were rapidly undercutting it by World War I. The elite perceived change intellectually, but in their hearts the sense of place endured. Place being central to elite values, I will describe it first before charting other features of regional society such as the family and urban culture. Finally, the analysis will focus on the main socializing agencies, which included the communications media, voluntary organizations, education, and the Church. Throughout, my objective is to recreate the provincial ethos, the setting for politics from 1890 to 1937.

We begin by examining the childhoods of three prominent Mineiros: Alice Dayrell Brant's girlhood in Diamantina, Cyro dos Anjos's coming of age in Montes Claros, and Carlos Drummond de Andrade's origins in Itabira.[2] Extracting common themes from an adolescent's diary, a novelist's memoir, and a poet's collected works is a legitimate but regrettably abstract and cursory view of some rich creative literature. And if these vivid, compelling books evoke the essence of Minas, it is well to remember that the authors lived in the Center and North zones, the most traditional regions. What matters is to touch upon a telluric sense of place which these Mineiros share with authors from the American South, as for example *North Towards Home,* a memoir of Willie Morris's Mississippi boyhood in Yazoo City. To grow up in the intensely human surroundings of the small Mineiro city was supportive, judging from the affection, mixed with humor and respect, with which these Brazilian authors recall their origins.

All belonged to families locally prominent since the eighteenth century. The Caldeira Brants, to whom Alice with her English father was related first by blood and then by marriage, were Diamantina diamond traders. The dos Anjos and Versiani families were leading merchants, fazendeiros, and physicians in Montes Claros. And, in Itabira, the Drummonds had once owned gold mines and ranches. To these children, the ancestral presence was palpable in the big, old houses, in the social history, even—as for the boy Cyro—in the unveiling of his grandfather's bust in the town square. Fathers ruled the family with a severe authority that commanded the children's respect and obedience into adulthood. Anjos and Drummond both left the careers their fathers would have wanted for them, and not without stress, especially for the poet whose father had to manage the faltering family fazenda alone. If to later generations the "Traditional Mineira Family" (TFM) would seem constrictive, repressive toward women, and hypocritical in its genteel respectability, there is no hint of this in the three books. Alice, a happy child, had the town for her stage and closed her diary as the most courted girl in Diamantina. In short, the family with its multiple relations and hovering retainers was a formidable and affective institution.

The bitter poverty in these isolated towns is described as a given, a fact of everyday life. In traditional society, the vast gulf between rich and poor served not to challenge, but rather to enhance and to legitimize the social order. Maintaining a genteel life-style was not easy in the impoverished interior, where status was so clearly revealed in dress, possessions, and access to education. Cyro dos Anjos tells how his merchant father earned only enough to keep a large family in modest circumstances, and to educate the two eldest sons in Rio, at great strain on a carefully watched budget. Cyro discovered the poverty hidden within many households where, if food was plentiful and cheap, the amenities often were in short supply.[3] Alice's Aunt Madge struggled bravely to support herself by teaching. Drummond's father lost the fazenda. This disaster, a break in the continuity of things, is evoked in the poet's lament for his lost local world:[*]

> Tive ouro, tive gado, tive fazendas.
> Hoje sou funcionário público.
> Itabira é apenas uma fotografia na parede.
> Mas como dói!

Despite manifest social inequalities, small-town life is portrayed as a theater of easy interaction, not of conflict. Rich and poor alike all know each other. Travelers, so often kinsmen from the country, are treated with traditional Mineiro hospitality. Toward the few foreigners there is the same open curiosity that Richard Burton noted several years before. Black people invariably appear in humble roles—as domestics, storytellers, mendicants, felons—but race is not a measurement of personality. Taken collectively, the poor do not have aspirations. Acceptance and passivity blur the socioeconomic contrasts of a society that is fundamentally conservative and hierarchical. Above all, there is a *joie de vivre*, an openness in human relations, that Yves

---

[*] "I had gold, I had cattle, I had estates./Today I am a public employee./ Itabira—only a photo on the wall./That hurts!" Confidência do Itabirano," p. 102.

Leloup, the French geographer, notes was still pervasive in Minas of the 1960's.[4]

That the quality of town life reflected the stable, conservative values of an agrarian society is not surprising. The small urban concentrations of that era faced toward the countryside they serviced. Noteworthy is the frequency with which fazendeiro relatives were mentioned in these books. Culturally, however, the townsmen felt superior to their country cousins. As Marvin Harris discovered, these old, established towns produced a distinctly urban ethic.[5] For the elite, there were secondary schools (usually seminaries) and normal schools that nurtured the Western humanistic values. The local men of letters had great prestige. For the masses, there were festivals that recalled colonial traditions—band concerts and market days—all of which provided *movimento,* that quality of hustle and bustle so prized in the interior.

Isolation restricted opportunity, but it also preserved the provincial spirit. All three authors grew up in towns that longed for rail service. And just as the two men left for Belo Horizonte the motor age arrived, heralded for Cyro by a flamboyant Protestant pastor on a motorcycle. The recent pessimism of Mineiros at their failure to develop rapidly is far removed from the satisfaction with which these authors recall their pasts. Childhood in these circumstances was deeply supportive for the *gente graúda,* as "good families" used to be called. Municipal culture marked our authors with a strong sense of place, which lingered as they all moved on to Rio, to swell the ranks of a familiar Brazilian type, the transplanted Mineiro.

This close relationship of community and family was cast in the classic Iberian mold of a stable, two-class society where a privileged few monopolized the high-status roles in commerce, agriculture, and politics.[6] Persons who can name and place over 200 living relatives are not rare in Minas. The art of placing was important because the famous TFM was a useful kinship network (*parentesco*) that sustained social and economic power. Through his parentesco, a man gained privileged information and private access to all institutions at the local, zonal, and state levels. The extensive genealogies that form the core of many municipal histories attest to the strength of this family-community nexus. It is not that this family-centered system was unique to Minas. It was that the Mineiro social order had great staying power in the face of swift economic changes and the physical transfer of people in large numbers. The durability and legitimacy of this society in part explains why Minas achieved political coherence despite the centrifugal economic forces that disunited it.

Elite society, with its agrarian roots and municipal ethos, was fully formed by 1850. Having made the transition from a mining to an agropastoral economy, Minas developed the clan-centered social order that Oliveira Vianna depicted in his *Populações meridionais do Brasil*. Although the social history of these extended clans remains to be written, their outlines may be followed in Cid Rebelo Horta's exploratory essay on the ruling families of Minas.[7]

As is clear in Rebelo Horta, the clan networks spread beyond their municipal bases to form zonal power groups that were interlocked by ties of parentesco. In the North and West, ranching families ruled. In the Center, some of the old mining-commercial families maintained their power through agriculture while others colonized the Mata and became the so-called *Nobreza do Café*, or coffee barons. As the most powerful of the Mineiro family clans, many Mata families were ennobled by a grateful Emperor for their political and economic contributions to the Imperial war effort against Paraguay in 1864–70.[8] In fact, the coffee barons with their large slave holdings were a pillar of the Second Empire until Abolition. The Sul and the Triângulo formed two more subsystems, each having extensive family and commercial links with São Paulo. Thus the subregions into which the state was divided by economics and geography also had distinctive clan links.

So central were these clans to the historical ethos of each region that the regional stereotypes with which Mineiros encapsulated their past often derived from the supposed qualities of the local families. The most traditional zone was held to be the North. There, clans ruled in the most unadulterated form, including large areas of the West where for generations the heirs and relations of Joaquina de Pompeu, the legendary Pitangui matriarch, held sway. The most Mineiro (*mineiríssimo*) region was of course the Center, the source for Drummond's "nostalgic sense of origins." It is this traditional stereotype that serves him when he locates the "real" Minas not in Uberaba, Cataguazes, or Ponte Nova—all nineteenth-century agrocommercial centers—but in the old mining cities: Ouro Preto, Diamantina, São João del Rei, and his beloved Sabará.[9] Others have praised the Center for its civility, the qualities of tolerance and open-mindedness born of a cosmopolitan past. To be sure, all this was considered decadent, even colonial, by the Republican generation. Toward the Triângulo there was in Minas a feeling of unease; its identity was uncertain. However progressive economically, the Sul and especially the Mata were typed as the most conservative regions. As the closest zone to Rio, the Mata, reputed for cautious dealings, tight-fistedness, and authoritarianism, typified Minas to Cariocas in the nation's capital.

Landed wealth and commerce formed the base for clan power in 1850. However, economic differentiation began quite soon in southern Minas, where several families branched out into textiles, railroading, and food processing. In zones remote from transportation, such as the North and West, limited markets helped to preserve the old career patterns of fazendeiro, merchant, or practitioner of the liberal professions. Given the opportunity, entrepreneurship began there too, notably in Curvelo and Montes Claros with cotton spinning. Thus the generation born after 1870 did not break new professional ground. Their fathers, from whom they inherited the Republic, had in many cases already branched beyond the traditional careers.

Multicareers were common in the Minas elite: a man might be in banking, own textile mills, and manage his fazenda while serving as a deputy in the state legislature. Playing many professional roles gave him access to informal networks of friends, called *panelinhas*. These small circles shared information and access to the powerful and influential at state and national levels. Anthony Leeds, an anthropologist, has called this behavior critically important for the functioning of Brazilian society.[10] Typical as these networks were in Brazil and Minas, they must have existed elsewhere in the West, at least in Latin countries. And since multicareers in the elite are a common feature of societies at the outset of modernization, informal circles similar to panelinhas may still function, or have recently existed, in many different cultures in the underdeveloped world.

This elite was neither a landed aristocracy nor a patrimonial oligarchy like the Northeastern sugar barons. Rather, it was an economic elite known not for great wealth, which in fact did not exist in Minas, but for its hard work and business sense.

To this economic elite, what mattered was not how the money was made but rather the fact of wealth itself. According to Sidney Green-field, a sociologist who has worked in Minas, traditional society was divided between the few who commanded the means to consume and the many who could not. New money arose with the changing econ-omy, while the once powerful who could not adapt to change declined. Thus, the absolute numbers in this class probably varied considerably over the years since colonization. Heterogeneous in its origins, this economic elite did not necessarily have class interests in common. "They do not constitute a group organized around some social or economic activity. What they share in common is a means—highly diverse in nature—of access that enables them to consume large amounts of material goods and services."[11] This surely overstates the case. New money was still comfortably allied to—when it did not derive from—the rural world of fazendas. Through 1937, there was no break with the agrarian past, which *did* constitute a common bond and tradition among the elite. Thus the premise of an open-ended economic elite, although suggestive, cannot be pushed too far.

Stratification was based largely on wealth, and the elite wanted symbols to differentiate themselves from the nonconsuming masses. During the Empire, leading notables received life peerages and other titles, whereas lesser figures enjoyed military rank in the National Guard (militia). The Republic abolished titles but continued to distribute colonelships and other ranks until 1917. The role of aca-demic titles is discussed below. Lineage, also, was a badge of distinc-tion. However, to a fluctuating elite with varied origins, these symbols of status were contingent on wealth. Because of economic change, it follows that the famous TFM must have been a weaker institution than is commonly supposed.

Sylvio de Vasconcellos, the architectural historian and himself from a famous Sulista clan, wrote recently that the ties of parentesco were in fact quite fragile. With rare exceptions, few of the original founding families remained in Minas. "In general, they lacked an enduring economic base, [so that] illustrious ancestors are followed by anony-mous descendants." Over the years, estates were subdivided among heirs who did not cherish the land but exploited it. Given the historic mobility of Mineiros, elite family ties were eroded by migration. Vasconcellos claimed that the TFM offered little support to these offspring when they left the family nest. In the sweep of Mineiro history from the gold rush, he maintained the role of leading individuals was much more important than the clans.[12]

The conclusion must be that the history of Minas Gerais cannot be written solely as the history of its leading families. And yet it is difficult to relegate the TFM to the role of myth. Did an economic elite in flux need to create such a myth as it searched for stability? Probably this is so. Nevertheless, Rebelo Horta's vigorously stated argument about the families' enduring political role is also compelling. Although more research into the clan networks and fortunes is needed, it seems probable that the apparent contradiction between the model of a heterogeneous, economic elite and that of a family-centered political elite is not real.

This is so because economic change was not sudden or drastic enough to destroy the families in one generation. Examples are the gradual shift out of mining to agriculture between 1780 and 1830 and, in more recent history, the move from coffee to dairy ranching in the Mata. Furthermore, the ebb and flow in family fortunes to which Greenfield and Vasconcellos allude is less compelling if 1850 is taken as the historical baseline. By then, the economic elite was organized on the agro-pastoral-commercial base that dominated the Mineiro economy until World War II. In this foreshortened time perspective, the continuities are more convincing.

Furthermore, several families appear to have organized themselves flexibly in order to exploit the shifting economic frontiers. It was not at all uncommon for the sons to move on with each generation, leaving the old and the less able behind to care for declining properties or to enter local service jobs. Many descendants of the old families now active in Paraná or Mato Grosso can trace their origins back from Minas to Rio de Janeiro state. Having opened coffee fazendas there in the early nineteenth century, their ancestors moved into the Mata in the 1830's and 1840's, then shifted to São Paulo in the 1870's, and later pushed into Paraná. Clans who specialized in ranching followed a similar pattern in the Triângulo and southern Goiás; some moved northward across the Bahia frontier.

Imbued with a conservative ethos, the spatially mobile family stressed affective ties within large parentescos. This had political consequences, for the family network could be mobilized for electoral support outside a man's own town. Several Mineiros made political careers in the capital, a phenomenon picked up in the collective biography. Yet having a parentesco in the interior was no minor asset for the Belo Horizonte–based politician. The cultural consequences of this spatially mobile family system also were important. It fostered a common view of social class and also a common culture; it reinforced "Mineiro-ness" (*mineirismo*), the sense of regional identity.

That there was a strong sense of traditional families, even among families without much in the way of tradition, is striking. It is apparent that the system was such as to create out of a mobile population, with a relatively high turnover of elites, a sense of one of the strongest and most stable regional elites. The sense of place, the myth of stability, the flexible response to changes in the economic base—all were facets of an ingrained, profound belief in the innate legitimacy of social hierarchy. The elite's almost classical sense of the appropriate social order was a source of conservatism, flexibility, and staying power. Fundamentally, the vertical organization of power was congruent with this self-image.

It bears repeating that the elite in Minas was not a closed elite. Marrying up was an accepted mobility channel for talented men without family connections. João Pinheiro da Silva, the Italian immigrant's son who was twice governor, bolstered his career by marrying into the Arantes family, which linked him to the Mata coffee barons. If cousin marriage was typical of the elite, so was their willingness to admit able sons-in-law to family councils. In short, this elite valued talent and business acumen.

After 1850, the elite not only redefined itself in terms of new economic activities; it also invigorated itself with infusions of new money. Precisely because it was an economic elite, it accepted the rise of the newly rich. This was to be expected, for, as Raymundo Faoro has shown, the old patrimonial fazendeiro clans became heavily dependent on urban merchants for credit and marketing during the latter half of the nineteenth century.[13] Increasingly, bankers, merchants, and industrialists appeared among the elite.

Elite mobility probably accelerated with the Republic, as shown in the biographies of several self-made men. For example, Colonel Benjamin Ferreira Guimarães (1861–1948), the banker and textile magnate, started out by clerking in a Rio merchant house and then peddled

goods in his native western Minas.[14] With the partial exception of the
Mineiro coffee zones, the relative impoverishment of the fazendeiro
class was notable. (The Triângulo, as a newly developed zone with
links to São Paulo, ranks apart.) This facilitated differentiation and
accommodation. The railroad that made Montes Claros the commercial center for northern Minas attracted many newcomers, often
of humble origin. As Cyro dos Anjos recalls, the old elite of doctors,
lawyers, and normal school graduates accepted the new merchants into
elite society and the running of town affairs. In ratifying the new
monied group, the older elements preserved their influence and
prestige despite very rapid change.[15]

The willingness of new groups and individuals to accept the terms
of this accommodation is very significant. It shows that there was no
fundamental redistribution of power or prestige symbols during the
period under review. The persistence of old values in the face of
economic change, improved communications, and the rise of cities was
of course not unique to Minas Gerais. However, it must be said of
Minas that the family-community ties that oriented these values were
widely accepted as both legitimate and desirable. Furthermore, the
existence of a very large, dependent rural population was the context
and foundation for these values. As mentioned, many leading Mineiros
managed to combine "modern" careers with agriculture. Thus the
fazendeiro and the industrialist shared much in common. Even those
who had no direct economic stake in the countryside valued fazendas
and small farms as the proper place for weekend relaxation.

The landed group was highly visible, however modest its life-style
and self-effacing its speech, comportment, and dress. Farmhouse in-
teriors were simple and austere by all accounts. The motif of Mineiro
rustics in the big city was popular in contemporary literature, notably
in Artur de Azevedo's comedy *A capital federal*. In this turn-of-the-
century spoof, a fazendeiro family from the Mata and their black maid
blunder through several misadventures in Rio before fleeing home.
Country ways amused the sophisticated Cariocas. Because landownership was concentrated, however, great wealth and conspicuous consumption were not required of power-holders in the countryside.

The old Iberian ideal of a rural middle class found some champions
in Minas, but their reforms got nowhere. Redistribution through a
rural property tax was adamantly opposed by landlords; the opening

of public lands by a homestead act died in the legislature; and colonization was a failure. Land titles in the Mata and Eastern frontier zones were chaotic, which suited those who had access to lawyers and the militia, and a legion of squatters who burned their way into the forest and burned out those who tried to fence them in. The Bureau of Lands and Colonization was crippled for lack of funds. Nobody wanted to register his title. And as squatters on the public domain told officials, "The state won't take our lands." The result was a rough-and-ready frontier land grab for all social groups, lasting well into World War II.[16] Throughout Minas, in fact, migration and subsistence farming were solvents to a stratified and exploitive rural order. Squatting in the advanced zones was perhaps more viable earlier, before overpopulation and the decline of soil resources.

Ethnically, the landed group was Portuguese. Some Indian blood came via the caboclos, and African traits came from miscegenation under conditions familiar to readers of Gilberto Freyre. On the whole, the elite descended from old European stock. Foreigners and naturalized Brazilians were conspicuous for their absence in the countryside. In 1940, less than 2 percent of either group owned farms or fazendas.[17]

The Negro was highly visible in the countryside, although by reputation he was poor, powerless, and unreliable. Pierre Denis, a Frenchman, while touring through the Minas coffee belt, found his belief in the black man's "moral and economic inferiority" confirmed at every turn.[18] Yet racist polemics were muted; and comparatively rare in Minas. Unlike their Paulista, Carioca, and Pernambucano counterparts, Mineiros seemed to have been less troubled by thoughts that their state might be doomed to poverty and backwardness because of the heavy infusion of black blood. A low estimation of the Negro continued, and the elite believed in the whitening myth. In the absence of Europeans, however, there was no alternative to the freedman's labor and thus one reason less to dwell upon themes of Negro inferiority.

Such, briefly, were the rural roots of elite society. The urban culture that flourished in municípios servicing this vast hinterland can now be seen in clearer perspective. Alice, Cyro, and Carlos Drummond were urbanites for whom the countryside was real, but also marginal to their intense experiences in the urban theater. If place is a hallmark of Mineiro culture, then the small city is its heartland.

To be sure, few people lived in real urban environments, defined in Chapter 1 as cities with more than 10,000 people. Although these true cities grew rapidly from five in 1920 to 22 in 1940, they accounted for only 2 and then 8 percent of the state's total population. Cities between 5,000 and 10,000 held from 3 to 4 percent. Most townsmen, or 6.2 (1920) and 13 (1940) percent, still lived in what Leloup calls "concentrated rural populations" having fewer than 5,000 inhabitants.[19] Before urbanization began in 1920, these small towns were, therefore, relatively important.

The urban ethos flourished in the old gold cities; yet there was more to urbanism than faded glories of the baroque era in which several leading centers in other zones did not participate. Throughout Minas, the local notables who ran these towns played ancient roles. Something of the Roman *civitas* survived in Minas, or at least the Roman tradition of legitimacy and continuity. Consider, in this regard, the "sense of order" and dislike of social innovations for which the Mineiros were famous. The pride in one's locality, what Brazilians call *localismo*, went beyond considerations of crass self-interest on the part of local rulers. Only a few men had enough education or experience to administer these towns, but this, too, was sanctioned by old traditions. Certainly the classics, on which the elite was nourished, reinforced the Roman legacy. Ferreira de Rezende, the judge, recalled how reading the classics instilled in him a love of liberty and a respect for the Romans' civic virtues. Cassio, Flamino, and Manlio were the names that he, in common with many in his generation, chose for his sons. "I am," Ferreira de Rezende concluded, "to the depths of my character extremely conservative."[20] Vestiges of the Roman spirit lingered in the public and domestic architecture, in the segregation of women, and in the images of saints which reminded some nineteenth-century travelers of pagan household gods. By 1890, however, these aspects were disappearing.

With their schools, clinics, and bureaucratic services, the cities were valued outposts of that wider world the elite called civilization. The leading fazendeiros, who since colonial times had kept town houses for their participation in religious festivals and civic events, discovered new reasons for maintaining urban residency. Those who could afford to do so often transferred their households to the city when the children reached school age. The automobile accelerated this trend to urban living. Until the 1930's, moreover, few bureaucratic functions transpired below the município. The taxing, mail, and police services all took place there, as did the registering of land titles and commercial transactions with the notaries. Merchants, who were the dominant source of rural credit, were located in the cities. These activities attracted educated people, to whom newspapers, dramatics, and literature appealed. Thus the sense of being in a cultured place was part of the urban ethos. Hardly cosmopolitan, the Mineiro city still received a wide variety of influences from outside.

One recalls that persistent regional type, the unsophisticated countryman who in Belo Horizonte or especially Rio felt vulnerable and inadequate. A famous example was Crispim Jacques Bias Fortes (1847–1917) from Barbacena, a leading political boss and former governor who never went to Rio, reportedly for fear of being ridiculed by the Cariocas. However, it is difficult to believe that this São Paulo Law School graduate and skilled manipulator was not consciously playing up the country style in his political and business dealings. In fact, Bias knew all about cosmopolitan values, coming as he did from Barbacena, which was no hick town. Rather, he preferred to play the role of representative type: "sure of his rights and privileges, respectful of others, honest in all situations, liberal, tolerant, and respectful of religious traditions, perhaps a believer. He raised cattle, made good cheese, lived for hunting and fishing, and was deeply involved in municipal affairs. . . . No Mineiro politician was more in harmony with the patterns, habits, and aspirations of his electorate."[21] Or consider Francisco da Silva Campos (1893–1968), the cabinet minister, international lawyer, and adviser to presidents, who énjoyed the company of ranchers and even on the streets of Belo sometimes wore the black hat, brown pants, and high boots of his native western Minas. Or Wenceslau Brás Pereira Gomes (1868–1962), a governor, president, and political chief, who chose in retirement to become "the fisherman of Itajubá." In short, these shrewd men were localists by choice; in style and frame of mind, theirs was at most a relative isolation.

By the 1880's the cities were well articulated to Rio and São Paulo merchant houses, although the North was still linked to Salvador. Regional centers, such as Uberaba and Juiz de Fora, developed in the late nineteenth century, but Belo did not rise commercially until after 1920. Mineiro merchants often served out their apprenticeships in Rio houses, and they made frequent buying trips to the capital, where they stayed in lodgings furnished by their commercial correspondent. In turn, these houses dispatched *cometas* (traveling salesmen) to the interior with goods, credit, and advice on the latest styles. To areas still remote from railroads the cometas came with sometimes elegant trains of matched mules, in silver trappings, there to dispense "the latest songs from Rio for the girls, the latest anecdotes for the boys, and the newest products for the merchants, all eight or ten months out of date."[22] Peddlers, many of whom were Middle Easterners called "turcos," plied the byways with drygoods and ladies' finery. And with the opening of the East zone in the 1920's, salesmen of all nationalities descended from Vitória, Rio, São Paulo, even Salvador and Recife to offer goods on easy terms in a breezy style salted with off-color jokes.[23]

As bearers of news, the cometas were especially important to localities where the mail and telegraph services were inadequate or lacking. Efforts to improve the mails were given high priority in the 1880's, and soon all of Minas was served (in theory) on a regular basis. Mail volume increased dramatically from 7.1 million pieces in 1896 to 56.2 million ten years later, and Minas led the nation with 831 postal agencies. To be sure, complaints then (as now) about letters lost, opened, late, or money not arriving were frequent. The federal telegraph reached Juiz de Fora from Rio in 1871, and was extended northward to Ouro Preto (1884), on to Diamantina, then to northern Brazil. Zones with good railroad service—the Triângulo, West, Mata, and the Sul— also used the railroad wire service. By 1926, some 200 telegraph posts provided Minas with the largest network in Brazil. Interestingly, the line from Belo to the Triângulo was not established until 1926.

Several private telephone companies sprang up. As might be expected, the Sul was well connected to Santos and São Paulo through the Companhia Telefónica Paulista, but direct phone service between Belo and Rio was delayed until 1926. Except for the North and East, few Mineiro cities by then were without phone service. Regular airline service between Rio and Belo began in 1936, the same year in which the state radio network (Radio Inconfidência) was set up.[24]

The shrinking of time and space accelerated, but this says little about the content of messages sent over the new means of communication. Doubtless, the quality of life improved for those who could take advantage of this medium. Doubtless, too, the vast majority received few if any letters, rarely employed the telegraph, which was expensive, did not use the telephone, and certainly never flew by plane. In fact, these new communications media did not rapidly erode the Minas mosaic. Perhaps the radio could serve this purpose, as Secretary of Agriculture Israel Pinheiro hoped in announcing plans to place a receiver in every município. The radio, he said, "would make Mineiros realize that they belong to a single community which is tied by common sentiments and traditions, and that they now, and soon will, share reciprocal interests." Radio Inconfidência was supposed to unify Mineiros with a statewide scope and influence that newspapers never had.[25]

The local press was another hallmark of Mineiro regionalism. Typically, a small-town newspaper carried political news and commercial advertisements in a weekly edition of under 500 copies. Often it was owned by the local political boss, whose dominance was disputed by a rival chief with his own press. That newspapers played a key role in local politics is abundantly clear.[26] As a forum for sustained verbal combat, the press gave local notables a means to sustain violence on a lower level than shootouts or assassination.

Equally important, however, was its role as booster for municipal affairs; optimism for the future of local enterprise was its stock in trade. Not to be slighted was the cultural patina that often graced its pages. Poetry, book notices, and literary commentary enhanced its prestige for those who valued civilization. In fact, the number of journals (often ephemeral) devoted to literature and humor themes was second only to the religious press among special interest publications. Thus the press was a pillar of politics, commerce, and culture at this state's center of gravity, the local level.

To a public hungry for news, the press was already an important institution when Richard Burton visited Minas in the 1860's. Newspapers proliferated after 1880 with the quickening pace of municipal life, and the peak was reached in 1920, when some 187 weeklies circulated, slightly more than the 176 extant in 1940. Minas ranked second in the Brazilian periodical press, and was the nation's third largest employer—1,817 people in 1933—in this sector. See Table 3.1.

It bears repeating that Mineiro journals were overwhelmingly localistic and limited to small press runs. That few dailies circulated outside Belo Horizonte and Juiz de Fora is explained by the small eco-

TABLE 3.1

*The Periodical Press in Brazil,* 1933

| State | Number of journals | Percentage |
|---|---|---|
| São Paulo | 312 | 24.4% |
| Minas Gerais | 212 | 16.6 |
| Federal District | 195 | 15.3 |
| Pernambuco | 135 | 10.6 |
| Rio Grande do Sul | 93 | 7.3 |
| Bahia | 78 | 6.1 |
| Estado do Rio | 56 | 4.4 |
| Other states | 197 | 15.4 |
| TOTAL | 1,278 | 100.1% |

SOURCE: Mario Cunha, citing state and federal statistics in *Minas Gerais,* April 25, 1935, p. 9.

nomic base provided by the state's compartmentalized markets. Owing to poor communications, newspapers from the state capital did not circulate beyond Belo Horizonte and its environs until the late 1920's. State leaders continually lamented the fact that large areas of Minas were served more efficiently by the São Paulo and Rio dailies.[27] Belo itself was firmly in the Rio orbit, while the Triângulo and the Sul depended on Paulista papers.

At first, only one Mineiro publication circulated statewide, and this was the *Minas Gerais* (state gazette), which started in 1892 with a press run of 4,100 and leveled off around 20,000 copies after 1923. The *Minas Gerais* employed politicians on the rise and the intellectuals, notably on its famous literary supplement. In 1927, Pedro Aleixo and others founded *O Estado de Minas,* which soon became the leading daily in Minas Gerais. By contrast, *O Diário de Minas,* the party newspaper from 1899 to 1930, circulated on a very limited basis outside the capital.*

Belo Horizonte did not monopolize opinion; rather Juiz de Fora, the Mata emporium, was the undisputed journalistic center until the 1930's. The Associação de Imprensa de Minas was founded there in 1921, in distinction to the capital's Sociedade Mineira de Imprensa, established in 1920. Uberaba, another economic center, spoke authoritatively for the Triângulo, as did Montes Claros for the North. Sharing

---

* *O Estado de Minas* had several owners, and lapsed frequently. The paper in its modern form started in 1927. The *Diário de Minas* was opposition until 1898, when the PRM captured it from Mendes Pimentel.

most of the wealth and municípios between them, the Sul and the Mata far outdistanced the other regions. Many journals were ephemeral and the content varied, so they were not equally influential. But Table 3.2 does correlate roughly with economic and social trends, and it seems clear that the local press was relatively less vital after 1920. See Table 3.2.

Another trend was the wider distribution of dailies: Uberaba and Uberlândia each had one in 1940, as did São Sebastião do Paraíso in the Sul, São João del Rei and Barbacena in the Center, and Teófilo Otoni in the frontier East zone. Belo Horizonte became the undisputed center, with five daily newspapers. Only three remained in Juiz de Fora, however, a sharp decline from the nine that flourished there in 1920. The *Gazeta de Leopoldina* had been the Mata's only small-city daily; by 1940 it was again biweekly. In part, this distribution reflected shifts in power. It also seems safe to say that journalism was becoming more specialized, perhaps to meet the Rio and São Paulo competition. Furthermore, the press had lost its cultural monopoly under the impact of a powerful new medium: imported motion pictures.

If newspapers were a cultural lifeline for the literate, the movies opened up new vistas of style and fantasy to the masses. Wildly popular, the films gained immediate acceptance from an eager, wider public. From a handful of commercial theaters in 1907, the halls showing movies mushroomed to over 300 in the early 1920's. In Montes Claros,

TABLE 3.2

*The Periodical Press in Minas, 1897–1940*

| Zone | 1897 | 1905–6 | 1920 | 1940 |
|------|------|--------|------|------|
| North | 5 | 12 | 13 | 12 |
| East | 1 | 3 | 9 | 3 |
| Center | 22 | 42 | 42 | 42 |
| Triângulo | 12 | 14 | 20 | 35 |
| West | 18 | 19 | 21 | 21 |
| Sul | 39 | 56 | 79 | 67 |
| Mata | 31 | 49 | 82 | 93 |
| TOTAL | 128 | 195 | 266 | 273 |

SOURCE: Compiled from "Actual imprensa periodica mineira," *Revista do Arquivo Publico Mineiro*, 3:234–36; Nelson de Senna; *Annuario*, 2:489–500, which I corrected for repetitions; Minas, *Annuario estatistico, 1921*, Anno I, pp. 279–307; "A imprensa periódica em Minas," special edition of *Minas Gerais*, April 21, 1942, pp. 10–12, but not including bulletins.

people couldn't see enough of the early films starring Priscilla Dean
and Laura La Plante. Thanks to cowboy films, the fazendeiros' sons
now wore Tom Mix outfits instead of traditional vaqueiro garb for
their Sunday gallop through town.

In Belo Horizonte, the Church's Morality League was active by
1920. "Sinister Mast," a serial, the League found inoffensive, but "Iron
Man" (which had tavern scenes) was viewed with reservation. "Cleo-
patra," starring Theda Bara, was rated prejudicial, "because the ac-
tress, with her gestures, her attitudes and attire, exudes voluptuous-
ness." As for "Illusion of Love," it was completely unacceptable.[28]
Moralists sprang up in every country. It was not the impact of foreign
ideas that bothered Mineiros; it was their fear that the broad new
public might emulate the vice and violence that so delighted it on film.
The very popularity of films increased the danger to society, said
Governor Artur Bernardes in 1921. He called for regulation. But
Bernardes also thought the state should look into their possible uses
in the public schools.[29]

Voluntary organizations were conspicuous for their absence in the
cities Burton saw. "As usual in the Brazilian interior," he observed of
Diamantina, "the city is guiltless of club, cafe, Mechanics' Institutes,
Christian Young Men's Association and Mutual Improvement Societies,
except for musical purposes; the bands, however, are all things considered, good."[30] Music, dramatics, and landscaped plazas were amenities without which no self-respecting city could be called civilized.
Thus remote Jequitinhonha city on the Bahian frontier seemed "beauti-
ful and civilized" to a 1913 traveler who had enjoyed the dulcet tones
of its Filharmonica Ypiranga.[31] Starting in the 1890's, however, there
was an upsurge of associations throughout the state. This showed that
an increasingly complex society was becoming better organized.

Club life became the focal point for elite family recreation. Commercial associations, sports clubs, and literary societies proliferated.
Notable, also, were the workers' benefit societies and associations.
Some of them were started by Italian, Portuguese, and Spanish immigrants in the anarchist tradition, some were sponsored by the Catholic
Church, and a few were founded by employers who were influenced
by Pope Leo XIII's new social doctrine. By 1910 the emergent middle
groups in Belo Horizonte were forming associations for civil servants.
And when motor vehicles increased the movement of people and

goods throughout Minas, voluntary organizations became even more important.

Some 2,600 associations are listed in the 1920 census, of which slightly more than half were of the traditional religious and charitable kinds, such as lay brotherhoods and medical relief societies. Organized clubs, bands, and dramatic groups followed next, with 588. In almost 350 sports clubs the elite's passion for British football was spreading rapidly to other social groups. Professional and benefit associations followed, with 106. That these voluntary organizations existed throughout Minas is made clear by subtracting the total for Belo Horizonte, which had 117, and Juiz de Fora, where 99 associations of all kinds existed. Not surprisingly, these two centers shared one-third of the professional and benefit associations between them.[32]

Among interest groups, the merchants, with their commercial associations in Belo Horizonte (1901) and in Juiz de Fora and São João del Rei (both 1903), were the first to organize, followed by similar groups in Barbacena (1912) and Pitangui (1921), a Western textile town. Typically, these organizations included industrialists as well as leaders in wholesale and retail trade. By 1935, some 50 commercial organizations were distributed as shown in Table 3.3. The lion's share was found in the developed southern part of Minas. The Associacão Commercial, Industrial e Rural of Uberaba spoke for the Triângulo, just as that for Montes Claros led northern interests, and that for Juiz de Fora was preeminent in the Mata. As expected, Juiz de Fora's merchant association rivaled the capital's organization in power and influence until the 1930's.

The Sociedade Mineira de Agricultura was organized in 1909, but, in a now familiar pattern, the Mata coffee growers had their own Centro de Lavradores Mineiros, which they founded as an independent

TABLE 3.3

*Commercial Associations by Zone, 1935*

| Zone | Number | Zone | Number |
| --- | --- | --- | --- |
| North | 4 | West | 5 |
| East | 1 | Sul | 13 |
| Center | 11 | Mata | 11 |
| Triângulo | 4 | TOTAL | 49 |

SOURCE: "Associações commerciaes existentes no Estado," in Pereira Brasil, pp. 121–22.

pressure group. Following the trend in Rio and São Paulo, Mineiro industrialists moved out of the commercial associations in the late 1920's to form more specialized groups, one each in Belo Horizonte and Juiz de Fora. In cultural affairs, both cities took the lead in developing Mineiro counterparts to national institutions. Thus, in 1907 the Instituto Histórico de Minas was founded in the capital, to be followed closely by the Academia Mineira de Letras, begun three years later in Juiz de Fora. Yet because so many writers lived on state patronage, the Academy was moved to Belo in 1915. Inevitably, Juiz de Fora's claim to cultural, economic, and political leadership suffered from the rise of Belo Horizonte.

That Belo Horizonte was becoming the new focal point for regional culture was not so obvious, even in 1940, when it was a city of almost one-quarter million. The cultural mosaic of regions persisted. Nonetheless, the basis for a true urban center was being formed. Conceived as a political capital, the city's commercial and light industrial base began to support a society more diverse than that of the politicians and functionaries who were the first to settle. It became a medical and educational center, also a garrison town, and this encouraged and attracted the middle classes. Working-class districts sprang up, as did the first shanty towns built by migrants from the interior. Well supplied with food, water, and urban services, Belo Horizonte was not yet overwhelmed with intractable poverty. The tree-lined streets of jasmine and magnolia, the neat middle-class bungalows, the blue sky studded with thunderheads gave a fresh, open aura to this growing but still provincial city.

Ouro Preto passed on a literary tradition to Belo Horizonte when the bureaucrats, including several writers, moved to the new capital. The historian Diogo de Vasconcellos never transferred his allegiances, but most others, including the poet Augusto de Lima, did. The city also drew writers from the other subregions, notably from the Sul, Mata, and North. These intellectuals and the literarily inclined brought the small-city ambience with them, so that an interest in local themes continued. From the founding, a small book-reading public existed for these authors, who produced historical essays, chronicles, poetry, and criticism. Thus the modernist movement began in a city where intellectuals enjoyed prestige and already had an established role.[33]

Starting in 1923, a core of some ten young writers, friends and sympathizers began meeting to discuss avant garde ideas and to re-assess their Mineiro roots. Their interest in the art and architecture of the eighteenth-century cities was sparked when a motor caravan of Paulista intellectuals visited Ouro Preto in 1924, a few years after Manuel Bandeira wrote his famous guide to the former capital. The Paulistas searched their past for the legacy of bandeirantes and the Indian. The Mineiro modernists traced their own origins in the mining boom and acknowledged the African's contribution. In focusing upon the black man, they were closer to the Recife regionalists under Gilberto Freyre, who examined a wide range of Afro-Brazilian themes.

Gustavo Capanema and Milton Campos (among others in the movement) went on to high public office; Drummond de Andrade, the physician Pedro Nava, and the historian João Dornas Filho achieved national renown in letters, to name three more of this small group which disbanded in 1930. Toward Minas they had been ambiguous—deploring its backwardness while seeking the sources of its vitality in art, architecture, and language. Basically, they were sympathetic to tradition, and this reflected both their small-city origins and the supportive yet provincial ambience of Belo.[34]

Far from dominating them, the capital was a meeting place, or convergence point where authors wrote about their subregions while sharing a common sense of "Mineiro-ness." This happened to Cyro dos Anjos, who passed through Belo briefly in the early 1930's before moving to Rio. João Guimarães Rosa wrote about the sertão in brilliant, innovative prose while living most of his life abroad or in Rio. Drummond and several of the former modernists were professionally active in the nation's capital. Thus, for many intellectuals, Minas with its new capital was a place to be from.

Belo Horizonte grew in the shadow of Rio de Janeiro, and this fostered a provincial insecurity in Belohorizontinos, to whom their city seemed an overgrown interior town. In fact, almost all of them did come from some small town. Cosmopolitan Rio offered patronage and status rewards that the provincial center could not match. And although Belo Horizonte slowly became a cultural center, Mineiros still looked to Rio for city lights. For those who stayed in Minas, the sense of inferiority toward the nation's capital was a subtle, pervasive, and perhaps eroding influence on regional culture.

Paulistanos living in São Paulo city never had this problem, and their metropolis had a firmer hold on its hinterland than Belo Horizonte did. Recifenses with their port-city mentality held the interior in contempt, something Belohorizontinos did not do. Yet the Mineiro and Pernambucano transplant was a common type on the streets of Rio. Talented and ambitious Paulistas were more likely to find opportunity at home. That São Paulo did not exert more influence on the Minas elite is notable. Except for those living on the Sul and Triângulo borders, Rio was the cultural reference point. The dynamism of Paulistas was impressive, as was their pride, underscored by the patronizing attitudes of wealthy Paulistas on vacation at the Mineiro spas of Poços de Caldas, Caxambu, and São Lourenço. But Rio had that mix of patronage and culture which, combined with easy access from Minas, was compelling.

Education had a high priority for the Republicans who wanted to invigorate Minas Gerais with new institutions under the new federalism. They raised a monument to Tiradentes, until then deferred out of respect for the Imperial family, and serialized the *Federalist Papers* in the new state gazette. Having evoked these symbols of sovereignty, the state legislature established a law faculty in order to train its lawyers, judges, and politicians at home. Attendance at the São Paulo and Recife law schools fell off drastically as Mineiros repudiated the Imperial system of rotating elites in order to socialize them in a unitary regime. Graduates of the São Paulo faculty averaged 23 a year in the decade up to 1896. Subsequent to the founding of the Minas faculty, those receiving Paulista law degrees declined to around six each year through 1900. Eighteen Recife law degrees were conferred on Mineiros between 1889 and 1893, which was six more than in all the following years to 1941.[35]

Graduating students cheered when their speakers exhorted: "Hail the intellectual autonomy of the State of Minas Gerais!" However engagé, the rhetoric was not empty. Before, most medical doctors had been educated in Rio, but after 1911 they could attend the faculty in Belo Horizonte. That same year an engineering school was founded. In Ouro Preto, a faculty of pharmacy attracted students from beyond the Minas borders, including Getúlio Vargas and his brother, who were expelled in 1897 after a shooting incident.[36] The Ouro Preto Mining School (begun in 1876) continued as the nation's only faculty for metallurgical engineers, and Juiz de Fora obtained its own law school. This list of higher institutes lengthened steadily after 1910. Suffice it to say that with the founding of the state university in 1927, Minas was a major center of Brazilian higher education.

These state faculties legitimized the new order with an aura of academic culture. Professors moved easily into top political and administrative posts, and the students could expect to rise rapidly once they were certified *bacharéis* (bachelors of law) or *doutores*. Law and medicine, especially, were pillars of a recruitment system that, except for the new regional focus, emerged unchanged from the Empire. Although the faculties were less elitist after 1930, the middle groups continued to esteem degrees as the hallmark of an educated man. Access to the corridors of power was much easier for him who wore the lawyer's ruby ring and had been reinforced by the companionship of status-secure classmates. This was a national pattern, but what distinguished Minas from all of the other states (except São Paulo and Rio) was the claim to academic excellence. The founding of *Revista Forense*, the national legal review, in 1904 enhanced the law faculty's prestige. (Thirty years later, its removal to Rio was a blow to regional pride.) The establishment of clinics and hospitals (often sanatoriums for tuberculosis) made Belo Horizonte, with its medical faculty, a national health center. To a state claiming leadership in the national federation, these faculties were important.

But a contradiction existed between the training of professionals and the granting of degrees for status. Physicians who did not practice, agronomists who spurned the countryside, and pharmacists who left their professions were all too common in Minas. And whereas the Law Faculty, unlike Bahia's law school, was not a diploma mill—only 119 degrees were conferred between 1892 and 1925—it was the degree that counted in a culture where the bacharel syndrome had deep roots.

To be sure, "*bacharelismo*" was attacked even in the heyday of the generalist before World War I. The lack of specialists was cited by men like Ignacio Burlamaqui, president of the Junta de Comércio, and Fidelis Reis, who led the Sociedade Mineira de Agricultura. In calling for a new, practically oriented business school, Burlamaqui said in 1903 that it must not become another focus for "*doutorismo*" like the recently defunct Commercial Academy in Juiz de Fora.[37] Reis helped to create the Engineering Faculty and founded a technical school in his native Uberaba. Later, as a Federal Deputy, he championed the cause of technical education in Brazil. Yet tradition died hard, especially when there was a shortage of certified degree holders to manage a largely illiterate population.

The hunger for degrees extended to the ranks of paraprofessionals, including the self-trained provisional lawyers who obtained temporary state licenses to practice law. Often in league with local politicians, large numbers of them served in the expanded state judiciary after 1892 as district attorneys, judges, and court clerks. Popularly known as *"rabulas"* (shysters), they organized to defend their licenses against reformers led by the young Francisco Campos. After 1920, only those already holding provisional licenses were admitted to legal practice.[38] In upgrading professional standards, the reformers also wanted to tighten state control over local police work and the municipal courts. The plan of Campos and his colleagues to centralize political power is discussed in the next chapter.

In the interior, educated men were needed to run town councils and, especially, to act as prestige links to the larger state system. Service as district attorney or judge was the time-tested rite of passage for young bacharéis or doutores whose political acumen was tested locally before they were tapped for higher office. Marriage into a leading local family often helped to establish a political base. Not only in the statehouse but also in the município the bacharel system was firmly rooted.

Bacharelismo was also compatible with multiple role-playing, which helped to cement elite control. Many lawyers and physicians were also successful fazendeiros, journalists, and bankers or industrialists. Strength of character and connections rather than technical or specialized training still counted the most. Probably the state could not have absorbed many more specialized people until industrialization began in the 1930's. That better opportunities existed in Rio and São Paulo was in any case the reason why so much Mineiro talent emigrated. Whether a more modern educational system could have stemmed this drain is doubtful.

Access to higher education was through the elite secondary schools, some of which enjoyed a national reputation. Church seminaries dominated in the nineteenth century, notably at Mariana. Some studied the classics at Caraça, that forbiddingly austere academy high in the misty mountains of central Minas. Others attended the Ouro

Preto Gymnasium, or prepared at the Colégio Pedro II in Rio. After 1891, the state gymnasium, with branches in Belo Horizonte and Barbacena, and the American Methodist institute, O Granbery, in Juiz de Fora were the most important. Young women could attend the Methodist-run Colégio Isabela Hendrix in Belo Horizonte. On a lower prestige level the normal schools, of which almost all were private, brought humanistic culture to several small cities. By 1908, there were 51 secondary schools of all kinds in Minas. That only one small federal military school existed (in Barbacena) proved that few Mineiros were interested in military careers. Native sons were conspicuously absent in the nation's officer corps.

The role of these schools as a regionalizing influence on the elite cannot be overestimated. Afonso Arinos de Melo Franco remembers being asked by Governor Bernardes, a Caraça graduate, why he did not attend the state gymnasium instead of the Pedro II in Rio. Ranchers from the São Francisco Valley region of Bahia and eastern Goiás often sent their children to Minas for schooling, just as neighboring Paulista students attended the colégio at Muzambinho in the Sul.[39] This formed interregional ties, although in reverse, many Mata students were sent to nearby Rio according to long-established pattern. The schools were stepping-stones for the well-placed. If most of the people were ignorant and lacked the rudiments of a civic culture, then at least, said Augusto Franco, the journalist, the state was fortunate to have good elites.[40]

Taken as a whole, the educational system from primary schools to faculties of higher learning was both impressive and lamentable. Aiming toward a universal system on the American model, Mineiro educators created a large public and private establishment virtually without benefit of federal funds. In the 1890's, Minas led the nation in new schools founded, and under Interior Secretary Francisco Campos in the 1920's it was a leader with São Paulo and Rio in the national movement to upgrade primary education.

In 1926, Campos convened a state congress on teaching methods and management problems at the primary level. Teachers were retrained under educators contracted in Europe, while the number of schools more than doubled. Caught up in the Atlantic world's postwar enthusiasm for pedagogical innovation, Campos and his staff were leaders in the national campaign to focus attention on education—in short, "to build a public opinion to support education." This was a principal theme at the Second National Education Congress held two years later in Belo Horizonte.[41]

Sadly, despite much vigor and idealism, these schools educated the urban population poorly and the rural masses almost not at all, and the few quality institutions were bastions of privilege. Virtually two-thirds of all Mineiros over seven years of age were still illiterate by the 1930 Revolution. For a state committed to education, these results were inadequate, and the governors said as much in their annual reports to the legislature.

Mineiro education was bogged in the economics of scarcity, and this demoralized it. Governor Silviano Brandão closed almost 400 schools during the 1898 depression, and later the reform momentum of the 1920's was slowed drastically by the 1929 crash. Furthermore, the granting of teaching posts and bureaucratic jobs for purposes of patronage filled the ranks with placemen. Almost 80 percent of the population lived outside urban areas, so that distance and dispersion were massive problems in their own right. Perhaps, after all, one should question the intent. Did a conservative, hierarchical society want to risk an open, modern system? Francisco Campos, the innovator, on becoming Minister of Education in 1931 recoiled from the logic of popular education, which was greater participation. Consider, also, the middle groups that moved into higher education in the 1920's without altering its basically elitist structure. For all of Minas's prestige in education, the limited resources coupled with a dispersed population and a conservative ethic did not favor the growth of a modern system.

Mineiros born in the Second Empire were touched by rationalist thinking, especially by the scientism of Spencer and the positivism of Comte, which was disseminated at national law schools or by the medical faculty. Many lost their faith at law school, but few repudiated Catholicism outright, and they were, on the whole, displeased when the national Constituent Assembly voted to disestablish the Catholic Church and to secularize public education in 1891. Catholics at the 1891 state convention successfully beat down the laicist clause, despite Republican doctrine. Religious instruction was allowed in Minas until Governor João Pinheiro, a Positivist, abolished it along with state subsidies to the seminaries in 1906. However, in bringing

Minas into line with the federal constitution, Pinheiro, a reform governor who believed strongly in secularism, stirred up an issue that for a Church then struggling to rebuild was made to order. The latent religiosity of Mineiros was mobilized in the ensuing anti-laicist campaign. Thus members of the generation born after 1889 were far more Catholic than their rationalist fathers.

The Church responded vigorously to Pinheiro with a press campaign and also urged Catholic householders to put pressure on their political representatives. Starting in 1910, several statewide congresses were held in which educators and professional men took leading roles. In 1913, the União Popular, a lay group, petitioned the Legislature to allow religious instruction after-hours in the public schools. It obtained 202,192 signatures on petitions throughout the state, many from registered voters. Governor Bernardes responded to this demand in 1920, and as the mobilization spread, Republican orthdoxy bent to practical politics. Following the first national Catechism Congress in Belo Horizonte (1928), Governor Antonio Carlos de Andrada directed Francisco Campos to allow one hour of catechizing in the schools. For signing this measure into law in September 1929, the governor was presented with a gold cup, inset with jewels.[42]

The Church in "this most Catholic of Brazilian states" was now much stronger, thanks to the education issue and to the organizing talents of Dom Silvério Gomes Pimenta (1840–1922), the Archbishop of Mariana. A humbly born Negro whose rise through the hierarchy took him four times to Rome, Dom Silvério carried out the Papacy's directive to re-Catholicize Minas. Under him, the Church was transformed from a weak dependency of the Empire to a self-confident, multilayered organization by World War I. Subsequently, the Mineiro Catholic movement outgrew its regional base as Belo Horizonte became a leading Catholic center under the overall direction of the Cardinal in Rio. The youth organization (União dos Moços Católicos), with 15,000 members nationwide, was transferred to Rio in 1928. And the Church, having won its 20-year battle against lay education by 1929, marshaled nationally to amend the federal constitution, which it did in 1934.[43] For his part, the immensely influential Dom Silvério was elected to the National Academy of Letters in 1920, taking the chair of a celebrated freethinker.

Dom Silvério pushed the Catholic revival on many fronts. Institutionally, Rome created three archbishoprics and nine new bishoprics between 1906 and 1924. Both Mariana and Diamantina (two of the new metropolitan sees) had depended on Salvador since colonial times, whereas parts of the Mata were affiliated with Rio de Janeiro, and the Sul and the Triângulo were ruled from São Paulo. Under the new governance, however, the Minas Church administered Goiás and in 1917 replaced Vitória's control of the disputed territory with Espírito Santo. Financially, Dom Silvério established a system of tithing and Church investments to replace the defunct Imperial subsidy. Disestablishment in 1891 was thereby turned to good advantage. Organizationally, the Church reached out to new groups, including workers, students, and professional men. Participation was stressed as an adjunct to revitalizing the clergy. This was a new departure from the routinized Catholicism described so vividly in Brant's *The Diary of Helena Morley*. Doctrinally, Dom Silvério declared war on the Protestants with their schools, and on the proliferating spiritualist movement. Moralizing films and the press were another of his priorities.[44]

In politics, the Catholic movement was an effective pressure group, with a large, multiorganization base. Dom Silvério's attempts to establish a clerical party failed (see Chapter 4), but as the Church's influence waxed, this hardly mattered. The revival was so successful that Minas did not develop the clerical-secular cleavages of post-Napoleonic Europe, or Mexico and Argentina. For one thing, the Church sponsored voluntary organizations just as society was becoming more complex. For another, the movement appealed to Mineiro conservatism in a period of accelerating change. The net effect was to mediate change with a set of symbols and organizations that gained wide acceptance among the elite.

The Minas revival began as an international missionary effort that relied heavily upon the organizing talents, élan, and experience of foreign priests, especially from France and the Low Countries. In the late Empire, Italian Capuchins were active among the few remaining Indians, and French Lazarites specialized in teaching the elite, notably at Caraça. French religious architecture of the pinched Gothic Revival style replaced some Portuguese colonial churches, owing to the influence of French priests. (Belo Horizonte's cathedral was designed by the French; Caraça's chapel was revamped by them.) Starting in 1892,

Pope Leo XIII stepped up the flow of Europeans to assist the thinly spread Brazilian clergy, and Dom Silvério personally recruited Dutch and Belgian priests in Europe. The new lay groups, Catholic labor unions, and the congresses all owed much to the European priests with their ideas for Catholic social action.

Since the new Catholicism depended upon European models and personnel, foreign influence was substantial. Missionary teachers, including Protestants, were well received by the general population, and they propagated foreign values in the course of what they regarded as their civilizing mission to an exotic and backward Catholic country. Future political leaders, such as Juscelino Kubitschek de Oliveira, often formed their first impression of the advanced nations through missionary teachers. Making tiny Belgium better known was an inducement for the Premonstratensians in Montes Claros, who saw themselves as "the first white priests" to serve in northern Minas.[45] A reservoir of sympathy was built up, as when the Belgian consul decorated Dom Silvério for his fund-raising on behalf of Belgian war relief. And the warmth with which King Albert was received in 1920 sprang in part from the elite's enthusiasm at speaking French. His visit to Belo Horizonte paved the way for Belgian investment in the charcoal steel industry.

Foreigners in the mass had little impact in a state where immigration largely failed. Outsiders were well received as individuals, not as members of a threatening alien group. Nativism hardly existed in the cultural sphere; rather, it was limited to a historic fear of foreign domination over natural resources. Even so, foreign investors were courted if they were culturally adept. The Belgians charmed Bernardes, who disliked Percival Farquhar of Itabira Iron for his patronizing ways. With the exception of iron ore concessions and the Leopoldina Railway (a British firm that crossed swords often with the Mata planters over freight rates), there were few symbols of foreign ownership.

In an elite on the whole attuned to foreign styles and roles, some stood out more than others. The politician and diplomat Afrânio de Melo Franco "when not in office is legal advisor to the Leopoldina and professes admiration for things British."[46] He received the K.B.E., and in 1934 became president of the Brazilian Society for English Culture. Afonso Pena Junior, a former cabinet minister and leading state politician, followed him in this post. Daniel de Carvalho, a rising young politician in the 1920's, did legal work for foreign firms. (He also frequented the Clube Floriano Peixoto, a patriotic society in Belo Horizonte.) Ties like this were not unusual in what was, after all, an exporting region. What matters is that there were not enough foreigners in key economic and cultural roles to threaten the elite's self-image and identification with Mineiro values.

No outsider was more highly regarded than George Chalmers (1856–1928), who in his obituary was hailed as "the perfect gentleman, a constant and dedicated friend of our country." A Cornish mining engineer, Chalmers was for 43 years superintendent at the Morro Velho gold mine, the state's largest industrial employer. It might be expected that a powerful man like Chalmers would arouse envy, perhaps resentment. Instead, he was seen as an innovator who was a stern but benevolent paternalist at the mine. He was a trusted economic adviser to the state. The English had their own club and Anglican Chapel at Morro Velho, but the superintendent cultivated good relations with Mineiros and saw to the needs of politicians, who were taken in tow discreetly by Jacques Paris, a fun-loving Uruguayan aide. The model of an English gentleman, Chalmers owned Jaguára, a huge fazenda outside Belo Horizonte that had belonged to Henrique Dumont, turning it into a model farm and game reserve. His scrupulous management of Jaguára and his love of fishing were virtues with which many identified.[47]

Low-status foreigners were kept on a tight leash. Spanish workers striking at Morro Velho in 1897 were faced down by Chalmers, who called for troops. Most of those jailed after the abortive Campanha revolt (1892) were Italian laborers. In 1896, Italian railroad workers rioted with Brazilians at Sabará over immigration policy. Until the militia arrived, it was feared some 2,000 compatriots helping to construct Belo Horizonte would join them. The leaders of these incidents, mostly anarchists, were deported. Foreigners who were dissatisfied with the low wages left for São Paulo or returned home. Those who stayed found their way in urban occupations; several foreign surnames among leading merchants and industrialists proved that mobility existed for the hardworking, the able, and the lucky.

Middle Easterners, the famous "turcos," were accepted grudgingly, but the congressional delegation voted in the 1920's to bar African immigrants. Armed Gypsy bands provoked several interstate police

actions on the Rio and São Paulo frontiers. By 1920, they were resigned to pot-mending and card tricks, although townsmen still kept
watch on their horses when the Gypsies were encamped. Traditional
anti-Semitism was felt by the small Jewish business community, and it
is true that, of all the immigrant groups, Northern Europeans had the
most prestige. However, no nationality or group was singled out for
cultural or political opprobrium, save the African, and even the
Negro freedman's stock was rising.[48]

Open to change but never having to break with traditional society,
the Mineiro elite was conservative, place-centered, and innocent of
role or identity crises. Dissatisfaction with the rate and direction of
economic development was present since the eighteenth century.
But the realization of Minas as a backward, underdeveloped region
dawned late, in the 1930's. Despair over these socioeconomic lags
was a post–World War II phenomenon. In a period of accelerating
change, the elite worried about urbanization, which made farm labor
(at low wages) hard to get, but they felt no political or social pressure
from below. The middle groups, as mentioned, accommodated to a
social contract still dominated and defined by those at the top of a
hierarchical social order. There was no crisis of modernization in the
conventional sense.

Yet regional culture was not static. Urbanization, mass communications, and mass education were under way by 1920, but so were a
revitalization and renewal of regional culture. Modern social change,
however tentative and imperfect in the case of education, was not incompatible with regionalism. Economic change reordered power and
population among the zones; the old Center again took the lead.
However, the essential facets of Mineiro identity survived economic
dislocations, an extensive emigration, and the rise of state and national
power. Far from being swamped by the inrush of modern values,
regional culture flourished.

What can be called the programmatic core of regionalism—the new
capital, the efforts at integration, the "loss of substance" argument—
was change-oriented. From Tiradentes onward, the thrust of regional
thought was to create a more viable unit based on a stronger identity
among the parts, but not to destroy them. Regionalism was thus
compatible with subregional identities, and Brazilian literature is the
richer for it.

To carry the point further, regionalism was not antithetical to strengthening a national identity or to maintaining a zonal identity. The Mineiro's emphasis on family and the small community did not preclude loyalty to state and nation, or identification with North Atlantic culture. So-called primordial loyalties survived and were adapted to meet new demands for identity to state and nation. Far from being unique to Minas, the growth of multiple identities appears to have cropped up in several regions and nations undergoing the impact of modernization.[49]

If regional culture faced change and helped Mineiros to mediate it, the very stability of Mineiro society may have been a long-term liability. A self-confident identity, coupled with the elite's belief in their capacity to cope, was essential to a pluralistic view of locality, region, and nation. This eroded in the 1930's, when Minas no longer led the nation in politics. But the sense of identity was still strong in the postwar generation, to which Juscelino Kubitschek belonged. The politics of federalism was doubtless compatible with a hierarchical social order, a subject to which we now must turn.

## CHAPTER FOUR

# State Politics: Men, Events, and Structures

SHOTS RANG OUT in Montes Claros, the capital of northern Minas, before Manuel Tomás de Carvalho Brito could address a political rally there on the night of February 6, 1930. Vice-President Melo Viana was wounded next to him, and three men were killed. Not that violence had been unexpected in this railhead town. Brito's men brought in two trainloads of supporters from Belo Horizonte, who got drunk, picked fights, and milled around with the prostitutes before marching behind Brito and the vice-president to cheers, exploding rockets, and a brass band. Then came the gunfire, followed by reports that the Juiz de Fora Army garrison might come North to "restore order." Meanwhile, the state militia was denied access to the federal telegraph and railroad. Thus the incident was staged, probably to provoke intervention. The governor was not deposed, but even Minas was vulnerable to federal intervention for daring to oppose a sitting president in what proved to be the last and most hotly contested election of the Old Republic.*

Federal pressure was common in the weaker states but new to Minas, which had cooperated closely with all the presidents to rule the system of unequal federalism favoring the big, powerful states of Minas Gerais, São Paulo, and Rio Grande do Sul. Committed to orderly government, Minas was a pillar of the presidential system,

* An ally of President Washington Luís and Júlio Prestes (the majority candidate), Brito led the Conservative Concentration group in Minas against the Partido Republicano Mineiro (PRM), the dominant state machine, which backed Getúlio Vargas for the presidency.

just as it had once been a mainstay of the Bragança monarchy. Adept at the legislator's game of compromise and maneuver, Mineiros led the congress for most of the Old Republic. They held the federal presidency three times and enjoyed the role of kingmaker. They were always represented in the ministry. Internal cohesion at home was the key to this national influence. For most of this period, the PRM machine was a highly successful adaptation to *coronelismo,* the patron-client politics run by rural bosses and orchestrated from the state house. In fact, dissident movements like the Conservative Concentration had been rare. But in 1930 the PRM was split, and Brito astutely analyzed the causes in his undelivered speech.

Minas politics developed in three phases, he wrote. At first the state was preoccupied with internal matters and did not seek leadership in the federation. In 1898, however, Governor Francisco Silviano Brandão projected Minas onto the national stage, in close cooperation with President Campos Sales of São Paulo. Silviano ended the internal feuding that had weakened Minas and set up the disciplined congressional delegation, which gave Minas great influence. For three decades this formula worked well: nationally, Minas stood by the president while at home the orderly functioning of state government and the transfer of power from one governor to another was not disturbed by what Brito called "ephemeral minorities."

But in 1929 a third phase began. Rather than supporting Washington Luís, a "legitimate and powerful president," the PRM broke with precedent to back the opposition candidate, with predictable results. Weakened by internal dissent, Minas faced disaster unless it rebuilt the all-important ties to Rio: cohesion at home was the key.[1]

These views were widely held in Minas, and in fact the idea of three political phases in state politics is historically accurate. As an end to this story, Brito's dissidents were forced out of political life following the Revolution, which brought Getúlio Vargas to power. After 1930, the traditional ability of Mineiros to unite behind their governor again assured them of national influence, but on terms that made Minas a political client of Vargas, well before the federal system was abolished in 1937, the end of phase three. After examining the three political phases, with emphasis on narrative synthesis and chronology, I will discuss the structures of state politics, and then, in the next chapter, will analyze the state elite in detail.

## Men and Events

Unlike São Paulo, where the Republican Party was primed to take power, or Rio Grande do Sul, where the disciplined Republicans contested leadership via civil war, the Minas Republicans were still disorganized when the monarchy collapsed in 1889. The last provincial governor (a Liberal) harassed Republican organizers and purged their sympathizers from government jobs.[2] Until the end, in fact, the Liberal and Conservative parties were stronger despite defections to the Republicans after slavery was abolished in May 1888. These "eleventh hour" recruits strengthened the so-called Historical Republicans, who until then had been unable to articulate a statewide organization.

Slavocrat until the end, most of the Imperial elite adhered to the Republic after the bloodless coup in Rio, which caught the Minas Republicans unawares. A few unreconstructed monarchists moved to Rio, where they helped to found the law school and were active in cultural affairs. The adherents tried, and in large part were able to keep their municipal bases intact, fully expecting to absorb, co-opt, and manipulate the less experienced historicals.

The Republicans' program went over well among broad sections of the elite. Their call for a new democratic order based on broadened local power appealed to grass roots loyalties. Their program of regional development under decentralized, federal institutions drew on the still compelling legacy of Tiradentes. Upgrading government services, which meant more jobs for professional degree holders (lawyers especially), was considered a necessity. Rising coffee revenues were available to fund this. Under federalism, the newly "sovereign" state of Minas Gerais would also have a larger share of taxes.

The Mineiros also shared a well-developed political culture, a mixture of regional patriotism, political experience, and civic values. In part, this was a legacy of the Empire, when the three parties competed for seats in the 20-man national delegation and the 40-man provincial Assembly. By 1889, the elite was familiar with modes of interaction that tended to be more sophisticated than coronelismo and clan warfare of the northeastern type. Despite broad agreement on goals and methods, however, the elite was divided by regional cleavages and factionalism for almost ten years.

Cesário Alvim, an eleventh-hour Republican with connections in the Center and Mata zones going back to his days as a Liberal leader, consolidated the first ruling coalition over the objections of the historicals, who had expected to take power. Closely linked to General Deodoro da Fonseca, the first president, Alvim appointed ex-Liberals to patronage posts and ignored the historicals.[3] He also took over the Republican Party with the help of João Pinheiro da Silva, its leader, who agreed with Alvim's policy of attracting seasoned and electorally powerful adherents into a strong coalition. Power and patronage having escaped them, some of the historicals asked the Army to intervene, but Alvim, now Deodoro's Minister of Interior, headed off a coup in June 1890. Crispim Jacques de Bias Fortes, another ex-Liberal, was appointed governor to oversee the upcoming elections for both the federal and state Constituent Assemblies.[4]

The historicals met in August at Juiz de Fora to protest the official slate of candidates for the *federal* elections, which included many adherents. The nominations, they said, should have come up from the municipal grass roots, not down from the party Executive Committee under João Pinheiro. Yet they did agree to support the mixed slate on the ground that Minas needed a united and experienced delegation to uphold state interests in Rio.[5] Pulling together won over principle.

They met again at Juiz de Fora on Christmas Day 1890 to oppose the official slate for *state* elections. Led by Fernando Lobo Leite Pereira, a Juiz de Fora lawyer, and Antonio Olinto dos Santos Pires, an engineer, they fielded their own rival slate and tried to build a counterforce in the Sul and Mata, with Juiz de Fora as their base. But the Alvim coalition won all 72 state seats in the January 1891 election, including 13 deputies and four senators whose names appeared also on the opposition slate.[6] Thus the historicals were denied a separate identity outside the broad official coalition. This was to be the fate of all opposition groups until 1930.

Meanwhile, several adherents not on the federal slate formed an opposition faction called the Partído Católico. Ex-monarchists in a few other states also formed Catholic parties to fight their exclusion from federal election lists. In Minas, they sought neither to win elections nor to protest the Church's recent disestablishment. Their real aim was to be co-opted into Alvim's coalition, the Partído Católico being a signal of who was regionally influential. Prominent were Francisco Silvano Brandão, a Sulista Republican turned Liberal, and Sabino

Barroso, a northern Conservative.[7] Their tactic worked, and in December seven "católicos" appeared on the official list for the State Constituent Assembly, to which they elected six senators (out of 24) and one deputy.

The state delegation was more cohesive and conservative than its federal counterpart, which included several historicals. To Oliveira Torres, the late monarchist historian, this signaled the return of powerful rural landowners, newly regrouped after abolition and the coup. However, the distinction he found between younger, more ideological federal deputies and the establishment state delegation is blurred by the fact that both groups included many sons and sons-in-law of ex-monarchists.[8] Fundamentally, Alvim regarded the state convention as the more important body, not only to consolidate his power base at home, but also because the elite was preoccupied with devising a viable political system for its newly "sovereign" state. In fact, the state electoral list was very tightly monitored. Only a handful of state deputies were ever elected off the ticket (extra-chapa) in the 1890's, whereas the federal elections were relatively more open and contested until the end of phase one. The assembly elected Alvim governor, but he was suddenly weakened by Vice-President Floriano Peixoto's coup against Deodoro in November 1891. The congressional delegation moved immediately to the new power pole, João Pinheiro being replaced as leader by Antonio Olinto. The historials also expected to gain the governorship and purge adherents, as their Paulista counterparts soon did against Governor Américo Brasiliense. They urged the federal garrison in Ouro Preto to act. Despite the historicals' close ties to Floriano, broad sections of the state elite abhorred the prospect of federal intervention, and they rallied to Alvim, the legal governor. In a strongly worded telegram signed by Afonso Pena, Bias, and other notables, they warned Floriano not to intervene.[9] But Alvim's days were numbered, and the catalyst for his fall was a regional revolt in the Sul.

The city of Campanha declared itself the capital of a new state, Minas do Sul, an option much discussed by planters during the late Empire who felt ignored by Ouro Preto. Minister of Justice Fernando Lobo, who came from the Sul, appeared to sympathize; at least, by not condemning it outright he raised the possibility of federal intervention to "restore order." Alarmed, the state elite again rallied to

Alvim, who sent a joint state-federal force against the rebels. A rising in the Mata município of Viçosa also was suppressed, once it became clear that Floriano would not actively support local revolts.[10] Unlike São Paulo, to be sure, the historicals were not strong enough to exploit these risings at the risk of civil war. Alvim resigned after insisting that the lieutenant governor take over, which he did, preparatory to ex-Liberal Afonso Pena's election in May 1892; this upheld the legal niceties.

Floriano soon reaped the benefits of conciliating the Mineiros. The 1893 navy rising against him had no chance to win after Governor Pena publicly asured him that the heartland would stay loyal. Cooperation between the legalistic Mineiros and this astute, supple military president lasted through a difficult civil war in Rio Grande do Sul until the return of civilian rule in 1894, which the Mineiros wanted. badly.

Alvim's fall also spurred a realignment of regional forces while the state Constituent Assembly was still in session. Power flowed from the old mining zone, where Alvim was strongest, to the coffee regions, which paid the bulk of export taxes, the budgetary mainstay. The decline of Alvim also strengthened advocates of a new, centralizing capital: Belo Horizonte was selected over other sites, including Juiz de Fora, in 1893.

In the Mata, revitalized historicals allied themselves with Carlos Vaz de Melo, an anti-Alvinista who led the Viçosa revolt. Vaz de Melo was a super-coronel, or boss, of the type that would dominate zonal politics for the next quarter-century. With Antonio Olinto he formed the Constitutional Republican Party (PRC) to unite the congressional delegation behind Floriano during the naval revolt. Ideologically, the PRC fought the revisionist views of monarchists on the right and Republican radicals on the left who claimed that federalism was not working. Holding the line against constitutional changes became dogma with the Minas establishment, which saw its own legitimacy thus upheld. (Ironically, it was Vaz de Melo's own son-in-law, Artur Bernardes, who as governor and then as president in the early 1920's changed this line.) The PRC was a congressional caucus party, although power did not lie with the lawmakers. To assure an orderly processing of election lists, the PRC was dominated by the governor and his Secretary of Interior in alliance with the key regional bosses.

In the Sul, meanwhile, Senator Silviano Brandão rallied fellow coronéis against the Campanha rising, which fortified his influence at the Constituent Assembly, and in turn led to his being made Interior Secretary. Having emerged as a super-coronel in his own right, Silviano used his office to erode the electoral bases of Alvim, who was still strong enough to contest the 1894 election. Bias Fortes won, thanks to Silviano's selective use of the police and control over the polls. As president of the senate, Silviano continued to build up his own faction, the "Silvianistas." His close associates were all Sulistas, including brother-in-law Júlio Bueno Brandão, an ex-Liberal, protégé Wenceslau Brás Pereira Gomes, from a Conservative family, and Francisco Bressane de Azevedo, a historical who was amnestied by Floriano for his part in the Campanha rising and reintegrated. With Silviano in the state senate, and Júlio Bueno serving as majority leader of the Chamber, the Silvianistas were well-positioned to dominate the PRC.

Thus power shifted to the coffee zones without federal intervention or institutional breakdown, and unprecedented coffee revenues helped ease the transition. Patronage increased throughout the state, however unequally distributed. Between 1894 and 1899, for example, the Sul received more than half of all state subsidies and loans for railroad construction (see Chapter 8). Only the Triângulo, with its links to Paulista markets, railroads, and credit, had a viable economic alternative to the emerging state system. Another reason why the transition went well is that no faction was cohesive enough to impose itself; no regional chief could rule without making pragmatic alliances with other bosses. State politics centered on a de facto collegium of regional bosses analogous to a mini-federal system.

Bias, Silviano, and Vaz de Melo were the superbosses in whose orbits lesser leaders jockied for position, power, and influence. Sabino Barroso enjoyed an independent northern base, thanks to Conservative Party clan ties. He defied the PRC and was one of few deputies elected extra-chapa to the state congress. In the Sul and Center zones, Francisco Antonio de Sales was a rising star. A historical, "Chico" Sales had parentesco in both zones and was a leading merchant who supplied produce to Belo Horizonte from his nearby fazenda. In 1897 a crisis over the national succession plunged the PRC into turmoil, from which emerged a new party, the famous Partido Republicano Mineiro.

On September 1, all Mineiro legislators were called to Ouro Preto to nominate Silviano for governor and to deliberate on the split between Francisco Glicério, who led the national Republican Party (PRF), and the president, who supported Manuel Ferraz de Campos Sales of São Paulo. Publicly, Silviano refused to take sides; privately, he was one of the leading state bosses on the basis of whose support Campos Sales ignored Glicério and the party. Silviano's indifference to the ideological issue, and indeed the manner of his own prearranged nomination were challenged by an opposition group led by Francisco Mendes Pimentel, a 28-year-old lawyer whose father was president of the state Supreme Court. This group moved to debate the national issue first, before discussing state politics, and then followed with a second motion to nominate the governor democratically, in an open convention, with delegates chosen by the municípios.* After losing two close votes on the motions, the dissidents walked out.[11]

At issue were two models of Republican party politics. One, the caucus party, was openly manipulated by the governor in league with leading bosses. This was the only practical way to rule a vast state like Minas, or so the "ins" always said. The other, a convention party, was to be run by delegates elected by new party branches at the district level. Starting with the historicals' meetings at Juiz de Fora in 1890, the "outs" always called for open conventions and free elections. Ironically, several of the 1897 dissidents were former Alvinistas, including Mendes Pimentel, their leader. The 65 congressmen who stayed on at Ouro Preto chose a new PRC Executive Committee under Vaz de Melo. The 35 who bolted began calling themselves the PRM and, having elected their own Executive Committee, prepared to meet at Belo Horizonte on December 20, one day after the new capital's inauguration.[12]

The creation of two rival factions threatened to weaken the governor and split the delegation in Rio, a scenario played out often in Bahia and the northern states. But the risk of competitive party politics was avoided when both factions agreed to meet at Belo Horizonte. (Bressane arranged this.) In exchange for endorsing Silviano for governor and Campos Sales for president, the convention

---

* Most delegates felt Glicério's national party was premature. The exceptions were a few historicals, to whom Glicério appealed when he chose Fernando Lobo to run for vice-president.

would vote new statutes vesting the nominating process in locally chosen delegates. The convention's mandate would then be carried out by a fusion Executive Committee.[13]

Silviano had in fact risked nothing by agreeing to an open convention; the spirit of reform did not long survive his uncontested election for governor in February 1898. Bressane himself represented 29 of the 73 municípios sending delegates, and he made full use of duplicate delegations, an effective way to weaken the opposition. A master manipulator, Bressane dispelled any doubts about who controlled the votes when the PRM Executive Committee met in July to process nominations for a federal senate seat. He personally laid the votes of 47 local party branches on the table for Júlio Bueno, thus overwhelming Antonio Olinto (the historical), who was next with 20.[14] Mendes Pimentel was not among those voted to the Executive Committee "by acclamation" at the next PRM convention in August 1898, and he also lost control of O Diário de Minas, the party daily he founded. The upshot was that by 1898 the old fault lines were closed: Alvinistas, historicals, adherents all bent to the new machine or, like the disillusioned Mendes Pimentel, left active politics. Phase one was over.

"Rounding up the herd" under one state party was greatly aided by the onset of economic depression in 1897. In his classic study of coronelismo, Nunes Leal, the political sociologist and jurist, showed how the 1891 Constitution underfunded municipal governments, making the local bosses economically dependent upon the state government for public works and patronage.[15] In return for economic favors, the coronéis delivered votes. Thanks to prosperity, municipal revenues in the more productive zones of Minas increased in the 1890's. This fortified the coronéis, as did the expanded electorate, which doubled after the Empire, and the increase in the number of appointive and elective offices at every level. But the depression weakened their revenue base, and this helped the rising PRM to consolidate its hold on most local governments by 1898. Some of the richer municípios, such as Leopoldina in the Mata, enjoyed more freedom to maneuver in the PRM structure than most localities. And the Triângulo, prosperous but geographically isolated from Belo Horizonte, enjoyed a looser affiliation than other zones; this worried the PRM. For most coronéis, however, there was but one commandment: never oppose the governor.

Silviano used the economic crisis to project Minas onto the national scene as a close ally of Campos Sales, who carried out a drastic austerity program. Both men also used the crisis to increase executive power at the expense of their respective legislatures. Campos Sales established his "politics of the governors" in close consultation with Minas and Bahia. The states were given control over federal patronage in exchange for supporting the president's program in congress. It was Vaz de Melo who, as president of the Chamber in 1899, set up the credentials review system to manipulate election tallies and weed out mavericks.[16] Starting in 1900, all 37 members of the Minas delegation often voted as a bloc. These were the national ground rules for phase two.

Under the PRM, Minas enjoyed a political stability unmatched by Republican parties elsewhere except in São Paulo and Rio Grande. Of particular interest is the institutionalized relationship between governors and superbosses on the party Executive Committee. The PRM did not charge dues, as in São Paulo, nor was it anything like the monolithic Rio Grande party. In Minas, the Executive Committee functioned as a collegium, responsive to the governor. Its role was advisory and procedural. It also legitimized the governor's compact with the superbosses, serving, in Bias's words, as his umbrella.[17]

Upon receiving the governor's selection of candidates for state and federal office, the committee sent his "suggestions" down to coronéis under their control for nomination. Bressane, the perpetual party secretary, articulated this system by wire. Wearing a green eyeshade, "Coronel Pisca-Pisca" (for his facial tic) poured over party ledgers on the locally influential, which included after each name a notation on the nearest telegraphic post. Bressane told each coronel how to distribute his vote, and worked out the opposition tally. In return, the coronel expected almost unquestioned access to local taxes, "which the more scrupulous put into roads and bridges near their own fazendas, or those of relatives and close friends."[18]

Yet the Executive Committee was something more than a front for the governor, as critics charged. Negotiations over the succession were held in this committee, then ratified by it in a public bulletin. The transfer of power was resolved without resort to unstable coalitions or the use of force, including federal intervention. Thus the chronic succession crises that debilitated other states and destroyed Bahia's national power after 1900 were contained and institutionalized in the Executive Committee. To be sure, each power transfer in Minas was a potential disaster: the literature is clear on this point.[19] During the succession debates, the committee played a stabilizing and a legitimizing role, which conferred a certain power on it. In the flexible PRM structure, therefore, it is accurate to say that the executive ruled in tandem with his committee. See Appendix B, pp. 255–56.

Governors served four-year terms and could not be reelected, but committeemen were subject only to the realities of regional power plays and the onset of old age. When Silviano died in 1902, the committee divided into three loosely defined blocs, which coexisted uneasily but effectively until 1918.

1. *The Silvianistas* were led by Júlio Bueno and by Wenceslau Brás, who did not come on formally until 1919, when he stepped down as the nation's president. Silvianistas held the state house for 15 years, until 1918. They furnished a president, two vice-presidents (one of whom did not take office), and several leaders in the federal legislature. Their durability is explained by Silviano's early articulation of the two coffee zones and by the staying power of loyalty and family ties.

2. *The Biistas* were under Bias Fortes of Barbacena, who presided over the Executive Committee from 1898 until his death in 1917. Bias was entrenched on the senate Finance Committee, and controlled the flow of legislation. "Let the Chamber pass any bill it wants," he boasted, "but when it reaches the senate I can knock it down."[20]

3. *The Salistas*. Francisco Sales was very active in federal politics, but he knew personally a great number of local notables, and scores of lesser bosses were beholden to him. He enjoyed the role of kingmaker and go-between in Rio. In 1898 he led the delegation, and then, having been governor in 1902–6, he was federal senator, Minister of Finance, and senator again until 1922. Bressane, his close ally, was a long-time federal deputy.[21]

The leaders of these factions shared a similar talent for nonideological politics based on pragmatic manipulation. They ran their factions on a patron-client system of reciprocal rights and obligations, in which personal loyalty was the guiding principle and patronage the cement of politics. While thoroughly rooted in the small-city ethos, they were, nonetheless bourgeois in their career patterns, as profiled in Chapter 5. Their ability to cohere in order to buffer the transfer of power was perhaps even more developed than that of their colleagues in the Republican Party of São Paulo (PRP), organized on similar lines. João Pinheiro's reform governorship (1906–8) is a case in point.

Having retired from politics after Alvim's fall, Pinheiro's return was sponsored by Sales as a compromise candidate. While he talked political reform, Pinheiro surrounded himself with fellow businessmen and engineers who shared his preoccupation with economic growth. He replaced Bressane as party secretary, elected some of his own men to the legislature, and allowed minority candidates to win elections, but did not revitalize the convention model or shake up the Executive Committee. When Pinheiro died suddenly in October 1908, the three factions cooperated to purge his brightest talents and closed ranks behind Júlio Bueno as governor while backing Marechal Hermes da Fonseca for the presidency. Cast adrift, Pinheiro's men joined Rui Barbosa's civilista campaign, but could not carry the state or even win local elections with the Executive Committee united against them. Consequently, this first of three contested presidential elections in the Old Republic was in Minas a machine-run show.[22]

The PRM took pride in its ability to bring young talent up the ranks by the *sargentação* system, or making one's career by the numbers. Artur da Silva Bernardes inherited Viçosa from Vaz de Melo and served a conventional apprenticeship within the Silvianista faction. Tested first in local politics, then in the state legislature, he moved to the federal congress, to the Secretary of Finance, and to the congress again before becoming governor in 1918. Raul Soares de Moura, another rising star from the Mata, returned from a São Paulo teaching career to take over Rio Branco município when his brother was assassinated there in 1909, served in the legislature, and as Secretary of Agriculture. Both assumed the image and the rhetoric of a new generation, and were eager to speed up economic growth. Sure of their young men, the PRM was taken by surprise when Bernardes, backed by Soares, imposed one-man rule in a dazzling display of executive power, starting in 1918.

The decline of the PRM founders gave him the opening to reform.

Generational change was manifested in the recent death of Bias Fortes, and in the poor health of other leaders. Thus enfeebled, the Executive Committee lost power to the governor. This intraparty shake-up, which paralleled a similar change in São Paulo a few years later, is worth examining in detail.

Bernardes first revamped the legislature, forcing a high turnover— 72 percent of the deputies and half (the maximum) of all senators— by far the most drastic during the Old Republic.[23] Almost all of the new deputies had university degrees; prominent civilistas won election; two canons of the Church became senators. This signaled his appeal to talent, to João Pinheiro's exiled band, and to the new Catholic vote. Sales controlled four of the seven Executive Committee votes, but did not challenge Bernardes for fear of splitting the party.

Next, Bernardes modernized the party statutes and machinery at the PRM convention of September 17, 1919. The new platform stressed that "politics is not the end, but the means to promote the general welfare," which was a slap at the old-style patronage politics typified by Sales. The convention voted to upgrade state services, tax reform, and a public health service. The revolutionary fears then gripping postwar Europe were fashionably echoed in the party's pledge "to conciliate the interests of capital and labor." Sincere or not, this platform was an ingenious cover for the statutory changes Bernardes used to break Sales's hold on the party machinery.

For one thing, each delegate now could represent no more than five local party branches. At the convention nominating Bernardes in 1917, Sales alone sat for 28 localities. For another, the Executive Committee was expanded to pack the voting against Sales, its president. All the ex-governors—Sales, Júlio Bueno, and Wenceslau—became lifetime charter members, which opened up three slots for Bernardistas. These were Astolfo Dutra, president of the Chamber of Deputies and a long-time Sales enemy in the Mata, Francisco Badaró, a Catholic intellectual from the North, and Raul Soares. Finally the convention voted to rotate the Executive Committee president and secretary each year, thus ending the hegemony of Sales and Bressane.[24]

Bernardes had a flair for identifying his political personality with reform and imposed one-man rule without splitting the party. He wanted to be an activist governor, but was also a manipulator who packed the PRM with his own supporters in order to run for the presidency in 1922.* Certainly his next move was radical. To break the power of local governments, he proposed a constitutional amendment making the office of mayor appointive. This would have transformed the 172 municípios into administrative arms of Belo Horizonte, with strict limits on local spending. The case for central control was argued very ably in the Chamber by Francisco da Silva Campos, a 26-year-old lawyer who later authored the 1937 fascist constitution and the 1964 Institutional Act number one, which legitimized military rule. After lengthy debates, in August of 1920 the legislature rejected this proposal 17 to 12. The majority did not want "outsiders" running the localities. In effect, they told Bernardes that he could not dismantle, or drastically alter, the coronelistic system.[25]

Bernardes wanted reform but not fundamental change. His paternalistic appeals to labor and the middle classes were in the tradition of co-optive politics. Old-style personalism was congenial to a man whose roots ran deep in the small-city ethos of Minas. Governor Raul Soares's death in 1924 abruptly closed the brief era of one-man rule. Now an isolated, unpopular president in Rio, Bernardes lost control of the PRM, which reverted to a collegium of regional satraps grouped around the new governor, Fernando de Melo Viana.

Yet political output did not return to lower levels, because state government in the 1920's was notably more activist. Minas responded to the twin stimuli of postwar economic growth and the demand for more government services at every level. State revenues doubled, owing in part to Bernardes' tax reform. A road construction program was begun, the embryonic steel industry was established, and Minas was a leader in the national movement for primary school reforms. In this optimistic climate, the state's political system appeared to work well enough, especially under the light, sure touch of Antonio Carlos Ribeiro de Andrada, governor from 1926 to 1930.

Andrada ranks with the great Mineiro politicians, but unlike Bias or Francisco Sales he cut a modern, contemporary figure. He held more elite offices (11, as defined in this work) than any other public figure in Minas, São Paulo, or Pernambuco. Well connected in business and

* Assis Barbosa points out that Bernardes' attack on the coronéis was not directed against the violent, outland areas of the North and West, or the bosses loyal to him. Rather, his purge was aimed at uprooting coronéis from the more densely populated agricultural-manufacturing center of the state, in the Sul and Mata, and especially against the Salistas. *Juscelino Kubitschek*, pp. 256–57.

professional groups in Juiz de Fora (his base), Rio, and abroad, he had an expert knowledge of banking and finance. Andrada ran a modern government, without changing the substance of politics. When law students became a power in Belo Horizonte city politics, he met their reform demands by instituting the secret ballot, knowing that elections would still be run by friendly coronéis. And he reestablished religious instruction in the public schools in a way most Mineiros could accept while winning the large Catholic vote (see below). What accounts for the October 1929 party split, an inter-elite upheaval from which the apparently secure PRM never recovered?

Throughout phase two (1898–1929), the leading bosses always pulled together at election time. Agreeing on the governorship was fundamental to preserving the state's bargaining position in Rio. Furthermore, the PRM always backed the majority presidential candidate until 1929. The decision to support Vargas put great strains on the party, unprecedented since the 1897 PRC convention at Ouro Preto. Unlike Silviano, however, the bosses in 1929 not only thwarted a sitting president but also failed to agree on the succession at home, which opened Minas to the cruder forms of federal punishment that Alvim and the other leaders had all successfully avoided.

Within the Executive Committee, a three-day deadlock between Melo Viana, Bernardes, and Wenceslau was broken in October by choosing senate president Olegário Maciel as a compromise candidate, and the state Chamber's presiding officer as his running mate. Elder statesman Maciel was acceptable to everyone except Vice-President Melo Viana, who wanted to be governor again. He bolted the party, along with the lieutenant governor, five federal deputies, and eight state deputies. These dissidents joined Carvalho Brito's Conservative Concentration, and Washington Luís backed Melo Viana's campaign, which was something new in Minas politics.[26] The president stopped federal patronage and credit, made it difficult for Minas to negotiate foreign loans, and came close to intervention. Fourteen PRM deputies lost seats in the new congress; the credentials of dissidents were validated instead. The PRM's great days were over. Phase three began with the 1929 split: Minas moved increasingly into a client relationship with the central power.

At first, the result of presidential pressure encouraged a traditional willingness to accommodate. The Vargas forces thought (correctly) that the PRM did not fully mobilize for the national ticket. Júlio Prestes garned one in every five votes cast in Minas, but Melo Viana won only 882 votes![27] The PRM made overtures, but Washington Luís would not call off his "punishment" campaign. It seemed also that São Paulo was determined to cut the political power of Minas down to size. Reluctantly, Minas joined the Gaúcho-led revolution. "There was no reforming zeal or thought of a new order behind this determination," the British Ambassador reported. "The old order in Mineiro eyes was quite a good one, provided their own State were in control."[28]

Minas mobilized in October and there was some fighting, but the victory belonged to Vargas, to the junior officers (*tenentes*) with authoritarian leanings who staffed his campaign, and to a group of younger politicians under Oswaldo Aranha of Rio Grande, who called for a new Republic. To these reformers, the PRM under Bernardes, Andrada, and Wenceslau was no different from the discredited Paulista establishment. To survive, Governor Maciel cooperated closely with Vargas, who needed Minas to consolidate his own shaky presidency in the confused cross-currents of the Provisional Government (1930–34).

Maciel, an ex-Liberal from the Empire and nearly 80, ruled with unexpected vigor. Other states were intervened by federal officials, but Maciel insisted on remaining and, over tenente objections, was allowed to stay as the legally elected governor. He could have been replaced at will, however, and this contributed to Maciel's interest in a working partnership with the president. He ordered the first of several cabinet shake-ups in November and three Bernardistas left, the result of tenente pressure. The key posts of Interior and Finance were given to protégés of Francisco Campos, who, as the new Minister of Education, wanted to orient Vargas and control Maciel. With the governor's approval, Campos set up the neo-fascist Legion of October movement and built up local support. By May 1931, Antonio Carlos and Wenceslau adhered, 80 percent of the municípios were said to be in the Legion's camp, and the PRM was declared officially dead. And when what was left of the PRM Executive Committee met in Belo Horizonte, Gustavo Capanema (Interior Secretary) cabled all the mayors that Maciel regarded this meeting as "an unfriendly act."[29]

The PRM that convened in Belo Horizonte in mid-August 1931 was still very much alive. Bernardes kept it going by force of personality and evoked old loyalties. Minister of Justice Oswaldo Aranha saw the PRM as a useful counterweight to Campos and his Legion. Aranha's friendship with Virgílio de Melo Franco, one of the few Mineiros with revolutionary credentials, and with Minister of Foreign Affairs Afrânio de Melo Franco, his father, who was also on the PRM Executive Committee, gave this political convention a certain sponsorship from Rio. Torchlight parades, fervid oratory, and milling about the streets were background for the main event, which was staged from Rio: a coup attempt against the aged governor by elements of the Força Pública.[30] The troops having revolted on schedule, Aranha instructed the federal garrison commander to assume the governorship until "order" was restored, at which point Virgílio would be named interventor. But Maciel refused to play his assigned part. He stayed in the palace, and as Capanema ringed it with loyal militia units, the federal commander hesitated. With Maciel holding, Vargas telegraphed his support and the coup aborted.*

This event helped Maciel in the same way that the 1932 São Paulo revolt strengthened Vargas. There were few arrests, and the Legion was broadened so that any politician willing to support the governor was expected to join. (The Legion and the PRM were merged formally in February 1932.) Campos, who had played no part in the coup, declined politically. Aranha and Melo Franco appeared inept; in Rio the incident was quickly dubbed "The Mistake." Vargas displayed good timing—and his famous grasp of men and events. From then on, the era's equivalent of the political hot line hummed frequently between Liberdade Palace and Catete. State and federal politics were increasingly intertwined.

When São Paulo tried to move national politics back to the old state-centered system, Maciel refused to join. Minas mobilized and in hard fighting secured both the military rear to Rio and the northern approaches to São Paulo. Politically united, Minas was in a strong position to contest elections for the federal Constituent Assembly in May 1933. Yet during the Paulista revolt Minas played a secondary role to the Army, and the depression-bound state was heavily de-

* This sequence of events had parallels with those of 1889–92: the historicals —like the tenentes in 1930—expected to take power when the government changed in Rio but were blocked by experienced senior politicians, whose ouster they then sought by coup.

pendent upon federal credits, both of which contributed to client status. Furthermore, Vargas knew all the details of the governor's new coalition, the Partido Progressista (PP), which was formed in November 1932.

The PP was run by a 19-man Executive Committee grouped roughly into Antonio Carlos, Wenceslau, and Maciel wings, with Gustavo Capanema, Virgílio de Melo Franco, and Bias Fortes Júnior forming the so-called youth wing. Twelve committeemen had held legislative office and/or high executive posts during the Old Republic. Among the others, only three were newcomers since the 1930 Revolution: Capanema, Pedro Aleixo, a former student leader and now a law professor, and Otacílio Negrão de Lima, a contractor, with good ties to the Catholic Youth movement. With strong municipal support, the PP won 31 seats to the Constituent Assembly and Antonio Carlos was elected its president.

The PRM elected only six deputies and had difficulty forming an Executive Committee, when Bernardes—who was still in exile for his part in the Paulista revolt—ordered it revived in January 1933. This was the first serious opposition party to be organized in Minas since the Empire.[31] The PRM sheltered under new federal election laws assuring minority representation, but its municipal base was tiny. More than half of the new Executive Committee were local politicians without statewide prestige. Two of the winners had the Church vote; Joaquim Furtado de Menezes, the Catholic leader, used the PRM to launch Catholic programs in the Assembly.

The balance of forces changed abruptly at Maciel's death in September 1933. Capanema and Virgílio were thought to be the leading choices for interventor, the one because of his proved administrative ability and ties to the Vargas clan, the other because of friendship with Vargas and Aranha. In fact, neither candidate suited Vargas, who was maneuvering to be elected president by the Assembly. Virgílio's appointment would have lent support to Aranha's own presidential drive while antagonizing the governor of Rio Grande, who wanted Capanema. Aranha, of course, wanted Virgílio. The rabbit in Getúlio's hat was an obscure young politician from western Minas named Benedito Valadares Ribeiro. In December, as the PP deputies caucused in well-publicized (and contentious) meetings, Vargas asked delegation leader Antonio Carlos to prepare a "representative list" of candidates, at the end of which would appear Valadares. On December 12, the president named Benedito Valadares to the post.[32]

Outmaneuvered and furious, the Melo Francos and their friends bolted to the PRM, which grew to about one-third the size of the Minas delegation. Demoralized and split, the PP never recovered its élan. With Minas neutralized under a presidential surrogate, there would be less opportunity for the congress to maneuver independently or for Rio Grande and São Paulo to revive the state power system. Telegrams and letters between the two men leave no doubt of who was master. Valadares' every move was cleared first with Vargas, including requests for permission to make political trips within his own state. In contrast to the elaborate courtesy with which Vargas treated Maciel, his communiqués with Valadares were terse and curt.[33]

Critics charged that Benedito was chosen to be the president's "pau mandado," or hatchet man. Valadares was a Vargas client, but in the next four years, before the 1937 coup, he astutely upgraded the status of their relationship, and soon emerged as a Mineiro politician of the first rank. There existed between himself and Vargas an intense personal bond, almost a father-son relationship.[34] Always the shrewd judge of men, Vargas treated Valadares first with stern contempt and then, increasingly, with affectionate, if paternalistic regard. Thus Benedito won his place as first lieutenant in the Getulian system by loyally supporting the chief out of motives that were based on more than calculation. This psychological dependence would have shocked the old Mineiro leaders like Alvim.

Mineiros abhorred outside control, and Valadares played up his parentela, which went back to Tiradentes. Election to the governorship in April 1935 legitimized his status—to be sure, Vargas instructed the state Constituent Assembly to so vote. Federal aid reached Minas via Valadares, who mediated the growing federal bureaucracy and became an acknowledged master at dispensing patronage. Firmly in control of the administration, he built his own political base. As for uprooting the coronéis, Valadares was no reformer and scores of local bosses fell into line. "He knows how to use the government machine and the tradition of obedience," one Vargas crony observed admiringly.[35] Yet there was room for talent, notably at Agriculture, where some early economic planning was initiated by Israel Pinheiro, the former governor's son. A mixture of the old and the new, Benedito's cadres survived the 1937 coup intact. In fact, he was the only state leader retained by Vargas and the Army. And in 1945 this durable politician set up the Social Democratic Party, which in Minas was a typical coalition of the bosses grafted onto the new political-administrative base created in the 1930's.

Valadares' famous remark "I'm neither for it nor opposed, quite the contrary" ranks with his mentor's well-known motto "Let things be to see how they turn out." But both men were decisive when it suited them. In 1936, they plotted the destruction of Antonio Carlos, who still harbored presidential ambitions. He resigned as Assembly president and Valadares ordered the PP and the PRM to unite in one party in order to prepare for the upcoming presidential campaign.[36] Once, in mid-1937, he wavered. Vargas and the Army were preparing to preempt the elections by coup. Fearful that the legalistic Mineiros might fight, and hoping to gain some room to maneuver, Valadares sounded out the Paulista opposition under Armando Sales. This was like "being gored by a tame steer," Vargas said, while fixing Valadares in the eye. Very soon his political son returned to what has been called "the Mineiro art of supporting the government and staying in it."[37] Minas mobilized to support the coup. The federal system was abolished, ending phase three of Mineiro politics.

Having established three political periods—specifically the ten years of consolidation from 1889 to 1898, then the high point of the state system to 1929, followed by the client phase—I want to leave the role of individuals and examine structures.

## Political Structures

The broad patterns of elite political behavior include an ability to downplay differences at home in order to present a united front in Rio, a strong tradition of uniting behind executive authority, and, consequently, a lack of interest in sustained opposition politics at the zonal or state levels. The Mineiro elite did not lose legitimacy or confidence in their capacity to govern during this period. Yet their political institutions were disorganized, their politics hindered modernization, and they did not arrest the economic decline of Minas relative to São Paulo and Rio Grande. Put broadly, Mineiro politics is another example of a phenomenon in Latin America, Italy, and Iberia, where, starting in the late nineteenth century, modern democratic forms were adopted, then shaped to fit the needs of Latin societies in transition.

Contemporaries were troubled by the gap between democratic ideals and corrupt politics. At first, Brazilians blamed it on their social backwardness, their immorality, and sometimes on their Negro blood. By the 1920's, however, it was fashionable to attack the imported North American federal model as neither suiting Brazilian realities nor reflecting the Portuguese-Imperial legacy of central authority. The Mineiros were rather less troubled by the moral arguments than were opinion-makers in Rio and São Paulo. The Republic's institutions suited Minas, which to the urban middle classes seemed willfully backward and provincial. Critics also blamed "the oligarchy," as though the elite and their methods were isolated from the whole social process. Recent research has brought the durable features of this politics into sharper focus. Sidney G. Tarrow's study of postwar politics in the Italian Mezzogiorno region is a good departure point.

As in Minas Gerais, political capacity in southern Italy is highly developed, but "modern political forms perform functions their creators never intended." Vertical relationships survive and in fact inhibit the development of horizontal social and political structures. In Tarrow's words, "bureaucratic organizations become infused with personal and particularistic tendencies. Legislatures, which function as organs of representation in the West, become solidarity-generating institutions. Political parties, bureaucratic and well articulated in the West, assume the character of broad political movements with poorly articulated organization. Similarly, the interest group phenomenon, almost synonymous with politics in Western models, assumes a different form and process."[38] Comparable permutations in democratic structures occurred in Minas. Several examples come to mind, following this scheme, after first a statement of basic reservations.

Politics of this type may be inherently unstable, and may also produce immobility while restraining social change and a wider, more equitable distribution of goods and services. Unlike the postwar Mezzogiorno, however, oligarchic democracy had not yet run its course in Minas by 1937. Elite politics was still able to introduce and channel change without destroying the foundations of a hierarchical social order. New groups were co-opted and linked to an expanding state apparatus, which had resources to dispense. The major challenge came not from within, but from institutional changes in the federal system.

Clientelism was a way of expressing the hierarchical relationships in society. It was deeply rooted in Mineiro culture and political institutions. And in the absence of an ethic of equality, it was both visible and legitimate. Seen not as an anachronism in "Western" politics but rather as a durable and adaptive power system, clientelism can introduce certain features of modernization. In fact, clientele relationships between individuals and groups of unequal status have been identified not only in Ibero-American societies but "as a generic trait of political systems regardless of their stages of development."[39]

In Minas, as (probably) in several other Latin polities of this era, change through clientele politics was authoritarian, from the top down, but garbed in democratic forms. This resulted in technocratic policies, the co-option of interest groups by the state, and the conscious suppression of class politics. Whereas clientelism eroded the development of collective interests, the state government was also beholden to special interest groups and gave them favors to secure their loyalty and prevent tax revolts. Here reciprocity—the key element of clientele politics—hindered basic structural change and was perhaps a high price to pay for short-term political peace.

There were sharp contrasts in political effectiveness among Brazil's regional elites. The Minas record compares favorably with Bahia, where the elite split in the early 1900's and went into swift national decline. This behavior is all the more remarkable because the two neighboring states were not that different: both had disarticulated, subregional economies, in short, the classic conditions for localism and coronelistic politics. Why did Minas act less like Bahia and rank alongside the strong state machines of Rio Grande and São Paulo? Analysis of political structures in this period will indicate some of the reasons why.

The public service in Minas Gerais was infused with personalism and functioned in large part as a patronage machine. While correlating Belo Horizonte bureaucrats with elite family names, Moema Siqueira (the Mineira historian) found that in 1900 about 38 percent belonged to well-known parentelas. By 1913, with the state bureaucracy eight times bigger, she matched up 21 percent of the functionaries with prominent families.[40] If placemen from the "good families" declined, there was still ample room for special relationships across the social spectrum. Other social groups were effectively co-opted by a pervasive clientelism.

Talent was welcome in the faculties of higher learning, the law courts (Juiz de Direito and above), and the engineering services, but these positions were also subject to loyalty and patronage criteria. "The employment and protection of intellectuals by the state seems to be a Mineiro tradition," writes Correia Dias.[41] Political conformity was expected in return. Barbacena under Bias Fortes was the state's emporium of patronage. In 1906 we find him, typically, asking President Afonso Pena to appoint a prominent banker's son to the newly created chair of tropical medicine in Rio.[42] Positions of all kinds passed through his hands. The Federal Mint was said to be overloaded with the friends of politicians from Rio, Juiz de Fora (the base of Antonio Carlos), and Barbacena.[43] Granting public employment conferred power on the superbosses, and the best positioned of all was the governor. Local, state, and federal posts were mediated this way until well past the 1930's.

Personal interests were satisfied by clientage politics, but the state government also had enough resources to offer something to every zone, however unequally the shares were divided. Jobs, city improvement loans, and other public works, especially railroads, were dispensed by an increasingly powerful governor, especially when the budget doubled after 1918 (see Chapter 8). Bahia had little to offer its backlands, which were commercially isolated from the capital until the 1930's.[44] Northern Minas, by contrast, hoped for better transport links to southern markets, and this was an incentive for cooperating with the governor and the PRM.

In theory, both houses of the state congress were co-equal branches of government, with the right to initiate legislation and power of the purse. Debate at the 1891 Constituent Assembly was vigorous; questions of taxation, regional autonomy, and the role of local government were freely raised. With the rise of Silviano, however, the legislature and the federal delegation were both relegated to supporting roles, with little power of initiative or review. Sanctioning the governor's decisions helped to fortify the united front in Rio, based on bloc voting. As the importance of floor debate declined, the key committees such as Finance, Municipal Affairs, and the special Mixed Commissions of both houses became more prominent. Committee chairmen guided legislation through the requisite patronage channels before bringing it to debate, while preventing many bills from ever reaching the floor. To this extent the Minas congress was a "solidarity-generating" institution. Why would anyone want to serve in such a powerless body, when dissent was tantamount to loss of office at the next election?

Coronéis with safe seats served for years, while enjoying life and contacts in the capital. Rising politicians paused there on the way to higher office. The governors recruited some members with special expertise to serve on the committees. Typical was the rancher from Sul Minas who was called to the senate when Governor Raul Soares needed a friendly agricultural expert. In return, he secured the "emancipation" (município status) of his town and was rewarded with various public works, including a bridge and a new town hall.[45] This smattering of talent relieved what was otherwise a tame arena for placemen, careerists, and patronage seekers. Occasionally, however, deputies voted against legislation their constituents did not want, and the land tax is an excellent example.

Sustained opposition by landed interests through the legislature prevented all governors from Silviano to Bernardes from shifting a significant share of the state tax base away from exports to a more rational and equitable statewide land tax.[46] The idea was to put state finances on a sounder footing, while taxing unproductive units heavily. Large areas of fertile lands along transportation routes were held for speculation because there was no serious property tax.[47] The concept of breaking up estates in order to implant colonies of middle-class farmers had been talked about since the late Empire, and, in the absence of a homestead act to redistribute the public lands, this tax was heralded as a way to improve productivity while modernizing the countryside. A broad coalition of ranchers, planters, and land speculators objected vigorously to this aspect of the land tax.

Most of the coffee planters did not want to change over to a new, direct tax; nor did they trust the government to be fair. They were accustomed to having the coffee commission agents in Rio and Santos discount all export taxes, freight charges, and expenses from their gross earnings. Mata planters held two protest congresses, one at Juiz de Fora in 1899, the other at Cataguazes in 1916, and throughout phase two they threatened to organize a powerful interest association. Implicit was the threat of a tax revolt and political opposition such as Silviano confronted in 1899, when the first land tax bill came to a vote.[48]

Pressured by the planters and the ranchers, Silviano could not get his original legislation through congress and saw his reform-minded Secretary of Agriculture forced from office. The watered-down bill he signed omitted any mention of a tax on the land area, opposed by ranchers, or the tax on improvements, attacked by planters, which left only a small tax on land values. And in the absence of a state cadastral survey, the owners themselves declared these values, with predictable results. This one-sided compromise was worked out by Antonio Carlos and other Mata politicians who, in pacifying the planters, made themselves indispensable to the new PRM and rose rapidly. Having advocated a strong land tax, Finance Secretary David Campista was distrusted by the bosses, who in 1909 blocked his presidential hopes.

In Rio Grande do Sul, the land tax became the leading source of revenue some ten years after it was introduced in 1904.[49] Neither Minas nor São Paulo was able to make this legislation work, which says a good deal about the relative abilities of three state machines to extract resources from the landed interests. This failure was more significant in Minas, which in contrast to São Paulo did not have a strong economic base or the same capacity to borrow abroad. Bernardes pushed the land tax up from an average of 5 percent of state revenues during 1901–19 to nearly 9 percent for the 1920's. (Francisco Campos, who advocated stronger central government, voted with the ranchers of his zone against a rate increase in 1919.)[50] Under Valadares the land tax reached 13 percent, in part because of falling export tax receipts but also because the governor had more power to extract resources.[51]

For 20 years, the landed sector used delaying tactics in the state legislature to avoid taxation. This shows that the usually docile, captive congress could function as a representative body, although the failure to provide an adequate revenue base was serious. In this sense, the representation of special interests reinforced immobility in the system. On the other hand, groups did not organize to bring sustained pressure on the legislature. Nor could the governors count on private organizations to help them implement their programs. One conclusion is that in the absence of strong interest groups, representation in the Western European–North American sense was incomplete. Another, quite different conclusion is that applying this concept to Latin politics is not very productive, for the following reason: the lack of strong, independent interest groups does not mean group demands failed to reach the government. Boycotts and other pressure tactics worked in the land tax episodes. But demands also reached the authorities through more or less captive, semiofficial associations.

The corporatist spirit pervades Mediterranean–Latin American politics, and Minas was no exception. Both the Commercial Association (founded in 1901) and the Agricultural Association (1909) worked closely with the governors on legislation. Opposition was generally limited to lobbying against taxes they did not like, and the leaders belonged to the governor's inner circle.[52] For these and other associations formed during this period, the seeking of favors and advantages rather than the use of power tactics at the ballot box or in the legislature was standard. It is not that Mineiros lacked the ability to associate —note that as early as 1893, state employees organized a statewide league "to represent their interests in the legislature and to defend their rights and interests before the public administration."[53] It is that association building was eroded by close ties to power holders and leached by co-optive politics. The planters are a case in point.

Starting in 1896, the fazendeiros began to organize agricultural centers and leagues at the local level to protest falling coffee prices and to agitate for lower freight rates, more and better credit, and tougher labor legislation. By 1898, "lavourista" groups were forming throughout Minas, as were their Paulista counterparts for similar reasons.

At the 1899 Juiz de Fora congress they blocked the first land tax bill. Although some planters wanted to channel their momentum into a political movement based on agricultural, ranching, and commercial groups, the majority thought a show of power would be enough to warn the government, and they cautioned against politicizing what were essentially demands for economic relief. Whether to oppose the governor's new PRM with an interest-oriented party or to get in close to the source of power and funds was soon resolved in favor of those who argued for co-optation.

Seven candidates from the Partido de Lavoura e Comércio won

seats in the December 1899 federal elections, and the party maintained some local bases in the Triângulo and the Mata for at least ten years. Alvimistas and ex-PRF men found a home in it; so did some of those who bolted the Ouro Preto meeting in 1897 to set up the original PRM, only to lose it to Silviano. The Andrada brothers belonged, as did Ribeiro Junqueira of Leopoldina. Thus the "outs" really did find shelter in the lavourista clubs, as the PRM charged.[54]

The economic grievances they raised were real enough. Only when Silviano modified the land tax bill and secured some freight rate relief did the planter clubs decline. "Those that survive can constitute the nucleus of an agricultural federation when and if we want it," a Barbacena leader warned in 1907, and this threat too was real.[55] To contain it, "a flood of National Guard commissions" descended on the Mata. This was the tactic that sapped "the spirit of collectivity and unity" among the planters.[56] Leading lavouristas were also welcomed into the PRM, including Ribeiro Junqueira and the Andradas. This wrecked the party as a statewide force. Others had their credentials challenged by Secretary Bressane at the PRM conventions, and were outmaneuvered by the rival delegation tactic that he used so well. And finally, the traditional appeal that always worked was made again: coalesce to preserve the united front in Rio.

That political capital could be generated from economic grievances seemed likely to the civilistas in 1909–10, and later to leaders of the Conservative Concentration in 1929—who took this party label to evoke support from the so-called conservative classes. In the first example, Carvalho Brito, who was João Pinheiro's Interior Secretary and an industrialist, tried to enlist the retail merchants, the planters, and the bankers for whom the prospect of having an Army general as president seemed bad for business and a risk to Brazil's foreign credit rating. The PRM responded with the traditional carrot and stick. Many northern leaders preferred Rui over Hermes, it was learned, were it not for the fact that prospects for obtaining a railroad were very promising now, with a Mineiro (Francisco Sá) in as Transport Minister. The public would tolerate no moves that might jeopardize this project. Faced with these tactics, the civilistas were unable to mobilize the economic groups, although they did reach new groups such as students and women, who in Minas were traditionally against conscription.[57] In 1929, Brito planned a series of regional economic congresses to air grievances, of which the Montes Claros meeting, described early in this chapter, was to have been the second.

Organizing businessmen into political action groups was also hindered by their preference for the corporatist approach. In 1933, leaders from industry, commerce, and agriculture formed a Minas branch of the Economist Party to contest seats for the Constituent Assembly. Their campaign poster featured a racing V-12 motor car, and their program was corporatist and elitist. But their main reason for organizing was probably to signal Vargas their unhappiness with his plan to force all the professional associations to syndicalize themselves and register in the new Ministry of Labor. (Unless they organized as any other productive group, they could not, under the new laws, send delegates to the Assembly.) The Economists were not a true opposition party; rather, their tactic was similar to Silviano's "católicos," who, in 1890, attempted successfully to retain some freedom to maneuver in the new state system being organized by Alvim. They did stay clear of the Labor Ministry, and the election of Euvaldo Lodi, a Mineiro industrialist, to lead the block of class delegates at the Assembly did much to satisfy their desire for inputs to the new federal system without being controlled.[58]

Starting in 1910, Minas became a center of the Catholic lay movement, and it is not surprising that groups which as early as 1913 could mobilize 210,000 signatures against divorce became a political force.[59] Having reorganized the bishoprics after disestablishment in 1890, the Church in Minas became a Brazilian proving ground for Catholic action movements along German, French, and Belgian lines. Missionary priests from Europe began recruiting middle-sector urbanites, as well as working and professional classes. Rechristianized in the Catholic youth movement, the political generation of Francisco Campos and Benedito Valadares was far more sympathetic to Catholic causes than their free-thinking fathers. Religious instruction in the public schools was reestablished in 1928, thanks to almost 20 years of intense organizational work and by mobilizing voters to elect Catholic political leaders like Canon João Pio de Souza Reis, who joined the PRM Executive Committee in 1925. That Catholic views were well represented at the 1933 Constituent Assembly owed much to the Catholic lay movement that started first in Minas and then became national in the 1920's.

Both the PP majority and the opposition PRM delegations included Catholic deputies who had strong electoral bases. Given the vote-getting power of these Catholic groups, it is significant that they, too, chose to work within the established party structure rather than to form their own political party.

By separating Church and State in 1890, rationalist Republicans sincerely wanted to keep religious issues out of politics. The tentative effort of Silviano Brandão and other "outs" to exploit the issue in 1890 was attacked by Republican journals that claimed the Partido Católico was an attempt to use the grass-roots clergy, and an effort at mystification, since there was no danger of irreligion in the new state government.[60] Religion was not in fact a serious issue in Minas until Governor João Pinheiro, a Positivist, and Interior Secretary Carvalho Brito barred religious instruction in the schools and stopped subsidizing the seminaries. The schools conflict in France was doubtless a powerful example. Alarmed, the Vatican instructed Mineiro prelates to test whether a Catholic political party could win elections. And in December 1908, Dom Silvério Gomes Pimenta, the black Archbishop of Mariana who had done so much to revitalize the Minas clergy, called on the faithful to send Catholic candidates to congress.

Joaquim Furtado de Menezes, a professor of engineering who had founded the St. Vincent de Paul Society in Minas, led the new Catholic party. Organized formally as the Regenerator Party in early 1909, the party dedicated itself to countering the threat of "dechristianização pública," meaning the schools issue. Initial forays into electoral politics were discouraging. The Regenerators lost every seat they contested, including Menezes's. His plurality in the third electoral district was ignored by the Credentials Committee.[61] The party was organized on the German model, being a lay movement that was to have complete freedom of political action while conforming to Church doctrine. But the strong-willed archbishop controlled it, and upon the nomination of Marechal Hermes, who was a Mason, Dom Silvério committed the Regenerators to rooting out masonry, which was one of his old crusades from the Empire. Hermes hastened to confirm his essential Catholicism, but not before the prelate threatened to excommunicate any of his parishioners who voted the Hermes ticket. Delighted, the civilistas fanned this issue; appalled, the PRM hastened to mollify Dom Silvério —it was rumored that the state's purchase of two fazendas owned by the archbishopric had something to do with his decision to become neutral. But he was also having second thoughts about the Church's approach to party politics, and by October he advised Menezes that "Catholics shouldn't be disunited over politics when they have the school issue to fight." The Regenerator Party was shelved, its director having resigned for health reasons. Furtado de Menezes then threw himself into organizing the first statewide Catholic congress at Juiz de Fora in January 1910.[62]

The experiment with organized opposition politics having failed, the Church decided to work within the PRM while alerting the voters to Catholic causes, of which education held first priority. "We should not be hostile to the PRM," a lay leader wrote in 1921. "Only in cases of necessity and when we have a good chance to win should Catholics run their own candidates."[63] By 1927, the Catholics were strong enough to form an electoral pressure group, the Centro Popular Mineiro, which fought for Catholic causes and passed judgment on the suitability of political candidates. Both Vargas and Júlio Prestes were asked to return a detailed questionnaire on their attitudes toward the Church and its issues. Vargas got high praise for his pro-Catholic response, but Prestes threw his questionnaire away and was judged less friendly.[64] Meanwhile, Furtado de Menezes returned to active politics under the auspices of Bernardes in 1918. He was the leading Catholic voice in state politics until the 1937 coup.

By mobilizing the voters and organizing social groups, the Catholics proved that the social bases of politics were becoming more complex than the relationship of patron and client that underlay the PRM. It is of course true that the bosses moved to co-opt all voluntary associations within their area. And after 1930 the old coronéis did not vanish; rather, several adjusted to the expanding state and federal bureaucracies, which offered them more patronage.[65] But to focus exclusively on the highly personal networks that structured politics at all levels would be to miss the growth and impact of horizontal groups. For example, urban labor in Juiz de Fora was asking to be reached as early as 1905, and was brought in.[66] Anarchists and Communists (organized in 1922) refused accommodation on these terms and were harassed by the police. Similarly, the Integralists (fascists) in Minas posed no threat, probably because the middle classes were already tied into Catholic lay groups.

Bust of João Pinheiro in the praça at Sêrro, his birthplace.

President Wenceslau Brás (center) with PRM colleagues at Poços de Caldas,
18. Antonio Carlos is on his right.

Governor-elect Artur Bernardes in 1918.

5. George Chalmers, the British mining
engineer, as a young man, c. 1886.

6. Dom Silvério Gomes Pimenta in 1920, when elected to the Brazilian Academy of Letters.

Minister of Finance Francisco Sales in 1913.   8. Carvalho Brito in 1920.

Getúlio Vargas (left, in auto), with Governor Antonio Carlos, campaigning for
the presidency in Juiz de Fora, 1930.

10. President Vargas with Governor Valadares, c. 1937.

That "modern" politics intermingled with "traditional" personalism is to be expected in a society undergoing rapid commercialization and early industrialization. The two modes coexisted, as the Catholic penetration of the PRM reveals. In part, this was because cleavages between agriculture and industry, and especially between city and countryside, did not yet exist. Class conflict was most unlikely under these conditions. In part, also, it was because the direction and rate of change was still mediated by clientelism in ways a hierarchical society could accept. A few words about leadership and the role of violence will help to explain the persistence of older patterns.

Lawyers and professional men dominated the PRM, as they had the old Imperial parties, and they were well integrated into a society that was still overwhelmingly agrarian. Some of the most prominent PRM bosses divided their time between legal practice, running fazendas, and managing their banks and small factories. Like any rural coronel, Carvalho Brito registered all the workers at his Belo Horizonte power plant to vote for him as a bloc. It would take a full-scale study of coronelismo in Minas to determine whether industrialists were less able to maintain their political dynasties in the small towns than the fazendeiros, as was recently suggested.[67] The essential point is that fazendeiros and clerics, businessmen and bankers could all play the same power role. Put another way, the social distance between a Belo Horizonte lawyer and a Montes Claros rancher was much more one of style than of role when it came to politics. Returning to Minas from his Rio law practice, Francisco Campos often dressed in the fazendeiro's black hat, buff-colored pants, and stout boots, and enjoyed the company of ranchers until his death in 1968.

In its heyday, the PRM always claimed that it recruited talented individuals to serve in politics who otherwise would never be elected from their home districts. Without fraudulent elections and the recognition of powers, it was argued, the coronéis would have entrenched themselves in the federal congress, where the prestige and perquisites of being a deputy were attractive.[68] Impatient of placemen, Governor Bernardes purged large numbers of state deputies, showing that reform from the top down was possible in this system. The Executive Committee helped to arrange and legitimize the transfer of power. Starting in 1918, this institution lost power to the governor. However, committeemen were integrated with the state's economic elite (see

Chapter 5), so there was no obvious or lasting cleavage between political and economic groups. To reach high office, furthermore, a man still had to prove himself in the sargentação system, usually by starting as a district attorney or councilman in the interior. This assured a leavening of talent while helping to stabilize what could otherwise have degenerated into warfare among the bosses, as happened in Bahia and the Northeast. Finally, certain norms and habits of political interaction—notably, the ability to unite—raised this politics above the level of mere factionalism.

Running for office could be grueling and expensive, as a political wife lamented in 1922. All those coffees to serve, telegrams to send, the late nights out, the rented house with help, and the costly political journal might be worth it if her husband finally won election in Muriaé after three years of effort. But he was exhausted and she had four children to raise. It was, in short, a difficult way of life for them. In contrast, she continued, "one thinks of politicians like Junqueira . . . and Antonio Carlos, who get practical results. My compadre Antonio Carlos never has to register a voter, or spend a penny on politics, and it's hard to get access to him, but for him politics is a veritable fountain of income."[69]

Dissenters were purged from party ranks, were punished at the ballot box, and were often threatened with physical violence. Having lost his bid for governor in 1910, Carvalho Brito found that all of the state's patronage and propaganda organs were mobilized against his campaign for federal deputy in August. Predictably, he lost massively. In the last issue of *Correio do Dia*, the civilista journal, Brito and Afonso Pena Junior announced they were leaving politics until the minority would no longer be treated as "a social danger" to be crushed by the state machine.[70] Even in the freer atmosphere of the early 1930's, with the press liberated from economic retaliation and the ballot secret, containing the opposition was no great problem. Concerning supplementary elections to the State Constituent Assembly in December 1934, Valadares informed Vargas: "We'll modify the PRM's slate for them by electing their more moderate and less popular candidates."[71]

Violence crackled through Minas, especially at election time. Raul Soares left his teaching career in São Paulo to take up the family leadership of Rio Branco in the Mata when his brother was shot. In 1919, Bueno Brandão's faction won a bloody shoot-out in Ouro Fino on the

Paulista frontier. One thinks of Júlio Bueno serving over 30 years on the Executive Committee and, with his dark suits, conservative habits, and cautious, squinting glance, symbolizing to the point of caricature the Mineiro's famous "grave sense of order." This happened in the Sul, where communications were much better than in the West, North, and East. Ambushings, assaults by hired thugs, burnouts, and dynamite bombings were facts of political life in these more remote zones.[72] Thus face-to-face violence was suffused throughout state politics, and was a major restraint on political change.

Normally, the governor only intervened in local conflicts when the violence threatened to spill over into other towns, or when an armed faction became too powerful. During the Bias Fortes regime (1894–98), two rival bosses fought for control of Viçosa. Members of the so-called dirty faction held the town hall and its tax records against the "cleans," who besieged them behind barbed wire. Governor Bias Fortes said he would crush the first group to open fire. Then he invited the two leaders to a banquet at the capital, where he toasted their patriotic example of backing off from combat.[73]

Until the 1920's, moreover, the governor did not approach having a monopoly on violence. The civilian police were underpaid and unprofessional; the militia was hard pressed to patrol a state twice the size of São Paulo or Rio Grande, each of which had superior state troops (see Chapter 7). Force levels were fixed at 1,500 officers and men in 1890, barely adequate to defend the capital while policing the more developed southern half of Minas. Budgetary restrictions kept the forces under 3,000 men until 1922. With better transportation and equipment, the Força Pública Mineira increased its range and gradually brought the outlying regions under effective state control. In addition to suppressing bandits, the Força Pública was used against strikers and to police the polls.

In Minas, where rigged, forced balloting was the rule during the Old Republic, elections were an important part of politics. Elections certified changes in personnel by methods short of coup and constant warfare. In part, the electoral game was played to control minorities. The "outs," from historical Republicans in 1890 to the opposition PRM in 1933, always promised to restore democratic rights usurped by the machine. Manipulated tallies were also used to break independent groups, as the Catholic Regenerator Party discovered in 1909. Controlled balloting symbolized the relative power of the zones while bolstering a united front in congress. Finally, voting was an important way to show Mineiro strength in national elections.

Imperial elections were relatively free after the 1881 Saraiva Law encouraged competitive voting, but the Republic soon limited electoral fair play in order to strengthen the new state governments against the coronéis who controlled more votes now that literate males 21 and over were enfranchised. Alvim himself, while serving as Minister of Interior, introduced the "garrot law," which removed the power of judges to count votes, so important in the Imperial electoral system. Placing the counting and the policing powers in state hands assured the desired results.

Managing the vote was taken one step further in 1894 when state electoral districts were reduced from eight to six, while the number of candidates in each district went from six to eight. The purpose of this maneuver was to squeeze minorities out. Under the first scheme, one voted for four of the six candidates, a ratio of two to three. Under the revised formula, it became six out of eight, raising the ratio three to four in favor of those running on the official ticket. Despite factionalism in the 1890's, the state ticket was rigidly controlled. Redistricting was another device for assuring stability at home.[74] As for the Rosa e Silva law to give minorities a few places on the federal delegation, Minas Gerais ignored it.

The number of registered voters in each zone corresponded roughly with population, showing that, despite rigged voting totals, the electoral system was not a total sham. The Mata was the largest source of votes, befitting its role as the leading zone. By 1921, the Sul's voting strength was more in line with population, but the North's was less so. Both the Center and the rapidly growing East were poised to demand a larger electorate.[75] See Table 4.1.

City voting rolls were kept small, both for purposes of patronage control and to prevent independent groups from mobilizing the vote. In 1921, for example, Belo Horizonte with 4,662 registered voters ranked ninth behind such Mata strongholds as Carangola, Muriaé, and Viçosa, and was only some 600 voters ahead of Montes Claros, an electoral bastion of the North. It is true that the coronéis usually limited their electorates to the size one man could conveniently service and control, which was a few hundred in each locality. Another prac-

TABLE 4.1

Registered Voters and Population by Zone, 1898–1921

| Zone | Voters, 1898 | Population, 1900 | Voters, 1921 | Population, 1920 |
|------|------|------|------|------|
| Population | 173,118 | 3,594,471 | 313,031 | 5,888,174 |
| Center | 22% | 25% | 19% | 16% |
| Mata | 23 | 18 | 24 | 18 |
| Sul | 16 | 20 | 21 | 21 |
| Triângulo | 8 | 6 | 7 | 6 |
| West | 11 | 11 | 11 | 12 |
| North | 13 | 16 | 9 | 15 |
| East | 7 | 4 | 8 | 11 |

SOURCE: Minas, Secretaria do Interior, Relatório, 1898, pp. 81–98; Minas, Annuario estatistico, Anno 1, v. 4, part 2, pp. 351–53. Electors by município were correlated by zone to construct this table.

tical reason for limiting the rolls in many rural areas was that, as coronéis on the governor's side knew well, their "best ballot was the state trooper's saber."[76] Among those registered were the living (supposedly literate), the fictitious (created by a penstroke), and the dead (who may once, perhaps, have voted). The electoral farce was often satirized in carnival floats. One such display rolled through the streets of Leopoldina in 1898, bearing ferns, lit candles, and a coffin from which a skeleton reached out to deposit his ballot in the voting urn.[77]

Opposition for anything but local posts was nearly hopeless under these conditions. With the machine able to arrange elections in advance, the pressures for co-optation dovetailed with the Mineiros' traditional instinct to join forces. Electoral competition for the post of federal deputy was rare after 1903. Of three contested gubernatorial elections, only the 1894 fight between Alvim's candidate Francisco Bernardino and Bias Fortes was anything like an equal battle, and Bias owed a good deal to Interior Secretary Silviano Brandão s selective use of the police. See Table 4.2. Among presidential races, the 1910 Rui-Hermes election is interesting because Rui carried the First District (Belo Horizonte and the Center-North) by over 3,000 votes, ran less than 1,000 votes behind Hermes in the Fourth (Lavras, including parts of the Sul and West), and slightly more than 2,000 votes behind Bias's own Third District. The Mata heartland, the Sul, and the extreme North went massively for Hermes, and this produced the machine's winning margin. Given PRM cohesion, this outcome was never in doubt. However, Rui's strong showing in the cities bears out the civi-

TABLE 4.2

Voting for Governor and President in the Old Republic, 1894–1930

| | Governor | | | President[a] | | |
|---|---|---|---|---|---|---|
| Year | Candidate[b] | Percent | Number voting | Candidate[†] | Percent | Number voting |
| 1894 | Bias Fortes | 59% | 44,431 | | | 28,701 |
| | F. Bernardino | 41 | 30,487 | | | |
| | TOTAL | | 74,918 | | | |
| 1898 | | | 113,088 | | | 52,334 |
| 1902 | | | 162,317 | | | 138,939 |
| 1906 | | | 69,098 | | | 44,530 |
| 1909 | | | 90,272 | | | — |
| 1910 | Bueno Brandão | 86 | 99,604 | Hermes da Fonseca | 61% | 85,765 |
| | Carvalho Brito | 14 | 16,174 | Rui Barbosa | 39 | 54,249 |
| | TOTAL | | 115,778 | TOTAL | | 141,267 |
| 1914 | | | 185,709 | | | 142,527 |
| 1918 | | | 54,562 | | | 64,554 |
| 1919 | | | — | | | 91,814 |
| 1922 | Raul Soares | 93 | 175,180 | Bernardes | 92 | 186,790 |
| | F. Sales | 7 | 13,293 | Nilo Pecanha | 8 | 15,723 |
| | TOTAL | | 188,473 | TOTAL | | 204,937 |
| 1926 | | | 191,067 | | | 144,705 |
| 1930 | | | 330,105 | Getúlio Vargas | 79 | 284,458 |
| | | | | Júlio Prestes | 21 | 77,563 |
| | | | | TOTAL | | 369,766 |

SOURCE: For the state, Minas, *Annaes da Camara*, 1894–1926, and *Diário do Congresso Mineiro*, Aug. 14, 1930; federal tallies are in Brazil, *Diário do Congresso*, 1894–1930.
   [a] The Minas Gerais breakdown in presidential contested elections is slightly below the final adjusted totals.
   [b] Contested elections.

lista claim to have reached and partially mobilized the urban vote.[78] Following the 1930 Revolution, the separate federal and state districts were replaced by a 150-district scheme, which encouraged statewide voting. The ballot was free between 1933 and 1937. With power and patronage concentrated in the governor's office, however, it was advantageous to support him. Massive losses in the July 1936 municipal elections convinced most of the PRM to fold their tents and join the Valadares camp.[79] The governor welcomed them into his one-party coalition, organized to fortify Minas in the upcoming presidential election, and rewarded several with patronage posts after the coup d'état.

As the nation's most populous state, Minas Gerais had the largest federal electorate, but turnouts for gubernatorial elections were always higher than presidential tallies until 1910. Delfim Moreira in 1914 and

Antonio Carlos in 1926 both won by margins far above the presidential results. After 1894, these state races were virtually uncontested, the vote being a show of solidarity at the transfer of power. João Pinheiro in 1906 and Artur Bernardes in 1918 had the smallest returns of any Mineiro governors in the Old Republic, hardly bothering with the election ritual. Voting went up in the 1920's as the machine paid more attention to the formal aspects of democracy, including the secret ballot in 1927, and mobilized for the 1930 presidential race, this time in opposition to a sitting president.

At every turn of the political wheel, Minas adapted to the new power situation without sustained political crisis or social upheaval. Continuity was featured over change, witness the relatively smooth transition from Empire to Republic, the comparatively easy adaptation to the Estado Novo. Committed to orderly government, Minas was a pillar of limited democracy and the presidential system, just as it had once been called (by the Emperor's son-in-law) "the Empire's last, best hope."

Such stability is explained in part by institutional factors, traced in the first part of this chapter, which focused especially on the Executive Committee. The political culture of Mineiros was a not unimportant contributing factor, notably the urge toward unity. It is also partly explained by power factors, as I have attempted to show in this section on political structures. One concludes that Minas politics controlled and adequately mirrored the main social forces of a society in transition from isolated, rural conditions to an increasingly commercialized, market-oriented, and industrial environment. There was no crisis of participation. In fact, Minas was perhaps excessively stable, as a result, seemingly, of relatively inadequate economic growth. Additional reasons for this behavior appear in the next chapter, based on a quantitative study of the state elite.

## CHAPTER FIVE

# The Political Elite

MINAS GERAIS—a new society with traditional values—believed it-self to be in evolution, keeping up with modern trends while the generations connected comfortably with each other. The sense of continuity, of nonthreatening change, suited the Mineiros with their conservatism, provincial habits, and strong sense of place. However, this conservative self-image was widespread among the counterpart elites in other states—so much so that one could view the Brazilian elite as homogeneous. They were, after all, shaped by similar sec-ondary schools and faculties. They participated in a national culture that was predicated on the export mentality and that borrowed heavily from abroad. And structurally, they were undergoing embourgeoise-ment: the land-based elites of mid-nineteenth-century Brazil were dif-ferentiating rapidly into an urban-based, business society. Having said this, we argue that there is a place for the regional perspective. Tri-angulation on our three uniformly defined political elites points up de-grees of difference and nuances of similar behavior. These regional data suggest explanations for actions that from the national per-spective cannot be fully appreciated or understood. The Mineiros knew they were not cut from the same cloth as their contemporaries. Computer analysis shows they were right.*

* Our quantitative study, which uses an SPSS program (version five) is dis-cussed in Appendix A, "A Note on Elites." A brief list of the almost 100 variables used to record the elite's characteristics, including values by state and the com-posite values, also appears in this appendix.

The political elite in Minas was notorious for being both homogeneous and closed to outsiders. They were indeed, but not much more so than Pernambucanos and Paulistas. Only six Mineiros out of 214 (just under 3 percent) had one or more foreign parents. This is to be expected of a state where foreign immigration was a failure. That the three-state mean was only 4 percent is interesting. The other states were slow to admit the sons of immigrants to their own elite ranks, despite the role and importance of foreigners in São Paulo and Pernambuco. By comparison, Minas was hardly less closed, but for different reasons.

Nonetheless, the insularity of Minas Gerais is striking. Parents of the six included three Portuguese, two Italians, and one Greek. In the entire group of 214, only one person bore an Anglo-Saxon surname, Mário Caldeira Brant, whose English grandfather settled in the Diamantina diamond region long before. Aside from one French surname, Northern European family names were conspicuously absent. The two Wernecks probably descended from seventeenth-century Dutchmen in Recife. Otherwise, the ranks of Luso-Brazilian surnames were untouched, with the possible, exotic exception of Aleixo Paraguassú, the son of a Portuguese, who took the name of a river where his Indian grandmother had been captured.

Foreign-born Mineiros did not appear in this elite. Amaro Lanari, Argentine-born of Italian parents, was the one exception, and he was a political outsider. (Lanari was an industrialist and fazendeiro who became Secretary of Finance during Francisco Campos' short-lived Liberal Legion in 1931.) None of the Minas group had foreign wives. Dark skins were rare in this elite, indicating biological as well as social distance from the lower classes. The one black Mineiro to figure in this narrative is outside the political elite. I refer to Dom Silvério Gomes Pimenta, the Archbishop of Mariana, whose rise in the Church hierarchy began during the racially more tolerant Imperial era. The only labor leader is Paraguassú, a militant Catholic layman who involved himself in the Church-sponsored Liga Operária Mineira.

On another test of homogeneity—out-of-state birth—Minas at 13 percent ranked lower than Pernambuco, with 15 percent, and São Paulo, which, as a population growth pole, had almost 19 percent. This confirms Assis Barbosa's observation that with rare exceptions, only native sons served in Mineiro politics.[1] Furthermore, Minas exported talent to São Paulo and the Federal District, which reinforced the perceived insularity of its elite at home.

Family ties, education, and money were the customary pathways to elite status. Of money, little is revealed in the biographical data. This elite considered itself to be historically well established: the oldest families traced their origins to the eighteenth-century mining boom via Portugal or São Paulo. Many families made their money later, in coffee and commerce; as in fortunes made in Boston after 1840, their blood was not thought to be true blue. But for all its aristocratic pretensions, this elite was open to new money and to talented young men who could bolster family fortunes. In turn, the making of money was facilitated by ties of parentela, and by protection by the established families.

The interlocking nature of this elite through kinship ties was outlined descriptively by Cid Rebelo Horta some years ago.[2] A look at the elite Mineiros for whom data could be found ($n = 177$) bears him out: 46 percent were related to at least one other member of the elite through first cousin, directly or by marriage. This probably understates clan ties—the data are not complete on parentela—but it is interesting to find Minas leading the other two states on this important variable, for which the mean is only 41 percent. On family ties with analogous elites in other states, Mineiros and Paulistas ranked very low, 4 and 1 percent, respectively, and the data are probably weak. Clan ties with the Paulista elite were very few, an important finding that sheds light on the ability of Mineiros to maintain a distinct regional identity in the face of São Paulo's sustained economic boom. Pernambuco's 12 percent ranking on this variable points up the importance of parentela in its Northeast satellite region. Only 16 percent of Mineiros were members of, or related to, the old Imperial elite.[3] Forty-seven percent had at least one of the three types of ties.

Parentela ties were probably the most salient at the higher echelons of this elite. Among the 15 governors, all but one had identifiable clan ties within the state, while four (27 percent) descended from Imperial figures. But only one had out-of-state links, and this was João Pinheiro through his wife's Paulista relatives. Brothers-in-law Silviano Brandão and Júlio Bueno Brandão were the only close relatives among the governors, a pattern quite unlike the nepotistic chief executives of São

Paulo. Two-thirds of all governors came from the Sul and the Mata. Interestingly, all three governors in political phase one (1889–98) had power bases in the Center zone; during phase three (1929–37), it was two western governors, serving at the sufferance of Vargas. The apogee of Mineiro power (1898–1929) was dominated by governors from the coffee zones, as Afonso Arinos pointed out.[4]

By comparison, one-third of the entire elite was based politically in these two zones, less than the governors, but still indicating the political power wielded by the coffee elite. The Triângulo, West, North, and East between them accounted for but 16 percent of all personnel surveyed (see Table 5.1). If the Center at 54 percent seems too strongly represented, this is partly because all magistrates were coded for Belo Horizonte. Nonetheless, just over one-third of the whole elite spent the most important years of their political careers in Belo.[5] This shows that the capital, despite its small electorate, did indeed function as the state's political center of gravity.

The bacharel, with his ruby ring for law and his sapphire for medicine, was a familiar Brazilian type. True to form, almost three-quarters of the total (adjusted) group were bacharéis, and two-thirds had law degrees. The bacharel's services were essential for drawing up contracts and laws and for court decisions—in short, for serving the powerful with legitimizing rhetoric from the Roman law tradition. He read, quoted from, and sometimes published literature, something that continues to be a source of pride and prestige in Minas today. Physicians, with their clinics and lists of clients, were well positioned to launch a political career; being indispensable, they were less vulnerable to political pressuring than the lawyers, who outnumbered them nearly six to one.

Mineiros fortunate enough to be certified as educated men in a land of illiterates enjoyed an exalted social status. Professional degrees were virtually a prerequisite to an elite political career, as the statistics show for all three states. Only 9 percent of the (adjusted) Mineiro elite lacked degrees beyond the secondary school level, and almost all of these were concentrated in the first political generation, born before 1869. A number of men without higher degrees practiced law nonetheless: 9 percent of the lawyers—13 of 144—were licensed "provisionals," popularly known as *rábulas* (shysters). They fought tenaciously for

this right, and their social status, against the efforts of reformers like
Francisco Campos who tried to require the degree. Júlio Bueno was
one of the best-known rábulas.

Only 30 (all lawyers) of 155 bacharéis were educated wholly in the
new state faculties of law and medicine. Nearly three-quarters received *all* their higher education elsewhere, notably at the São Paulo
Law School or at the Rio School of Medicine. Fourteen percent of the
entire group took some or all of their secondary schooling in another
state. The education of so many away, at a formative stage in life, is
notable.[6] That so few out-of-state marriage ties resulted is thus remarkable, a testament to Mineiro provincialism. The "Traditional
Mineiro Family" expected its young people to marry at home. Some
wives living away returned especially to give birth; the Melo Francos,
living in Rio, were a highly visible example.

Religion played an increasingly important role in the social and
political life of Minas, notably after 1909. Traditionally, the social life
of small towns revolved around the Church. But the third political
generation was far more involved in Catholic issues than their rationalist fathers. Many first generation Mineiros lost their faith at law
school. Having arrived in São Paulo with his beliefs intact, Ferreira de
Rezende sought confession in secret to avoid the ridicule of fellow
students.[7] Yet a rundown of the Minas group shows that almost nobody in this first generation repudiated the Church outright. Nine
were identified as leading Catholic lay leaders, authors, or major bene-
factors, including the group's one priest. João Pinheiro was the only
Positivist. In the second political generation, seven elite actors were
identified as leading Catholics. Camilo Rodrigues Chaves from the
Triângulo presided over the Mineiro Spiritualist Union, but there were
no Protestants. The third generation for whom data were available included two Catholic lay leaders. In sum, 9 percent of the entire group
was identified as having strong religious convictions, and of these, 18
were Roman Catholics. Most of the rest were doubtless nonpracticing
Catholics. Religious cleavages did not cut deep in Minas, but the
generations did feel differently on the separation of Church and State.
Otherwise, the intense campaign to reinstate religious instruction in
the schools would not have taken 20 years.

As mentioned, only one cleric appears in the Minas group—but only
because of the way we defined political elite. (This was Canon João

Pio de Souza Reis, a state senator on the PRM Executive Committee.) In fact, there was always at least one priest in the state legislature, usually two for each congressional term.[8] Nor does the group include some of the politically active Catholic laymen, men like Furtado de Menezes, Bernardino de Lima, and José Campos do Amaral. Yet another omission is of course the wives. Intensely religious, Governor Francisco Sales's wife, Dona Nicota, was very active in Catholic activities in the new state capital. The overview, then, remains the traditional one of Minas as "the most Catholic state" in Brazil. Certainly, the contrast with São Paulo's less religiously involved elite is striking. The parallel with Pernambuco, however, is suggestive. Both states underwent a religious revival that affected politics.

Fazendeiros are certainly underrepresented in the statistics on professions in the Minas group: only 35 individuals (17 percent) were so identified. Data on rural property ownership are poor, but I assume that many, perhaps the majority, of this elite held fazendas and/or were closely related to fazendeiros. Many repaired to *sítios* (small farms) for weekend relaxation or between sessions of the legislature. Newspaper biographies and obituaries usually focused on a man's educational and professional achievements rather than his assets, including rural properties. The available data do reveal that all but four of the fazendeiros exercised other professions in addition to farming or ranching for profit. And these four men all lived in the North and West, relatively backward zones. Two-thirds of the fazendeiros had two or more careers, from manufacturer to banker to teacher and pharmacist. This multiple career pattern suggests there was no conflict of interest between landowners and the other professions. It also indicates a society in the early stages of modernization. But only one in ten fazendeiros was based professionally in Belo Horizonte—far below the elite rate as a whole, which was 36 percent.

Despite conventional wisdom, the conclusion is that "the fazendeiros" as a group did not control Minas politics at the state elite level. Murilo de Carvalho reached the same conclusion for the Imperial elite in his doctoral dissertation. However prestigious landownership was, it was not necessary for membership in the political elite, whereas education was all but essential. If the fazendeiro data are suspect—Minas and Pernambuco are only half the São Paulo rate!—it is still worth mentioning that after lawyer (68 percent) the most common occupations were educator (32 percent), journalist (24 percent), and industrialist (18 percent). But again, bear in mind that multiple careers were common in this elite group.

The sense of place, of roots in the small town, of coming from somewhere, is to the literature and folklore on Minas what the *basso continuo* line is to Bach: inevitable, expected, and ordering. Sure enough, the large majority of regional bosses were based politically in the municípios of their birth—Bernardes in Viçosa, Bias in Barbacena, Wenceslau in Itajubá. Taking the Minas group as a whole, however, one notices that almost 70 percent of those for whom birthplaces are listed were politically active *elsewhere* for most of their careers.[9] And they often lived in more than one place before settling down. Figures of the second rank, such as Afrânio de Melo Franco, were expected to troubleshoot around the state as the PRM directed. For Afrânio, this meant politicking in the Triângulo outside his native West, running for office in the North, or leading some of Bressane's duplicate delegations to party conventions. In short, the highest leaders were more firmly rooted in the município of origin than lower-echelon types.

The system they controlled was also more flexible than is usually supposed. Politically, the sargentação system encouraged this geographical circulation of elites. Economically, the search for better professional opportunities reinforced it. Geographical movement within the state occurred at virtually the same rate (69 percent) as in São Paulo, a state in full frontier expansion.

In Minas, however, this mobility was largely toward the new capital. Old bastions of the Imperial elite—notably Serro, Campanha, and Ouro Preto—exported several native sons, and most zones actually "lost" people to Belo Horizonte. The Triângulo's extraordinary isolation from the elite is underscored again, as is the East's political potential owing to population growth. See Table 5.1. The Sul exported talent; the Mata, led by Juiz de Fora's industrial and commercial growth, attracted it.

Two-thirds of the Center's group based itself in the capital, and almost half of the Mata's personnel operated out of Juiz de Fora. Eighty-eight individuals, thus, representing 44 percent of the Minas elite ($n = 198$), carried out their political activities in large cities.[10] Clan ties linked them to the countryside, yet the stereotype of the small-town politician is clearly wrong above the level of coronel.

TABLE 5.1

Distribution of Elite by Zone, 1890–1937

| Zone | Birthplace | Political base |
| --- | --- | --- |
| Center | 59 | 106 |
| Mata | 22 | 38 |
| Sul | 40 | 22 |
| Triângulo | 3 | 3 |
| West | 21 | 12 |
| North | 22 | 12 |
| East | 3 | 5 |
| Out of state | 27 | — |
| Foreign | 1 | — |
| TOTAL | 198 | 198 |

NOTE: Figures include only those whose birthplaces are known.

That Belo Horizonte was the quintessential bureaucratic city is one reason why the Minas elite appeared to be less well integrated with its corresponding economic elite than São Paulo's. Recall that the capital had no commercial-industrial base to speak of until the late 1920's. Later, it still had to share these economic functions with Juiz de Fora until the war. It follows that the Minas elite should include relatively fewer merchants, industrialists, and bankers, but lead São Paulo in teachers and engineers, the service-oriented occupations.* Differentials in socioeconomic development are not the reason, because on the composite variable "business," Minas and São Paulo ranked 35 and 41 percent, respectively. In turn, Minas outranked Pernambuco in the above-mentioned professional groupings, and was 11 points above it on the business variable.[11] If there was a gap between the political and economic elites, it appeared in the third political generation, as I discuss below.

Why, then, are there so few interest-group leaders in the Minas elite? Nearly 7 percent in each of the other two elites were agrarian leaders, 4 percent in each were commercial leaders. This compares with less than 2 and 1 percent, respectively, for Minas. Presidents of the Commercial and Agricultural Associations did not enjoy less prestige in Minas, nor was the elite closed to these leaders. They did

* Since the São Paulo elite was larger (263 to 214), it actually led Minas in the first category by 151 individuals to 82, roughly two for every one. Minas, with 96 of its elite in teaching and engineering to São Paulo's 75, had an absolute lead of four to three in the service-oriented professions. Because of multiple occupations, these ratios are suggestive, not definitive.

have to contend with the division of economic roles and rivalry between Juiz de Fora and the capital, owing to which duplicate associations existed. This meant they were less visible politically and probably
easier to control than their counterparts elsewhere.* Findings such as
this suggest that generalizations about the national elite must be made
with care. Note, also, a major point in common: all three elites had
virtually the same percentages of lawyers and magistrates, showing the
degree to which the legal-formal culture they shared had spread
throughout the national elite.

Lacking a seaport, Mineiros did not have the same easy access to
foreigners and Atlantic Basin cultural trends as did their counterparts.
But their insularity is striking, nonetheless. Less than 8 percent resided abroad for more than six months. Compare this to the 32 percent
of Paulistas and the 20 percent of Pernambucanos who traveled for
extended periods outside Brazil. On the composite variable for all
foreign ties, Mineiros trailed the others by a ratio of roughly three-
two-one.[12]

Limited travel abroad explains why Rio and the famous Carioca
chic had such a hold on the Mineiro imagination. Federal patronage
was another reason why one-sixth of the Minas elite—and one quarter
of Pernambuco's—at some point worked in Rio or moved there for
professional reasons and returned. Plugging into the federal pipeline
was far less important to Paulistas: a mere 7 percent sought out the
capital's professional opportunities, and only one-third of that elite
served in the federal congress. Interestingly, half of the other two
elites were in the national legislature at some point. But when it came
to holding political and administrative offices out of state (excluding
the Federal District), Minas ranked behind São Paulo, confirming thus
its insularity. In this regard, Pernambuco's career patterns were very
different because of its links to northern satellites.

---

* Valadares did not recruit leaders of the state's economic elite to top political
posts, but Vargas did. The president was close to Euvaldo Lodi and Walter
Gosling, two Mineiro industrialists who were class deputies in congress and who
led the National Industrial Confederation in Rio. The extent to which the state's
economic elite was redirected toward Rio in this period should be investigated.
In reaction, two ex-association leaders served Governor Milton Campos in 1947
when the federal system was restored. José de Magalhães Pinto, a banker who
led the Commercial Association in 1938, became Secretary of Finance. Industrialist Américo Gianetti, who led the Minas Federation of Industries in 1939–47,
was made Secretary of Agriculture.

Generational change appeals to historians, for whom the slice-of-life approach used often in the other social sciences seems simplistic, at times misleading. For example, aggregate data on the three political generations (i.e. those born before 1869, between 1869 and 1888, and afterward) are remarkably proportionate across the states: roughly 50, 33, and 18 percent, respectively. The median age for entering the first elite status job was 43.3, which is again quite consistent: 42 for Minas and Pernambuco, 45 for São Paulo. Data indicate that the recruitment patterns must have been the same. However, a closer look at generations shows some different patterns for each state.

If a man was 29 or under, he had a much better chance to enter his first elite post in Pernambuco, where 17 percent did so, compared with only 5 percent in Minas and 4 percent in São Paulo. Thirty-seven percent of the Mineiros entered in their thirties, 32 percent in their forties. A Paulista was most likely to enter between age 40 and 49—in fact, 40 percent did so. In all three generations, more Mineiros advanced before age 40 (the percentages are 31, 42, and 70, respectively) than their Paulista counterparts (23, 12, and 68 percent).[13] The PRM prided itself on being able to bring in young talent, and these figures validate that claim. The better-organized PRP was not so open to new blood, notably in the second generation, where, as Joseph Love points out in his parallel study on São Paulo, there was a career bottleneck for youth. As for the Pernambuco state machine, it was disorganized: this is probably why men in their twenties could aspire to high political office there.

Another difference in political careers emerges from the data on legislative service, both state and national. A majority of the elite in each state served, but Mineiros served more, and more consistently, as is shown by the following figures:

|         | Pernambuco | Minas | São Paulo |
|---------|------------|-------|-----------|
| Federal | 55.7%      | 51.2% | 31.7%     |
| State   | 30.9%      | 47.4% | 48.6%     |

To conclude that Pernambucanos put a premium on federal legislative experience, while Paulistas valued state service more, is tempting. Possibly, also, the Mineiro system of sargentação demanded more legislative participation. In Minas, roughly two-thirds of each political generation were elected senator or deputy to either legislature.[14]

TABLE 5.2

*Percent of Tenure in More Than One Post*

| State | First post | Second post | Third post | Fourth post | Fifth post | Sixth post |
|---|---|---|---|---|---|---|
| São Paulo | 100 | 46 | 22 | 14 | 9 | 6 |
| Minas Gerais | 100 | 42 | 21 | 11 | 6 | 3 |
| Pernambuco | 100 | 25 | 8 | 3 | 1 | 1 |

Data on office groupings by the sequence of positions held, shown in Table 5.2, contain a number of interesting patterns for Minas and São Paulo. Pernambuco has few patterns, indicating the disorganized state of politics there and the fact that few men held more than one post.

A glance at Table 5.3, with reference to the analogous tables in the other studies, shows that service in the state cabinet and executive posts fell off rapidly in both Minas and São Paulo. Having been tested in these posts, one moved on to the governorship or federal service. (Pernambucan data show no clear patterns except a rise in ministerial posts.) In similar federal posts, the trend rose rapidly for Minas but was ambiguous for São Paulo, indicating, perhaps, that Paulistas were less attracted than their counterparts to high federal office. Senior São Paulo politicians were more likely to serve in top positions in their state legislature than was true in the case of Minas; top federal legislative posts were more often held by senior Mineiros, by contrast. Evidently, the two elites valued state and federal legislative posts differently. As for the judiciary, almost all state-level judges entered the courts on their first post and the Supreme Court justices on their second, with some exceptions in the case of Minas. Pernambucan judges joined both courts at the third post level: this percentage rate may indicate that the judiciary there was more politicized.

Returning to the Minas elite, variations among the three political generations are sometimes interesting, but on the whole they are slight and not very important. Clan ties were important to each generation, especially to the first and third; foreign ties were unimportant, except to the second generation. Those born after 1888 appear to be more insular, perhaps more professionally specialized than the middle-generation group. For when generation was cross-tabulated by occupation, the only statistically significant results (other than for magistrate) emerged for the industrialist and (almost) for the business variables. See Table 5.4. The second generation again led the other groups, implying that it was more cosmopolitan.

That third generation Mineiros were still at mid-career by 1937 should raise a note of caution when conclusions are drawn. After this is said, it does seem that third-generation "politicians" were more specialized in service careers, especially law and teaching, than the others. If so, there was now less congruence between the political and economic elites in Minas. Certainly, the rising incidence of Belo Horizonte–based political careers suggests this is so. No third-generation personnel were active in Juiz de Fora.

Concerning ideology, 49 percent of those eligible in the total Minas

TABLE 5.3

*Office Groupings by Sequence of Positions Held*

(Adjusted frequency)

| Office group | First post | Second post | Third post | Fourth post | Fifth post | Sixth post | Seventh post | Eighth post | Ninth post |
|---|---|---|---|---|---|---|---|---|---|
| State | | | | | | | | | |
| S1 | 1.4 | 3.4 | 15.6 | 8.3 | 16.7 | 0 | 50 | 0 | 0 |
| S2 | 19.7 | 16.8 | 8.8 | 0 | 0 | 0 | 0 | 0 | 0 |
| S3 | 29.9 | 18.0 | 17.7 | 0 | 8.3 | 0 | 0 | 0 | 0 |
| S4 | 12.1 | 11.2 | 0 | 8.3 | 8.3 | 0 | 0 | 0 | 0 |
| S5 | 5.1 | 2.2 | 0 | 0 | 0 | 0 | 0 | 0 | 0 |
| S6 | 22.9 | 19.1 | 20 | 33.3 | 8.3 | 0 | 0 | 50 | 100 |
| Federal | | | | | | | | | |
| F1 | 0 | 0 | 4.4 | 0 | 0 | 0 | 25 | 0 | 0 |
| F2 | 2.7 | 11.1 | 8.9 | 12.6 | 16.6 | 0 | 0 | 25 | 0 |
| F3 | .9 | 2.2 | 4.4 | 12.5 | 0 | 16.7 | 0 | 0 | 0 |
| F4 | 2.8 | 10.0 | 17.8 | 16.7 | 41.6 | 83.4 | 25 | 25 | 0 |
| F5 | 2.3 | 4.5 | 2.2 | 4.2 | 0 | 0 | 0 | 0 | 0 |
| All federal | 8.7 | 27.8 | 37.7 | 46.0 | 58.2 | 100.0 | 50 | 50 | 0 |
| All state except S6 | 68.2 | 51.6 | 42.1 | 16.6 | 33.3 | 0 | 50 | 50 | 0 |
| Absolute number in each group | 214 | 89 | 45 | 24 | 12 | 6 | 4 | 4 | 1 |

S1. Governor.
S2. Secretaries.
S3. Other state executive posts (prefect, police chief, top administrator, bank president, lieutenant governor).
S4. State legislative posts (president of the senate, president of the chamber, majority leader).
S5. President, state court.
S6. Executive committees of the Republican parties and opposition parties.
F1. President of the Republic.
F2. Minister.
F3. Other federal executive posts (president of the Bank of Brazil, etc.).
F4. Congressional posts.
F5. Supreme court.

TABLE 5.4

*Generation by Select Variables*

| Generation | Clan ties | Foreign | Industrialist | Business | Magistrate | Residence in Belo |
|---|---|---|---|---|---|---|
| 1 | 58% | 13% | 17% | 34% | 28% | 23% |
| 2 | 47 | 28 | 30 | 48 | 9 | 42 |
| 3 | 61 | 12 | 9 | 24 | 3 | 58 |

NOTE: Significance for the cross-tabulations of generation by select variables: clan tie, .3954; foreign, .0481; industrialist, .0348; business, .0613; magistrate, .0008. Generation by Belo Horizonte residence is part of a comprehensive table on residence by município, for which the statistical significance figure is irrelevant. Clan ties is a composite of variables 67–69; foreign, of variables 16–28; and business, of variables 54–56, 63–65 (see Appendix A). Significance is at the .05 level.

group were Historical Republicans; 51 percent were monarchists who adhered in 1889 or later. This corresponds with São Paulo's breakdown, but superficially. For included in the variable "historic" are seven "eleventh hour" Republicans such as Cesário Alvim, who switched after abolition, in May 1888. One in six Republicans was a latecomer; almost nobody in the other two elites played this wait-and-see game. Moreover, the data surely underrepresent the Mineiro fence-sitters. Many biographies are vague on the specific nature of a man's Republicanism. Retrospectively, it was good to say one had been a Republican. Weak, disorganized, and on the defensive at the time, the Minas Republican Party was more like Pernambuco's—Republicans there were only 21 percent—than São Paulo's well-organized militants. Consider, also, the low incidence of abolitionists among the Mineiros—only 9 percent of those eligible in what was almost to the end a slavocratic bastion of the Empire. Twice this number come down to us as abolitionists from the other two states.

Historical Republicans were strongly represented on the early PR and its successor, the PRC. But they lost men in the political battles up through 1897, while the adherents gained access to top posts. During phase two, the two groups split 50–50 on the PRM Executive Committee. That one-third of the PRM's "Historical" committeemen were in fact eleventh-hour converts in revealing. And, if the truth be known, many historicals wore their ideological wounds from the late Empire like dueling scars.

Data on conflict participation in state and national politics support the analysis in Chapter 4: the Mineiros fought at home but pulled together in the federal arena. State political cleavage was high during phases one and three. Never less than 15 percent of the eligible elite broke with the establishment during each of three crisis periods in the 1890's—over Alvim's government (1890–92), with the PRC (1893–96), and at the PRC's Ouro Preto Congress (1897). The same happened in phase three, when 15 percent broke at the Valadares nomination (1933), and when he set up a fusion party (1936). Twenty-two percent broke at some point with Olegário Maciel's administration (1930–33).

Except for the 1910 civilista campaign, when nearly 11 percent of the elite broke, the incidence of cleavage on the federal level was only one-third the magnitude of state breaks. Thus, 6 percent backed General Deodoro's coup in 1891; 5 percent joined the Nilista forces in 1921; and only 6 percent broke with the PRM in 1929–30. The other elites behaved quite differently during the three contested presidential elections. Pernambucanos were much more volatile, Paulistas somewhat more stable.

To carry the three-state comparison further, the rate of cleavage when Governor Bernardes purged the legislature and moved to one-man rule (1918–20) was, at 8 percent, nearly identical with rates during crises within São Paulo's PRP in 1915 and 1924. Both machines were more stable than they had been, and the PRP with its dues-assessing system was of course more institutionalized. In the case of Minas, legislative turnover was matched by efforts to attract top politicians like the old civilistas into Bernardes' camp. To this extent, Bernardes' reforms were limited. Data on Pernambuco's internal conflicts do not seem comparable. Breaks there during the three contested national elections are worth reviewing, because any state showing rates of 24, 7, and 22 percent, respectively, was bound to weaken itself in the federation. See Appendix A for cleavage data.

Turning now to look systematically at political parties, we find many more similarities than differences between those who served on party executive committees (39 percent) and those who did not. As a whole, committee members were slightly more business-oriented, and more of them had clan ties, but on neither variable are these findings statistically significant.[15] The one difference occurs with the variable "away job": committeemen worked outside the state in a proportion of less than one in five, but one in three of the noncommittee members did.[16] Just as the superbosses were more place-centered than most, so top personnel in the party hierarchies were less likely to seek greener pastures elsewhere. Insularity at the top, contrasted to geographical and career mobility at the second echelon, is the clear pattern here.

Comparing all executive committee members with all nonmembers revealed few differences. Some interesting variations do appear when the four Executive Committee groups are compared with each other, and against the elite as a whole. These four groups include the PR (1889–90) and the PRC (1893–97);* the PRM in power (1897–1930); the PRM in opposition (1931–36); and the Partido Progressista committee, which ran the new PP establishment party in the 1930's.

The first committee members were more radical in their politics, but not more "modern" in their professions. Nine of the 12 men were Historical Republicans, including an eleventh-hour convert. Most did not survive the turbulent 1890's; only four historicals were politically active by 1898. Among those accommodating to Silviano Brandão's new order were three PRC committeemen who joined the new PRM Executive Committee. Interestingly, all three were ex-Liberals like Silviano himself; two were adherents; and one (Antonio Martins Ferreira da Silva) was the last-minute convert to Republicanism. Professionally, this early group mirrored the whole elite, with lawyers leading. It is tempting to say they were rather more business-oriented than their compatriots as a whole, but the sample is too small.

Forty-three men served on the PRM Executive Committee through 1930. Over two-fifths belonged to the second political generation, showing that, unlike the situation in São Paulo, injecting new blood was not a serious problem for the state machine.[17] Compared with the entire Minas group, PRM committeemen had a few more lawyers and ranked somewhat higher in the business professions: merchants (12 vs. 6 percent), industrialists (26 to 18 percent), and bankers (21 to 15 percent). Thirty percent of them were fazendeiros, but comparison is meaningless because the overall data are so weak. But there were one-third fewer educators and only half the engineers.

Seven of these men stayed loyal to the PRM when it went into opposition in May 1931. Led by Artur Bernardes, this rump group was less distinguished than its predecessor; biographical data for five of its 27 members are incomplete, indicating the party had difficulty re-

* Defined as leaders signing voting slates.

cruiting top personnel. Eduardo Amaral, who was lieutenant governor under Bernardes and a leading Catholic layman, was the only man from generation one. At first, the party could not attract young men, but four third-generation politicians joined in January 1933 as the PRM reorganized to contest the upcoming Constituent Assembly elections. Later, Virgílio de Melo Franco and Bias Fortes Júnior adhered, which boosted the young contingent to one-third, the rest being from generation two.[18] Lawyers led the professions with 67 percent, just the level of the entire elite. The business professions ranked within a few percentage points of the entire group, making this committee less distinguished than the old PRM, which ranked higher than the norm. Twenty-six percent were fazendeiros. The service occupations were low: 7 vs. 14 percent for engineers, 7 vs. 32 percent for educators.

Only four of the old PRM Committee joined forces with a notably younger political group to found the Partido Progressista in November 1932. Led by Antonio Carlos, the new establishment party included one first-generation fixture: Wenceslau Brás. Men born after 1889 were the majority, or exactly half the 19-man committee.[19] The PP's success in attracting young political talent probably spurred the PRM to do likewise. Lawyers and teachers dominated this committee—79 percent and 32 percent, respectively—proving that the PP was well rooted in the bureaucratic and service-oriented ambience of the capital. PP committeemen involved themselves in the business professions at almost the same rate as the entire elite. Fazendeiros were well represented at 26 percent. After a strong beginning, the PP lost its élan in late 1933 when Valadares was appointed interventor and the Melo Franco group defected, making the two parties more equal, if equally irrelevant.

Comparing the four Executive Committees, it is clear that the old PRM (and perhaps the early PR and PRC) was relatively more "business-oriented" than its successors in the 1930's. That the third generation tended to follow bureaucratic and service-oriented professions is a trend that also runs through these later-day committee. The old PRM congressional delegation was modernized by men of Bernardes' generation, which of the three age-groups was the most active in business careers. However, comparison between generations one and two on the old PRM turned up few professional differences. In purging Francisco Sales and his allies in 1919, Bernardes seems to have deliberately overstated their attachment to narrow local loyalties and the fazenda. The university degree did become almost a prerequisite for legislative service under Bernardes. Thus, it is likely that he encouraged the trend that showed up in generation three, where more service-oriented career men appeared in the top political posts.

Enough has been said so far to show in what ways the Minas elite did or did not conform to tri-state norms and to national patterns. The dominance of lawyers is clear. Fazendeiros did not run politics at the highest level, although they were well represented on party Executive Committees, and the great majority for whom data were available followed multiple careers. Bacharelismo was the template to which at least 70 percent of the three state elites was cut, but four in every five Mineiros received his higher education out of state. Insularity was nonetheless the mark of Minas, judging from marriage patterns, the low incidence of interstate ties, and foreign travel. However, Mineiros were more "legislative-minded" than their counterparts. This underscores the central role of Minas in congressional politics. Belo's growth as the region's bureaucratic and, later, economic center was unique, the divergence of political and economic elites by generation three being a possible consequence.

These conclusions are based on numerical relationships. Having measured the Minas group, one can more confidently trace the careers of representative men. Brief sketches of a few such individuals will conclude this chapter, after first posing our "typical" Mineiro in a composite portrait to gain perspective.

After taking his law degree at São Paulo, the typical Mineiro worked his way up the ranks to his first elite status job, held usually by his early forties. He served first on the local level as Public Prosecutor, sometimes as Municipal Judge, and often, but not always, in his home town. Perhaps he married into the local elite and became a councilman, then prefect. Or he practiced law in one or more towns before moving to Belo Horizonte. Election to the state legislature followed logically. There he learned the patterns of interzonal bargaining while the superbosses watched how he worked within one of the three dominant political factions and estimated his general suitability. At that point he might go on to the Rio delegation or accept his first elite job.

It might be an administrative post: 27 percent of the group took one as their first of our elite-defining positions. One-quarter began in the secretariat, including a few governors and lieutenant governors. Eighteen percent joined a party Executive Committee as their first top job. After this, the typical Mineiro might then go to Rio, where the majority of his compatriots served at some point in their careers. Some posts were political dead ends. If he became police chief, the odds were two to one that he would never take another top position, and if he did so, it would be another administrative post or the judiciary. Directors of the state press did not usually advance to other posts. The most likely route to multiple responsibilities and to a governorship was through the secretariat.[20] But the majority of Mineiros (see Table 5.2) never held more than one top post.

Typically, our Mineiro lived in Belo Horizonte but kept in close touch with rural relatives, on whose fazendas he would spend vacations if he did not have rural properties of his own. He respected friends who held strong religious views, but was himself a nonpracticing Catholic. He engaged in at least two professions other than the one for which we know him best: politician. And he took the overnight train to Rio frequently, laughing when Cariocas satirized the Minas rustic type in print and on the stage. Well educated, he himself had hardly just arrived from some fazenda in the Mata. Still, the federal capital with its patina of elegance and sophistication was not his world, and he did not venture overseas.

José Monteiro Ribeiro Junqueira (1870–1946) was the model superboss from generation two. Upon graduating from São Paulo Law School in 1893, Junqueira entered Leopoldina politics, where he served briefly as Public Prosecutor, then as city councilman of this important Mata município. In 1895 he was elected to the state legislature from the Sul, where his father had family and political connections. Marriage to Helena de Andrade Ribeiro allied him to the Andrade Botelhos from Lavras in the Sul. This put him in Francisco Sales's camp. Through his mother he inherited the Monteiro family base in Leopoldina, a coffee town this family founded in the 1830's after migrating from the mining zone. Under Junqueira, his brother Custódio (a physician), and his niece's husband Carlos Coimbra de Luz from a leading Sulista family, the Monteiros controlled Leopoldina politics almost uninterruptedly through World War II. This Mata base sustained Junqueira for another term as legislator (1899–1902), as a leading federal deputy (1903–30), and then as federal senator for Minas (1934–37).

His influence extended to the highest councils of the state machine, on whose ruling Executive Committee he served for almost 30 years before switching to the Partido Progressista for another five years.

Politically, Junqueira was nonideological, in short, a familiar Minas type. For several years he battled Astolfo Dutra Nicásio (1863–1920) for control of the south Mata. That Junqueira was the scion of a leading Liberal family while Dutra came from the Conservative elite in nearby Cataguazes doubtless set the scene for conflict, although they were both too young for Republican flirtations. At the 1897 Ouro Preto Congress, they lined up on different sides when the PRC split. Dutra stayed with Silviano; Junqueira joined the Mendes Pimentel reform group and then the Partido da Lavoura before switching in 1900 to the mainline PRM. Meanwhile, Dutra pressed him for control of Leopoldina, where brother-in-law Joaquim Dutra led the local Silvianista faction. By 1909 Junqueira had won, and a truce was called as the PRM closed ranks to fight the civilistas. Junqueira joined the Executive Committee and was soon made leader of the congressional delegation, having emerged as a superboss in his own right within the Salista camp. The rise of Artur Bernardes did not catch him off base: Junqueira was the only top Salista left after the 1919 purge. He almost went with Carvalho Brito's Conservative Concentration group, but pulled back in time. In 1931 he bolted Bernardes and the rapidly declining PRM to become Maciel's Secretary of Agriculture just as the contract for his light and power company came up for renewal.

In Rio, Ribeiro Junqueira was a pillar of the committee system, which Mineiros dominated for most of the Old Republic. From 1903 to 1913 he served various years on the Finance and Agriculture committees. And for three years until 1914 he led the Finance Committee while Francisco Sales, his political ally at home, headed the Ministry of Finance. Coffee policy was his area of expertise, and Junqueira often represented Minas at the interstate coffee congresses, starting at Taubaté. For almost 30 years he was the state's chief negotiator in its dealings with the other coffee states. A leading member of the Mineiro Coffee Institute, he was its representative on the National Coffee Council until 1933.

Junqueira's many business interests were interwoven with his politics. From his fazendeiro parents he inherited a large stake in the Mata coffee industry. As a leading fazendeiro he helped to develop dairy ranching as old coffee lands gave out on the estate he grandly called "Niagara." In fact, his Companhia Leiteira Leopoldinense became the largest milk supplier to the Federal District. With his brother-in-law, State Senator Francisco de Andrade Botelho, Junqueira founded a savings bank with branches in several Mata towns and the nation's capital. The electric light company that he and other fazendeiros began in 1906 to service the Leopoldina-Cataguases area was built in part with capital from the treasuries of the towns they controlled. Being the largest employer in Leopoldina assured him several hundred votes. Junqueira patronized the local secondary school and owned the *Gazeta de Leopoldina*. He also owned the local textile plant. Upon his death in 1946, Junqueira was a leading entrepreneur in Minas, with interests in Santa Catarina coalfields and holdings in the capital. Joaquim, a son, managed the bank and the fazendas, while Vanor, another son, was entrusted with the power company. And although Junqueira belonged to the leading clubs in Rio, there was never any doubt that the ties of family, politics, and business began and ended at Leopoldina.[21]

João Luís Alves (1870–1925) typified a political career of the second rank. An intellectual, Alves offered his brains to the superbosses and served the party well. Born of a well-connected Mata family in modest circumstances, Alves was sent through law school by his godfather, the Baron of Santa Helena, who ran the Juiz de Fora gasworks with his father. Service in another município was the usual first post for bacharéis without large fortunes, so Alves chose Campanha, where he was Public Prosecutor, married, and practiced law. Shrewdly, he refused to join the separatists in 1892, although his friend Francisco Bressane was secretary to the abortive junta that tried to found the state of Minas do Sul. Instead, Alves attached himself to Silviano Brandão and, after being mayor of Campanha, rode Silviano's coattails into the legislature from another zone in 1898 and moved to Belo Horizonte.

In the new capital, João Luís became the PRM's polemicist as editor of *O Diário de Minas*, the newspaper Bressane had wrested from the PRM reform group. He also taught law at the new faculty in Belo Horizonte. In 1903, Alves went to Rio for a Mata district and led the protectionist movement, discussed in Chapter 2. He also presided over the Justice Committee for two years. And although he joined the Jardim de Infância reform group under Carlos Peixoto, he was no rocker of party boats. In 1908, he stood for the senate from Espírito Santo, at that time a satellite of Pinheiro Machado (the gaúcho kingmaker), which Peixoto, as president of the Chamber, was anxious to infiltrate. Ties of parentesco eased his way into Capixaba politics, but he did so on command. Ever alert to shifts in power, Alves moved in close to Pinheiro Machado when Peixoto's star set, and supported the Hermes ticket against Peixoto and the civilistas. Pinheiro admired João Luís's quick mind, just as the younger man liked power and the gaúcho's finesse. Alves served in the senate ten years, distinguishing himself as a moving force behind the 1916 Civil Code and as president of a special joint committee to revamp Brazil's Commercial Code.

The rise of Artur Bernardes brought him back to Belo as the governor's Secretary of Finance. At the important 1919 Convention it was Alves who wrote the party platform which legitimized one-man rule and the purge of Francisco Sales and Bressane. In 1921, he was one of three Bernardistas who joined the PRM Executive Committee. Next he served as President Bernardes' Minister of Justice, taking a tough line on dissenters, against whom detention camps and torture were used. Ill health forced his retirement from the ministry in 1925. But before João Luís died in a Paris clinic, he was rewarded with a Supreme Court justiceship. Election to the Brazilian Academy of Letters assured his stature as a leading cultural light, the most brilliant in the stable of intellectuals brought onto the national scene by the PRM.[22]

For the third echelon, a glance at the career of a city administrator and the feud of two rival coronéis, men acting just below the level of the state elite, will round out this portrait of typical Mineiros.

Menelíck de Carvalho (1897–1949) was a Mata-born protégé of Antonio Carlos who began by clerking at the Secretariat of Agriculture. His father and father-in-law were both public functionaries; his mother, though distantly related to the Visconde de Ouro Preto, was a primary-school teacher. The upwardly mobile Carvalho worked his way through the state ginásio and the law school (1932), becoming the top administrative officer at Agriculture while also teaching. In 1915 he was briefly a police officer in Juiz de Fora before returning under Governor Antonio Carlos to direct the Belo Horizonte police and the Motor Vehicle Department. There he installed the capital's first traffic lights. Election to the Automóvel Club marked him as having socially arrived.

During the 1930 Revolution, Carvalho commanded the state's Fourth
Military region (the Mata) and supervised the Juiz de Fora police, an
important job, since that city was headquarters for a hostile army garrison. In 1932 he rounded up Bernardes and other Paulista sympathizers while coordinating police work in the Mata. Appointed mayor of
Juiz de Fora in 1933, Carvalho typified the new breed of civil servants
who studied public administration. In fact, he wrote two books on it.
Valadares switched him to Uberaba three years later when local factions in that Triângulo hub city failed to agree on a candidate for
mayor. The fall of Antonio Carlos probably was a factor, but Carvalho's
reputation as a *realizador* (doer) reflected well on Valadares, who retained him. In 1942, Carvalho left the public service for a career in
business, banking, and teaching back in Juiz de Fora.[23]

Montes Claros was for years divided into two armed camps. One,
the "Upper Party" in the town's higher plaza, was led by the Alves
brothers, Honorato (1868–1948) and João José (1876–1935). Theirs
was the old Conservative faction called the "cockroaches," inherited
by the brothers from a physician whose practice in North Minas and
Bahia the Alveses also continued. The other, the so-called "Lower
Party" (for another plaza), was under Camilo Filinto Prates (1859–
1940), a normal-school teacher. His group traced back to the old Liberal clique known as the "cowbirds." Each faction had a marching
band, its own newspaper, its hired thugs and allies in neighboring localities. Children whose families were beholden to one party dared not
play with the sons of fathers in the other. Inevitably, the two camps
in their Republican colors received new nicknames: the "bald ones"
and the "busybodies." In 1915, the early years of nonviolent competition gave way to open warfare. Montes Claros, a railhead town and
regional cattle mart, grew and prospered despite the ping of Winches-
ters and the crash of dynamite bombs.

The Alveses and Camilo spanned two worlds, that of respectable
elite society and that of crude backlands politics, all of which made
their careers a noteworthy example of how the system worked in the
remoter Minas zones. Born in Diamantina, the Alves brothers attended
fashionable secondary schools in Ouro Preto and Caraça before taking
medical degrees in Rio. Honorato's marriage to the daughter of Senator Virgílio de Melo Franco linked him to the circle of Law School
founders in Ouro Preto and to clans in the West and North. Afrânio

de Melo Franco was his brother-in-law and young Virgílio was a
nephew on his wife's side. At Caraça, João José was a classmate of
Bernardes, Melo Viana, and Raul Soares, all of whom became governors. Camilo was yet another Northerner (from Grão Mogol), also
schooled in Ouro Preto. Like many men in the first generation, he
chose not to take a higher degree and moved to Montes Claros, where
he taught physics and mathematics. It was there he married Amélia,
sister of Antonio Gonçalves Chaves (1840–1911), who was the Liberal
Party chief of the North and would soon himself become a Law School
founder. Camilo served the Liberals as a provincial deputy, and in
1891 Alvim, a former Liberal, appointed him the first Republican
mayor of Montes Claros just as Honorato Alves arrived from Rio to
practice medicine.

Alvim's fall from power saw the local situation shift to Honorato's
group, the ex-Conservatives. Having consolidated his base by 1897,
Honorato held the mayorship until he moved to Belo as a state deputy
and then to Rio, where he was a long-time delegation member, 1906–29.
For years he held court in Rio's summer colony, Petrópolis, which became an obligatory stopover for northern visitors who wished him well
and requested favors. Brother João José in the meantime took over the
clinic and looked after Montes Claros politics for the family. The
Alveses had been loyal to the PRM since 1902, and enjoyed a large
network of allies throughout the North. Loyalty to the party cost
Honorato and brother-in-law Afrânio their seats in congress in 1929,
and he left active politics. But João José retained the strong local base,
and in 1932 he was a PP founder and committeeman, serving as a
deputy to the Constituent Assembly.

Camilo and Gonçalves Chaves, the ex-Liberals, kept their Montes
Claros base despite Alvim's demise and stayed loyal to him, which
brought them close to João Pinheiro. In 1897, both men voted with the
anti-PRC group at the Ouro Preto Congress. Silviano tried to purge
them both, but in Pinheiro's government (1906–8) they held high
posts—Camilo as Inspector of Education under Carvalho Brito and
Antonio as president of the state senate. Antonio Gonçalves lined up
with the civilistas in 1910, but Camilo, though close to Brito and the
others, was now a federal deputy from the North, which wanted a railroad badly. Discretion, and the fact that Minister of Transport Francisco Sá was related through his mother, led Camilo to support the

PRM. This was the usual pattern: support the governor, but fight the other local faction. Soon with the Alveses it was war, and though Montes Claros for years had two federal deputies, their feud did the town little good when it came to public works and patronage. In 1929, Camilo adhered to Brito's Conservative Concentration movement. It was his group, the Lower Party, that organized those enthusiastic Brito partisans in February 1930. Through the streets they went, into territory belonging to the Upper Party, parading right past João José Alves's house, where the shooting started.

Violence in Montes Claros was not new, but this particular violence almost brought on federal intervention. Within the year Camilo was permanently out of office, the two-party division ended, and the North, seemingly the changeless home of old-time coronéis, began to modernize its politics. Valadares appointed a bright and well-connected young mayor, who installed the town's first water and sewage system, for years delayed by political strife.[24]

## CHAPTER SIX

# State and Nation: Political Dimensions

REPUBLICAN INSTITUTIONS based on a loose, unequal federalism meshed with the socioeconomic realities of Minas Gerais. As a mosaic of different regions, Minas itself was organized as a mini-federal system. It seems clear that working with power disparities among the state's seven regions conditioned the Mineiros' approach to federalism. In sum, they regarded the federation as an extension of their region. By looking at federalism from their perspective, this process is easier to perceive and perhaps more faithful to the actors' view of themselves and what they did.

But while they accepted inequality among the states, Mineiros also tried to build a more integrated nation. This was the counterpart to policies aimed at making their own region more viable. Along with other states, Minas accepted and in fact depended upon the Union while attempting to structure this relationship advantageously. State and nation were always interrelated, but the dynamics changed. In phase one, Mineiros looked more toward their own state than the nation. From 1898 to 1929, they hoped to perfect both governmental units. And in the last phase, they linked their own fate more tightly to the Union by force of circumstances.

There is one central proposition that I think clarifies and informs the Mineiro approach to federalism. Stated succinctly, the state's main asset was not economic power, or fiscal resources, or military strength, but political unity. United, Minas was well positioned to demand economic favors from the federal government in return for offering political support. After examining presidential politics and the national legislature in this chapter, I will deal with the problem of integration in a companion chapter, focusing on military affairs, congresses, and meetings. A final chapter will analyze the fiscal aspects of federalism.

## The Presidential System

In the regionalistic Old Republic, no single state could dominate the federation. For lack of a viable national party system, politics centered on unstable coalitions during presidential election campaigns, which were negotiated among the unequal state parties and factions. Minas, São Paulo, and Rio Grande do Sul dominated; yet the secondary powers of Bahia, Rio de Janeiro, and Pernambuco also played important roles in these temporary coalitions. Each national election was a potential crisis of the system, a situation paralleled in the states during gubernatorial successions.

The system worked when the interests of Minas, the leading political power, and São Paulo, the economic giant, coalesced in the informal alliance known as *café com leite* that functioned from 1898 to 1929. But even in the inward-looking period, Minas was not isolated in national politics as was Rio Grande under the regime of Julio de Castilhos. Minas collaborated actively with São Paulo to secure the nomination of Prudente de Morais (1894–98) and Manuel de Campos Sales (1898–1902), the first civilian presidents. In turn, the Paulistas' search for allies to consolidate the civilian regime after 1894 meant that the Mineiros, once united at home, would inevitably become prominent in national affairs. Since the main outlines of these and other events are well covered in the literature, only the high points need be given here.[1]

The presidential system stabilized in 1900 with the famous "politics of the governors." This pact between Campos Sales and the leading states allowed him to purge dissidents in congress while securing support for his austerity program. Taking the nominating power away from congress had been the first step toward fortifying the executive. In 1897, Campos Sales won the presidential nomination with the support of Minas and Bahia, outmaneuvering the PRF in congress.* Gaining control of the legislative branch was the next step before the execu-

---

* The Federal Republican Party (PRF) was a congressional caucus led by Majority Leader Francisco Glicério of São Paulo. In staying with the PRF, several historicals from Minas refused to accept Campos Sales and soon left politics.

tives' agreement could work. Under Carlos Vaz de Melo, an ally of Silviano's who presided over the Chamber, all deputies-elect were reviewed by a Credentials Committee, which nullified the elections of those the president did not want. Having purged the congress with Silviano's help, Campos Sales winked when the Mineiro governor "rounded up the herd" in his own assembly.[2]

Coalition politics suited the Mineiros, who collaborated with other parties, states, and groups, but would not take orders from them. In fact, this strategy predated the Campos Sales–Silviano pact. Mineiros associated with the PRF in 1893 to support Prudente, but never carried this alliance to the point where their state-based Constitutional Party (PRC) was absorbed into the national organization.[3] With their strategy of staying united, the main factions in the PRC were reluctant to take sides when the national party split in 1897. Once having agreed to support Campos Sales and Silviano, however, they closed ranks in the new PRM. Their uneasy association with Pinheiro Machado, the gaúcho kingmaker, is a case in point.

As vice-president of the senate, Pinheiro orchestrated the so-called bloco in 1904, a loose coalition of state bosses that in 1910 he replaced with a congressional caucus party like the defunct PRF but under his control. Active collaboration with Pinheiro began when Afonso Pena, the Mineiro compromise candidate, won the presidential nomination in 1904. But Pena refused to accept Pinheiro's tutelage: he and Carlos Peixoto, the legislative leader, moved quickly to offset Pinheiro's influence in the Chamber.[4] In the next succession, Pinheiro recouped by forming an alliance with Bias Fortes to block David Campista, Pena's chosen successor after João Pinheiro's death, whom Bias considered a dangerous reformer. Pinheiro swung the nomination to General Hermes; the vanquished Pena forces joined the civilistas, setting up the first contested election of the Republic.

The 1909 succession crisis fortified Pinheiro's influence in congress over the PRM bosses, but for all his power this political ringmaster could not control the Minas state machine. The Mineiros closed ranks again and in 1913 collaborated with São Paulo to block Pinheiro's bid to control the nomination, thus initiating his swift decline. The upshot was that Wenceslau Brás, not Pinheiro's man, moved into the Catete Palace in 1914, and Minas controlled the presidency for the next five years.

Minas continued with coalition tactics in the postwar period, although the growth of executive authority under Governors Bernardes and Raul Soares (1918–24) and, on the federal level, under President Bernardes (1922–26), altered the play of power. President Epitácio Pessoa, from a weak northeastern state, relied heavily on the Mineiros to pass his legislative program. In fact, Pessoa's budget is an interesting mixture of drought-relief projects for the North, balanced with a new valorization plan for São Paulo, and railroads for Minas and Rio Grande. Bernardes carefully nurtured this collaboration to secure the nomination.

The presidencies of Bernardes and Washington Luís were marked by revolts, dissent in the cities, and a crisis of authority which they met by strengthening executive power. The Brazilian federal system was in trouble, but it bears repeating that from the Minas perspective, there was little desire to replace it with a different system. Upon the death of Raul Soares, the superbosses regained some power; Bernardes could no longer dictate state politics on the basis of one-man rule. This restored the illusion of normalcy. Minas fully expected to continue the Paulista alliance while accommodating the rise of Rio Grande.

The 1909 succession excepted, Minas and São Paulo usually worked out a basis for agreement well in advance of the official nominating conventions. But in 1929 the two state machines diverged as Washington Luís imposed his successor (Governor Júlio Prestes), and punished the PRM. Unable to unite behind a gubernatorial candidate at home, the party split and declined in congress. All of the big three lost power to the central government after the 1930 Revolution. Hoping to restore the old state system, São Paulo tried to revive the Minas alliance through Artur Bernardes, who headed the opposition PRM. Governor Maciel, as mentioned, stood with Vargas during the São Paulo war in 1932 but had to accept client status.

Almost all the Mineiro political factions anticipated returning to the old state party system at the 1933 Constituent Assembly. This they did obtain with São Paulo and the other state groups, only to have real power elude them as Vargas became constitutional president in his own right. Meanwhile, the Vargas-Valadares team molded a new axis of executive power into the Estado Novo.

A united Minas Gerais gave presidents the legitimacy and support they needed to make the federal system work. No president except for the ill-fated Washington Luís attempted to rule the nation without Minas. In turn, Minas moved in close to incumbent presidents, whose role in the succession was critical, often decisive. As a national institution, the presidency symbolized unity of purpose. The chief executive also managed payments on the foreign debt and saw to Brazil's credit rating abroad, matters of great importance to Minas and São Paulo. Thus the presidency transcended purely regional aims. Minas Gerais, as a pillar of the system, expected to benefit from cooperating.

Federal intervention in the weaker states upheld the principle of authority, which Minas supported. Until the post-1918 period, however, presidents held the line against constitutional revisions. This was ideological bedrock to Mineiro politicians, although they considered the 1891 constitution an imperfect instrument. Revisionism, to them, was a mask for dissidents—monarchists, parliamentary purists, and state factions unwilling to accept presidential authority. Having been muted by the politics of the governors after 1900, the constitutional issue revived again, but this time prominent Mineiros pressed vigorously for reform.

To Francisco Campos, the main problem of Brazilian federalism was restraining "the excesses of democracy and regionalism," and he called for the strengthening of central authority in an important address to fellow law students in 1913.[5] Revisionism was still a radical concept in Minas, but it soon became clear that men in the Bernardes camp were prepared to use constitutional reform as a weapon to upgrade central authority. Campos and Bernardes used it in their attempt to break the power of local governments in 1919, discussed in Chapter 4. They collaborated again in 1925–26 to push through reforms in the federal constitution, including the power to intervene in states that could not manage their finances, and to supervise the states' foreign debts. Bernardes also rationalized the budget-making process in congress, and brought the government into social welfare with federal pension plans.[*]

These institutional changes presaged the decline of Minas and the

----

[*] Bernardes campaigned on an antirevisionist platform. But he was preoccupied with foreign credit, especially with payments on the consolidated funding loan. According to Marly Ribeiro, he had to achieve political stability to reassure foreign bankers. The constitutional reforms were one means, repression another. To be sure, Bernardes also feared American intervention in the Amazon region, and was a centralizer by conviction. To this extent the credit problem was a convenient pretext for upgrading presidential power.

state system, even before the 1929–30 crisis. But as long as Minas remained united and strong in congress, the shift toward presidential power was not considered unacceptable, especially with a Mineiro in the presidency. This focuses attention upon the congress, where Minas was well entrenched.

## The Federal Congress

As the most populous Brazilian state, Minas Gerais had the nation's largest electorate and the most congressional seats—37, to São Paulo's and Bahia's 22, Pernambuco's 17, and Rio Grande's 16. During the inward-looking phase, Minas did not or could not mobilize its electoral potential for full effect in the national system. São Paulo, with its smaller population, had almost the same number of votes in 1894. Starting with the 1902 presidential election, however, Mineiros usually returned at least 20 percent of all votes cast in national elections. Almost three times as many voters turned out to elect Rodrigues Alves as had filed to the polls for Campos Sales in 1898 (for the presidential vote, consult Table 4.2, p. 138). "With tallies like these," the *Correio da Manhã* commented, "Minas will be assured of preponderant power over all other states."[6] This electoral strength, coupled with the large and disciplined bancada—nicknamed "the flock of sheep"—was the instrument of Mineiro power.

After the 1920 census, it was clear that booming São Paulo would soon overtake Minas in population. The Paulistas called for reapportionment, while charging that Minas inflated its own population count for political ends. It is true that Minas claimed to have 7,400,000 people by the 1930 election. This was 700,000 above the 1940 census count! Most or all states overestimated their populations in 1930 because of the inflated 1920 census, but it was widely believed that Minas overestimated more than most. Measures short of reapportionment were, however, available to fortify the strong and undercut the weak.

Enfeebled by internal strife, Bahia could not prevent the erosion of its electoral base between 1898—when 103,000 ballots were cast—and the 1910 elections—when only 61,000 of their votes were officially recorded. Bahia's ebbing power was reflected in the congress: not only were Bahiano ballots voided in large numbers, but their men lost leadership posts and the key committee chairmanships. Rio Grande do Sul, led nationally by Pinheiro Machado, replaced Bahia as the third major power.[7] In 1929, it was the turn of Minas to be squeezed as São Paulo moved to dominate the system.

Divided, the PRM could not prevent the loss of 14 seats to the pro-Paulista opposition under Carvalho Brito, cutting the machine's bloc to 23. This was reapportionment, Paulista style. They compounded the disaster by taking away committee chairmanships and by imposing federal economic sanctions. Having been treated like a small state, the Mineiros expected to recoup by accommodating as they always had, but Paulista intransigence turned them, reluctantly, to revolution. Concurrently, São Paulo developed a larger electorate. In 1933, Minas registered 311,374 voters to São Paulo's 299,074; but in the final vote for Constituent Assembly delegates the Paulistas pulled ahead by some 10,000 votes and the gap has widened ever since.[8] São Paulo gained five congressional seats; with minor changes, the other state delegations stayed the same, and Minas, with 37 deputies, was still the largest.

Factionalism in Minas allowed Vargas to manipulate state politics, including the appointment of Benedito Valadares in late 1933. In the meantime, Getúlio created his own congressional voting bloc of 40 "class" (professional) deputies, larger than any state delegation, and highly vulnerable to presidential pressure.[9] This was reapportionment, Vargas style. Under Euvaldo Lodi, a Mineiro industrialist, this bloc backed Vargas in the Assembly and assured his election to the presidency. Lodi was elected vice-president of the Chamber in 1934 and became a longtime Vargas crony and interest group leader. These maneuvers undercut Antonio Carlos de Andrada, who, as president of the Chamber, hoped to revive the traditional legislative dominance of Minas. Lodi's corporatist style was perhaps more modern and effective with economic groups than Andrada's. In phase three, power flowed through the client relationship with Vargas, and derived much less from the congressional delegation or the vote.

Coalition politics in the congress suited the Mineiros, with their skills at bargaining and negotiating. Unlike the Gaúchos under Pinheiro Machado, they did not seek long-term satellites. Nor did they have regular clients like the Paulistas, who controlled the senate vice-presidency after Pinheiro's death in 1915 and several politicians. The sheer weight of the Minas delegation explains their relative indifference to making permanent allies or satellites. Starting in 1898, Mineiros moved in very close to the presidency when they did not actually hold it. Even in the

1890's, they never adopted Rio Grande's strategy of isolation as the best guarantee of state autonomy in periods when the gaúcho machine had little influence over the president.[10] Their role at the center of power enabled them to confer favors and to offer security to lesser politicians. The smaller states came to Minas for favors and protection; in turn, the Mineiros called in their political debts at election time.

Maximum involvement at the center drew Minas into the political management of dependent states on the periphery, usually on Mineiro terms. This stewardship included seeing to the election of friendly deputies, as in 1900 when Epitácio Pessoa, who led the minority faction in Paraíba, asked Silviano's aid to prevent the majority from winning control of his state delegation. The "politics of the governors" was supposed to fortify the dominant state groups, but in this case Campos Sales readily agreed to bend the rules.[11] Minas was often asked to referee disputed gubernatorial elections, which helped the PRM to choose friendly faces among the supplicants. Having successfuly backed one faction in Espírito Santo against the other championed by São Paulo in 1920, Minas was then asked to support the governor's candidates in congress and to help him get railroad credits. In return, Espírito Santo supported Bernardes' maneuvers for the presidential nomination.[12]

Stewardship failed to secure stability in the case of Amazonas, Brazil's largest state, which was in fiscal and administrative chaos after the rubber boom collapsed in 1913. Each of the governors-elect, with their camps in the state legislature, asked Governor Bernardes to intercede with President Epitácio Pessoa in 1920. Minas backed the "winner," Rego Monteiro, who after taking office asked Bernardes to help him obtain a federal loan, to regain the Acre Territory for revenue purposes, and to assure that all of his congressional candidates were recognized by the Credentials Committee.[13] Despite these good offices, chaotic Amazonas turned against Bernardes in the 1922 election. And when the governor at Manaus was kidnapped by local revolutionaries in July 1924, Bernardes intervened. The Chief of Police from Minas took charge on presidential orders. The next elected governor, Efigênio de Sales, was a transplanted Mineiro with good political connections. He infuriated Bernardes by granting a large concession to Standard Oil of New Jersey.[14] Amazonas was an extreme case, but also a highly visible situation where the Mineiro brand of federalism based on tutelage and congressional management did not work.

Family bonds were relatively unimportant in coalition politics, as shown by the low rating of Minas on the tri-state variable "clan ties" discussed in Chapter 5. There were some notable exceptions. Although Francisco Sá began his political career in northern Minas, he married into the Accioli clan and represented Ceará for many years in congress. Twice Minister of Transport, Sá also served on the Senate Finance Committee, specializing in the public works budget. He was a friendly advocate for Minas and helped his native state obtain railroad credits and equipment. Alfredo Sá, his cousin, was the police chief who ran Amazonas for Bernardes, and was later lieutenant governor of Minas.

Antonio Prado Lopes Pereira, an engineer from the state of Pará, rose in Mineiro politics to become president of the state legislature, federal deputy for Minas, and professor at the state Engineering School. For many years he was the PRM's contact man with the Pará delegation, because of his parentesco there. After moving to Rio he joined the Pará delegation and chaired the Chamber's Public Works Committee when Bernardes was president.

Clan ties across the border regions of Bahia and Goiás were important at the zonal level, but relatively unimportant in interstate politics. Family connections in Espírito Santo reinforced the nearest thing to a satellite relationship that Minas had. João Luís Alves was federal senator there for a decade, while Heitor de Souza led the Capixaba delegation for two terms in the early 1920's. Yet this "special relationship" with its weak coastal neighbor did not discourage other leaders from trying to muscle in. Alves was a close associate, if not a client of Pinheiro Machado, whom the agile Mineiro intellectual much admired.

Pinheiro's decline was sealed at the so-called Pact of Ouro Fino, the Sul de Minas town where representatives of the PRM and the PRP agreed to support a common presidential candidate in 1913. Although Ouro Fino was the ancestral home for many socially prominent Mineiros and Paulistas, it happened to be the governor's home town and political base, and was not chosen for symbolic value. A competitive spirit and regionalism attenuated the pull of family ties over this frontier. Much more significant was the cultural and political grip of Rio de Janeiro on the thoughts and actions of Mineiros.

The making of presidents, governors, and congressmen was an important attribute of Mineiro power. Little wonder that the Mineiro saw themselves as the balance wheel, straddling the solid center with São

Paulo, between what one writer called "the extreme combativeness of Brazilians to the north and to the extreme south. But for the equilibrating role of Minas, regional politics would be self-destructive." The smaller states had no right or claim to national leadership, another journalist observed. "For example, it would be ridiculous for Sergipe to have any decisive political influence, with its delegation of only four members, of whom at least two are nothing more than tools of local factions." No, the role of this and other small delegations "is to vote intransigently with the president, following the majority docilely so it won't lose official favors . . . such as the modest resources to pay salaries of their state functionaries ten months in arrears, or a minor dam or two, while singing the president's praises as a great statesman."[15] The weaker states cried domination; Mineiros saw their role as central, but not predominant.

As can be seen in Table 6.1, the weight of Minas in the federation correlated roughly with the incidence of tenure in the three most important and politically sensitive ministries: Finance, Justice, and Public Works. It did not correlate exactly because the ministers served the president and were not, therefore, direct agents of their state. Note, however, that the three leaders and the three secondary powers held these key ministries 70 percent of the time in the Old Republic. During the first four presidencies, Minas and Pernambuco ranked closely in the distribution of posts: 16 and 13 percent, respectively. São Paulo controlled the Finance Ministry more than half of the time. From 1898 to November 1929—when the PRM split—Minas dominated; Pernambuco was displaced by Rio Grande; but São Paulo's ranking was illusory. If São Paulo rarely held the Ministry of Finance in phase two, this means little because for the most part Minas was the faithful executor of its economic policies.[16] In phase three, no Mineiro held Finance or Public Works, but Mineiros served as Justice Minister during crisis periods—before the 1930 Revolution, during the Paulista revolt, and on the eve of the 1937 coup—indicating their role in legitimizing presidential acts.

The priority given to legislative service shows up clearly in the many congressional posts Mineiros held.* Recall that Minas ranked highest on the tri-state variable for legislative activity, discussed in the last

* No data were collected on the senate, which in the Old Republic played a secondary role.

TABLE 6.1

*Ministerial Tenure by Phases, 1889–1930*

| State | Finance | | Justice (11 yrs) | | Public Works | | Total ministerial years[a] | |
|---|---|---|---|---|---|---|---|---|
| | Years | Percent | Years | Percent | Years | Percent | Years | Percent |
| I. Nov. 15, 1889, to Nov. 15, 1898: 9 years[b] (inward phase) | | | | | | | | |
| Minas Gerais | 0 | 0% | 2.77 | 25% | 2.01 | 22% | 4.78 | 16% |
| São Paulo | 4.76 | 53 | 1.21 | 11 | 1.35 | 15 | 7.32 | 25 |
| Rio Grande | .24 | 3 | .93 | 8 | .85 | 9 | 2.02 | 7 |
| Pernambuco | .38 | 4 | 2.64 | 24 | .83 | 9 | 3.85 | 13 |
| Bahia | 1.18 | 13 | .50 | 5 | 0 | 0 | 1.68 | 6 |
| Rio de Janeiro | 0 | 0 | .35 | 3 | 1.28 | 14 | 1.63 | 6 |
| TOTAL | | | | | | | | 73% |
| II. Nov. 15, 1898, to Oct. 3, 1930: 31.83 years (apogee) | | | | | | | | |
| Minas Gerais | 9.71 | 31% | 10.80[c] | 34% | 6.02[d] | 19% | 26.53 | 28% |
| São Paulo | 3 | 9 | 1.26 | 4 | 3.32 | 10 | 7.58 | 8 |
| Rio Grande | 5.82 | 18 | 6.72 | 21 | 2.78 | 9 | 15.32 | 16 |
| Pernambuco | 1 | 3 | 1.41 | 4 | 0 | 0 | 2.41 | 3 |
| Bahia | 0 | 0 | 4.00 | 13 | 4.99 | 16 | 8.99 | 9 |
| Rio de Janeiro | 2.92 | 9 | 0 | 0 | 2.10 | 7 | 5.02 | 5 |
| TOTAL | | | | | | | | 69% |

SOURCE: Based on Max Fleiuss, *História administrativa do Brasil* (Rio, 1922), and Dunshee de Abranches, *Governos e congressos da republica dos Estados Unidos do Brazil, 1889 a 1917* (São Paulo, 1918). For the 1930–37 period, consult Alzira Vargas do Amaral Peixoto, *Getúlio Vargas, meu pai* (Rio, 1960).

NOTE: After the 1930 Revolution, Education and Health (a new ministry) was reserved for Minas, which, with the exception of a few days at Justice, did not hold any of the three key cabinet posts.

[a] Total ministerial years for the first period is 29 years, and for the second period is 95.49 years.

[b] The period covered for the Ministry of Justice is 11 years, which includes two years in the Deodoro government when Justice and Interior were separate; starting with Floriano, they became one ministry.

[c] Includes the year after Oct. 1, 1929, when the Justice Minister abandoned the PRM for Washington Luís.

[d] Includes 5.4 years of service by Francisco Sá, a Mineiro ally.

chapter. Except for Deodoro's brief presidency, however, Mineiros were conspicuously absent from the key positions of majority leader and president of the Chamber until phase two. More often than not, Minas held one or both these posts until 1927. And in 1933–37 Antonio Carlos and others attempted to revive this power base, quixotically as it happened. A few words about the leadership are in order, before discussing the committees where Minas was entrenched.

Majority leader Francisco Glicério managed the voting in congress from 1892 to 1897, and attempted to control alliances through his caucus party, the PRF. Rio Grande was isolated and at war. The Northeast's importance—especially Bahia—was reflected in the president of congress: following a brief tenure by Minas under Deodoro, the post was held by São Paulo and then by Ceará, Pernambuco, and Bahia. Divided, the Minas delegation could not pull its weight. The accession of Mineiros to the posts of majority leader and president of the Chamber in 1899 began the politics of the governors. The Fourth Legislature (1900–1903) was dominated by Minas, in concert with São Paulo and Bahia, which shared control of the majority leadership. Then Bahian power declined and Pinheiro Machado emerged as the main contender with Minas for control of congress. Except for a three-year hiatus under President Afonso Pena, Pinheiro controlled the majority leaders for 11 years (1904–14) while Minas dominated the presidency of the Chamber. His fall delivered congress lock, stock, and barrel to the PRM. Starting with the delicate maneuvers of Bernardes to win the presidential nomination, however, Minas had to share power in congress with the other two of the big three. Under Washington Luís, for the first time in 20 years a Mineiro did not hold the majority leadership, the presidency, or both. In sum, from the end of the Third Legislature in 1899 through the Twelfth (1924–26), Minas was first in congress.

Little need be said about the brief constitutional period under Vargas. Antonio Carlos de Andrada presided over the Assembly with dignity and great parliamentary skill gained in three decades of experience in the old congress. And yet, well before Andrada was forced out—in 1936 as delegation leader and in 1937 as Assembly president—real power had slipped away with the Valadares appointment and the PP's demoralization. Vargas named a boulevard after him in downtown Rio.

When completed in 1936, the magnificent new congress hall in Rio was called Tiradentes Palace, and most of the committee rooms were named after prominent Mineiros from the Old Republic: Antonio Carlos, Carlos Peixoto, Bueno Brandão, Sabino Barroso, and Afrânio de Melo Franco were all memorialized. This evoked the days when at least one deputy from Minas was always to be found on the key committees—Finance, Justice, Credentials, and Public Works.[17] Control of these four committee chairmanships often rested in Mineiro hands. Thus the committees were a major arena of state power, whether exercised directly or with the help of allies and clients. A glance at Table 6.2 confirms by now familiar trends.

Judging from committee chairmanships, the isolation of Minas was

TABLE 6.2

Mineiro Chairmen of Key Committees, Chamber of Deputies

| Year | Public Works | Finance[a] | Credentials | Justice |
|------|-------------|---------|-------------|---------|
| 1891 | Rio Grande | São Paulo | Bahia | Bahia |
| 1892 | Minas | São Paulo | Bahia | São Paulo |
| 1893 | Minas | São Paulo | Bahia | Rio de Janeiro |
| 1894 | Pernambuco | Ceará | Bahia | Rio de Janeiro |
| 1895 | Pernambuco | Ceará | Ceará | Minas |
| 1896 | Pernambuco | Ceará | Maranhão | Minas |
| 1897 | Pernambuco | Minas | Bahia | Minas |
| 1898 | Minas | Minas | Bahia | Bahia |
| 1899 | Pernambuco | São Paulo | Minas | Bahia |
| 1900 | Minas | São Paulo | Bahia | Bahia |
| 1901 | Minas | Bahia | Minas | Bahia |
| 1902 | Minas | Bahia | Paraíba | Bahia |
| 1903 | Minas | São Paulo | Paraíba | Bahia |
| 1904 | Minas | São Paulo | Maranhão | Bahia |
| 1905 | Minas | São Paulo | Maranhão | Bahia |
| 1906 | Ceará[b] | Minas | Paraná | Minas |
| 1907 | Ceará | Minas | Paraná | Minas |
| 1908 | Minas (?) | Minas | Paraná | Ceará |
| 1909 | Rio Grande | Minas | Pernambuco | Ceará |
| 1910 | Rio Grande | Minas | Maranhão[c] | Ceará |
| 1911 | Minas | Minas | Maranhão | Ceará |
| 1912 | Minas | Minas | Minas | Maranhão[c] |
| 1913 | Minas | Minas | Minas | Maranhão |
| 1914 | Minas | Rio Grande | Minas | Maranhão |
| 1915 | Minas | Minas | Minas | Maranhão |
| 1916 | Minas | Minas | Minas | Maranhão |
| 1917 | Minas | Minas | Minas | Maranhão |
| 1918 | Minas | São Paulo | Minas | Maranhão |
| 1919 | Minas | São Paulo | Minas | Maranhão |
| 1920 | Minas | Minas | Minas | Maranhão |
| 1921 | Minas | Pernambuco | Pernambuco | Maranhão |
| 1922 | Minas | Minas | Pernambuco | Maranhão |
| 1923 | Pará[d] | Minas | Minas | Minas |
| 1924 | Pará | Minas | Minas | Minas |
| 1925 | Pará | Minas | Minas | Minas |
| 1926 | Pará | Minas | Minas | Minas |
| 1927 | Rio Grande | São Paulo | Minas | Minas |
| 1928 | Rio Grande | São Paulo | Minas | Minas |
| 1929 | Rio Grande | São Paulo | Minas | Minas |
| 1930 | Pernambuco | São Paulo | São Paulo | Bahia |

source: Culled from Brazil, *Annaes*, and Brazil, *Diário oficial*.
note: No survey of the 1933–37 legislature was made.
a Called the Budget Committee until 1905.
b Sergio Saboia of Ceará, probably allied to Minas.
c Cunha Machado of Maranhão, allied to Minas.
d Antonio do Prado Lopes Pereira of Pará, former president of the Minas Gerais Chamber of Deputies, 1907–11, allied to Minas.

relatively much less than that of Rio Grande before 1899. Mineiros were most active on Public Works and the Justice Committee, this latter post coinciding with the return to civilian rule under Prudente de Morais. The importance of railroad construction projects in Minas was underscored also by the tenure of Antonio Olinto dos Santos Pires in the Public Works Ministry during 1895–96. The deal Campos Sales made is reflected nicely in the chairmanships for 1898: two each went to Minas and Bahia for supporting him.

Bahia held several chairmanships through 1905, when Pinheiro Machado elbowed that divided state aside. However, Rio Grande's rise as the third power in the federation does not show up directly in the list of chairmen, except for Public Works in 1909–10, when patronage was doubtless a potent weapon for use against the civilistas. São Paulo ran the Finance Committee during Campos Sales's austerity program and under Washington Luís; otherwise, Mineiros usually held this post. Especially noteworthy was the fact that Minas and its allies controlled Public Works for 25 of the 31 years in what I have called phase two. Note that Washington Luís purged all the Mineiros in 1930, but he elevated sitting members to the chairmanships, indicating he never intended to reform congress or the committee structure. And while the president moved to dominate, he retained a dissident Mineiro as Minister of Justice to legitimize his acts.

Far from being a cipher, submissive to an all-powerful executive as is often thought, congress had power because it represented the interests of strong state machines.[18] For one thing, it could deny a president's program or simply render it unworkable by inaction and delay. For another, congress was an important forum in which decisions over allocation—often arrived at in private—were debated, certified, and legitimized in public. For lack of a detailed analysis of this institution, one can only hint at the structures and personalities involved, while hitting the highlights of Mineiro activity.

Each year, what has been called "the political budget" was reviewed in the Finance Committee, where deputies from Minas were entrenched. To put it gently, they assured that the interests of Minas would not be overlooked. Once sent to the senate and returned, the president's budget was customarily voted in the final hours of each legislative session, when riders by the score were tacked on for friends and special interests. Power of the purse was a right even the managed congresses after 1900 never alienated to the executive: they shared it. Thus, executive credits outside the budget were regularly approved. One of Bernardes' principal reforms in 1926 was to gain control of this chaotic budgeting. As long as Minas remained strong in congress, this reform was not incompatible with state interests. All in all, control over the budgetary process was a principal instrument of clientelistic politics, as well as a check on presidential power. Keeping the amendments within tolerable limits—specifically, balancing what the president and the treasury could accept with what the states and interests wanted— was the job of the committee chairman. Not surprisingly, Minas held this chairmanship 17 years, and São Paulo ten years during phase two.

*Federal Favors and Support*

Patronage was an important federal resource, and Mineiro placemen were found throughout the government. Typical was this telegram from Governor Olegário Maciel to Vargas in 1930: "José Braz, the son of Dr. Wenceslau, wants a federal post and we are sympathetic." Dr. Júlio Bueno Brandão Filho wanted to be an auditor on the Tribunal das Contas, he wrote in similar vein. The pursuit of government posts was doubtless more successful after phase one. However blatant, the search came to be less stridently proclaimed than it was, for example, in 1891 when Deputy Américo Lobo contrasted São Paulo with its gathering of the spoils to Minas, which "hasn't a single native son in the diplomatic corps or on the Supreme Court."[19] (Lobo was nominated to the Court in 1894.) Five of the 12 Mineiros who served were appointed between 1919 and 1926, during the Bernardes period. These justiceships, to be sure, were filled by distinguished men.

Most of Minas lay within a day's train ride of Rio de Janeiro, giving Mineiros easy access to the capital, where many settled permanently. Paying a call on one's congressman was customary for visitors from the interior. In Rio, Mineiros founded banks, businesses, notary offices, and contracting firms—tapping into the flow of federal funds. A Mineiro usually headed the federal lottery, and, if one report is true, most of the profits were distributed to schools and charities in Minas. (Mineiro lotteries, until 1913 banned in the state constitution, were tolerated on grounds the National Lottery Company was draining too much money out of state!) The fact that Minas had the largest post and telegraph network in Brazil produced many jobs.[20] Juscelino Kubitschek, a future president, and his crony from Diamantina, José Maria de Alkmim, a future vice-president, got their start as telegraph operators and rose to high positions under Valadares.

Securing federally funded projects was another form of patronage. Consider José Bonifacio de Andrada, who was close to Bias Fortes (the patronage king of Barbacena) and who was also the brother of Antonio Carlos. Thanks to him, Barbacena received a farmer's apprentice program, a dairy-farming school, a military secondary school, and an agricultural research station. To draw a U.S. parallel, José Bonifacio's Barbacena was the functional equivalent of Congressman Mendel Rivers' Charleston, with its ring of military plants and bases.

Railroad credits and equipment led the list of economic favors required from the federal Union. A principal objective of state policy was to create a viable internal market at home and to link the major production centers more efficiently to port cities. When private railroad construction virtually ceased in 1898, Minas asked the Union to buy out deficit lines, assume some of the burden of subsidies and interest payments, and construct new lines. To be sure, the nation was moving anyway to "recapture" some lines to avoid making interest payments in gold. And there was foreign pressure to consider. German creditors of the financially hard-pressed Oeste de Minas Line protested energetically to the Brazilian Foreign Office when Minas canceled that company's 1873 contract, with its interest guarantee. The state's credit rating would be threatened unless it reconsidered, the Germans said in a press campaign and in representations by their legation in Rio. Two years later the crisis eased when the Union purchased German equity for 1,117 contos (about $268,000) while also buying out British shareholders, the majority.[21] And so this deficitary line serving the cattle ranches of western Minas came under federal ownership and operation. Concurrently, the Central do Brasil resumed construction north from Belo Horizonte—all this despite austerity and depression.[22]

The high point came after World War I: almost 40 percent of all federal railroad construction in the 1920's occurred in Minas. By contrast, São Paulo continued to rely on still-profitable private lines. The big three also rented railroads from the Union, starting in 1919. Minas assumed operating responsibility for the Rêde Sul Mineira in 1920 after the private concessionaire could not meet operating costs, in part because the state would not grant rate increases.[23] Under Governor Bernardes, the state began operating three railroads and initiated large construction and equipment purchases on its own account.

Another objective, obtaining lower freight rates on exports, became politically feasible when Minas emerged from its inward-looking phase. Governor Silviano Brandão agreed to support Campos Sales's drastic austerity program, and in return asked for tariff protection and new, uniform freight rates on cereals. Within two years, corn, feijão (beans), even rice, from Minas began to displace foreign imports in the Rio market. This was a brilliant use of the state's bargaining power.[24] On the negative side, however, it began a trend to politicize freight rates, which reduced railroad operating revenues to the point of decapitalization. This constituted a hidden subsidy for producers, with the nation as a whole picking up the large railroad deficits on government lines. The Central do Brasil was particularly vulnerable to such pressures. Mineiro politicians often crossed swords with Irineu Machado, the Carioca lawyer-politician who mobilized the railroad worker vote out of the Federal District. This is an interesting example of political conflict among different interests. The one wanted the Central do Brasil to expand its system northward while lowering freight rates on export crops; the other sought higher salaries and the nation's first federal pension plan.[25]

Relations with the British-owned Leopoldina Railway were often strained. In 1898, the Leopoldina was consolidated by foreign creditors to serve in the Mata and Rio de Janeiro state with a unified system, making it the largest British railroad in Brazil. Renegotiating rates with Minas, in line with changing capital, exchange, and profit criteria, was often a delicate matter for the British, who had also to reach agreement with Rio de Janeiro state and the Union. For years, Minas resisted the company's request to unify freight rates while supporting the Mata planters, who wanted lower rates. The company's roller-coaster ride from profits to deficit and back is extensively reported in the British diplomatic records. In 1921, Governor Bernardes' refusal to grant rate increases was said to have brought the Leopoldina to the point of "certain collapse." If, as the line desired, it had only the federal authorities to deal with, "it is likely that the freight rate situation would have been solved long ago in favor of the company, for even shippers are willing to pay higher rates if they can get regular, efficient service." On the other hand, as the British Ambassador observed, "it is only fair to add, from the Brazilian point of view, that the present management are said to be suffering the sins of their predecessors, who in years of prosperity did little to win the favour of their public or to assist in the development of the country."[26] In the Leopoldina case, therefore, state power was used to extract resources even when the federal government would have settled for lesser terms.

In the distribution of power, Mineiro resources were greater than any other state outside the big three. Clearly, however, Minas was relatively less impressive than the other two in its economic strength and potential and, as will be shown in the next chapters, in its military strength and ability to generate state revenues. And because of this *relative* weakness, most notably economic, it follows logically that Minas was more dependent on the Union than the other two leaders. Put another way, Minas had no choice but to play a central role in national affairs.

This was a deliberate shift in policy. In the 1890's, the state attempted to finance its own development without recourse to large transfers from the Union. Initially, Mineiros tried to do what the Paulistas did throughout the Old Republic. Large sums were expended on immigration, railroad loans and subsidies, and the new state capital at Belo Horizonte (see Chapter 8). Fueled with domestic loans and expanding coffee revenues, these expansionary budgets in the 1890's mirrored the buoyancy, optimism, and confidence with which Mineiros faced their future as a "sovereign" state in the federated Republic.

Starting in 1897, the coffee depression hit Minas hard, ushering in nearly 15 years of deficits and austerity budgets. Pessimism ruled the day; the elite never quite regained its former optimism. As shown, the depression coincided with and, in fact, facilitated and justified the PRM's rise to dominance. When Silviano Brandão told his compatriots that the foreign bankers were making very tough demands and that, consequently, they would have to submit to discipline, he had a ready-made cover for his own desire to be a strong governor and to project Minas onto the national scene. *

Yet Silviano moved with caution, realizing that the maturing inter-

---

* Foreign demands, which led to the debt consolidation and funding loan of 1898, forced Campos Sales to secure congressional support for austerity through the politics of the governors. Assis Barbosa argues this point forcefully in his article. That the crisis also provided opportunities for both Campos Sales and Silviano to consolidate political institutions is also clear. The parallel with Bernardes' constitutional reforms in 1925–26 is also suggestive.

dependence with the Union could degenerate into a dependency relationship. Mineiros had actively sought federal railroad credits before then in the congress, indicating again that the inward-looking phase was relative. With the onset of depression, however, the guidelines shifted: new opportunities and new dangers arose. Unable to pay the salaries of the Força Pública and of state functionaries, Silviano refused a loan from the Bank of Brazil and turned instead to the British at Morro Velho for a £50,000 loan at 6 percent, which was redeemed over the next few years. As taxpayers on their gold exports, the British would not try to extract political advantages. "To owe money to the Bank of Brazil can be nothing but threatening to our autonomy," Silviano said bluntly. "The federal government could use this to restrain Minas politics and crimp our freedom of movement. Minas supports the president, but wants to remain independent and will never put itself under feudal obligations to the government of the Republic."[27] Thus he stated an axiom in all federal systems, which is, to accept money is to face the inevitable consequence: the benefactor will want to call the turns.

As long as Minas was strong in congress, Silviano's brave words were backed by political power, which compensated for but did not solve the structural situation of a relatively weak economy. This congressional strategy worked well, but still the disparity between Minas and the two other leaders grew. Stripped of its congressional base in 1929, Minas faced disaster. It soon moved into client status which the Great Depression reinforced. What this meant is revealed in the Secretary of Finance's comments on his efforts to offset alarming rises in the floating debt with federal credits. Spending "day after day in Rio, neglecting normal duties while seeking these short-term funds by any and all means is a distasteful, demoralizing task," he said in early 1934.[28] Skillful bargaining by Valadares did upgrade the role of Minas, but Vargas's supremacy was never in doubt. After 1930, the Union called the financial turns.

Bargaining in congress was another way the states adjusted their often conflicting interests. A brief look at the beef tariff issue shows how bargaining worked during phase two.

Cattlemen from Minas, Mato Grosso, and Goiás wanted to increase their share of the market for beef cattle in the Federal District, an idea that became increasingly attractive in the 1890's, because of exchange depreciation and improved rail service between Rio and the fattening centers in southern Minas. To placate lower- and middle-class consumers hit by inflation, however, the Rio city authorities controlled prices by a slaughtering monopoly and by importing, or threatening to import, beef cattle from the Plata. The cattlemen claimed with reason that this policy disrupted domestic production and reduced their chances to capture the Rio market. Their efforts to secure tariff protection against foreign imports were fought by a combination of the northern states, Rio politicians speaking for consumers, and Rio Grande do Sul charque producers who wanted free imports of cattle from Uruguay and Argentina. In turn, however, the charque interests could not survive in the domestic market without protection against La Plata charque, while the North and the cities wanted lower prices for this mainstay of the lower-class diet. Why, asked the Mineiro deputies, should Gaúchos continue to enjoy protection, when a promising new industry in central Brazil had to compete with foreigners?

Efforts to impose a tax of 15 milreis per head of cattle imported for consumption failed in 1895. With the Minas delegation divided—as it often was in this period—the Budget Committee threw out the tax on grounds it would weigh heavily on the poor by raising the price of meat, especially in the Federal District. In 1896 it became part of the budget law over violent objections from the Federal District representatives, who presented petitions from the workers. Rio Grande demanded and received exemption from the tariff as the price for going along with the central states led by Minas.[29]

In 1903, during debate on the federal budget bill, the two pastoral states agreed to coordinate their policies, despite the fact that they reached different markets. On the bill's second reading, Rodolfo Paixão from Minas lost his amendment to raise the beef tariff 100 percent, to 30$000 a head. Speaking for the cattle interests of Minas, Goiás, and Mato Grosso, Paixão immediately proposed another amendment, this time to raise charque duties, which passed. The beef tariff carried on the third reading, owing to the Gaúchos, who probably intended to smuggle what they needed from La Plata.[30]

In fact, the two state delegations cooperated to pass a number of protectionist measures that encouraged domestic producers of rice, lard, potatoes, charque, butter, and beef cattle. Rio de Janeiro state voted with them against the North and free-trade spokesmen and some

deputies who spoke for Paulista coffee interests. Afonso Pena, the first
Mineiro president, was initially partial to protectionism: this is one reason why Pinheiro Machado worked to secure his nomination. And in
late 1906, in an apparent bending of Rio Grande's policy of fiscal conservatism, Pinheiro supported David Campista's controversial Exchange
Bank bill, a measure the coffee states wanted badly.[31] Unlike Minas
with its large coffee sector, Rio Grande was both resolute and consistent in demanding stable domestic prices, and the two states competed
for federal railroad credits. On issues affecting cattle, however, the two
governments continued to cooperate. In 1916, for example, in return
for supporting President Wenceslau's sales tax bill, Gaúchos got exemption from this levy for their charque.[32]

Minas usually followed São Paulo's lead in coffee policy, and helped
to convince the nonproducers that coffee was a national resource, not
a regional problem. Yet the café com leite alliance was not based on a
genuine reciprocity of interests, because Minas was the weaker partner
and had to follow São Paulo's lead in economic policy. Mineiros
blamed the whole problem of surplus coffee on Paulista overplanting.
This obscured the basic truth of São Paulo's comparative advantage.
The accelerating drain of Mineiro manpower to Paulista fazendas was
resented, as was the growing disparity between the two regions. As the
gap between them grew, their different objectives in the federal arena
became clearer. Aside from coffee and monetary policy, São Paulo did
not depend upon the federal government (until the 1930's) for economic favors. Minas, by contrast, had a large shopping list. United, the
two states made the state system work; disunited, they opened up political space for others to maneuver, as Vargas proved after 1930. In
addition to keeping them apart, Vargas reinforced Minas's militia as a
counterforce to São Paulo state's troops, which brings up the role of
military power in the states.

## CHAPTER SEVEN

# Toward Integration

INTEGRATION, the search for and movement toward closer ties in the federation, gained momentum after the turbulent 1890's, accelerated by World War I, and was redirected in the Vargas years. Just as the federal system suited Minas, a point worth repeating, so integration there had a distinct regional impact.

On the territorial level, integration occurred with the Union and among the states, but also within the region. From the Inconfidentes on, the program of Mineiro regionalism was to provide an economic base in order to support political autonomy. Belo Horizonte was the unifying central symbol, and (after 1889) separatism was treasonous. Political and economic forces eroded this regional ideal, starting in 1898 but most notably in the 1930's when Minas became a client of Vargas, and even more clearly than before performed a neo-colonial economic role.

Loyalty to Minas Gerais as a "sovereign" entity became less sharply focused and explicit early on as the requirements of interdependence took hold. By 1898, the need to set the terms of allocation within the federation drew Minas forthrightly to the center of national politics. There was less emphasis on the parts, more on how the parts fit together. Loyalties shifted with the play of forces across zone, state, and nation. Far from disappearing, however, these subnational allegiances were essential layers or parts of the Mineiro's identity.

Two kinds of integration took place at once in the social and organizational fabric. One occurred on the horizontal dimension between groups that wanted to upgrade their relationship by creating something new. Interstate congresses and meetings are a good example of this type. The other, vertically structured, was the process of change among unequal but interdependent units. The Força Pública Mineira's changing role exemplifies this kind. By use of these concepts with appropriate case studies, it is easier to understand what changed and how, from the regional perspective.[1]

### Military Federalism

Neither Minas nor the Union achieved a monopoly over the instruments of violence until the 1930's. The growth of military power at both levels was a response to the crisis of internal order, beginning after World War I. From the state perspective, this involved a trade-off between the old advantages of military independence and the new necessity—as the elite saw it—to improve the national defense and strengthen the military bonds of internal cohesion.

This period has been called "the era of armed federalism," because well into the 1930's the big three fielded state military forces.[2] Counterbalanced by state forces, the federal Army did not win strategic superiority or control over the organized use of force until it had defeated São Paulo troops in 1932, co-opted the Força Pública in 1933, and faced down the large Rio Grande forces in October 1937. Until then, the big states used their forces to bolster autonomy of the central power; executives of the weaker states were subject to frequent federal intervention.

Militarily, however, the Mineiro forces were inferior to the Gaúchos, if not in number then in seasoned fighting men, and to the Paulistas, who had twice as many men under arms until the 1930's and who could afford good equipment, including a French training mission. Never larger than 3,000 men until 1922, the Força Pública Mineira was hard pressed to police a state that was roughly twice the size of the other two units. Even in the politically troubled 1920's, Minas had under arms a maximum of 4,000 poorly armed, low-paid men. After the 1930 Revolution, however, this force was expanded to almost 7,000 regulars, rising to nearly 10,000 men, with again as many serving in volunteer battalions, during the Paulista revolt in 1932. On the eve of the 1937 coup, it rose again to nearly 10,000 men, using federal funds, equipment, and officers.[3] See Figure 4.

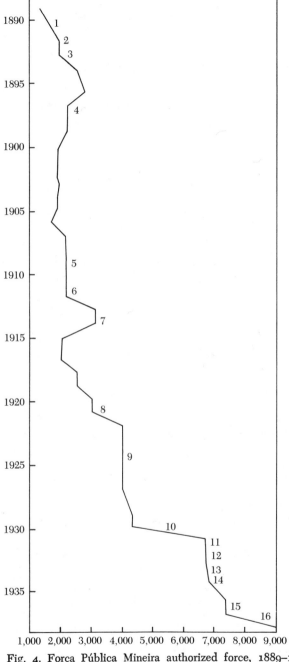

1. July 1890, coup tried
2. Dec. 1891, threat of federal intervention, followed by Campanha Revolt (Jan. 1892); Nov. 1892 coup planned
3. 1893–94 civil war
4. 1897, depression begins
5. 1909, civilista campaign
6. May 28, 1912, incident with the Army
7. 1913–14 force raised 50% to forestall Pinheiro Machado
8. Oct. 1920, Minas becomes a military region; Bernardes presidential campaign begins
9. 1924, Army revolt in São Paulo
10. 1930, October Revolution
11. Aug. 18, 1931, coup
12. 1932, mobilize against São Paulo
13. Oct. 2, 1933, agreement
14. 1934, Army training mission
15. Jan. 17, 1936, Law 192 promulgated
16. 1937–38, mobilize for Estado Novo coup

*Active-duty strength for selective years:*

Oct. 24, 1932, c. 9,700 men still active after Patriotic Battalions dissolved

Oct. 1937, 9,792 men active, including 1,064 reservists

1938, actual force level of 8,268 officers and men

Fig. 4. Força Pública Mineira authorized force, 1889–1938. (For sources, see note 3, p. 289.)

Until 1930, Minas did not require large forces for federal politics; rather, a constant theme of official speeches and reports was the lack of funds to field a force sufficient for internal *state* requirements. Minas held an excellent strategic position as the military rear to Rio de Janeiro, and it stood alongside the Rio–São Paulo corridor. When Minas stayed loyal to the president—as it always did except in 1930— it freed federal forces for action elsewhere. Also, the state machine could mobilize several thousand irregulars, or Patriotic Battalions, in the event of a showdown with the central power. This happened in 1930, when civilians fought alongside the Força Pública to bottle up federal garrisons in the southern half of Minas. It happened again on a larger scale in 1932, when Minas confronted São Paulo in alliance with the central power.

General Floriano Peixoto, having failed in 1891 to engineer a military coup in Ouro Preto against Alvim, treated the Mineiros with great care. In turn, they supported him during the 1893 naval revolt and the Rio Grande civil war. Marechal Hermes da Fonseca restrained some junior officers in the Belo Horizonte garrison who seemed eager to intervene in 1912. Washington Luís threatened intervention and placed the federal garrison at Juiz de Fora on alert for most of the 1929–30 campaign. In pressuring Minas, he deliberately and recklessly weakened a major pillar of the presidential system, and the Mineiros, reluctantly, moved to revolution. Vargas himself disavowed a 1931 putsch attempt to overthrow Governor Olegário Maciel. In return, he received political and military backing against São Paulo in 1932.*

The governors were remarkably successful in seeing to the loyalty of their militia, thus making unlikely a federally inspired coup from a rival faction. State forces (under federal command) crushed the Campanha separatist revolt in early 1892, and their presence in Ouro Preto helped to restrain at least three plots by Army officers in league

---

* Both the 1891 and the 1931 movements were miscalculations, when it seemed in Rio that the governor was weaker than he really was. In 1891, the state elite rallied behind Alvim, just as the Liberal Legion majority, the secretariat, and the militia stayed loyal to Olegário Maciel 40 years later. Alvim did resign in 1892, but he was careful not to split the elite, which would have encouraged federal interference. Maciel, a canny 76-year-old, appeared inept to Minister of Justice Oswaldo Aranha and Virgílio de Melo Franco, two influential members of the revolutionary group in Vargas's entourage. Their failure helped open the way for Vargas to select a surrogate governor in 1933. The 1912 incident, by contrast, was not of the same importance.

with civilian dissidents. Their loyalty shows the strength of state patriotism and the spirit of autonomy.

Recruitment of qualified officers in these early years was hindered by political uncertainties, low pay, and the fact that almost all officers had to serve as police chiefs in the small towns until the PRM gained the upper hand over the coronéis. Furthermore, the forces were under-manned because, as one governor put it, "Mineiros hate the uniform. Conscription won't work, and was evaded while our women tore up enlistment records. Sending recruiting agents out does not work well, either."[4]

Despite this anti-military tradition—there are no Army officers in the Minas elite profile—patriotism was readily aroused whenever the state, or the Union, appeared to be in danger. Several volunteer bat-talions were readied, but did not march on Canudos to fight Anthony the Councilor in 1897. More than once civilians accompanied Army units sent down to quell revolts in Rio and São Paulo. Sons of the Belo Horizonte well-to-do volunteered for weekend military training start-ing in 1909. These civilian training groups (linhas de tiro) were organized in a few other cities under regular army officers. And for years the Clube Floriano Peixoto hosted patriotic gatherings where local garrison commanders, militia officers, and politicians met in Belo Horizonte to celebrate their solidarity in support of the Union and federal institutions.[5]

Minas offered legitimacy and strategic security to federal presidents in return for being left alone. This freed the militia for routine police work—political duties at the governor's command, rounding up va-grants, and chasing bandits (often in cooperation with other state forces) on the frontiers. The officers served out their obscure, low-paid, bureaucratic careers with remarkable dedication; none rose by regular or irregular means to high political office, and as we have seen, the post of civilian police chief was more often than not a political dead end. Budgetary restrictions kept the forces small, which is what Mineiros, with their anti-military tradition dating back to the Para-guayan war, preferred and what this vast state, with its tradition of private controls over local violence, could manage.

The National Guard, with its hundreds of paper brigades and thou-sands of commissioned officers, was politically important. Granting these federal commissions was an important patronage resource and conferred prestige on local notables in a rank-conscious society. Floriano granted commissions liberally to his supporters in the Triângulo, we are told. This resource passed into state hands after 1900, along with other types of federal patronage. In 1901, Colonel Júlio Pinto Coelho from the Mata became state commander in a move to quiet restive coffee growers: hundreds of them received commissions, and Pinto himself obtained the first streetcar concession in Belo Horizonte. Abolished in 1917, this militarily useless but highly visible pork barrel merits further study.[6]

The Força Pública Mineira kept a very low profile in federal politics until 1912, when a handful of Army enlisted men clashed with municipal policemen in Belo Horizonte. President Hermes quickly assured the PRM that this was an isolated incident, and the troops were transferred to Niteroi. Nonetheless, Minas raised its forces by 1,000 men as a warning to the Army and Pinheiro Machado not to meddle in state affairs, as they had in the Northeast and Rio de Janeiro state. São Paulo increased its forces with fanfare; however, the sounding of war drums in Minas was more discreet. "We could not justify fabulous expenditures to maintain a useless militia," the Secretary of Finance reported while at the same time quietly hiring an American military instructor, Colonel Robert Drexler. The force was still small—as he put it, "manifestly inadequate" for normal police duties. Nonetheless, it was cut back to 2,000 men when Wenceslau entered the presidency and Pinheiro Machado fell from power.[7]

It was Governor Bernardes who launched the Força Pública into the national arena during his presidential campaign, by adding another battalion. Minas and São Paulo were prepared for joint intervention if the Rio military school revolt in 1922 had not been suppressed, the British learned. Secretary of the Interior Melo Viana also impressed them with his assessment of Minas's military and strategic strength.[8] Though still too small for domestic police duties, the force saw action in São Paulo against Army rebels in 1924, in Mato Grosso, and against the Prestes Column. Committed to order on their own terms, Bernardes and the PRM used their forces nationally when they had to compete on more equal terms for national leadership with São Paulo and Rio Grande, and to quell unrest by dissident Army and civilian elements during the 1920's. That it could again be sent across the border was the message of a November 1929 memorial service when state officials dedicated a monument to the men who fell in these campaigns.[9]

Mineiro officers were politicized in the upheavals that reduced Minas to client status, beginning with the threat of intervention in 1930 and followed by revolution, the attempted coup against Maciel, and the 1932 São Paulo war. Force levels rose rapidly, encouraging politically ambitious officers, which worried the Army high command. A militia far above peacetime needs was created in the Paulista campaign. Reductions to the 1930 level could be made, the Finance Secretary reported in 1933. "But if it is decided to keep the current force levels as part of the Army's reserve, then we will need a federal credit."[10]

Unlike the other states, Minas did not have to place its forces under federal control (the Code of Interventors) after the 1930 Revolution. But in 1933 the Army wanted to tighten control. Reluctantly, Minas agreed to transform its force into Army line reserves, which meant using national equipment, uniforms, and training methods.[11] Among the reasons why Vargas selected Valadares to govern Minas in late 1933 was the convenient fact that Ernesto Dorneles, Commandant-designate of the Força Pública, was not only Gétulio's cousin but also Benedito's brother-in-law.

Federalization, whether outright or by degrees, was unpopular in Minas. Dorneles never did assume command, and Valadares took care not to alienate the state officer corps. Instead, Dorneles ran the Army training mission. In 1936, he became police chief just as the Força Pública came under full Army tutelage while remaining a separate military entity. Two battalions were federalized in October 1937. Dorneles commanded one of the two federal-state blocking forces that secured the strategic routes to Rio before the coup.[12]

Ever since the Ouro Preto incidents in 1891, the Army was extremely sensitive to Mineiro public opinion. Federal units were twice withdrawn from the capital after clashes: in 1893 they went to the Rio Grande front, and in 1912 they were entrained for Niteroi. Governors Alvim, Pena and Maciel were each in their time made honorary generals. And the Army's customary policy of stationing local boys in their home town garrisons helped to integrate soldiers and their families with the region. Mobilizing these regiments for overseas duty proved quite difficult in 1943, but for domestic purposes the policy worked well.[13]

State forces outnumbered federal troops ten to one until Minas became a federal Military Region in 1920. Significantly, it was Calógeras, a Mineiro politician serving as the first and only civilian Minister of

War, who raised the federal garrisons in Minas to over 4,000 men in 1921.[14] This was done for reasons of national defense. President Afonso Pena introduced national conscription in 1907, including draft registration boards, which Mineiros, as was their custom, evaded. President Wenceslau Brás carried out the first draft in 1916, which Army officers chosen for their tact and Mineiro family ties moved very carefully to enforce.[15] After 1891, therefore, the Army's role in Minas was almost invariably tailored to terms and conditions set by Mineiro political leaders. Even Army tutelage of the force after 1933 was accomplished under the political coverage of Valadares.

Badly demoralized after surrendering to state forces in the 1930 Revolution, men of the 12th Infantry Regiment in Belo Horizonte were encouraged to fraternize with their state counterparts. They joined the União Católica dos Militares, a Rio-based group.[16] This brought the regiment into line with the Força Pública, whose welcome to Catholic chaplains in 1928 had been controversial. For many years, units from both forces commemorated the Belo Horizonte siege—the Army its glorious defense, the force its victory over the Army and, by extension, the national government's defeat. These parades were abolished by the military government after 1964 on grounds it was not in the national interest to commemorate an event that had once divided these two forces.

### Congresses and Meetings

Another way to assess the elite's response to integration is to examine its congresses, where elite groups shared information and symbols, demonstrated intentions, and made social contacts. Mineiros participated in a great number of meetings at the zonal, state, and national levels. What might be called the "congress phenomenon" was stimulated by conditions of rapid commercialization and industrial growth, both characteristic of modernization in the early states. Professional, economic, and religious groups organized and spread through Minas, as shown in Chapter 3. The quickening pace of associational activity, and the greater complexity in social interactions this reflected, showed up in the meetings these groups held.

The sequencing, scope, and content of Brazilian national congresses were influenced by events abroad. International meetings of all kinds show a rapid rise in the 1870's, and tremendous sustained activity just before World War I.[17] No full count of Brazilian congresses is available, but the takeoff in such phenomena began in the 1890's. Congresses in Minas proliferated about 1900. These linkages from Atlantic Basin to the Union, to the states, and to the subregions are suggestive and ought to be surveyed systematically. Brazil also competed actively with Argentina to host international meetings of all kinds. Yet Brazilians on the periphery were not merely following issues raised at the center.*

Within Latin America, the Brazilian congresses were unique because a great number of meetings followed a federalist format. Several groups rotated their congresses among the state capitals, showing that Rio did not dominate this activity the way Buenos Aires or Santiago did. The Mineiros, having organized themselves in a kind of mini-federalist system, seemed well prepared mentally to work with this arrangement.

Mineiros eagerly promoted congresses, expositions, and specialized professional meetings in Belo Horizonte. The publicity and visitors coming through put their new capital on the political, commercial, and cultural map. The Paulistas, with their dynamic economy, generated a good deal of congressional activity. And the Pernambucanos, who exercised an ambivalent leadership over the northeastern states, had their own reasons for convoking meetings.

The first political generation (born before 1869) was occupied with political and economic problems: abolition, institutionalizing the Republic, inflation, and the foreign debt. The Agricultural Congress held in Rio in 1878 was the first of several dealing with commodity prices, production techniques, and the export market.[18] Congressional activity took place on a sustained basis first over economic issues. The next two political generations (dividing at 1888 in birth dates) were interested in a broader range of social and administrative problems, reflecting greater social complexity and the worldwide spread of social issues and wider government initiatives. But this was more of a shift in emphasis than a break between generations.

João Pinheiro's generation believed in the demonstration effect of

---

* The São Paulo, Recife, and Belo Horizonte–based modernist movements in literature, with their search for folk traditions, followed European and North American precedents. (Gilberto Freyre organized the first regionalist congress in Recife in 1926.) However, Brazilians were searching for their own, separate identity within the West. How Mário de Andrade and other intellectuals coped with the problems of imitation and originality is discussed in Joan Dassin's recent dissertation.

new techniques. Their expositions, trade fairs, and model farms also reflected the idea of progress and a fascination with change through economic development. The 1903 Agricultural, Commercial, and Industrial Congress held in Belo Horizonte attracted national attention for its wide-ranging inquiries into regional economic problems. That the Minas economy was so obviously lacking in direction and coordination challenged the talents of this generation, which believed it could cope. Protectionism was coming into vogue. The cooperative movement of producers was also discussed in 1903, and became state policy under João Pinheiro.

Expositions were held throughout the Atlantic world to enhance prestige, show new products, and attract investment capital. Ouro Preto hosted the first industrial exposition in Brazil in 1861. The Juiz de Fora Exposition of 1886 was considered a great success because it attracted crowds from Rio de Janeiro and the other zones of Minas. A similar blend of the progressive spirit and regionalism inspired the Permanent Exposition in Belo Horizonte, a fairground where each município was to have its own display pavilion. "This will be more than an industrial fair," the organizers said in 1901. "It will symbolize our capacity to cooperate, and will stimulate the municípios to progress through common action."[19] (The exposition closed after several localities failed to subscribe their shares.) Later, the Feira de Amostras (Exposition Hall) in downtown Belo Horizonte displayed regional products in a central tower, around which were placed new offices for officially recognized interest groups. Built in art deco style, this landmark of the Valadares era symbolized "common action by the producing classes to end the depression."[20]

Mineiros sent products and samples abroad, and participated in the glamour of international expositions while hoping to attract foreign capital. They sent a delegation to Santiago (1904), and attended the Columbian Exposition in Chicago (1897), the Paris Exposition (1900), and the Pan-American Exposition in Buffalo (1901), as well as the great Saint Louis Fair (1905). The practical results were minimal. When foreigners finally did invest in mining—after the 1908 Stockholm Congress set off a rush to acquire deposits around the world—they mostly held the iron ore in reserve, and except for the Belgians were reluctant to found a heavy steel industry. Foreign investment outside mining was very low. Yet the sense of participating in foreign events (at state expense) was an important benefit to this generation. Making Minas better known abroad was also important to them. The National Exposition of 1908 was held in Rio de Janeiro to commemorate 100 years of open ports and free trade, and the theme was internationalism. Minas erected a fanciful pavilion in the French style of art nouveau. The official guide to this exposition was printed in three languages—Portuguese, French, and Esperanto. To impress European visitors, Negroes and beggars were removed from downtown streets. The vision of an industrializing, progressive, and Europeanized Brazil that this event promoted was widely held in Minas.

The National Centenary Exposition of 1922 featured cooperation between the states, with national unity as its theme. Times had changed, although these were the usual halls of products on display. The Americans stole the show with models of tropical diseases at their medical exhibit, upstaging the French, who donated a full-size replica of the Petit Trianon, to later house the Brazilian Academy of Letters, and much outdrawing the British, whose pavilion modeled after a Roman law forum was dull.[21] In keeping with the centennial spirit of self-discovery, Minas presented a chorography, a detailed topographical map, and the state's first statistical annual. The new state Department of Statistics had been organized by Mário Augusto Teixeira de Freitas, who ran the 1920 census in Minas and now directed the national statistical agency. Teixeira used Minas as his testing ground to work out techniques of coordinated data-gathering at the município level. The two departments were closely linked, a connection the Centenary Exposition dramatized well.[22]

The first generation sponsored regional stock shows and model farms as the rural counterparts to industrial expositions, and used them to dramatize the idea of regional integration. Held at Belo Horizonte in February 1908, the first Exposição Agropecúaria de Minas featured the Zebu, a rugged breed of cattle from India used to improve the domestic herd.[23] These stock shows and fairs publicized the state's large cattle industry, and were supposed to encourage innovation while promoting the habit of intra-zonal cooperation. The first Congress of Agricultural Cooperatives was held in 1911, although the movement soon declined.

Governor Francisco Sales convened a Congress of Municipalities in 1902 to discuss the adverse effects of illegal local taxes on the circulation of goods. In 1907, Pinheiro sponsored municipal congresses in the

Sul, Mata, and North zones. Each congress had an agenda, and delegates pledged themselves, among other things, to subscribe 15 percent
of their budgets to primary education, to abolish intermunicipal taxes,
and to set up model farms and cooperatives. More than forums for the
airing of good intentions, these early meetings with the governor were
highly charged politically because the balance of fiscal and political
power was tipping toward the state (see the next chapter).[24]

More of these congresses were held in the 1920's to discuss common
problems and means to coordinate local services, but sometimes to assert regional demands on Belo Horizonte. Congresses in the Mata
(1927), the Northeast (1927), and the West (1929) discussed zonal
economic problems and public services. Delegates at the northeast
Congress also called for political redistricting to give their zones more
power in the competition for public works. Political mobilization and
vote pooling at the zonal level seemed possible for the first time, now
that Antonio Carlos had brought in the secret ballot.[25] For their part,
the governors wanted local governments to implement state policies,
not assert demands. Raul Soares convened a carefully controlled congress of all the municípios in 1923; Valadares held another in 1941.[26]

Conflict between the Mata coffee planters and state authorities was
symbolized by two very different congresses held in March 1917.
Three hundred delegates to the Congresso de Lavradores do Café at
Juiz de Fora set up the Confederação Agrária Mineira to agitate for
tax relief, among other things. Whether to limit it to the Mata planters
or open the membership to other groups was debated at length.
Proponents of a broader, statewide pressure group carried the day.
The new confederation was authorized explicitly to join other groups,
if convenient, "to defend, help the progress of, or develop the interests
of the productive classes." Meanwhile, the official Sociedade Mineira
de Agricultura was meeting in Belo Horizonte under Senator Francisco
Sales, president of the PRM Executive Committee. Instead of registering protests, the SMA congress was a typical solidarity-building affair.
Numerous state and federal deputies attended, as did mayors, merchant spokesmen, and leading agriculturalists.[27] As for the confederation, it expired when Governor-elect Bernardes pledged to lower the
coffee export tax, which he did in 1919.

The second political generation—those born between 1869 and
1888, who came to maturity by the middle of the Old Republic—

widened the scope of congress activity. Rio was the most important of several regional capitals where congresses were held after 1900. These forums dramatized a very wide range of issues at a time when the capital was only one of many active centers generating congress activity.

Physicians were apparently the first professional group to hold regular national meetings in the state capitals. Belo Horizonte welcomed the seventh national medical congress in 1912. Other groups holding regional meetings included engineers, lawyers, pharmacists, and bureaucrats. São Paulo students organized the first Brazilian student congress in 1909. Workers from the Federal District dominated the first labor congress (Rio, 1906), but at the second (1912), Minas had the largest delegation, having held its first state labor convention at Sabará in 1907. The desire of specialized groups to associate in these forums is evidence of increased social interaction, which is part of integration.

São Paulo and Minas were the first to sponsor a series of meetings to discuss primary and secondary education. The first was in São Paulo (1911), the second was held in Belo in 1912, and the third took place in Rio as part of the centenary celebration. Later, the Brazilian Education Society sponsored a new series of national congresses, starting in Curitiba (1927), then in Belo Horizonte (1928) and São Paulo (1929), and held several more in Rio during the early 1930's. Even the Esperanto movement switched from the Federal District— where its first congress met in 1907—to São Paulo, Juiz de Fora, and other cities for its conventions.

A series of geographical congresses were held in the state capitals to publicize Brazilian research and to popularize national issues. The Geographical Society of Rio de Janeiro hosted the first congress in 1909. The Sixth Geographical Congress (1919) was held in Belo Horizonte, and the theme was interstate cooperation to solve old border disputes. The congress itself was an elaborately staged extravaganza to underscore and to legitimize a series of border agreements already hammered out by the Geographical Society in Rio with the help of ex-President Wenceslau Brás—who had resolved the Paraná–Santa Catarina frontier dispute in 1918—and the Liga de Defesa Nacional, a Rio-based patriotic organization.

The rhetoric ranged from themes of cooperation to nationalism to the race issue. Surrounded by state flags, and with the slogan "For a United Brazil" festooned across the hall, Governor Bernardes told the delegates that Minas and São Paulo would soon sign their own border accord. He praised the society for holding these congresses in different parts of the country. It was time, he said, for Brazilians to know themselves better, "to study the good and the bad ourselves instead of finding this out from foreign pens." What better way to celebrate the independence centennial, another delegate said. Here in Belo "flat-headed Northerners and thin-faced blonds from the South" are mixing in the study sessions, tours, banquets, and parades of this conference, showing "that a miscegenated people can stay together. Gobineau is wrong!"[28]

The Belo Horizonte congress achieved some results, although some of the border disputes lingered until the Estado Novo, and the large contested region with Espírito Santo remained a shadow zone infested with bandits and adventurers, where rival state police units postured and customs inspectors wrangled over jurisdictions. For all its power, Minas could not move Espírito Santo to negotiate beyond statements of intent. The Capixabas never did settle, preferring to use this dispute with their large neighbor to generate political support at home.[29] Yet the need to forge institutional links across the fragmented state structure set up in 1891 was compelling. President Pessoa called a national congress to discuss the remaining border disputes in 1920. Even the touchy issue of constitutional reform was raised at the 1908 Juridical Congress in Rio de Janeiro.

Aside from education congresses, Minas's main contribution to the growing framework of federalized meetings grew out of the Catholic lay movement. At first the Church was preoccupied with institution-building at the state level. The Vatican encouraged frequent meetings at the provincial and diocesan levels, the first Concilium of Brazilian Bishops having been held in 1890 at São Paulo, and the first meeting of diocesan clergy at Mariana in 1903. Under the dynamic Dom Silvério, Mariana became an Archbishopric, and outlying parishes, including the Triângulo and parts of the new East zone, were transferred from bishops in other states to his jurisdiction. In 1916, Dom Silvério created the Caratinga Bishopric, which included the contested zone with Espírito Santo.[30] Following this vigorous institutional response to the Republic, the Church began to mobilize the laity, with Minas a main center of activity.

European priests led by the Redemptionist Fathers in Belo Horizonte organized a Catholic action movement called União Popular in 1909. Modeled along German lines, the União Popular organized workers and students, involved itself in the schools issue, and pressed Catholic moral values on the press and cinema. The União Popular set up branches across the state and ran the Federation of Catholic Associations. It also sponsored Catholic lay congresses, the first of which was held in Juiz de Fora in 1910 following the Regenerator Party's collapse in the civilista campaign. These congresses encouraged the middle classes and especially professional groups to actively support Catholic issues and causes.[31]

This activity generated a labor front, a woman's league, and, in 1915, the Union of Catholic Youth. Several third-generation politicians (those born after 1889) participated in Catholic Youth activities, of which there were a great many in Belo Horizonte. The Union of Catholic Youth outgrew its Belo Horizonte base in 1928 and moved to Rio, having become a federated organization with 15,000 members. The first of several national catechism congresses was held in the state capital in 1928. Originally planned as a regional event, it grew into a national meeting when many out-of-state Catholic groups adhered.[32]

While Minas remained a leading Catholic center, dynamism shifted to Rio in the 1920's under Dom Leme, the forceful archbishop and later cardinal of Rio de Janeiro. He organized the Catholic Confederation of activist laymen in the Federal District, and in 1932 created a nationwide political pressure group called the Catholic Electoral League (LEC).[33] Activities along these lines were pioneered somewhat earlier in Minas. Consider that the multiorganization approach Cardinal Leme used to mobilize the elites was similar to the strategy of União Popular, while LEC was formed after the state political pressure group, the Centro Popular Mineiro, established in 1927. Dom Leme owed more to Vatican directives and to the direct influence of European precedents than he did to the early Minas experiments with Catholic action; yet the link from Europe to Minas to Rio existed, as did the federalist dimension in these activities.

Congressional activities were shifting toward Rio, but this was not a process of accelerating centralism pure and simple because the federalist impulse remained strong. Activities increased at all levels after World War I. The first national highway congress held in Rio in 1916 was paralleled by a Paulista highway congress one year later. In fact, Minas in 1924 and São Paulo in 1926 set up modern highway departments well before the federal counterpart was organized in 1937. (Both states had more extensive road construction programs than the Union until World War II.) In 1918, the journalists held their first national congress in Rio, and divided into state sections. Twenty years later the National Union of Students was built upon state delegations, with a national directorate in Rio. In 1922, Mineiros joined the first Miss Brazil competition, which was sponsored by A Noite, a Rio daily, on North American lines. Local beauties went to Belo Horizonte for the state judging, and the first "Miss Minas Gerais" (from São João del Rei) led a motorcade through the business district. Competitions all over the country were held for the 1929 Miss Universe contest in Florida. Brazil lost, but won the next year, when it was held in Rio.[34]

These interactions followed a pattern: the organizations, meetings, symbols, and expectations at the center related to similar phenomena in the states. Minas was a main contributor to this interchange. However, Mineiros in the third political generation looked increasingly to national solutions, and they seemed less innovative in the Vargas years because the close ties to Catete Palace stifled initiative. Congresses seem to have lost some of the enthusiasm and élan they had during the heyday of the state system.

National congresses show a trend toward specialization, and also of co-optation under central government initiative. In 1927, for example, the then Minister of Finance Getúlio Vargas attended the Congress of Revenue Agents and Tax Collectors in Belo Horizonte. Later, such national meetings were usually held in Rio. In 1936, the Ministry of Agriculture convened a Conference of State Secretaries of Agriculture, while the Foreign Ministry hosted the National Statistical Convention. The education congresses which were innovative in the states moved to the Federal District, where they lost momentum and the reform spirit. This is significant, because Mineiros held the Ministry of Education. Francisco Campos, an innovator in state education, became a reactionary at the federal level. The feminist congresses are another case in point. Mineiro women had been active since the 1920's, and they joined a series of congresses held in Rio under the patronage of Sra. Darcy Vargas until her husband the president suppressed them. State congresses exhibited a basic continuity with the 1920's, when there was a surge of activity, but seemingly with more sponsorship and control from the Palácio de Liberdade. At least four commercial, industrial, and agricultural congresses were sponsored by the state Commercial Association, two being held in Belo Horizonte (1928 and 1935) and one each in Juiz de Fora and Itajubá in the Sul (both 1930). Restive Mata fazendeiros held several congressos de lavradores de café in the early 1930's until they were cut short by Valadares when Vargas federalized coffee policy (see Chapter 2). Local governments probably were better run by some of the appointed mayors like Menelíck de Carvalho, who took over in 1937, but the issues of local power, zonal and state cooperation raised at the early municipal congresses were only temporarily laid aside.

Integration did occur in Minas and Brazil, if not fast enough to satisfy the critics of federalism, then sufficiently strong enough to affect political actors at all levels of government. The federalist dimension was important, because the rate and direction of change was not only toward the national center. Efforts to upgrade relationships took place within the zones of Minas, as well as at the state and national levels. Thus a survey of military affairs, followed by a rundown of the congresses, indicates that a process of integration was under way. But was it meaningful?

In *The Uniting of Europe*, Ernst Haas defined integration as "the process whereby political actors in several distinct national settings are persuaded to shift their loyalties, expectations and political activities toward a new centre, whose institutions possess or demand jurisdiction over the pre-existing national states." This process is characterized by a combination of institutional and attitudinal changes. While integrating, Haas continued, the activities of certain key groups are "refocussed on a new set of central symbols and institutions." Habits, expectations, and conveniences develop which make the forging of new ties at first attractive, then indispensable.[35]

Still provocative, this classic definition of integration has been questioned by researchers, reevaluated, and buffeted by the course of European events.[36] Thus it is now clear that increased interaction does not necessarily lead to centralization. Nor is the process only one of movement toward the center, as other units retain and even expand upon their functions. Perhaps, in caution, the most that can be said about this highly complex process is that the interpenetration of social, economic, and political life across regional boundaries and the transfer of decisions and resources toward the center are two convergent and reinforcing parts of integration. Furthermore, it also appears that the actions (and nonactions) of the leadership, especially the bargaining over terms, have a central role in integration, which need not be cumulative or complete. Many examples in the Minas study support this conclusion.

The Minas elite looked to qualitatively richer, if not fundamentally different relationships with their neighbors and the Union. Since the mid-nineteenth century they had accepted national unity, but their approach to integration was weighted toward interactions between dominant and inferior actors, on the vertical plane. Relationships of power, prestige, and political weight in the federation were not expected to change very much. Client status after 1929 altered their strategy, if not their methods.

For integration to proceed, Haas wrote, expectations and commitments must shift toward a new center. As has been shown, Mineiro loyalties shifted at all levels. But the elite seems deliberately to have staved off the full impact of integration by strategies of selective change. Social mobilization, to be sure, was kept quite low.

These elite congresses served the interests of a basically conservative society in which co-optive methods, force, and the corporatist style all served to mediate the impact of change. The self-confidence and staying power of this elite is striking. And it may well be that the impact of integration on the horizontal level of association was blunted by the informal nature of this society, where panelinhas got things done and paternalism eroded the development of collective opinion and group action.

Integration at the state level did not go further because the governor had limited resources to finance communications and public services, and because certain changes were involuntary. Another cause was the hold of Rio de Janeiro on the aspirations, ambitions, and purse strings of Mineiros, who were all too well integrated into the Federal District's banking and patronage networks. This drained money and talent from the state even though the aim of congressional power was to secure federal favors for Minas. But the main obstacle to state integration was surely the basic fact that Minas, a mosaic of regions, was not a natural economic unit. This affected the integration process at all levels. That large parts of the state were somebody else's hinterland was neo-colonial integration. In the Center-South trading and industrial complex, Minas had to accept interdependence as the weaker partner.

Historically, the political-cultural thrust of Mineiro regionalism was directed against this situation, which geography reinforced. Yet purely regional solutions were believed to be inadequate as early as 1898, when the depression led to the forging of new national links. During the second depression Minas accepted client status, while astutely upgrading the terms of this new relationship with the Union. Business and professional groups looked increasingly to the Rio de Janeiro power nexus, which might lead one to conclude that regionalism had "lost its substance." Regionalism probably meant little to Euvaldo Lodi, the industrialist, president of the National Industrial Confederation, and a Vargas crony. It still resonated well in Minas, however, which recovered its élan when Vargas fell in 1945 and the federal system was revived. Power, heavy industry, and transportation were promoted by postwar state governments. In a classic maneuver, Força Pública units and the Army descended on Rio from the Minas highlands to depose President João Goulart in 1964. Ironically, this led to another centralizing dictatorship. But it had been years since Minas played the same central role in the federation.

## CHAPTER EIGHT

# Fiscal Federalism

STRONG IN CONGRESS, militarily autonomous as were few states in the Old Republic, Minas was fiscally weaker than its ranking as the federation's second economic power would at first glance suggest. Minas could realistically aspire to lead the Republic in tandem with São Paulo. But that state's dazzling economic growth generated large tax revenues and attracted foreign credit, whereas Minas lived close to cutbacks and austerity budgets. Compared with Pernambuco, Minas had some leeway. But if Minas was relatively well off within the federation, it was critically short of funds in relation to its very large, and for the most part painfully backward, population.

Mineiros acted cautiously because they wanted to keep their good credit rating abroad and because they disliked deficits, but also because they were constrained, even frightened, by a weak tax base dependent on exports. The drawbacks were well known: export taxes weighed heavily on producers, hindered the growth of interstate commerce, and were highly vulnerable to sudden shifts in international prices, so that the budgetary process was chaotic. When exports were strong, as in the 1890's and 1920's, revenues were still insufficient to finance schools, public health, and infrastructure projects. In lean times, for example the 1898–1909 period and the early 1930's, these state services were curtailed. Given this restricted and vulnerable tax base, the fiscal conservatism of this state was something more than a famous culture trait.

Mineiros were also famous for not paying taxes. Despite good intentions, no governor until Artur Bernardes (1918–22) was able to shift a

TABLE 8.1

Percent of Total State Receipts by Select States, 1897–1936

| State | 1897–1906 | 1907–16 | 1917–26 | 1927–36 |
|---|---|---|---|---|
| São Paulo | 29.3 | 30.4 | 34.5 | 37.8 |
| Minas Gerais | 10.6 | 13.4 | 14.9 | 15.7 |
| Rio Grande | 6.3 | 8.0 | 12.5 | 14.4 |
| Pernambuco | 5.5 | 5.7 | 5.5 | 4.9 |

SOURCE: Brazil, Anuário estatístico, 1939/40, Ano V, p. 1416.
NOTE: Receipts include both ordinary and extraordinary revenue but not extra-budgetary credits.

significant share of the tax burden onto rural property owners (see Chapter 4). The elite could have taxed themselves more heavily, and they should have stamped out illegal sales and transfer taxes that hampered the internal market. Charges that Minas did not pay its fair share of federal taxes were often raised in congress, notably by the São Paulo delegation. However, this very large state faced structural problems of underdevelopment that went far beyond tax reform. Not enough money came into government. This affected all aspects of regionalism and hindered integration.

State revenues increased, although not as rapidly as those collected in São Paulo and Rio Grande do Sul. See Table 8.1. In the periods 1897–1906 and 1927–36, the big three's share of total state revenues increased from 46 to almost 68 percent. The Minas share increased 5 percent, but the other two leaders grew at somewhat faster rates, and Rio Grande drew almost even in state revenues. Almost all the northeastern states declined, including Pernambuco. All states south of Bahia increased their shares of total state income except Rio de Janeiro, with its decadent coffee sector.

That the South grew while the North stagnated or declined is no surprise. That the income of southern states grew faster than federal income is, however, unexpected. The federal system favored states with strong economies: they had the bulk of export earnings and paid most of the federal import duties and consumer taxes, giving them leverage in Rio. Yet the expected growth of central fiscal power vis à vis the states did not occur, even in the Estado Novo. Rising revenues in the southern states indicate, first, that the demands for state services continued to expand and, second, that fiscal federalism based on regional economies was deeply rooted in the structure of Brazilian institutions.

TABLE 8.2

*State Income as Percent of Federal Income, 1891–1945*

| State | 1891–1900 | 1901–10 | 1911–20 | 1921–30 | 1931–37 | 1938–45 |
|-------|-----------|---------|---------|---------|---------|---------|
| São Paulo | 14.2 | 11.0 | 14.9 | 19.4 | 21.6 | 25.5 |
| Minas Gerais | 6.0 | 4.2 | 6.3 | 8.2 | 8.8 | 8.5 |
| Rio Grande | 3.3[a] | 2.6 | 4.0 | 7.6 | 7.9 | 8.4 |
| Pernambuco | 2.6 | 2.0 | 2.8 | 2.7 | 2.7 | 2.6 |

SOURCE: Computed from federal and state revenue tables in Brazil, *Anuário estatístico*, Anos V–VII.
[a] For the period 1897–1900 only. All data for 1891–96 are from state annual reports.

Again the share of Minas Gerais increased, if less rapidly than São Paulo's or Rio Grande's, while Pernambuco's declined. State incomes declined relative to federal receipts during the first depression, but increased (Pernambuco held its own) during the second depression. See Table 8.2. These data point to the states' increased capacity to extract resources from their populations. Fiscally, they were better able to cope with the second big slump. Two other trends also are clear. Thanks to prosperity and better revenue collection, Minas and Rio Grande surged ahead in the 1920's, which for both was a period of innovation in state government. São Paulo's sustained increase for virtually the whole period contrasts sharply with Pernambuco's secular stagnation.

The budgetary history of Minas Gerais is characterized by cycles of boom-bust-boom, but on a modest scale (this shows up clearly on Figures 5 and 6). The pattern was one of cautious fiscal management and a pay-as-you-go approach to the public debt. Note that general revenues and expenditures were closely phased; the expansive 1890's and the depressed 1930's were exceptional departures from the balanced-budget rule. Note also the efforts to restrain public indebtedness. In fact, the debt was virtually retired in the mid-1920's, a time of all-out borrowing in most of Latin America, including São Paulo (see note 7, p. 292). Perhaps the most remarkable aspect of the budget was the depressingly small income rise (about .5 in constant contos) for the period 1890–1920, years when the state population rose 85 percent. Thereafter, Minas was on a sounder fiscal footing: income more than doubled in the 1920's.

Fiscal problems were often blamed on the export tax, which fell on interstate trade goods and commodities as well as foreign sales. The Minas budget doubled in real terms between 1889 and 1891, when the

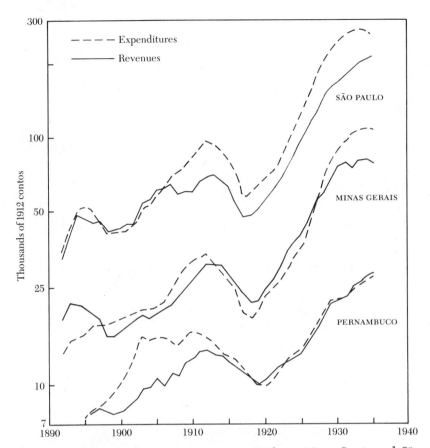

Fig. 5. General revenues and expenditures, Pernambuco, Minas Gerais, and São Paulo, 1892–1935. Five-year moving averages in thousands of 1912 contos. Data for Minas compiled from Appendix C, series A-3 and B-3; data for Pernambuco and São Paulo are in the companion books, forthcoming.

state received a broader revenue base than the old Provincial Government, but so much depended on coffee receipts.* Eighty-one percent of all tax revenues came from exports in 1895. The coffee crash spurred efforts to find a broader, more stable fiscal base, notably from the land tax. What amounted to a tax revolt against this new impost by coffee

* The Empire allowed double taxation, which meant that the central government taxed revenue sources such as provincial exports, property transfers, and professional activities that in the Republic were granted exclusively to the states. Chronically underfunded, the provincial governments required revenue supple-

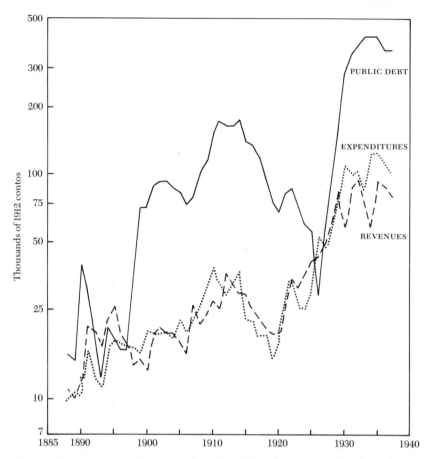

Fig. 6. Revenues, expenditures, and public debt of the state of Minas Gerais, 1888–1937, in thousands of 1912 contos. Compiled from Appendix C, series A-2, B-2, and D-2.

and ranching interests forced the state to continue collecting consumer taxes, which were illegal, and to rely upon expedients like the coffee surtax, discussed in Chapter 2.

There was some progress away from overdependence on exports, but little tax relief for producers. Between 1905 and 1932, the share of export taxes stabilized around half of all tax revenues, falling to one-

ments that made them dependent on the central government; Iglésias, p. 188. The Republic gave autonomy to the states, but only those with strong export economies were fiscally strong enough to avoid dependent status.

quarter in 1936 when the tax on sales and consignments was introduced. This was a turnover tax, applied to both industrial products and traditional exports. Although this new sales tax soon became the largest single source of revenue, it covered items in interstate trade, amounting to another way of taxing primary products. Movement away from the export tax was forced by depression conditions, especially in the 1930's. Until then, the revenue base remained narrow and vulnerable.[1]

Surpluses and shortfalls sometimes varied from the yearly budget bill by as much as one-third, or one-half, or even more. Revenues up to 60 percent above estimates buoyed the new state; shortfalls up to 20 percent then dogged the depression years from 1898 to 1909. Very large sums from coffee swelled state coffers after the war. In 1925, for example, income was almost 90 percent above estimates. Minas collected one-third more revenue from all sources in 1929 than expected, one-third less in 1930 than the legislature had budgeted. The gap between anticipated and actual receipts narrowed after that, as the state gained more control over the budgetary process.

Taxes weighed disproportionately on the dynamic and productive zones. Secretary of Finance David Campista estimated that two-thirds of all revenue in 1899 came from a narrow band along the Rio de Janeiro and São Paulo borders. The Center and North virtually escaped taxation, and most of the agro-pastoral sector was undertaxed. (In 1966, two-thirds of all receipts came from only 4 percent of the municípios, including Belo Horizonte.) Lopsided taxation discouraged fiscal integration while promoting widespread tax evasion and undercounting.[2]

Income fell short of needs in most years, partly because Mineiros evaded the fisc. In 1899, the State Secretary of Agriculture lamented that per capita a Mineiro furnished only one-fourth the state taxes that a Paulista did. Though less wealthy than São Paulo and Rio Grande, Minas by 1927 was still contributing much less per capita: the ratio was roughly 5:4:1. Smuggling, undervaluation of goods and property, and inefficient collection all contributed to a pattern of persistent tax evasion that was rooted historically in the Mineiros' resistance to Portuguese colonial rule.[3] Evasion was at least in part an unfortunate residue of a patriotic attitude.

Yet the state's fiscal history also records some successes at tightening up and tax reform, starting with the Bernardes administration. *Moody's Manual of Investments* for 1930 attributed the substantial revenue increases of the past decade to a "steady expansion of economic productivity, and also to improved methods in the collection of taxes."[4] The 1920's were a decade of innovation in state government, fueled by expanding revenues. That the political system was better able to extract resources from the productive groups is also clear. Looking back on what to them seemed a decade of fiscal progress, reluctant Mineiro revolutionaries in 1930 were not ready to condemn or abandon the state system.

Public borrowing was easier than tax reform, but taking on indebtedness through the recourse of extrabudgetary credits was considered dangerous fiscal medicine in Minas. São Paulo borrowed heavily and prospered; the northern states assumed obligations they could not carry; Minas borrowed prudently and worried when it did. Service on the funded debt (most of which was foreign) averaged about 20 percent of the actual budget between 1897 and 1923, then dropped off.[5] Most of the early foreign loan capital was French and was used to finance Belo Horizonte, municipal improvements, an agricultural credit bank, and some railroad construction. When payments threatened to reach 30 percent of the yearly budget, these French loans were consolidated in 1910.* Service was suspended for three years during the war and resumed amidst a controversy with French creditors over payment terms, which went to the International Court of Justice.[6]

Shaken by the long depression after 1897, and worried by the state's weak and vulnerable tax base, the government was reluctant to borrow more and aimed instead for balanced budgets and debt redemption. Although Minas was known abroad for a good credit rating, it did not depend so heavily on foreign transfers to supplement its revenues as São Paulo did. In the prosperous 1920's, for example, Minas spent only 8 percent of its budget on debt service and redeemed most of the prewar French debt. Despite the fact that American loans were scandalously easy to obtain after 1918, the Mineiros maintained their con-

---

* Bernardes called for austerity and strict budgets to meet payments on the 1915 funding loan (*Manifesto,* pp. 45–46). This was another motive for his drastic political reforms in 1918–19, discussed in Chapter 4. Note the parallel with Silviano Brandão's actions twenty years before.

servative approach to foreign borrowing.[7] After 1930, foreign capital
dried up and Minas relied heavily on domestic borrowing, as did São
Paulo.

Domestic public credit was the main source of extrabudgetary income during the late Empire and the boom period until 1897. For most
of the Old Republic, however, the state government was parsimonious
in its use of this source and relied more heavily on foreign lenders.
After 1897 the internal funded debt was less than half the foreign
debt. The floating debt, covering short-term payments—in effect, another form of deficit—was rigorously controlled after having risen
alarmingly to one-seventh of the total public debt in 1897. No mention
of the floating debt appears in official reports between 1902 and 1910,
possibly in order to escape the painful disclosure of higher deficits.
Later, the floating debt rose rapidly—from 32,000 contos in 1926 to
370,000 contos in 1934—forcing Olegário Maciel to ask Vargas for relief. This reinforced the development of client status, despite the good
repayment record on overall debt obligations. Concurrently, the
funded internal debt became the largest and fastest growing part of
the public debt after 1930.

Expenditures were allocated through the regular budget, and by
extrabudgetary credit operations. Data on these regular expenditures
through the state secretaries are generally more detailed and complete
than data on the credit operations.[8] Despite inconsistencies and gaps
in the yearly reports, however, some interesting findings appear. A
look at the first, optimistic decade of the Republic in Minas shows how
Mineiros wanted their new state government to spend its revenues and
gives a basis for comparing long-range trends in state expenditures.

Organized "not as a simple state, but rather like a great nation,"
Minas was overcommitted in public works and services, and as Silviano
Brandão, the hard-pressed governor, reported in 1899, it must retrench
and settle for less ambitious goals. The state had overreached itself—
Bernardo de Sena Figueiredo, chairman of the Budget Committee,
confirmed this in a long and thoughtful report to the legislature in
1904. Yet despite certain errors, he maintained, the early administra-
tions could not be blamed for doing "their patriotic duty to satisfy
pent-up demands." Thus the drawn-out budgetary crisis was caused, as
he put it, by "the aspiration of all Mineiros to see railroads built, the
new capital constructed, and public services put on a regular basis."

Education was deplorable under the Provincial Government; the militia had been too small; public works and the court system were also inadequate because of lack of funding. Now somewhat improved, these services could not be cut back to Imperial levels. In effect, the state assumed obligations that had seemed reachable in the era of free-spending but which now, in depression times, would be most difficult to fund.[9]

Expenditures in the regular, or actual, budget increased three and a half times over those in the last Imperial decade. Note in Table 8.3 that the relative share of education, the militia, and public works actually declined in the 1890's, while the judiciary became a major new item in the budget as the state took over and expanded the court system and gave employment to lawyers. The bureaucracy also increased: Sena Figueiredo estimated that the corps of functionaries doubled after the capital was moved to Belo Horizonte. Salaries for bureaucrats took a larger share of the expanded budget. By the late 1890's, debt service payments were climbing rapidly—to 23 percent of the actual budget—just as coffee revenues fell drastically.

Programs funded by domestic bond issues, notably railroad support, the new capital, and immigration subsidies, increased 11 times over the level of credit operations during the Empire. The lion's share of credit (54,000 contos) went to the railroads. One-quarter was expended on guaranteed interest payments and subsidies under terms negotiated between private companies and the old Provincial Government. The rest was loan capital, secured by mortgages on the lines, and 10,000 contos spent in 1899 to purchase the bankrupt Bahia e Minas railroad. The original intent of this large loan program was to finance a pioneer line across the virgin East zone and parts of the eastern Mata toward Espírito Santo and its ocean port, Vitória. After intense lobbying in the state congress, the bill that emerged (Law 64 in 1893) authorized loans to several existing lines, including two in the Sul that were on the point of abandoning construction.[10] Over half the loan capital under Law 64 was absorbed by the Sapucaí and Muzambinho railroads, whose tracks ran through the heartland of municípios loyal to Silviano Brandão. Silviano's Pouso Alegre benefited, as did Wenceslau's Itajubá. Campanha, capital of the recent regional revolt, was on the Muzambinho line. The result of Law 64 was to up-

TABLE 8.3

Expenditures in Minas Gerais:
Percent of Actual Budget by Decade, 1880–1937

(Thousand current contos)

| Period | Debt service | Education | Força Pública | Judiciary | Public works | Railroad support | Coffee support |
|--------|------|------|------|------|------|------|------|
| 1880–90   | 12 | 26 | 17 | —  | 14 | —  | —  |
| 1891–99   | 12 | 19 | 14 | 10 | 5  | 3  | —  |
| 1900–1909 | 24 | 14 | 13 | 7  | 4  | 7  | 3  |
| 1910–19   | 22 | 16 | 10 | 5  | 5  | —  | 2  |
| 1920–29   | 7  | 14 | 8  | 3  | 7  | 12 | 2  |
| 1930–37   | 15 | 12 | 9  | 3  | 3  | 17 | 4  |

SOURCE: Data for the 1880's, through the Provisional Government budget of 1890, are in Minas, *Blanço de tabellas de 1891–94;* the remainder are from annual *Relatórios* of the Minas Secretaria das Finanças.

NOTE: Credit operations are not included, nor are all expenditures.

grade rail service in the Sul. Railroad development along the Espírito Santo axis was delayed for several years.

The days of big railroad deals ended abruptly with the depression. Having invested heavily in several private lines, the state was forced into the railroad business while facing angry foreign creditors who demanded interest payment in gold and threatened diplomatic action (see Chapter 2). And although interest payments and subsidies continued, direct loans to railroads ceased, and Minas turned to the federal government for relief. The Sapucaí and Muzambinho were sold to the Union, which consolidated them into the Rêde Sul Mineira and later (1921) rented the system back to the state. Railroad support was shifted out of the credit operations column to the regular budget. Thus it appears as an increasingly large item in Table 8.3.

Over half of the 8,500 contos targeted for immigration benefited the Sul directly, which received the most immigrants. Starting in 1900, this program too became a regular budgetary item and was then phased out. Credits to finance Belo Horizonte reached nearly 29,000 contos before the funding for this very large public works project was shifted in 1897 to a 65 million franc loan from the Banque de Paris et des Pays Bas. After discounts for commissions, fees, etc., only 62 percent of the principal was delivered in this first of the state's large foreign loans.[11]

What benefits accrued from spending such large sums? Sena Figueiredo admitted that Law 64 "had not produced the desired results" and was a major reason for the current budget crisis. But the state was too deeply involved to abandon railroading. The money spent on railroads and immigration had not been wasted from the standpoint of increasing the value of private lands and of private fortunes, he added. If Belo Horizonte had been chosen with "a touch of caprice" and would not generate economic benefits for years, it did represent a long-standing goal fulfilled.[12] A good portion of this money flowed toward the coffee zones, but the North got some trackage and the promise of more, while the once-dominant Center received a new capital city and a new future. To this extent, the structure of Mineiro federalism was reinforced and the ideal of integration was furthered.

One fashionable area of state economic action, aid to infant industry, was quickly abandoned. Interest at 7 percent and other favors were granted the Rio Branco Sugar Central, a Mata concern, in 1885. The company was supposed to reserve 10 percent of its liquid assets in a special fund to advance short-term loans to cane suppliers. It also obligated itself to settle 500 colonos and to produce a certain sugar quota each year. Having failed on all three counts, the Rio Branco Company was fined and cut off by the state in 1894, just as Pernambuco, for example, was going heavily into the financing of sugar centrals. Officials concluded that mills not dependent on state aid functioned better.[13]

Usina Esperança, the pioneer steel plant founded in 1888, was heavily dependent upon interest guarantees and tax concessions that the state withdrew. Protectionism and aid to cooperatives were the preferred support policies up to World War I. For example, Federal Deputy Carvalho Brito added a rider to the 1906 budget bill raising duties on cast iron as an aid to infant industry. The promise of tax relief was offered to infant industries such as steel and meat packing after the war. In 1925, the legislature authorized a 20,000 conto credit to establish a steel works under state-private ownership, including German equity. This mixed enterprise was never carried out. Apparently, the state stayed out of industrial development loans until the Estado Novo.[14]

Allocation decisions taken during the decade of austerity (1900–1909) also appear in Table 8.3. Debt payments reached their highest level, all other services except railroad support were reduced, and there was a new category—coffee support. The Secretariat of Agriculture, which handled public works, was abolished between 1902 and 1910, its services going to other divisions on a reduced basis. Education's share of the budget fell to 14 percent after several schools were closed (including normal schools) and many teachers were laid off. It was again 14 percent in the 1920's, but there was more money available from the much larger budgets of that decade. The long-range trend was for education, the militia, and the judiciary to shrink still further, and for expenditures on public works (especially highways) and railroads to rise. Debt servicing took a smaller share of the budget than in Pernambuco and the poor states, showing that Minas with its growing revenues had more fiscal leeway after 1920.

Entries in the actual budget columns do not of course tell the whole story. Irregularities are hard to pinpoint and confirm. That no published report exists for 1921 is interesting in light of British comments that Bernardes used that year's surplus to finance his presidential campaign.[15] Recall that revenues from the coffee surtax exceeded outlays for coffee support in most years; 1909 was an exception. Agricultural loans of 7,000 contos were also granted during that election year.

Credit operations in the late 1920's bolstered coffee support, a regular budgetary item. Railroad support, long funded out of general revenues, received 84,000 contos in extrabudgetary credits between 1926 and 1930. The larger part went to the Rêde Sul Mineira, which the state rented and operated; the rest financed equipment and construction on the state-owned Paracatú line in west Minas. Financial transactions with the federal treasury and various lending institutions were the largest item under credit operations during the 1930's. Federal payments to support mobilization in 1932 and to expand the Força Pública do not appear under the standard budget headings. Before leaving this overview of expenditures, I want to examine the municipal loan program, which bears on the question of fiscal integration.

Aspirations for a better quality of life at the local level revived with prosperity in 1910. If the municípios stayed backward, Finance Secretary Bernardes said, "the state could never consider itself economically advanced, progressive, or civilized." Minas took out a 50 million franc loan at 4.5 percent from Perier, its French bankers, to construct water, sewage, and electric power systems. These improvements were financed from a fund that amounted to $8.2 million dollars after commissions and fees. The state acted as intermediary for the municípios, which thus received better terms from the French than they could have individually. Some Paulista municípios had to pay up to 8 and 9 percent for the same projects, Bernardes said. Governor Rodrigues Alves of São Paulo advised Uberaba's mayor not to seek a private bank loan in São Paulo, but instead to borrow from Minas at 6 percent, a rate Alves called "*dinheiro de pai para filho.*" Uberaba, one recalls, was firmly in São Paulo's trading orbit.[16]

Under the enabling legislation (Law 546 of 1910), the state made loans to local governments, supervised their improvements with a new bureau, the Municipal Improvements Commission, and collected their revenues to secure this French loan. The municipal loan program was popular. By 1914, four-fifths of the capital had been expended on nearly 60 projects. It was canceled during the war, and then brought back by Governor Bernardes, who had originally set the program up. Funded, now, with domestic bond issues, it remained a regular budgetary item into the 1930's.[17] The governors were careful to point out that state supervision did not imply interference with local autonomy, a touchy issue in Minas. Inevitably, however, the new loan program brought the state directly into municipal affairs.

João Pinheiro called municipal congresses in 1907 to upgrade local services, as we have seen. But his persuasive powers were limited to exhortation and political arm-twisting. Later governors had direct institutional and political leverage through this loan program. Conditions, both formal and informal, came with the improvements. But when Bernardes and Francisco Campos tried to change the Constitution in 1919 so the governor could control local government, congress refused. The public works were welcomed; the central appointment of mayors and the independent auditing of local finances by a nonpolitical council were measures the bosses did not want (see Chapter 4). It may be true that Bernardes acted "more for political than for technical objectives," as a leading analyst has written.[18] These proposals were consistent with purging the Salistas from their bailiwicks. Bernardes had reached the institutional limits of integration: attempts to move from financial tutelage to formal control failed to clear the legislature.

Integration, meaning here a growing state tutelage of the municípios, ran counter to the historic ideal of local autonomy and was controversial. Vertical integration of this kind reinforced an unequal reciprocity. It was held to certain limits in Minas: the mayors in several other states *were* appointed, for example. To be sure, these limits applied more to the few wealthy and more powerful municípios than they did to the majority of local governments that were poor and politically dependent on Belo Horizonte.

Municipal revenues increased sixfold in the 1890's over the last Imperial budget in 1889, and they were the equivalent of about 30 percent of state receipts until World War I. Making local governments independent of the legislature was the goal of delegates to the state constitutional convention in 1891. They failed, in part because income was concentrated in a few municípios and in part because the governor's political leverage increased during the first depression. After 1920, the proportional share of income going to town halls fell to 24 percent of state receipts, while the governor disposed of a larger budget. State powers to supervise, appoint, and control local government personnel all increased in the early 1930's.[19] Yet the issue of local autonomy remained very much alive, and it cannot be said that this third level of government ceased to matter in the play of power.

Minas received back from the federal government a good share of what it contributed in customs duties, excise and consumer taxes during the Old Republic. Just how large a share was controversial. A substantial portion of the federal debt service paid for railroad equipment, of which Minas was the main beneficiary. Also, many Mineiros were professionally active in Rio, where the bulk of federal funds was spent.

The actual contribution of Minas to federal coffers is difficult to estimate. The state had no customs house and kept no records on duties paid in Rio, Santos, and other ports. Also, Minas produced relatively few manufactured goods, so that most federal imposts on domestic manufactures were paid out of state before being shipped in by middlemen. By neglecting customs duties, while counting federal railroad projects in Minas as income for the state, it seemed to some that Minas Gerais was milking the nation and contributing little. One hostile critic proved to his satisfaction that, per capita, the Mineiro contributed only one-fifteenth the federal taxes of his Paulista counterpart. Minas did not lack for counterarguments. In 1926, it appeared that the ratio of federal to state revenues generated in São Paulo was roughly 4 to 3, whereas in Minas the proportion was only 1 to 3. But when customs duties were included, it was possible to contend that the Minas ratio rose to a respectable 5 to 4.[20]

Mineiros, to be sure, did not pay their fair share of federal taxes— they evaded state and local taxes, for that matter. The federal tax service in this very large state was inefficient, and fell behind with collections and its paper work. Calógeras estimated it was 2,000 contos behind in 1918; total federal receipts in Minas were only 14,686 contos ($4.7 million) that year![21] Nor was Minas growing as fast as the other two of the big three. Thus the federal sales tax brought in a larger sum in Rio Grande than in Minas for the first time in 1929 and continued to do so in the ensuing decade.[22] All in all, the visible share of Mineiro tax collections was very small. Questions about the fiscal role of Minas became more pointed in the 1920's, as demands for state and national services increased throughout Brazil.

Income flowed from the poorer regions of the North and West toward the wealthier Center-South, a trend beginning in the mid-nineteenth century. Southern state revenues grew faster than federal revenues after 1889, and the Union spent far more in the Federal District than anywhere else, not to mention its outlays for railways in Minas and Rio Grande. True, the bulk of federal receipts from São Paulo were applied elsewhere, implying that São Paulo was a large net loser. This does not take into account the important differential effects on the regions that exchange manipulation had. In the actual federal budget, Minas was a net contributor by a small margin between 1912 and 1930. "If federal expenditures on servicing the foreign debt could be allocated to the states which benefited from the proceeds of this debt," one analyst contends, "we might find that Minas Gerais was actually a net recipient of income."[23] This is improbable because customs duties exceeded federal expenditures on railroad projects in Minas by a large margin in most if not all these years. It is clear, nonetheless, that Minas relied heavily on federal transfers while São Paulo did not. The role of Pernambuco was to contribute.

The year 1930 was the last in which federal expenditures (in the actual budget) exceeded receipts in Minas. From then on, the balance tipped the other way by 43 percent.[24] Was this because Mineiros could no longer defend their vital interests in congress, which was abolished after the 1930 Revolution, and because they lost leverage on the presidency?

Federal transfers through the new social security agencies and the savings banks occurred. Loans from the Bank of Brazil also became available to the southern states, as they had been since the late 1920's for the bankrupt North. As of 1937, outstanding loans by the Bank of Brazil to states and municipalities totaled 571,733 contos ($49.4 million). Minas garnered one-fifth of the national total. But São Paulo, whose 1932 war debt was federalized by Vargas, held more than half of these outstanding loans.[25] That Minas did not fare as well as São Paulo is clear, but more research is needed on the fiscal dimensions of client status. In a situation of expanding federal services and internal market growth, allocations were no longer being made so much on regional criteria. This movement toward a more national fiscal policy accompanied the decline of state power.

Creating an internal market for the young United States was, to Brazilians, one of the most admired and discussed results of the American institutions they sought to emulate in 1891. The Brazilian states were not allowed to levy import duties, transfer taxes, and other surcharges in restraint of internal trade. Yet despite good intentions and the Constitution, the free flow of goods across state and local borders was restricted by interstate taxes for many years. Goods from other states were taxed for revenue, and sometimes for purposes of protectionism, which led to tariff disputes in the early 1900's. Later, more subtle means were found to advance regional interests through the fisc. This despite Supreme Court decisions (based on American case law) against duplicate taxation in restraint of trade, despite the wishes of commercial groups, the exhortation of presidents, and the Constitution. The struggle against these taxes climaxed after 1900. Minas at first stood on states' rights, and then reluctantly, and at times ambiguously, aligned itself on the side of market integration.

Interstate taxes were carried over from the Empire, when the provinces had a smaller tax base. These restraints on economic growth were frequently discussed during the Republic, which was unable to stamp them out. Regrettably, the British observed, "no Alexander Hamilton has arisen . . . to compel all parties to put aside their petty jealousies and sacrifice their private interests to the welfare of the Union."[26] It happened that Brazil did not lack for neo-Hamiltonians when the authoritarian Estado Novo abolished these taxes and unified fiscal policy.[27] To some extent, it was an institutional problem, as *Cor-*

*reio da Manhã* editorialized in 1903. "Unlike the United States, our model, where Congress and the President do not persist in applying unconstitutional laws, here the Federal President has little interest in the courts because the judiciary controls no votes." This, the Rio daily concluded, is the consequence of corrupting politics under the politics of the governor formula, and "Minas is the state that has most abused these imposts."[28]

Hindsight suggests that contemporaries did not appreciate the extent to which dynamic market forces helped to make Hamilton's policies work in the United States. Highly uneven economic growth in the follower nation divided Brazilian leaders who professed the same objectives. Mineiros thought they had little leeway on the issue. Their assessment of the play of forces determined their actions, and inactions, on this complex problem.

Fiscal crisis threatened Minas in 1904, when the national congress outlawed interstate taxes. The state legislature was convened in special session to find an alternative to the so-called consumer tax, which since the late Empire had been the second largest source of tax revenue. With export income down because of the coffee slump, the consumer tax accounted for $454,000, or 10 percent of that year's austerity budget. Finding a substitute that the population would accept was extremely difficult, and the fiscal crisis lasted into 1905 before the leaders found a way out.

The consumer tax fell exclusively on goods from out of state, both foreign and domestic. In 1892, federal authorities warned Minas that the consumer tax amounted to an import tax, and as such was illegal. Meeting in special session, the legislature determined to continue with it until the issue was settled in court. Other states, it was argued, imposed such taxes and they had not been challenged.[29] That the consumer tax imposed dual taxation was of course true. During the inward-looking phase, such arguments were brushed aside and Supreme Court rulings ignored. In the 1890's, there was no institutional means to compel Minas to change policy.

Furthermore, the consumer tax was popular with certain groups, like the butter producers and mineral water bottlers, who were protected by it. In 1901 and again in 1903 the rates on "imported" competing goods (*semelhantes*) were raised selectively, while agricultural machinery, plants, seeds, chemical fertilizers, and breeding stock now entered free. David Campista favored this protectionist approach, which was also used by Pernambuco and Ceará to foster local products. Such beggar-thy-neighbor policies were extreme manifestations of the protectionist movement, of which Minas was the nation's leading champion at that time. They were also depression-born expedients used by state governments under pressure from producers to "do something" about the contracting domestic market. Meanwhile, facile states' rights arguments on the legality of consumer taxes were made by men like João Luís Alves, the intellectual profiled in Chapter 5, who defended state fiscal policy in congress and the party newspaper *O Diário de Minas*.[30]

Voices on the other side were also heard. Francisco Mendes Pimentel, a PRM founder, Law School professor, and editor of *Revista Forense*, issued a scholarly attack on consumer taxes. Others argued that their state, which sold three-fifths of its exports within Brazil, would benefit from an expanding internal market. The Commercial Association opposed consumer taxes, especially the protectionist aspect. Having supported the stand of commercial groups in Pernambuco and Rio Grande against these "anarchic taxes," it joined with counterparts at the 1902 Sugar Congress in Bahia that called for federal legislation. Rio Grande do Sul, which sold mostly in the domestic market, came out strongly for free trade. Threats to retaliate against states that slapped duties on goods from Rio Grande soon led to a six-year tariff dispute with Pernambuco.[31] Mini-tariff wars broke out in the Northeast; commercial associations launched a national press campaign; and the issue came to a head in congress during 1903.

Minas opposed, tried to delay, and finally had to recognize the strength of anti-tax forces in congress. This was inevitable, after all the major delegations (except Minas) rallied behind draft legislation submitted by São Paulo in August. This bill prohibited consumer taxes on imports and interstate trade goods, but not on retail trade as long as all goods were taxed equally. Protectionist measures against another state's exports were forbidden. Having become a pillar of the congress, Minas had to go along, however reluctantly. There probably were certain trade-offs: protectionist legislation for certain products that both Minas and Rio Grande wanted, discussions on a joint coffee policy with São Paulo, negotiations for the up-coming presidential nomination. The precise mix of backroom maneuvers that led to Law

1185 of 1904 probably never will be known. Congress felt the weight of organized commercial groups and public sentiment against inter-state taxes.[32] President Rodrigues Alves also opposed the taxes. Thus the institutions were responsive, and Minas on this issue behaved quite differently than it had in phase one. But the thorny problem of a sub-stitute tax went deeper than a policy dispute.

The tax issue presented a crisis of authority. Mineiro leaders were extremely reluctant to tamper with a traditional tax to which the public was accustomed. Substituting a direct tax, on incomes for ex-ample, was considered impossible: the Mineiros would only go along with indirect levies. The tradition of tax evasion, even tax revolt, was very much alive in Minas. In 1900, a planter-rancher coalition had watered down the land tax, despite widespread belief that it was the solution to fiscal penury. Given the state's weak tax base, who would bear the burden?

The first solution was a uniform 1.5 percent gross receipts tax on retail trade. Merchant representatives in the legislature labeled this discriminatory. Merchants across the state vowed publicly to boycott the collection, which, in any case, was to be based on their own ac-count books. By year's end this scheme, though passed into law, was abandoned.[33] In 1905, the old consumer tax was collected under an-other name, giving Finance Secretary Antonio Carlos more time to come up with a formula to replace that 10 percent portion of the budget. The state constitution was amended so that the state could collect the industries and professions tax concurrently with the mu-nicípios, to which it had been allotted exclusively as the major local revenue source in 1892. Duties on alcoholic beverages were raised, an unpopular move that was satirized in carnival floats. But the crisis passed.

Meanwhile, the municípios had become accustomed to levying taxes "on anything they can dream up," including foreign imports, goods from out of state, products from their neighbors, prime consumer items such as salt, tobacco, and cachaça (rum), cattle by the head, contracts—all of which were doubly unconstitutional. These taxes were often applied selectively, as a means short of violence for hound-ing political opponents out of town.[34] The state legislature passed a constitutional amendment banning intermunicipal taxes in 1903. This is an interesting example of the PRM's ability to discipline the localities, whose assemblies under the state constitution had some legislative powers. Fiscal integration on the state level was possible because the state had increasing leverage on local governments. In fact, state officials were more eager to free the home market of intermunicipal taxes than they were to stamp out interstate taxation.

The export tax was another restraint on internal trade, which fell equally on goods for the domestic and foreign markets.* One of the strongest arguments for shifting to the land tax was that it would facilitate commerce. Export taxes gradually declined in the total share of state revenues, but, as mentioned, a state sales tax did not supplant them until the mid-1930's. Regressive taxes still dominated; the elite still refused to tax itself. Relatively weak economically, Minas had a horror of losing tax resources. It acted conservatively on this aspect of interstate taxation, and the constitutional reforms of President Bernardes in 1926 did not touch it.

Several states levied interstate taxes under other names well into the 1930's. Minas never returned to the old consumer tax, but it did impose differential export taxes on cattle and iron ore to encourage home production. This policy was attacked and ridiculed by contemporaries, notably by those tied into the international trading nexus. Yet readers from the energy-rich American West will appreciate Minas's intent. Garnering a larger share of profits and benefits from raw materials production through differential state taxes is a lively current issue in American federalism. In 1915, Minas levied a travel tax to finance highway construction. Whether this was tantamount to a tax on goods in transit between states—illegal under the Constitution —was debatable. These imposts gave the Mineiros a bad name in the export-import centers.

If the record was not as bad as hostile critics made it out to be, then Mineiro self-image as the federation's balance wheel hardly applied to its role in the issue of interstate taxation. A mosaic of land-locked regions, it was buffeted by two traditions, free commerce and

* The right of states to tax exports was a striking departure from the United States model, in which export taxes were forbidden. Attacked throughout the Old Republic as a retrograde holdover from the Empire, this tax power was controversial. Most of the states, including Minas, depended heavily on it. An 1896 Supreme Court decision limiting these taxes to foreign commerce was countermanded by congress (Law 410 of 1896). The Court reversed itself in 1897, but in 1910 again declared export taxes on goods sent to another state unconstitutional, only to reverse its position again in 1918. See James, pp. 39–40.

home development. That home development was a function of market forces most of the time was the fate of Minas. Perhaps this was the best result for the nation, but Mineiro policies to the contrary were not absurd. Whether these policies are called "selfish regionalism" or not depends on the point of view.

Federal transfers into railroads turned out not to be the key to economic development that contemporaries assumed; highways would be. Minas extracted fiscal resources from the nation when it could, in part to supplement a weak tax base and its relatively backward economy. Whether this strategy was detrimental, a prop to underdevelopment, is arguable. Contemporary modernizers did not intend so. The federal connection probably helped to postpone internal change but in complex ways, reflecting the multiple, subtle impact of a dependency relationship.

# Conclusion

PROGRESS, to João Pinheiro's generation, began with technological change and economic growth, which produced social differentiation, which in turn led logically, and in good time, to modern democratic politics. To Mineiros, and other late-nineteenth-century Brazilians, the goal of accelerating change along these lines was a reasonable assumption. The United States, with its new power, wealth, and capacity, demonstrated this model of social dynamics. Federal institutions would liberate the same change sequence in Brazil, freeing this very large nation of its colonial heritage, providing the right organizational framework for growth and development to occur. The role of government was to apply techniques and policies that promoted this progression. Given these aspirations, and the efforts that Mineiros made to implement them, the persistence of backwardness in Minas Gerais was shocking. What went wrong?

Development, with its discontinuities and unpredictable results, was more complex than the hopeful modernizers of Pinheiro's generation thought. Minas did not slumber in decadence: it cannot be said that nothing changed. There was moderate economic growth and twice the state was buoyed by prosperity; social differentiation occurred; and politics was not insensitive to new forces, such as the Catholic vote. But change did not produce the phased, sequential, cumulative impact of modernization as anticipated.[1] Instead, artifacts of older social processes survived in ways that only now are being better understood. Furthermore, key aspects of the change process were not controlled in Minas.

Vertical structures and relationships ordered this society far longer, and adapted to change far better than believers in the late-nineteenth-century idea of progress could have thought. Interactions between dominant and inferior actors occurred across the social spectrum of a society based on wealth. Mobility was through patronage and hard work as an individual, or family member, rather than through collective action. Clientelism and co-optive methods tied groups and individuals to the state machine and the administration while eroding several attempts at interest group formation and independent action. There was no crisis of authority, because the emergent middle groups played along and the masses were not yet politically active. Out-migration by elites and masses probably contributed to social stability and the maintenance of integration along vertical dimensions.

But in many ways Minas was no longer the traditional society of literature or social science folklore. Urbanization was under way. The elites were differentiating into a variety of modern occupations required of an increasingly complex socioeconomic order. Urban-rural cleavages did not exist. Yet fazendeiros did not run the state. Rather than living in small towns, many of the political elite gravitated toward Belo Horizonte, the economic center. The tremendous pent-up demand for transportation belied nostalgia for rural isolation or a static social order. Rather, this demonstrated a demand for markets and also to be plugged into happenings in the Atlantic world. These changes began, or were anticipated at least a generation before the Republic was declared. To be sure, they also occurred at different rates, and with different intensity, throughout the Minas mosaic.

During the period under study, the elite never lost confidence in its ability to manage and channel change in nonthreatening directions. There was massive migration and economic dislocation, but no crisis of authority or challenge to the established order. Inadequate economic growth contributed to the maintenance of elite rule on these terms. However, as frequently mentioned, relative economic decline vis à vis São Paulo was a condition that caused great concern in Minas, leading to policies aimed at finding a way out.

Politics was of the type called oligarchical democracy, with low voting and limited participation. Minas Gerais was but one of many examples found in the late-nineteenth-century Atlantic world, especially in the Latin culture areas. Geared to patronage, and dependent on loyalty and reciprocity, this politics was not a reliable means for implementing or following through development programs. João Pinheiro's cooperatives were a case in point. Yet Mineiros pulled together at key points to preserve political power and even to improve governmental output. Silviano's "rounding up the herd" in 1898 under the PRM is one example; Bernardes' 1918 purges of the legislature and the coronelistic grass roots is another. Reform was imposed from the top down, through authoritarian methods. The carrot of co-optation and the stick of violence were offered leading dissidents. Lesser leaders knew that there was but one commandment: never oppose the governor.

The causal link between political power and economic decline is complex. As mentioned frequently in this narrative, the age of Mineiro power began during a prolonged depression, and lasted until the onset of another, in 1929. But the key to political power, and the cause of its decline, was political organization: the capacity to unite for common action. This dynamic was not a direct consequence of economic forces, and owed much to the political culture, to the staying power of the social structure, which was dominated by an elite with a strong sense of place and family, and to the governor's having more income and disposable resources than all but a handful of his counterparts in the South. In aggregate national comparisons, the economy performed relatively well; stacked up against São Paulo and Rio Grande, however, Minas did relatively less well. The political consequences of this were far from obvious.

Minas and São Paulo had similar state machines: both had executive committees based on regional satraps, both were run by business-oriented elites, and both followed similar trajectories of internal cleavages and growing gubernatorial power during the Old Republic. While socially more diverse, the Paulista political domain offered little more room than Minas for newer types of political organizations to develop or compete. Like Minas, the elite there never lost control. Undeniably, São Paulo with its strikes and discontented middle groups experienced earlier, and to a greater extent, the sociopolitical tensions associated with modernization. Political culture there appears to have been less forthrightly conservative. Nevertheless, until 1930—and ambiguously so after that—it cannot be said that Paulista politics were more open and participational, owing to economic growth, and that by way of contrast Minas was politically more traditional because of a lower growth rate. Traditional modes based on co-optation, clientelism, and violence were equally important in the Paulista elite's kit of tools. The variables that best account for this similar behavior are convergent political organization and leadership, not divergent economic performance.

Having said this, one may speculate that if the Minas economy had stagnated (which it did not), the results would probably have been political fragmentation of the Pernambucan and Bahian type. Relative decline is after all much better than stagnation, and it bears repeating that Minas was part of the dynamic South, if ambiguously so as a marginal contributor. That Minas and São Paulo had different objectives in the federal arena is abundantly clear. While following São Paulo's lead in coffee policy, Minas sought federal transfers and patronage, whereas São Paulo with its international linkages was not dependent on the Union in this way.

Furthermore, there was no clear or sequential relationship between social differentiation and political change. The old politics were more altered by political and economic changes coming from outside the region than from internal social changes. New groups coming into politics could still be accommodated by old means. Valadares showed this. To say nothing changed would be false. Voting went up in the 1920's; urbanization and better communications affected politics, but not yet to the extent of undermining the old order by demands for a more participatory politics.

By the third political generation, the political elite appears to have diverged somewhat from the economic elite. Only intensive investigation of the Valadares years can substantiate this finding, which emerged from the quantitative elite data presented in Chapter 5. That several business and industrial leaders were put in top political posts, and with fanfare, after 1945 would suggest attempts were made to rebuild an interlocking elite, perhaps in preference to horizontal interest associations. As mentioned, this is a question for future research.

To sum up, there was economic growth, but not enough to energize society on the North American model; society became more complex, but in ways the old hierarchical order could still deal with; and oligarchical politics based on limited democracy did not of itself give way. Clearly, the nineteenth-century progress model, with phased sequences, did not happen.

Change impacted on a political-cultural unit that lacked a coherent economic base. And it occurred at different rates in the Minas mosaic. There were even two capitals: Belo Horizonte, the political center gaining economic power; Juiz de Fora, the manufacturing hub losing its preeminence. This state was an old administrative entity with a distinct history, literature, and backlog of political experience. The existence of a common political frontier around heterogenous subregions contributed much to regional coherence: politically, state and region were one. Economically, however, the regional identity was far more tenuous. Large parts of Minas were somebody else's hinterland. It belonged to the Center-South market and producing region, but it participated as a marginal producer of almost everything, as an exporter of raw materials, foodstuffs, and agricultural labor.

It appears that Minas Gerais was a dependent region of a special kind. Several nations have experienced the North-South problem during the early stages of development. The United States, Italy, and Brazil offer well-known examples of regional inequality, the process whereby capital, labor, and organizational capacity concentrate in one part of the nation at another region's expense. Regional inequality is likely to increase all the more sharply in the early stages of national development.[2] After 1870, the flow of factors was toward the Brazilian South, spurred by the coffee economy, ranching, and the new urban markets. As part of this newly favored region, Minas benefited. Further south, however, in states with better land resources, transportation, and the challenge of an internal frontier, the reference points were less favorable to Minas.

The political economy of this transitional unit was therefore different from strategies adopted in the North or the South. Because they belonged to the stronger southern region, Mineiros did not make common cause with the disadvantaged North. In fact, Minas joined with São Paulo to spread the costs of coffee valorization onto the nation as a whole. State policies that were aimed at getting a better share of the southern pie were another matter. Governmental actions such as differential ore taxes to force the establishment of steel plants, protectionism to foster Mineiro products, and the internal customs houses to fortify regional commerce were not well received in the export centers. To those benefiting most from the dynamic southern market and its foreign links, Minas's policies appeared backward and unworkable, the result of "narrow regionalism," hardly respectable and often embarrassing.

The long-term benefits of belonging to an emergent industrial heartland were not immediately apparent to Mineiros, for whom state and region still coincided as the logical and accustomed locus of policy and political action. They were by no means sure that market integration would work to their ultimate advantage. This explains their reliance on governmental action to counteract what they perceived to be a structural situation of neo-colonialism. Almost all these policies aborted, as we have seen. After World War II, however, their participation in the Belo Horizonte–Rio–São Paulo industrial triangle was heavily conditioned by state government investments in communications, power, and development loans. Postwar governments took new initiatives, but the idea grew out of earlier efforts to better the terms of Mineiro participation in the Center-South economy. President Kubitschek's developmentalism in the 1950's, then the move to Brasília, grew from concepts developed first on the state level.*

The transitional economic role of Minas between North and South showed up often in the tri-state comparisons. Consider the fiscal data presented in Chapter 8. State income grew, but less rapidly than that of São Paulo and Rio Grande, while Pernambuco's share declined. But the concept of transitional status and relative economic decline, while necessary, is not sufficient to explain this history. Recall the discussion of legislative service in the chapter on careers. Pernambucanos gravitated to the federal congress; Paulistas concentrated on state legislative service; Mineiros served more, and more consistently at both

---

* The move to Brasília was a national aspiration, going back to the early Empire, and explicitly called for in the 1891, 1926, 1934, and 1946 Constitutions. In light of the Mineiros' fascination with Rio, it is interesting that a Mineiro president carried out the move, breaking the hold of Rio—with its city-state mentality—on the federal system, focusing attention on the interior, building an explicit monument to the goal of national integration. Sixty years earlier, the Minas state capital was moved from parochial Ouro Preto to the centrally located, planned city of Belo Horizonte. Having been mayor of Belo from 1940 to 1945, Kubitschek was steeped in this approach. Israel Pinheiro, who was João Pinheiro's son, headed the government construction company (NOVACAP) that built the new capital and was Brasília's first mayor.

levels. One concludes that federal contacts were less important to Paulistas. Their time was perhaps better spent allocating the large state budgets, in comparison with which Pernambuco's much smaller pie was less worth cutting. But why did so many Mineiros want to serve at home? As mentioned often, the state had some resources to spread among the subregions. Equally important, if not more so, was the fact that politicians were expected to serve there, as in São Paulo, which, like Minas, had a strong state machine. The capacity for political organization was more developed in the two southern states, hence in part the higher incidence of state legislative service.

The foreign impact was profound, although Mineiros wished for more. Investments, immigrants, and trade links all pointed toward São Paulo. International events affected Minas in a complex way, and not by economics alone. More than once, for example, a foreign payments crisis triggered political reform from the top down: in 1898 under Silviano and Campos Sales, in 1918 under Governor Bernardes, and again in 1924 when President Bernardes was worried about meeting payments on the funding debt. In these cases, strong-willed leaders took advantage of the situation and under cover of foreign pressure imposed their reforms. The 1929 depression had a different result. Presidential power increased because of it, but also because the Minas state machine had broken down. In the case of coffee, moreover, the Minas growers faced ruin from international economic forces, had it not been for the staying hand of valorization, a political act.

Mineiros appreciated the role of government, although they lacked the political and administrative organization to support and sustain development plans. The leadership was not helpless in the face of change. On the margins of a dynamic new unit, the Center-South, they wanted to achieve better terms of participation. These Minas policies belong to the mainstream of Brazilian efforts at the state and national levels to reverse regional inequality through governmental action. In Minas, at least, implementing this concept was aborted by lack of governmental follow-through, hindered by the obstacles of topography, and confused by different historical patterns among the zones.

Zone, state, and nation interacted on a continuum, but the balance of forces shifted with integration. Controlling the allocation of power and resources between these units was a principal concern of state government. If in the 1890's state and nation were rather sharply counterposed, this hard-line brand of regionalism was muted after 1898, when it was decided that Minas could not develop unaided by the central government.

Viewed from this perspective, the thrust of Mineiro regionalism was to provide an economy for the fortifying of regional power. This goal was cross-cutting and contradictory. Market integration drew Minas into new configurations, on terms that seemed unfavorable to the unit as a whole while benefiting some of the parts, notably the Triângulo.

Regionalism was redefined with integration, but the process was not one of accelerating centralism pure and simple. All levels of government gained in capacity and took on new responsibilities, judging from the Minas case. State revenue actually grew faster than federal revenue during the 1930's, even though military and presidential power had been growing at the center since World War I. Integration meant tutelage, as well as cooperation. The municipal improvement loans are one example. The state Finance Secretary seeking relief in Rio from the short-term floating debt in 1933 is another. Integration at the state level was hindered by the disarticulated market. And one may speculate that it was hindered also by social patterns favoring informal, vertical relationships over horizontal solidarities. Recall the many failures of agricultural groups to organize. Finally, it seems clear that national integration for Minas took place on rather special terms, because of the state's location and economic deficiencies, but also because of its political power and importance to presidents.

Regional culture celebrated small-town roots, old families, and the mining past. Yet in many ways this was a new society formed in the early-nineteenth-century shift into agriculture and ranching, and branching into urban-centered occupations by the 1880's. The elite was schooled according to national norms and patterns, but displayed some regional twists. No homogeneous national oligarchy existed, as the computerized data reveal. Mineiros traveled less abroad, served less in other states, and allowed fewer nonnatives into politics than their Paulista and Pernambucano counterparts.

Belo Horizonte was far less dominant as a cultural center than Recife or São Paulo; this encouraged the survival and growth of subregional themes in literature. However, the typical elite leader was far from being the place-centered politico celebrated in novels, short stories, and plays. Geographical movement within the state occurred at virtually the same rate as in São Paulo, a state in full frontier expansion. But in Minas, this mobile elite gravitated mostly to Belo Horizonte, the bureaucratic center, and next to Juiz de Fora. This elite also went to Rio in large numbers, with Cariocas saying of Mineiros, "the best ones always leave."

The balance sheet for Minas Gerais is disappointing in light of João Pinheiro's goals and expectations. Given the resources and geography, however, Minas did not fare badly on a world scale. Underdeveloped and poverty-ridden it surely was, but there was also hope and expectation of relief through governmental action and economic growth. The quality of life for most Mineiros was bad—public health, literacy, income, and migration data show this well—but this society was not unrelievedly grim. Belo Horizonte with its broad boulevards and generous layout, and the towns with their lively civic culture, stood for qualities that were arresting and not just to be enjoyed by the privileged few.

# Appendixes

# A Note on Elites

THE POLITICAL ELITE examined in Chapter 5 is a group defined as holders of important positions in state parties and governments, plus the state's representatives in important federal posts, during the years from the birth of the Republic to the Estado Novo. Thus, statistically speaking, the elite is a population rather than a sample. Since some persons held office for as little as one day, a 90-day minimum tenure was required for inclusion during the period November 15, 1889, to November 10, 1937. All persons are included who could be identified by name and dates of tenure, whether or not any other information was discovered. In fact, however, virtually complete biographies were obtained for more than 90 percent of the elites of the three states—Minas Gerais, Pernambuco, and São Paulo.

The authors agreed on the inclusion of 17 to 18 state government posts and 17 at the federal level. In the states the list consisted of the governor and his important elected and appointed assistants in the executive, and top-ranking legislative and judicial figures. Federal posts were defined analogously, but were included only when held by representatives of the state under study.

Specifically, state elite members consisted of the governor; the lieutenant governor; the secretaries of justice, finance, agriculture, transportation, education and health, security, and the governorship; the state chief of police; the president of the state bank; the prefect of the state capital; leading administrators peculiar to each state (viz., presidents of the Coffee Institutes in São Paulo and Minas; director of the state press in Minas; director of the port authority and inspector of municípios in Pernambuco); the presidents of the state chamber and senate; the majority leader in the chamber; and the president of the state supreme court.

Federal officials included the president of the Republic; the vice-president; the ministers of justice, finance, agriculture, transportation, education, labor, and foreign affairs; the president of the Bank of Brazil; the prefect of the Federal District; the president of the National Coffee Department; the president of the federal chamber of deputies; the vice-president of the senate;* the majority leader of the chamber; the leader of the state delegation in the chamber; and members of the federal supreme court.

Thus the elites were defined uniformly except for the "leading [state] administrators" specified above. To have eliminated such key positions as the presidencies of the Coffee Institutes in São Paulo and Minas because the post did not exist in Pernambuco seemed unduly procrustean, since the central purpose of the definition of elites was to obtain comparable *wholes* from each state. The size of the elite populations ranged from 214 in Minas Gerais, to 263 in São Paulo, to 276 in Pernambuco.

Three nongovernmental positions are also included in the elites—the executive committee of the Republican Party (the "establishment" party in the Old Republic), and those of the most important non-Republican party before 1930, and from 1931 to 1937. (The roles of the Republicans and their opponents were reversed after 1930, or new establishment parties brought in many leaders of pre-1930 opposition groups.) It seemed essential to include this nongovernmental sector of the elite because of its leading role in the larger political process. Separate computer runs of party executive committee members against nonmembers tended to confirm our qualitative judgment on this point: committee members held more elite-defining positions than nonmembers, and they were more prominent in the economy and society. Thus, in the manner of Frank Bonilla's definition of the Venezuelan political elite, in *The Failure of Elites* (Cambridge, Mass., 1970), p. 16, party executive committees were included to better approximate the effective power structure.

The elite was defined to exclude military and naval officials, since these groups were members of virtually self-regulating corporations and had tenuous ties with the three state machines. In the cases of the ministries of war and navy, in only one administration (Pessoa, 1919–22) were civilians appointed to the posts; they were excluded from our elites, though officers holding the specified "civilian" posts were not. Regional military commanders, with the possible exception of those in Rio Grande do Sul, had no enduring ties with state political machines, and these career officers were rotated around the country. Commanders of the state military police forces were subordinated to the civilian political leadership, and in none of the three states did they play significant roles in political decision-making.

In each case our institutional definition omitted a few individuals who might have been included had the elite been defined on a "reputational" basis. Yet the exclusion of two or three persons in a group of 753 seemed an acceptable sacrifice to maintain a cohesive definition across the states: those left out would have changed the profile of the group only a percentage point, and many data were too "soft" to justify claims of precision at a fraction of a point.

Approximately 100 variables were recorded on the elite's characteristics. They were grouped under the headings of political ideology, roles in major political events at both national and state levels, social and cultural activities, foreign ties, interstate ties, age, education, occupation, *municípios*

* The vice-president of the Republic was ipso facto president of the senate.

and zones of political activity, and family ties. (For coding schemes, the reader may obtain code books from the authors.) Biographical data were strongest on educational and official positions held; they were weakest on economic assets.

Though the computer program was designed to show progression through the elite posts during the period studied, it does not cover whole career patterns, and thus we have not produced a political recruitment study analogous to Frederick W. Frey's *The Turkish Political Elite* (Cambridge, Mass., 1965). Frey's elite is much more simply defined than ours; it includes all members of the Turkish National Assembly serving between 1920 and 1957, i.e. occupants of one post rather than 37 (p. 7).

Data were obtained from a variety of sources: official obituaries in state gazettes, obituaries and centenary-of-birth notices in newspaper morgues, almanacs, membership lists of voluntary associations, biographies, interviews of elite members and their descendents, questionnaires to these groups, professional school graduation lists, publications of political parties, biographical dictionaries and encyclopedias, and commemorative albums.

An initial problem was to construct lists of officeholders and dates of tenure, since in the majority of cases none existed. For the executive committees of the Republican Parties in Minas and São Paulo, it was discovered that elections for state and national offices would always bring forth an "electoral bulletin" signed by the current members of the respective committee. Historical reconstruction of the committees therefore began with a search for the dates of elections in the annual reports of the secretary of justice. This was followed by an examination of the *Correio Paulistano* and the *Minas Gerais* on the day preceding the contests to discover the signers of the bulletins. (A similar procedure was used in Pernambuco, but with less success, because of the lower degrees of party cohesion in that state.) The compilation of lists of officeholders and dates of tenure should provide basic chronologies for the historian of institutions, and a complete listing for the state is found in Appendix B.

*Conventions Used in Classifying Elite Characteristics*

1. Members of the elite had to be Brazilian nationals.

2. If a member held the same post more than once, he was coded for each separate tenure of that office.

3. In the absence of data for a given characteristic in cases where data were virtually complete, it was assumed the elite member lacked the attribute, and the item was coded negatively. Only in those cases where the overwhelming majority of data were missing was "missing data" coded.

4. The "not applicable" code was entered whenever a member was too young to have participated in a given event, had already died, or had withdrawn from political activity.

5. All events and experiences that were coded positively occurred during the stated chronological limits, except those specifically referring to pre-1889 events and items pertaining to education, foreign parentage, and residence abroad, all of which included pre-1889 experience as well.

6. If a member represented a state in a federal post other than the one

for which he was coded, that portion of his career outside the state under study was not coded. (E.g. Rivadávia Correia in his youth was a member of the São Paulo elite, but later represented Rio Grande do Sul as a federal minister.)

7. Multiple professions were coded, viz., all those professions and occupations ascertainable in the 1889–1937 period. Specific conventions: an exporter was also classified as a merchant; a comissário was not classified as a banker, since the latter term implies a director of a larger operation (though there was considerable overlap); newspaper publishers, building contractors, and railroad builders were all coded as industrialists, and all magistrates were also classified as lawyers.

8. All state supreme court justices were coded as having their political base in the appropriate state capital. Since most were professional magistrates, they were so classified because they had no home constituency and depended on directives from the state government to which they were attached.

9. Presidents of the Bank of Brazil included only that group who held office between 1906 and 1937. The bank was completely reorganized in 1906 with a more fully national mission. Before the reorganization it had no agencies outside the Federal District, and by 1927 there were 70.

*The Brazilian Elite—Political Offices Held*

STATE

Secretary of Justice, or General Secretary
Secretary of Finance
Secretary of Agriculture
Secretary of Education and Health (Interior)
Secretary of Transportation (*Viação*)
Secretary of Security (*Segurança*)
Secretary of Governorship or Interventorship
Governor or Interventor
Lieutenant Governor
Prefect, State Capital
Police Chief of State
Top State Administrator (SP [São Paulo] def.: pres., Coffee Institute. MG [Minas Gerais] def.: director, State Press, and pres., Mineiro Coffee Institute. PE [Pernambuco] def.: dir., Port Authority and Inspector General of municipalities)
President, State-owned bank
President, State Senate
President, State Chamber, or President, Constituent Assembly
Majority Leader, State Chamber
President, State Supreme Court
Leader of largest non-PR party or coalition, through 1930 (SP def.: member, executive committee, Partido Democrático. [MG: not applicable.] PE def.: member, Martins Jr. and José Mariano factions; member, pre-1910 anti–Rosa e Silva group; member, anti-Dantas group, 1911–18; member, Partido Democrático, 1920's)

Leader of largest non-PR party or coalition, 1931–37 (SP def.: member, executive committee, PD [1931–34]; member, executive committee, Partido Constitucionalista, 1934–37. MG def.: member, executive committee, Partido Progressista. PE def.: member, dissident Partido Social Democrático bloc [anti-Lima Cavalcanti faction])

Member, executive committee, Partido Republicano (MG def.: PR, 1889–90; Partido Republicano Constitucional, 1893–97, defined as leaders signing voting slates; Partido Republicano Mineiro, 1897–1937)

FEDERAL

Minister of Justice
Minister of Finance
Minister of Agriculture
Minister of Foreign Affairs
Minister of Education
Minister of Labor
Minister of Transportation
President of the Republic
Vice-President of the Republic
Prefect, Federal District
President, Conselho Nacional do Café, or its successor, Departamento Nacional do Café
President, Bank of Brazil (1906–37)
Vice-President, Federal Senate
President, Chamber of Deputies, or President, Constituent Assembly
Majority Leader, Chamber of Deputies
Leader, state delegation (bancada), Chamber of Deputies
Minister, Supreme Court (Supremo Tribunal Federal)

*The six-page table that follows shows variables and values for Pernambuco, Minas Gerais, and São Paulo*

## Variables and Values in the Three Elite Studies
(Adjusted frequencies in percentages)

| Categories and variables | Pernambuco | | Minas Gerais | | São Paulo | | Composite | |
|---|---|---|---|---|---|---|---|---|
| | Value | Number | Value | Number | Value | Number | Value | Number |
| **POLITICAL EVENTS** | | | | | | | | |
| 1a. Monarchist who adhered to the Republic by public affirmation, Nov. 15, 1889–Dec. 31, 1891 | 73.8% | 80 | 48.2% | 83 | 49.5% | 105 | 56.3% | 268 |
| 1b. Monarchist who adhered to the Republic, 1892–1900 | 3.8 | 80 | 2.4 | 83 | 0 | 105 | 1.9 | 268 |
| 1c. Historical Republican: a self-proclaimed Republican before abolition (May 13, 1888) | 21.3 | 80 | 41.0 | 83 | 49.5 | 105 | 38.4 | 268 |
| 1d. Eleventh-hour Republican: publicly declared self a Republican between May 13, 1888, and Nov. 14, 1889 | 1.3 | 80 | 8.4 | 83 | 1.0 | 105 | 3.4 | 268 |
| 2. Abolitionist before Jan. 1, 1887, calling for complete termination of slavery within one decade or less | 16.8 | 95 | 8.6 | 116 | 19.8 | 111 | 14.9 | 322 |
| 3. Deodoro backer: supported Deodoro's attempted coup between Nov. 3 and 24, 1891 | 5.2 | 97 | 5.9 | 118 | 12.3 | 122 | 8.0 | 337 |
| 4. Break on valorization: break with the state establishment's position at any time | 0 | 114 | 0 | 131 | 1.0 | 206 | 0.4 | 451 |
| 5. Break with state establishment's position over presidential succession in 1909–10 | 23.7 | 135 | 10.7 | 149 | 7.9 | 164 | 13.6 | 448 |
| 6. Break with state establishment's position over presidential succession in 1921–22 | 6.8 | 117 | 4.6 | 151 | 0.6 | 178 | 3.6 | 446 |
| 7. Break with state establishment's position over presidential succession in 1929–30 | 22.1 | 113 | 5.9 | 136 | 3.2 | 125 | 9.9 | 374 |
| 8. Tenente or political associate of tenentes after Oct. 24, 1930 | 18.9 | 111 | 2.9 | 138 | 5.8 | 171 | 8.3 | 420 |
| **NONPOLITICAL LEADERSHIP** | | | | | | | | |
| 9. Magistrate: *Juiz de direito* or higher | 25.9 | 205 | 16.8 | 214 | 19.4 | 242 | 20.6 | 661 |
| 10. Cultural leader: member, state academy of letters, or national academy of letters | 8.2 | 196 | 4.7 | 214 | 5.8 | 241 | 6.1 | 651 |
| 11. Labor leader: officer, labor union (local), or higher unit or organization | 1.0 | 196 | 0 | 214 | 0 | 243 | 0.3 | 653 |

| | % | N | % | N | % | N | % | N |
|---|---|---|---|---|---|---|---|---|
| 12. Social club member: any one or more of the following: SP def.: Sociedade Hípica, Clube Comercial, Jockey Clube, Clube Atlético Paulista, Automóvel Clube. MG def.: Automóvel Clube, Jockey Clube. PE def.: Clube Internacional, Jockey Clube Sport, Centro Pernambucano do Rio | 15.3 | 196 | 11.2 | 214 | 27.4 | 241 | 18.4 | 651 |
| 13. Agricultural society officer: SP def.: Sociedade Rural Brasileira, or any of its constituent entities before consolidation—Centro Agrícola, Sociedade Paulista da Agricultura, Liga Agrícola Brasileira, or Associação de Lavradores de Café. MG def.: Sociedade Mineira de Agricultura. PE def.: Sociedade Auxiliadora de Agricultura de Pernambuco | 6.6 | 196 | 1.9 | 214 | 6.7 | 239 | 5.1 | 649 |
| 14. Officer, state Commercial Association | 4.1 | 196 | 0.5 | 214 | 3.7 | 242 | 2.8 | 652 |
| 15. Officer, Ordem dos Advogados or Instituto dos Advogados | 0.5 | 196 | 5.1 | 214 | 4.1 | 242 | 3.4 | 652 |
| FOREIGN TIES | | | | | | | | |
| 16. Lawyer for foreign company operating in Brazil. Def. of foreign: at least 51 percent of stock owned by foreign nationals | 4.3 | 187 | 2.3 | 213 | 0.8 | 240 | 2.3 | 640 |
| 17. Importer: manager or director of, or investor in, importing firm | 1.1 | 188 | 0 | 214 | 2.9 | 239 | 1.4 | 641 |
| 18. Exporter, manager or director of, or investor in, exporting firm | 7.4 | 189 | 0.5 | 214 | 6.7 | 239 | 4.8 | 642 |
| 19. Manager or director of, or investor in, foreign firm operating in Brazil; foreign defined under 16 | 2.7 | 188 | 2.4 | 211 | 9.2 | 239 | 5.0 | 638 |
| 20. At least one foreign-born parent | 4.3 | 188 | 2.8 | 213 | 4.6 | 239 | 3.9 | 640 |
| 21. Foreign-born wife | 1.1 | 188 | 0 | 214 | 2.1 | 238 | 1.1 | 640 |
| 22. At least one year of foreign study at any level | 6.9 | 189 | 5.1 | 214 | 13.4 | 239 | 8.7 | 642 |
| 23. Residence abroad for at least six months | 20.3 | 187 | 7.5 | 214 | 31.9 | 238 | 20.3 | 639 |
| 24. Consul for foreign government | 2.1 | 188 | 0 | 214 | 0.4 | 239 | 0.8 | 641 |
| 25. Decorated by foreign government | 1.6 | 188 | 0.9 | 214 | 8.8 | 239 | 4.1 | 641 |

NOTE: This is not a list of all variables tested; in some cases data were too incomplete to be recorded here. Values omit cases where no data were found and those for which the item was not applicable. Number refers to the number of valid cases from which the percentages were derived.

## Variables and Values in the Three Elite Studies (Continued)

| Categories and variables | Pernambuco | | Minas Gerais | | São Paulo | | Composite | |
|---|---|---|---|---|---|---|---|---|
| | Value | Number | Value | Number | Value | Number | Value | Number |
| 26. Procurer of immigrants: director or manager of, or investor in, private or government immigration-promoting enterprise | 0.5% | 188 | 0.9% | 214 | 4.2% | 239 | 2.0% | 641 |
| 27. Naturalized Brazilian | 1.1 | 188 | 0.5 | 214 | 0.4 | 239 | 0.6 | 641 |
| 28. Foreign title: holder of foreign or papal title of nobility | 2.1 | 188 | 0.5 | 214 | 0.8 | 239 | 1.1 | 641 |
| INTERSTATE TIES | | | | | | | | |
| 29. Political or administrative officeholder in another state: *Juiz de direito*, state deputy or federal deputy, or above (i.e. the defining positions—17 to 18 state posts and 17 federal ones) | 6.9 | 195 | 6.1 | 214 | 7.1 | 238 | 9.7 | 647 |
| 30. Professional career in another state, then returns: minimum time, one year | 12.9 | 194 | 3.3 | 214 | 7.1 | 240 | 7.6 | 648 |
| 31. Professional career in Federal District | 17.5 | 194 | 14.5 | 214 | 1.3 | 240 | 10.5 | 648 |
| 32. Professional career in Federal District, then returns | 7.2 | 194 | 2.3 | 214 | 5.8 | 240 | 5.1 | 648 |
| 33. Employee in any official interstate agency: e.g. an interstate coffee convention | 4.6 | 195 | 0.5 | 214 | 0.4 | 239 | 1.7 | 648 |
| 34. Out-of-state birth | 14.5 | 193 | 13.1 | 214 | 18.6 | 236 | 15.6 | 643 |
| 35. Political or administrative officeholder in another province or in the Município Neutro before Nov. 15, 1889: Def. officeholder is *Juiz de direito*, provincial deputy, general deputy, or above (i.e. imperial equivalents of posts cited in 29) | 21.2 | 193 | 4.2 | 214 | 12.5 | 112 | 12.3 | 519 |
| 36. Colégio in another state or Federal District: minimum time, one academic year | 8.3 | 193 | 13.6 | 211 | 19.7 | 234 | 14.3 | 638 |
| EDUCATION | | | | | | | | |
| 37. Law degree, in state | 71.8 | 196 | 14.1 | 213 | 62.5 | 240 | 49.8 | 649 |
| 38. Law degree, other state or Federal District | 3.6 | 193 | 42.3 | 213 | 5.0 | 241 | 16.8 | 647 |
| 39. Law degree split: at least one year at law school in a state (or Federal District) other than the one where he graduated | 1.6 | 193 | 5.1 | 214 | 2.9 | 242 | 3.2 | 649 |

| | % | N | % | N | % | N | % | N |
|---|---|---|---|---|---|---|---|---|
| 40. Medical degree, in state | 0.5 | 193 | 0 | 213 | 0.4 | 241 | 0.3 | 647 |
| 41. Medical degree, other state or Federal District | 7.3 | 193 | 10.4 | 212 | 5.0 | 240 | 7.4 | 645 |
| 42. Medical degree, split: analogous to 39 | 0 | 193 | 0.9 | 214 | 0 | 242 | 0.3 | 649 |
| 43. Engineering degree, in state | 3.1 | 193 | 8.4 | 214 | 4.5 | 242 | 5.4 | 649 |
| 44. Engineering degree, other state or Federal District | 2.6 | 193 | 2.3 | 213 | 2.1 | 242 | 2.3 | 648 |
| 45. Military degree: graduation from Agulhas Negras, Escola Militar in Rio, Colégio Militar in Pôrto Alegre, or its imperial equivalent in Ceará | 4.1 | 193 | 0.9 | 214 | 2.1 | 241 | 2.3 | 648 |
| 46. Pharmacy degree | 0.5 | 193 | 3.7 | 214 | 1.2 | 242 | 1.8 | 649 |
| 47. Other university degree | 4.1 | 193 | 0.9 | 214 | 10.4 | 241 | 5.4 | 648 |
| 48. Secondary school graduate, but no higher degree | 4.7 | 193 | 7.1 | 210 | 5.8 | 241 | 5.9 | 644 |
| 49. Up to secondary school, but no diploma | 1.0 | 193 | 1.9 | 209 | 1.7 | 241 | 1.6 | 643 |
| OCCUPATION | | | | | | | | |
| 50. Lawyer | 55.1 | 214 | 67.9 | 212 | 69.3 | 241 | 64.3 | 667 |
| 51. Physician | 7.1 | 197 | 12.1 | 214 | 7.1 | 241 | 8.7 | 652 |
| 52. Journalist | 35.0 | 197 | 23.8 | 214 | 26.6 | 241 | 28.2 | 652 |
| 53. Fazendeiro: owner of estate producing agricultural or pastoral goods primarily for cash sale | 18.8 | 197 | 16.7 | 210 | 37.7 | 239 | 25.1 | 646 |
| 54. Merchant | 13.3 | 196 | 5.6 | 213 | 16.6 | 241 | 12.0 | 650 |
| 55. Industrialist: owner of, or investor in, manufacturing or processing operation (e.g. usineiro) | 12.6 | 199 | 17.8 | 214 | 27.8 | 241 | 19.9 | 654 |
| 56. Banker: manager, director, or legal counsel of, or investor in, bank | 9.1 | 198 | 15.0 | 214 | 18.3 | 241 | 14.4 | 653 |
| 57. Educator: secondary- or university-level teacher | 27.3 | 199 | 32.2 | 213 | 21.2 | 241 | 26.6 | 653 |
| 58. Engineer | 9.4 | 202 | 12.7 | 213 | 9.9 | 242 | 10.7 | 657 |
| 59. Cleric | 2.5 | 198 | 0.5 | 214 | 0 | 253 | 0.9 | 665 |
| 60. Military officer | 4.6 | 197 | 0.5 | 214 | 2.5 | 242 | 2.5 | 653 |
| 61. Magistrate: Juiz de direito or above | 19.8 | 197 | 17.3 | 214 | 19.1 | 241 | 18.7 | 652 |
| 62. Rural land dealer | 1.0 | 197 | 0 | 214 | 2.9 | 241 | 1.4 | 652 |
| 63. Comissário: Short-term lender to fazendeiros | 0 | 197 | 0 | 214 | 3.8 | 240 | 1.4 | 651 |
| 64. Manager, director, or legal counsel of, or investor in, railroad company operating in Brazil | 0 | 197 | 5.6 | 214 | 9.5 | 241 | 5.4 | 652 |
| 65. Mine owner or investor in mining | 1.0 | 197 | 3.3 | 213 | 0 | 241 | 1.4 | 651 |
| 66. Other profession or occupation | 2.0 | 197 | 6.5 | 214 | 4.6 | 241 | 4.4 | 652 |

## Variables and Values in the Three Elite Studies (Continued)

| Categories and variables | Pernambuco Value | Pernambuco Number | Minas Gerais Value | Minas Gerais Number | São Paulo Value | São Paulo Number | Composite Value | Composite Number |
|---|---|---|---|---|---|---|---|---|
| FAMILY TIES | | | | | | | | |
| 67. Related to at least one other member of same state elite, through first cousin—consanguineal or affinitive | 34.3% | 198 | 46.3% | 177 | 42.5% | 240 | 41.0% | 615 |
| 68. Member of, or related to, imperial elite, through first cousin, con. or aff., or direct descendant through grandson. Def. of imperial elite: senators, or title-holders of *barão* or above | 27.4 | 197 | 16.2 | 185 | 19.7 | 239 | 21.1 | 621 |
| 69. Related to at least one member of any other analogously defined state elite (not just those of PE, SP, or MG), through first cousin—con. or aff. | 12.0 | 192 | 4.3 | 185 | 0.8 | 241 | 5.3 | 618 |
| 70. In federal congress: served at least once (appointed or elected) for 90 days or more, in chamber or senate | 55.7 | 192 | 51.2 | 209 | 31.7 | 252 | 45.0 | 653 |
| 71. In state legislature: served at least once (appointed or elected) for 90 days or more, in chamber or senate | 30.9 | 194 | 47.4 | 209 | 48.6 | 255 | 43.0 | 658 |
| OTHER VARIABLES: COMPOSITES OR ITEMS DERIVED FROM "POLITICAL OFFICES HELD" | | | | | | | | |
| Historical Republican: composite of 1c-1d | 22.5 | 80 | 49.4 | 83 | 50.5 | 105 | 41.8 | 268 |
| Adherent to the Republic: composite of 1a-1b | 77.6 | 80 | 50.6 | 83 | 49.5 | 105 | 58.2 | 268 |
| Age at first elite-defining position: | | | | | | | | |
| Minimum | 19 | 186 | 23 | 181 | 25 | 230 | — | 597 |
| Maximum | 78 | 186 | 80 | 181 | 85 | 230 | — | 597 |
| Mean | 43.0 | 186 | 43.3 | 181 | 46.0 | 230 | 44.2 | 597 |
| Median | 42.3 | 186 | 41.9 | 181 | 45.1 | 230 | 43.3 | 597 |
| Age at first elite-defining position, grouped in 10-year intervals: | | | | | | | | |
| 29 or less | 16.7 | 186 | 5.0 | 181 | 3.5 | 230 | 8.0 | 597 |
| 30–39 | 22.0 | 186 | 36.5 | 181 | 23.9 | 230 | 27.1 | 597 |
| 40–49 | 29.6 | 186 | 32.0 | 181 | 39.6 | 230 | 34.2 | 597 |
| 50–59 | 18.3 | 186 | 20.4 | 181 | 21.3 | 230 | 20.1 | 597 |
| 60 or over | 13.4 | 186 | 6.1 | 181 | 11.7 | 230 | 10.6 | 597 |

|  | % | N | % | N | % | N | % | N |
|---|---|---|---|---|---|---|---|---|
| **Political generation:** | | | | | | | | |
| First: born before 1869 | 50.8 | 193 | 50.3 | 181 | 46.1 | 230 | 48.8 | 604 |
| Second: born between 1869 and 1888 | 29.5 | 193 | 31.5 | 181 | 33.9 | 230 | 31.8 | 604 |
| Third: born in 1889 or later | 19.7 | 193 | 18.2 | 181 | 20.0 | 230 | 19.4 | 604 |
| Held first office after 1930 Revolution | 14.9 | 268 | 21.5 | 214 | 37.3 | 263 | 24.7 | 745 |
| Out-of-state job: composite of 29–33 | 43.6 | 195 | 22.4 | 214 | 16.8 | 238 | 26.7 | 647 |
| Out-of-state link (education, experience, family tie): composite of 29–34, 36, 38–39, 41–42, 44–45, 69 | 64.9 | 185 | 72.1 | 183 | 39.3 | 229 | 57.3 | 597 |
| Foreign tie: composite of 16–28 | 33.3 | 186 | 15.7 | 210 | 48.1 | 237 | 33.0 | 633 |
| *Bacharel*: composite of 37–42 | 81.3 | 194 | 73.8 | 210 | 76.2 | 239 | 76.9 | 641 |
| Lacking university degree: composite of 48–49 | 5.7 | 193 | 9.2 | 206 | 7.5 | 241 | 7.5 | 640 |
| Businessman: composite of 54–56, 63–65 | 24.4 | 197 | 34.9 | 212 | 41.3 | 240 | 34.1 | 649 |
| Member of agricultural export complex: composite of 13, 18, 53, 63 | 26.2 | 187 | 17.1 | 210 | 40.3 | 233 | 28.4 | 630 |
| Relative of Republican or imperial elite: composite of 67–69 | 45.3 | 192 | 52.9 | 170 | 49.6 | 236 | 49.2 | 598 |
| Member of PR executive committee | 14.9 | 276 | 32.2 | 214 | 28.5 | 263 | 24.6 | 753 |
| Opposition leader: composite of all members of non-PR executive committees | 10.5 | 276 | 8.4 | 214 | 20.5 | 263 | 13.4 | 753 |
| Party leader: composite of all members of PR and non-PR executive committees | 25.4 | 276 | 38.8 | 214 | 48.3 | 263 | 37.2 | 753 |
| Governor | 6.2 | 276 | 7.9 | 214 | 8.0 | 263 | 7.3 | 753 |
| Legislative experience: composite of 70–71 | 65.6 | 276 | 68.4 | 209 | 57.1 | 252 | 63.2 | 737 |
| INTRA-STATE VARIABLES: MINAS GERAIS POLITICAL EVENTS | | | | | | | | |
| Break with Alvim administration, 1890–92 | | | 16.2 | 111 | | | | |
| Break with Partido Republicano Constitucional, 1893–96 | | | 15.3 | 118 | | | | |
| Break with PRC, 1897 | | | 15.3 | 118 | | | | |
| Braek with Partido Republicano Mineiro, 1898 | | | 6.0 | 116 | | | | |
| Break with PRM under Bernardes, 1918–20 | | | 8.1 | 148 | | | | |
| Break with Olegário Maciel administration, 1930–33 | | | 22.0 | 132 | | | | |
| Break when Valadares appointed interventor, December 1933 | | | 15.1 | 126 | | | | |
| Break when the Partido Progressista and the PRM were fused by Valadares, 1936 | | | 14.5 | 124 | | | | |

# Tenure in Elite Posts

*Governor*

| | |
|---|---|
| José Cesário de Faria Alvim | Nov. 15, 1889–Feb. 10, 1890 |
| João Pinheiro da Silva | Feb. 11, 1890–July 19, 1890 |
| Domingos José da Rocha | [July 20, 1890–July 23, 1890] |
| Crispim Jacques Bias Fortes | [July 24, 1890–Aug. 5, 1890] |
| Domingos José da Rocha | [Aug. 6, 1890–Aug. 13, 1890] |
| Crispim Jacques Bias Fortes | [Aug. 14, 1890–Oct. 3, 1890] |
| Domingos José da Rocha | [Oct. 4, 1890–Oct. 17, 1890] |
| Crispim Jacques Bias Fortes | [Oct. 18, 1890–Dec. 27, 1890] |
| Frederico Augusto Álvares da Silva | [Dec. 28, 1890–Jan. 6, 1891] |
| Crispim Jacques Bias Fortes | [Jan. 7, 1891–Feb. 11, 1891] |
| Frederico Augusto Álvares da Silva | [Feb. 12, 1891–March 17, 1891] |
| Antonio Augusto de Lima | March 18, 1891–June 15, 1891 |
| José Cesário de Faria Alvim | June 15, 1891–Feb. 8, 1892 |
| Afonso Augusto Moreira Pena | July 14, 1892–Sept. 7, 1894 |
| Crispim Jacques Bias Fortes | Sept. 7, 1894–Sept. 7, 1898 |
| Francisco Silviano de Almeida Brandão | Sept. 7, 1898–Feb. 21, 1902 |
| Francisco Antonio de Sales | Sept. 7, 1902–Sept. 7, 1906 |
| João Pinheiro da Silva | Sept. 7, 1906–Oct. 26, 1908 |
| Wenceslau Brás Pereira Gomes | April 3, 1909–Sept. 7, 1910 |
| Júlio Bueno Brandão | Sept. 7, 1910—Sept. 7, 1914 |
| Delfim Moreira Costa Ribeiro | Sept. 7, 1914–Sept. 7, 1918 |
| Artur da Silva Bernardes | Sept. 7, 1918–Sept. 7, 1922 |
| Raul Soares de Moura | Sept. 7, 1922–Aug. 4, 1924 |
| Fernando de Melo Viana | Dec. 22, 1924–Sept. 7, 1926 |
| Antonio Carlos Ribeiro de Andrada | Sept. 7, 1926–Sept. 7, 1930 |
| Olegário Dias Maciel | Sept. 7, 1930–Sept. 5, 1933 |

NOTE: The question mark indicates uncertain tenure dates; brackets indicate a period served of less than 90 days, too brief a time to be counted in the elite study.

*Interventor*

| | |
|---|---|
| Gustavo Capanema | Sept. 5, 1933–Dec. 15, 1933 |
| Benedito Valadares Ribeiro | Dec. 15, 1933–Nov. 5, 1945 |
| (constitutional governor) | April 4, 1935–Nov. 11, 1937 |

*Lieutenant Governor*

| | |
|---|---|
| Eduardo Ernesto da Gama Cerqueira | June 15, 1891–Dec. 31, 1892 |
| João Nepomuceno Kubitschek | Sept. 7, 1894–Sept. 7, 1898 |
| João Candido da Costa Sena | Sept. 7, 1898–Sept. 7, 1902 |
| Pacífico Gonçalves da Silva Mascarenhas | Sept. 7, 1902–Sept. 7, 1906 |
| Júlio Bueno Brandão | Sept. 7, 1906–Sept. 7, 1910 |
| Antonio Martins Ferreira da Silva | Sept. 7, 1910–Sept. 7, 1914 |
| Levindo Ferreira Lopes | Sept. 7, 1914–Sept. 7, 1918 |
| Eduardo Carlos Vilhena do Amaral | Sept. 7, 1918–Sept. 7, 1922 |
| Olegário Dias Maciel | Sept. 7, 1922–Sept. 7, 1926 |
| Alfredo Sá | Sept.. 7, 1926–Sept. 7, 1930 |
| Pedro Marques de Almeida | [Sept. 7, 1930–Nov. 11, 1930] |

*Secretary of the Interior*

| | |
|---|---|
| João Pinheiro da Silva (Secy. of State) | Nov. 25, 1889–Feb. 10, 1890 |
| Francisco de Assis Barcelos Correia | Sept. 7, 1891–Dec. 2, 1891 |
| Teófilo Domingues Alves Ribeiro | ?Feb. 9, 1892–July 13, 1892 |
| Francisco Silviano de Almeida Brandão | July 14, 1892–Sept. 7, 1894 |
| Henrique Augusto de Oliveira Diniz | Sept. 7, 1894–Sept. 7, 1898 |
| Wenceslau Brás Pereira Gomes | Sept. 7, 1898–Sept. 7, 1902 |
| Delfim Moreira da Costa Ribeiro | Sept. 7, 1902–Sept. 7, 1906 |
| Manuel Tomás de Carvalho Brito | Sept. 7, 1906–Oct. 28, 1908 |
| Estevão Leite de Magalhães Pinto | Oct. 28, 1908–Sept. 7, 1910 |
| Delfim Moreira da Costa Ribeiro | Sept. 7, 1910–Dec. 6, 1913 |
| Américo Ferreira Lopes | Dec. 6, 1913–Nov. 26, 1917 |
| José Vieira Marques | Nov. 26, 1917–Sept. 7, 1918 |
| Raul Soares de Moura | Sept. 7, 1918–July 28, 1919 |
| Afonso Pena Junior | July 28, 1919–Sept. 7, 1922 |
| Fernando Melo Viana | Sept. 7, 1922–Sept. 11, 1924 |
| Sandoval Soares de Azevedo | Sept. 11, 1924–Sept. 7, 1926 |
| Francisco Luís da Silva Campos | Sept. 7, 1926–Sept. 7, 1930 |
| Cristiano Monteiro Machado | [Sept. 7, 1930–Nov. 26, 1930] |
| Gustavo Capanema | Nov. 28, 1930–Sept. 5, 1933 |
| Cândido Lara Ribeiro Naves (interim) | ?[June 25, 1932–Sept. 11, 1932] |
| Álvaro Baptista de Oliveira | Sept. 5, 1933–Dec. 15, 1933 |
| Carlos Coimbra da Luz | Dec. 15, 1933–April 5, 1935 |
| Gabriel Rezende Passos | April 6, 1935–Jan. 4, 1936 |
| Domingo Henriques Gusmão Junior | Jan. 4, 1936–Sept. 19, 1936 |
| José Maria de Alkmim | Sept. 19, 1936–1938 |

### Secretary of Finance

| | |
|---|---|
| Justino Ferreira Carneiro | July 14, 1892–Sept. 7, 1894 |
| Francisco Antonio de Sales | Sept. 7, 1894–Sept. 7, 1898 |
| David Moretzon Campista | Sept. 7, 1898–Sept. 7, 1902 |
| Antonio Carlos Ribeiro de Andrada | Sept. 7, 1902–Sept. 7, 1906 |
| João Braulio Moinhos de Vilhena | Sept. 7, 1906–June 1908 |
| Manuel Tomás Carvalho Brito | June, 1908–Oct. 28, 1908 |
| Juscelino Barbosa | Oct. 30, 1908–Sept. 7, 1910 |
| Artur da Silva Bernardes | Sept. 7, 1910–Sept. 7, 1914 |
| Teodomiro Carneiro Santiago | Oct. 26, 1914–Sept. 7, 1918 |
| Afrânio de Melo Franco | [Sept. 7, 1918–Nov. 15, 1918] |
| João Luís Alves | Nov. 26, 1918–Sept. 6, 1922 |
| Augusto Mário Caldeira Brant | Sept. 7, 1922–Aug. 26, 1925 |
| Djalma Pinheiro Chagas | Aug. 26, 1925–Sept. 7, 1926 |
| Gudesteu de Sá Pires | Sept. 7, 1926–Nov. 26, 1929 |
| José Bernardino Alves Júnior | Nov. 28, 1929–Sept. 7, 1930 |
| José Carneiro de Rezende | [Sept. 7, 1930–Nov. 27, 1930] |
| Amaro Lanari | Nov. 27, 1930–Dec. 17, 1931 |
| José da Silva Brandão (interim) | [Dec. 17, 1931–March 5, 1932] |
| Carlos Pinheiro Chagas | March 5, 1932–June 25, 1932 |
| Cândido Lara Ribeiro Naves (interim) | June 25, 1932–Sept. 11, 1932 |
| José Bernardino Alves Júnior | ?Aug. 1932–Dec. 15, 1933 |
| Alcides Pereira Lins | Dec. 15, 1933–Feb. 24, 1934 |
| Ovídio Xavier de Abreu | Feb. 24, 1934–1938 |

### Secretary of Agriculture

| | |
|---|---|
| David Moretzon Campista | July 14, 1892–Sept. 7, 1894 |
| Francisco Sá | Sept. 7, 1894–April 18, 1897 |
| Francisco Antonio de Sales | April 18, 1897–Sept. 7, 1898 |
| Américo Werneck (post suppressed 1901–10, placed under Finance) | Sept. 7, 1898–Sept. 16, 1901 |
| José Conçalves de Souza | Sept. 7, 1910–Sept. 7, 1914 |
| Raul Soares de Moura | Sept. 7, 1914–Nov. 28, 1917 |
| Artur da Costa Guimarães | Nov. 28, 1917–Sept. 7, 1918 |
| Clodomiro Augusto de Oliveira | Sept. 7, 1918–Sept. 7, 1922 |
| Daniel Serapião de Carvalho | Sept. 7, 1922–Sept. 7, 1926 |
| Augusto Viana do Castelo | [Sept. 7, 1926–Nov. 15, 1926] |
| Djalma Pinheiro Chagas | Nov. 15, 1926–Sept. 7, 1930 |
| Alaôr Prata Soares | [Sept. 7, 1930–Nov. 26, 1930] |
| Cincinato Gomes Noronha Guarani | Nov. 28, 1930–May 3, 1931 |
| José Monteiro Ribeiro Junqueira | May 3, 1931–March 4, 1932 |
| Ovídio João Paulo de Andrade | ?March 4, 1932–August 1932 |
| Carlos Coimbra da Luz | ?August, 1932–Dec. 15, 1933 |
| Israel Pinheiro da Silva | Dec. 19, 1933–June 1942 |

### Secretary of Security, 1926–30

| | |
|---|---|
| José Francisco Bias Fortes | Sept. 7, 1926–Oct. 29, 1929 |
| Odilon Duarte Braga | Oct. 29, 1929–Sept. 7, 1930 |

| | |
|---|---|
| *Secretary of Education, 1930–* | |
| Levindo Eduardo Coelho | Sept. 7, 1930–April 30, 1931 |
| Noraldino Lima | April 30, 1931–April 5, 1934 |
| José Bonifácio Olinda de Andrada | April 5, 1934–Sept. 2, 1936 |
| Cristiano Monteiro Machado | Sept. 2, 1936–Nov. 5, 1945 |
| | |
| *Secretary of Transport and Public Works, 1935–* | |
| Raul de Noronha Sá | April 5, 1935–Nov. 11, 1937 |
| | |
| *Mayor of Belo Horizonte* | |
| Adelberto Dias Ferraz da Luz | Dec. 29, 1897–Sept. 7, 1898 |
| Américo Werneck (interim) | [Sept. 7, 1898–Oct. 27, 1898] |
| Wenceslau Brás Pereira Gomes (interim) | [Oct. 27, 1898–Jan. 31, 1899] |
| Francisco Antonio de Sales | Feb. 1, 1899–Sept. 2, 1899 |
| Bernardio Pinto Monteiro | Sept. 12, 1899–Sept. 7, 1902 |
| Francisco Bressane de Azevedo | Sept. 7, 1902–Oct. 28, 1905 |
| Cícero Ferreira (interim) | [April 20, 1905–May 10, 1905] |
| Antonio Carlos Ribeiro de Andrada | Oct. 30, 1905–Sept. 7, 1906 |
| Benjamin Jacob | Sept. 7, 1906–April 15, 1909 |
| Benjamin Franklin Silviano Brandão | April 16, 1910–Sept. 7, 1910 |
| Olinto Deodato dos Reis Meireles | Sept. 9, 1910–Sept. 7, 1914 |
| Cornélio Vaz de Melo | Sept. 7, 1914–Sept. 7, 1918 |
| Afonso Vaz de Melo | Sept. 7, 1918–Sept. 7, 1922 |
| Flavio Fernardes dos Santos | Sept. 7, 1922–Sept. 7, 1926 |
| Francisco Álvares da Silva Campos (interim) | [Sept. 7, 1926–Oct. 16, 1926] |
| Cristiano Monteiro Machado | Oct. 16, 1926–Nov. 28, 1929 |
| Alcides Pereira Lins | Nov. 28, 1929–Sept. 7, 1930 |
| Luis Gonçalves Pena | Sept. 7, 1930–Dec. 18, 1932 |
| Otávio Pena (interim) | Dec. 22, 1932–Dec. 15, 1933 |
| José Soares de Matos | Dec. 15, 1933–April 8, 1935 |
| Otacílio Negrão de Lima | April 8, 1935–April 18, 1938 |
| | |
| *Police Chief* | |
| Aristides de Araujo Maia | Nov., 1889–July 1890 |
| Antonio Augusto de Lima | July, 1890–March 18, 1891 |
| Francisco de Paulo Ferreira e Costa | March 18, 1891–April 6, 1892 |
| Joaquim de Melo Jequiriça | April 6, 1892–Oct. 15, 1892 |
| Adalberto Dias Ferraz da Luz | Oct. 15, 1892–Feb. 26, 1894 |
| Alfredo Pinto Viera de Melo | Feb. 26, 1894–Aug. 15, 1896 |
| Aureliano Moreira Magalhães | Aug. 15, 1896–Sept. 7, 1898 |
| Eduardo da Cunha Pereira | Sept. 7, 1898–Feb. 21, 1902 |
| Antonio Gomes Lima | Feb. 21, 1902–Sept. 7, 1902 |
| Olinto Augusto Ribeiro | Sept. 7, 1902–Jan. 1903 |
| Juscelino Barbosa | January, 1903–Dec. 4, 1903 |
| Cristiano Pereira Brasil | Dec. 4, 1903–Nov. 6, 1905 |
| João Olavo Eloi de Andrade | Nov. 6, 1905–Dec. 7, 1906 |

| | |
|---|---|
| Josino Alcantara de Araujo | Dec. 7, 1906–April 7, 1907 |
| Rafael de Almeida Magalhães | April 7, 1907–July 16, 1908 |
| Francisco de Assis Barcelos Correia | July 16, 1908–Dec. 22, 1908 |
| Urias de Melo Botelho | Dec. 23, 1908–Sept. 7, 1910 |
| Américo Ferreira Lopes | Sept. 7, 1910–Dec. 6, 1913 |
| Herculano Cesar Pereira da Silva | ?Dec. 6, 1913–Sept. 7, 1914 |
| José Vieira Marques | Sept. 7, 1914–Nov. 26, 1917 |
| Antonio de Afonso de Morais | Nov. 26, 1917–Sept. 7, 1918 |
| Júlio Otaviano Ferreira | Sept. 7, 1918–Sept. 7, 1922 |
| Alfredo Sá | Sept. 7, 1922–Nov. 3, 1924 |
| Arnaldo de Alencar Araripe | Dec. 21, 1924–Sept. 7, 1926 |
| José Francisco Bias Fortes | Sept. 7, 1926–Oct. 29, 1929 |
| Odilon Duarte Braga (1930–33 held | |
|   by Secretary of Interior) | Oct. 29, 1929–Sept. 7, 1930 |
| Álvaro Baptista de Oliveira | Dec. 15, 1933–April 5, 1935 |
| Domingos Henriques Gusmão Júnior | April 5, 1935–Jan. 4, 1936 |
| Ernesto Dorneles | Jan. 4, 1936–Oct. 17, 1942 |

*Director of the State Printing Office*

| | |
|---|---|
| Jorge Alberto Leite Pinto | March 8, 1892–July 22, 1892 |
| Edmundo Veiga | July 22, 1892–Sept. 7, 1894 |
| Gastão da Cunha | Nov. 17, 1894–Aug. 26, 1895 |
| José de Andrada Braga | Aug. 26, 1894–Sept. 7, 1898 |
| João Nepomuceno Kubitschek | Sept. 7, 1898–June 3, 1899 |
| Francisco Bressane de Azevedo | Sept. 19, 1899–Sept. 7, 1902 |
| Carlos Domicio de Assis Toledo | Sept. 7, 1902–1904 |
| Álvaro Astolfo da Silveira | June 5, 1904–Sept. 7, 1907 |
| Francisco Barcelos Correia | Sept. 7, 1907–June 7, 1908 |
| Gabriel de Oliveira Santos | June 7, 1908–March 9, 1912 |
| Leon Roussoulières | March 9, 1912–Sept. 7, 1915 |
| João Carvalhães de Paiva | Sept. 7, 1914–Sept. 7, 1918 |
| Mario Franzen de Lima | Sept. 7, 1918–Sept. 7, 1922 |
| Noraldino Lima | Sept. 7, 1922–1927 |
| Abílio Machado | 1927–Sept. 7, 1930 |
| Noraldino Lima | Sept. 7, 1930–Apr. 30, 1931 |
| Mário Casasanta | April 30, 1931–Dec. 15, 1933 |
| Mário Gonçalves de Matos | Dec. 15, 1933–April 1935 |
| Romão Côrtes de Lacerda | April, 1935–Sept. 24, 1937 |
| Mário Casasanta | Sept. 24, 1937–1938 |

*President, State-Controlled Banks*
  (a) *Banco de Crédito Real*

| | |
|---|---|
| Francisco de Paulo Mayrink | ?Nov. 1889–June 1890 |
| José Joaquim Monteiro da Silva | ?1892–96 |
| Antonio Gomes Lima | ?1910–15 |
| Americo Gomes Ribeiro da Luz | ?1915–Nov. 17, 1927 |
| José Joaquim Monteiro de Andrade | ?Nov. 17, 1927–Sept. 1930 |

  (b) *Banco Hipotecário e Agrícola*

| | |
|---|---|
| Juscelino Barbosa | 1911–36 |
| Estevão Leite de Magalhães Pinto | 1936–43 |

*Director, Mineiro Coffee Institute*
  *(IMC)*
José Rezende     ?[1927– ]
João Gonçalves Pereira Lima     March 22, 1929–Sept. 7, 1930
Jacques Dias Maciel     Sept. 11, 1930–March 1934
Artur Felicíssimo     ?March 1934

*President, State Senate*
Crispim Jacques Bias Fortes     1891–93
Frederico Augusto Álvares da Silva     1894
Francisco Silviano de Almeida
  Brandão     1895–98
Antonio Martins Ferreira da Silva     1898–1906
Antonio Gonçalves Chaves     1907–10
Levindo Ferreira Lopes     1910–11
Crispim Jacques Bias Fortes     1912–15
Eduardo Carlos Vilhena do Amaral     1916–18
Levindo Ferreira Lopes     1918–20
Eduardo Carlos Vilhena do Amaral     1920–22
Diogo de Vasconcellos     1923–26
Olegário Dias Maciel     1926–29
João Jacques Montandon     1929–30

*President, State Chamber of*
  *Deputies*
Otávio Esteves Otoni     1891–92
Levindo Ferreira Lopes     1892–94
Francisco Antonio de Sales     1894
Eduardo Augusto Pimentel
  Barbosa     1894–96
José Tavares de Melo     1897
Francisco Ribeiro de Oliveira     1898–1902
Joaquim Domingos Leite de Castro     1903–5
João Braulio Moinhos de Vilhena     1906
Manoel Alves de Lemos     [1906]
Antonio do Prado Lopes Pereira     1907–11
Eduardo Carlos Vilhena do Amaral     1911–15
Odilon Barrot de Andrade     1916–18
Alfredo Martins de Lima Castelo
  Branco     1918
Emílio Jardim de Rezende     [1918]
Pericles Vieira de Mendonça     1919–21
João de Almeida Lisboa     1921–23
José Francisco Bias Fortes     1924–25
Enéas Câmara     1925–26
Pedro Marques de Almeida     1927–30
Abílio Machado     1935–36
José Rodrigues Seabra     [1936]
Dorinato de Oliveira Lima     1936–37

*Majority Leader, State Chamber of Deputies*

| | |
|---|---|
| Camilo Filinto Prates | ?1891–92 |
| Henrique Augusto de Oliveira Diniz | ?1893 |
| Júlio Bueno Brandão | 1894–98 |
| Júlio Cesar Tavares Paes | 1899–1902 |
| Carlos Peixoto de Melo Filho | 1903 |
| Afrânio de Melo Franco | 1904 |
| Bernardino de Sena Figueiredo | 1905–6 |
| Afonso Pena Junior | 1907–9 |
| Bernardino de Sena Figueiredo (post abolished after 1914?) | 1910–14 |

*President, State Supreme Court*

| | |
|---|---|
| João Braulio Moinhos de Vilhena | 1891 |
| Adolfo Augusto Olinto | 1892–97 |
| Francisco de Paulo Prestes Pimentel | ?1897–98 |
| Teófilo Pereira da Silva | 1898–1902 |
| João Braulio Moinhos de Vilhena | 1902–9 |
| Antonio Luís Perreira Tinoco | 1910–11 |
| José Antonio Saraiva | 1912–13 |
| Edmundo Pereira Lins | 1913–17 |
| Hermenegildo Rodrigues de Barros | 1918–20 |
| Artur Ribeiro de Oliveira | 1921–23 |
| Rafael de Almeida Magalhães | 1923–28 |
| Tito Alves Pereira Fulgencio | 1928–33 |
| Arnaldo Alencar Araripe | ? |

*Executive Committee, Partido Republicano, 1888–91*

João Pinheiro da Silva
Francisco Ferreira Alves
Domingos da Silva Porto
Domingos José da Rocha
Antonio Olinto dos Santos Pires†

*Executive Committee, Partido Republicano Constitucional, 1893–97*

| | |
|---|---|
| Antonio Olinto dos Santos Pires | 1893–94 |
| Joaquim Gonçalves Ramos | 1893–97 |
| Carlos Vaz de Melo | 1893–97 |
| Antonio Martins Ferreira da Silva | 1893–97 |
| Necessio José Tavares | ?1893–94 |
| Fernando Lobo Leite Pereira | ?1896 |
| Eduardo Augusto Pimentel Barbosa | ?1894–96 |
| Júlio Bueno Brandão | ?1894–97 |

*Executive Committee, Partido Republicano Mineiro 1897–1931*

| | |
|---|---|
| Carlos Vaz de Melo | Dec. 1897–Nov. 1904 |
| * Astolfo Dutra Nicácio | Nov. 1904–Nov. 1905 |
| José Raimundo Teles de Menezes | Dec. 1897–Aug. 1898† |
| Francisco Mendes Pimentel | Dec. 1897–Aug. 1898† |
| Sabino Alves Barroso Júnior | Dec. 1897–Aug. 1901; Nov. 1902–Sept. 1909; Nov. 1910–June 1919 |
| * Olimpio Júlio de Oliveira Mourão | Aug. 1901–Nov. 1902 |
| * Bernardo Pinto Monteiro | Sept. 1909–Nov. 1910 |
| (full member) | Sept. 1917–July 1924 |
| Júlio Bueno Brandão | Dec. 1897–Nov. 1908; Nov. 1914–Oct. 1930 |
| * Francisco Álvaro Bueno de Paiva | Nov. 1908–Nov. 1914 |
| (full member) | Nov. 1914–Aug. 1928 |
| Crispim Jacques Bias Fortes | Aug. 1898–May 1917 |
| Francisco Antonio de Sales | Aug. 1898–Nov. 1902; Nov. 1906–Nov. 1910; May 1913–Aug. 1920† |
| * Júlio Cesar Tavares Paes | Nov. 1903–Nov. 1906 |
| * Alvaro Augusto de Andrade Botelho | Nov. 1910–May 1913 |
| Antonio Martins Ferreira da Silva | Aug. 1898–April 1919 |
| * Francisco Ribeiro de Oliveira | 1903, for a few months |
| Francisco Bressane de Azevedo | Aug. 1898–Sept. 1921† |
| Carlos Peixoto de Melo Filho | Nov. 1905–Sept. 1909† |
| Acrísio Diniz | Nov. 1906–Dec. 1908 |
| José Montiero Ribeiro Junqueira | Sept. 1909–May 1931† |
| Delfim Moreira da Costa Ribeiro | Sept. 1917–July 1920 |
| Raul Soares de Moura | Sept. 1919–Nov. 1922 |
| * Levindo Duarte Coelho | Nov. 1922–Sept. 1925 |
| (full member) | Sept. 1925–1931 |
| Wenceslau Brás Pereira Gomes | Sept. 1919–May 1931† |
| Francisco Coelho Duarte Badaró | Sept. 1919–Sept. 1921 |
| Américo Ferreira Lopes | Sept. 1919–Aug. 1920† |
| João Luís Alves | Sept. 1921–Nov. 1922 |
| * João Pio de Souza Reis | Nov. 1922–Sept. 1925 |
| (full member) | Sept. 1925–1931 |
| Alaôr Prata Soares | Sept. 1921–Nov. 1922, Nov. 1926–1931 |
| * Waldomiro de Barros Magalhães | Nov. 1922–Nov. 1926 |
| Landulfo Machado de Magalhães | Aug. 1920–Sept. 1921 |
| João Nogueira Penido Filho | Aug. 1920–Sept. 1921 |

* Alternate.
† Date when broke with party or was purged.

256

256 APPENDIX B

| Getúlio Ribeiro de Carvalho | Sept. 1921–Jan. 1925 |
| Afonso Pena Junior | ?1922–March 1925, Nov. 1926–1931 |
| * Manuel Tomás de Carvalho Brito | March 1925–Nov. 1926 |
| Alfredo Sá | Sept. 1925–Oct. 1929† |
| Fernando de Melo Viana | Sept. 1926–Oct. 1929† |
| Artur da Silva Bernardes | Sept. 1922–1931 |
| José Bonifacio de Andrada e Silva | ?1928–1930 |
| Teodomiro Carneiro Santiago | Nov. 1929–May 1931† |
| Eduardo Carlos Vilhena do Amaral | Nov. 1929–1931 |
| Afrânio de Melo Franco | Nov. 1929–1931 |
| Augusto Mário Caldeira Brant | Nov. 1929–1931 |
| Antonio Carlos de Andrada | Sept. 1930–May 1931† |

*Executive Committee, PRM in Opposition, 1931–37*

| Artur da Silva Bernardes | 1931–37 |
| (in exile) | 1932–34 |
| Augusto Mário Caldeira Brant | 1931–37 |
| (in exile) | 1932–34 |
| Djalma Pinheiro Chagas | 1931–36† |
| (in exile) | 1932–34 |
| Afonso Pena Junior | 1931–32 |
| Alaôr Prata Soares | 1931–34 |
| José Francisco Bias Fortes | 1931–32† |
| José Carneiro de Rezende | 1931–36† |
| Cincinato Gomes Noronha Guarani | 1931–32 |
| Cristiano Monteiro Machado | 1931–36† |
| Eduardo Carlos Vilhena do Amaral | 1931–32 |
| Afrânio de Melo Franco | 1931–32 |
| Levindo Duarte Coelho | 1931–36† |
| Rubens Ferreira Campos | 1933–37 |
| Garibaldi de Castro Melo | 1933–34 |
| Ovídio João Paulo de Andrade | 1933–37 |
| Daniel Serapião de Carvalho | 1933–37 |
| Camilo Rodrigues Chaves | 1931, 1933–36† |
| Olavo Gomes Pinto | 1933–34 |
| Hugo Furquim Werneck | 1933–35 |
| Francisco Duque de Mesquita | 1933–34 |
| Waldemar Diniz Alves Pequeno | 1933–36† |
| João Sebastião de Paiva Azevedo | 1933–34 |
| Jefferson de Oliveira | 1933 |
| Joaquim Afonso Rodrigues | 1933–36† |
| João de Almeida | 1933–34 |
| José Maria Cançado | ?1935–37 |

* Alternate.
† Date when broke with party or was purged.

*Executive Committee, Partido Pro-
gressita, 1932–36*°

| | |
|---|---|
| Antonio Carlos Ribeiro de Andrada | 1932–36† |
| Gustavo Capanema | 1932–36 |
| Virgílio de Melo Franco | 1932–33† |
| Washington Ferreira Pires | 1932–36 |
| Noraldino Lima | 1932–36 |
| Wenceslau Brás Pereira Gomes | ?1933–34 |
| José Monteiro Ribeiro Junqueira | 1932–36 |
| Pedro Aleixo | 1932–36 |
| Idalino Ribeiro | 1932–36 |
| João José Alves | 1932–35 |
| Otacílio Negrão de Lima | 1932–36 |
| Luís Martins Soares | 1932–36 |
| Adélio Dias Maciel | 1932–36 |
| Augusto das Chagas Viegas | 1932–36 |
| João Tavares Correia Beraldo | 1932–36 |
| Waldomiro de Barros Magalhães | 1932–36 |
| José Francisco Bias Fortes | 1932–33† |
| Aleixo Paraguassú | 1932–33 |
| Odilon Duarte Braga | ?1935–36 |

FEDERAL POSTS

*President*

| | |
|---|---|
| Afonso Augusto Moreira Pena | 1906–9 |
| Wenceslau Brás Pereira Gomes | 1914–18 |
| Artur da Silva Bernardes | 1922–26 |

*Vice-President*

| | |
|---|---|
| Afonso Augusto Moreira Pena | 1902–6 |
| Wenceslau Brás Pereira Gomes | 1910–14 |
| Delfim Moreira da Costa Ribeiro | 1918–19 |
| Francisco Álvaro Bueno de Paiva | 1920–22 |
| Fernando de Melo Viana | 1926–30 |

*Minister of Justice* (formerly Interior)

| | |
|---|---|
| José Cesário de Faria Alvim | Feb. 10, 1890–Jan. 22, 1891 |
| Fernando Lobo Leite Pereira | Feb. 10, 1892–Dec. 8, 1893 |
| Sabino Barroso Júnior | Aug. 6, 1901–Nov. 15, 1902 |
| Alfredo Pinto Vieira de Melo | July 28, 1919–Mar. 10, 1921 |
| João Luís Alves | Nov. 15, 1922–March, 1925 |
| Afonso Pena Júnior | March, 1925–Nov. 15, 1926 |
| Augusto Viana de Castelo | Nov. 15, 1926–Oct. 26, 1930 |
| Afrânio de Melo Franco (interim) | [Oct. 26, 1930–Nov. 3, 1930] |
| Afrânio de Melo Franco (interim) | [Sept. 16, 1932–Nov. 1, 1932] |

° Valadares consolidated the PP and most of the PRM in Sept. 1936.

*Minister of Finance*

| | |
|---|---|
| Sabino Alves Barroso Júnior | [Sept. 2, 1902–Nov. 15, 1902] |
| David Moretzon Campista | Nov. 15, 1906–June 18, 1909 |
| Francisco Antonio de Sales | Nov. 15, 1910–May 9, 1913 |
| Sabino Alves Barroso Júnior | Nov. 15, 1914–July 8, 1915 |
| João Pandiá Calógeras | July 8, 1915–Sept. 6, 1917 |
| Antonio Carlos Ribeiro de Andrada | Sept. 6, 1917–Nov. 15, 1918 |
| João Ribeiro de Oliveira e Souza | Jan. 17, 1919–June 27, 1919 |

*Minister of Agriculture*

| | |
|---|---|
| João Pandiá Calógeras | Nov. 15, 1914–July 8, 1915 |
| João Gonçalves Pereira Lima | Nov. 28, 1917–Dec. 12, 1918 |
| Odilon Duarte Braga | July 28, 1934–Nov. 13, 1937 |

*Minister of Transport and Public Works*

| | |
|---|---|
| Antonio Olinto dos Santos Pires | Nov. 15, 1894–Nov. 20, 1896 |
| Afrânio de Melo Franco | Nov. 15, 1918–June 27, 1919 |

*Minister of Foreign Affairs*

| | |
|---|---|
| Fernando Lobo Leite Pereira | Nov. 28, 1891–Feb. 10, 1892 |
| Olinto Maximo de Magalhães | Nov. 15, 1898–Nov. 15, 1902 |
| Afrânio de Melo Franco | Oct. 24, 1930–Dec. 1933 |

*Minister of Education and Health*

| | |
|---|---|
| Francisco da Silva Campos | Nov. 14, 1930–April, 1932 |
| Belisário de Oliveira Pena (interim) | [Aug. 1931–Dec. 1931] |
| Belisário de Oliveira Pena (interim) | April, 1932–Sept. 16, 1932 |
| Washington Ferreira Pires | Sept. 16, 1932–July 26, 1934 |
| Gustavo Capanema | July 26, 1934–Nov. 1945 |

*President, Bank of Brazil, 1906–1937*

| | |
|---|---|
| João Ribeiro de Oliveira e Souza | Nov. 27, 1906–June 25, 1909 |
| José Joaquim Monteiro de Andrade (interim) | [July 30, 1919–Aug. 1919] |
| José Joaquim Monteiro de Andrade (interim) | Nov. 12, 1919–Dec. 20, 1920 |
| José Joaquim Monteiro de Andrade (interim) | [Oct. 24, 1930–Nov. 4, 1930] |
| Augusto Mário Caldeira Brant | Nov. 4, 1930–Sept. 5, 1931 |

*Mayor of the Federal District*

| | |
|---|---|
| José Cesário de Faria Alvim | Dec. 1898–Jan. 1900 |
| Alaôr Prata Soares | Nov. 15, 1922–Nov. 15, 1926 |

*Justice of Supreme Court*

| | |
|---|---|
| Evangelista Negreiros Saião Lobato | 1881–92 |

| | |
|---|---|
| Francisco de Paula Perreira de Rezende | 1892–93 |
| Américo Lobo Leite Pereira | 1894–1903 |
| Adolfo Augusto Olinto | 1897–98 |
| Edmundo Pereira Lins | 1917–37 |
| Hermenegildo Rodrigues de Barros | 1919–37 |
| Alfredo Pinto Vieira de Melo | 1921–23 |
| Artur Ribeiro de Oliveira | 1923–36 |
| João Luís Alves | 1924–25 |
| Heitor de Souza | 1926–29 |
| João Martins de Carvalho Mourão | 1931–40 |

*President, Chamber of Deputies*

| | |
|---|---|
| João da Mata Machado | June 18, 1891–Oct. 30, 1891 |
| Carlos Vaz de Melo | May 9, 1899–through 1902 |
| Carlos Peixoto de Melo Filho | May 9, 1907–through 1908 |
| Carlos Peixoto de Melo Filho | [May 5, 1909–May 17, 1909] |
| Sabino Alves Barroso Júnior | May 26, 1909–Nov. 15, 1914 |
| Astolfo Dutra Nicácio | Nov. 15, 1914–July, 1917 |
| Sabino Alves Barroso Júnior | July 1917–July, 1919 |
| Astolfo Dutra Nicácio | July 1919–May, 1920 |
| Júlio Bueno Brandão | May 1920–through 1920 |
| Antonio Carlos Ribeiro de Andrada | 1933–April 1937 |
| Pedro Aleixo | May 4, 1937–Nov. 11, 1937 |

*Majority Leader, Chamber of Deputies*

| | |
|---|---|
| Adalberto Dias Ferraz da Luz | 1899–through 1900 |
| Wenceslau Brás Pereira Gomes | 1903 |
| Wenceslau Brás Pereira Gomes | [Sept. 1904–Oct. 10, 1904] |
| Carlos Peixoto de Melo Filho | [June 1905–        ] |
| Carlos Peixoto de Melo Filho | May 1906–through 1906 |
| Antonio Carlos Ribeiro de Andrada | Nov. 15, 1914–Sept. 1917 |
| Astolfo Dutra Nicácio | July 1917–through 1918 |
| Antonio Carlos Ribeiro de Andrada | May 1919–through 1919 |
| Júlio Bueno Brandão | May 1921–late that year |
| Antonio Carlos Ribeiro de Andrada | May 1922–through 1924 |
| Augusto Viana do Castelo | May 1925–through 1925 |
| Júlio Bueno Brandão | May 1926–through 1926 |
| Pedro Aleixo | May 1936–Aug. 1936 |
| Pedro Aleixo | ?        –May 4, 1937 |
| Carlos Coimbra da Luz | May 10, 1937–Nov. 11, 1937 |

*Leader, State Delegation, Chamber of Deputies*

| | |
|---|---|
| João Pinheiro da Silva | July 1891–Nov. 1891 |
| José da Costa Machado e Souza | Nov. 23, 1891–through 1893 |
| Joaquim Gonçalves Ramos | ?May 1894–through 1896 |
| Adalberto Dias Feraz da Luz | ?1898 |

| | |
|---|---|
| Francisco Antonio de Sales | Sept. 1899–through 1899 |
| Sabino Alves Barroso Junior | May 1900–Aug. 6, 1901 |
| Wenceslau Brás Pereira Gomes | [1903] |
| Wenceslau Brás Pereira Gomes | 1904–5 |
| Carlos Peixoto de Melo Filho | 1906 |
| Astolfo Dutra Nicácio | 1907–9 |
| Francisco Álvaro Bueno de Paiva | 1910 |
| José Monteiro Ribeiro Junqueira | 1911–12 |
| Antonio Carlos Ribeiro de Andrada (interim) | [May 1912] |
| Antonio Afonso Lamounier Godofredo | ?1914–17 |
| Júlio Bueno Brandão | ?1918–19 |
| Afrânio de Melo Franco | May 1920–through 1920 |
| Júlio Bueno Brandão | May 1921–through 1923 |
| Augusto Viana da Castelo | ?May 1924–Sept. 1926 |
| José Bonifacio de Andrada e Silva | Sept. 1926–1930 |
| Virgílio de Melo Franco | 1933 |
| Antonio Carlos Ribeiro de Andrada | Dec. 1933–Sept. 1936 |
| Noraldino Lima | Sept. 1936–Nov. 11, 1937 |

# Select Budgetary Data, 1888-1937

## Notes to table column heads for the
## four-page table that follows

*A-1, B-1. Revenues, Expenditures.* Data are from the annual *Relatórios* of the Minas state Secretary of Finance, which present provisional balances. Revised balances were occasionally substituted after publication of the report in the early Republic, but less often thereafter, as follows: for A-1, 1891, 1894, 1901, 1905–10, 1933; for B-1, 1891, 1894, 1898–1901, 1904–10, 1913, 1919–21, 1933, 1935. These new, revised balances were found in *Annuario estatistico de Minas Geraes*, Anno II, pp. 1148–51, and in *Relatório financeiro 1935*, pp. 134–35 (for 1920–34), as checked against the more recent *Finanças do Estado de Minas Gerais, período republicano 1890–1953*, n.p., and the federal *Anuário estatístico do Brasil, 1939–1940*, pp. 1414–15. According to these state series, federal data on expenditures are incorrect for 1898–1900, 1905, 1913, 1918, and 1934.

*C-1. Price index, 1888–1937.* This index is a splice of a foodstuffs price index through 1929 and a general cost-of-living index from 1921 to 1939. Both were constructed for the city of Rio de Janeiro, for an upper-middle-class family. The price index is based on the prices of nine food staples, using a weight derived for the year 1919 (E. Lobo et al., "Evolução dos preços e do padrão de vida no Rio de Janeiro, 1820–1930—resultados preliminares," *Revista Brasileira de Economia*, 25, no. 4 [1971]: 235–65). The cost-of-living index was developed by the Instituto Brasileiro de Geografia e Estatística (IBGE), based on prices of food, clothing, rents, personal services, and general household goods; it is available in the Brazil *Anuário estatístico do Brasil, 1939–1940*, p. 1384. The cost-of-living index is clearly superior for our purposes, but it only covers the years 1912–39. The two have been spliced during the 1920's, a period when they behaved quite similarly. In 1921 the price index was given a weight of .9 and the IBGE index .1; in 1922 the former was weighted .8 and the latter .2; in 1929 the former was weighted .1 and the latter .9.

*L-1. Value of the Brazilian conto in U.S. dollars, 1892–1940.* For the period 1892–1918, the figures are from the *Retrospecto commercial do Jornal do commercio*, calculated from the mean of the highest and lowest quotation for the U.S. dollar in Rio. From 1919 on, the rates from New York as cited in the U.S. Department of Commerce, *Statistical Abstract of the United States*, various years.

*D-1. Public debt.* Included are internal bonded indebtedness, external loans, and the fluctuating debt made of local short-term obligations. The balances for 1899–1904 are estimates because the *relatórios* do not give national currency values for the foreign debt (see below). These balances are mostly from the *relatórios* until 1919; from the *Relatório financeiro 1935*, p. 133, for 1920–34; and from the yearly *relatórios* for 1935–37.

*D-3. Internal debt.* This includes the internal bonded debt, and the fluctuating debt (which in the early Republic was not always given in the yearly *relatórios*).

*D-4. State foreign debt.* For 1899–1904 the debt is given in francs and pounds; thereafter, national currency equivalents are given in the *relatórios*. The early foreign debt in milreis was computed from the yearly sterling rates given in *Anuário estatístico, 1939–1940*, pp. 1353–54, with one pound being equal to 25 francs. The foreign debt balances are from the same sources as D-1.

*D-6. Federal foreign debt.* Source: *Anuário estatístico, 1939–1940*, p. 1424.

*DS-1, E-1, F-1. Debt service, Education, Força Publica.* All are from current balances in the yearly *relatórios*.

I am grateful to Michael Conniff for helping to prepare these series.

| Year | Revenues (current contos) A-1 | Expenditures (current contos) B-1 | Revenues (1912 contos) A-2 | Expenditures (1912 contos) B-2 | Revenues, 5-yr. moving averages of A-2 A-3 |
|---|---|---|---|---|---|
| 1888 | 4.1 | 3.7 | 11.0 | 9.9 | |
| 1889 | 4.2 | 4.3 | 10.2 | 10.4 | |
| | | | | | |
| 1890 | 5.4 | 4.7 | 12.2 | 10.6 | 14.8 |
| 1891 | 11.8 | 9.3 | 20.8 | 16.4 | 16.1 |
| 1892 | 16.2 | 10.6 | 19.9 | 13.0 | 18.6 |
| 1893 | 14.9 | 9.7 | 17.2 | 11.2 | 21.3 |
| 1894 | 19.2 | 13.8 | 22.9 | 16.4 | 21.0 |
| 1895 | 20.5 | 14.4 | 25.8 | 18.1 | 20.5 |
| 1896 | 19.4 | 17.9 | 19.0 | 17.5 | 19.8 |
| 1897 | 21.0 | 20.7 | 17.4 | 17.1 | 18.2 |
| 1898 | 17.8 | 21.5 | 14.0 | 16.9 | 15.7 |
| 1899 | 18.6 | 19.9 | 14.9 | 15.9 | 15.7 |
| | | | | | |
| 1900 | 14.5 | 21.6 | 13.4 | 20.0 | 16.3 |
| 1901 | 16.6 | 17.4 | 18.7 | 19.6 | 17.3 |
| 1902 | 16.8 | 16.1 | 20.4 | 19.6 | 18.3 |
| 1903 | 16.2 | 16.6 | 19.3 | 19.8 | 19.1 |
| 1904 | 17.3 | 16.3 | 19.5 | 18.4 | 18.5 |
| 1905 | 14.1 | 17.9 | 17.7 | 22.5 | 19.6 |
| 1906 | 15.0 | 19.0 | 15.5 | 19.6 | 20.0 |
| 1907 | 24.0 | 20.8 | 26.1 | 22.6 | 20.9 |
| 1908 | 20.1 | 24.2 | 21.4 | 25.7 | 22.8 |
| 1909 | 21.2 | 27.4 | 23.7 | 30.6 | 24.8 |
| | | | | | |
| 1910 | 22.8 | 32.1 | 27.5 | 38.7 | 26.9 |
| 1911 | 23.4 | 29.7 | 25.3 | 32.1 | 29.1 |
| 1912 | 36.8 | 29.3 | 36.8 | 29.3 | 30.3 |
| 1913 | 31.5 | 33.2 | 32.2 | 33.9 | 30.6 |
| 1914 | 27.5 | 33.9 | 29.8 | 36.7 | 30.5 |
| 1915 | 38.3 | 30.2 | 29.0 | 22.9 | 27.4 |
| 1916 | 34.5 | 30.4 | 24.8 | 21.9 | 25.3 |
| 1917 | 37.7 | 32.5 | 22.4 | 19.3 | 23.2 |
| 1918 | 40.6 | 38.3 | 20.3 | 19.2 | 21.3 |
| 1919 | 51.6 | 39.7 | 19.5 | 15.0 | 21.7 |
| | | | | | |
| 1920 | 56.2 | 52.6 | 19.4 | 18.2 | 24.1 |
| 1921 | 63.4 | 65.4 | 26.8 | 27.6 | 26.4 |
| 1922 | 78.5 | 78.4 | 34.7 | 34.7 | 29.8 |
| 1923 | 90.3 | 72.5 | 31.7 | 25.4 | 34.2 |
| 1924 | 120.5 | 83.7 | 36.3 | 25.2 | 37.4 |
| 1925 | 141.1 | 107.8 | 41.4 | 31.6 | 40.3 |
| 1926 | 134.3 | 161.9 | 43.0 | 51.9 | 46.3 |
| 1927 | 151.6 | 143.7 | 49.2 | 46.7 | 55.5 |
| 1928 | 180.2 | 179.0 | 61.5 | 61.1 | 58.9 |
| 1929 | 232.1 | 206.3 | 82.6 | 73.4 | 67.5 |
| | | | | | |
| 1930 | 141.7 | 264.7 | 58.3 | 108.9 | 76.7 |
| 1931 | 201.2 | 240.3 | 86.0 | 102.7 | 79.6 |
| 1932 | 223.0 | 242.9 | 94.9 | 103.4 | 74.8 |
| 1933 | 177.6 | 200.2 | 76.2 | 85.9 | 81.6 |
| 1934 | 146.6 | 306.7 | 58.4 | 122.2 | 82.1 |
| 1935 | 245.1 | 328.8 | 92.5 | 124.1 | 79.3 |
| 1936 | 268.5 | 337.8 | 88.3 | 111.1 | |
| 1937 | 264.8 | 334.8 | 81.0 | 102.4 | |

| Expenditures, 5-yr. moving averages of B-2 B-3 | Budget surplus (1912 contos) A2-B2 | Price index, 1912 = 100 C-1 | One conto in U.S. dollars L-1 | Public debt (current contos) D-1 | Public debt in 1912 (1912 contos) D-2 |
|---|---|---|---|---|---|
| | 1.1 | 37.4 | | 5.9 | 15.8 |
| | −0.2 | 41.2 | | 6.0 | 14.6 |
| 12.1 | 1.6 | 44.4 | | 16.4 | 36.9 |
| 12.3 | 4.4 | 56.7 | | 16.4 | 28.9 |
| 13.5 | 6.9 | 81.3 | 244.4 | 13.4 | 16.5 |
| 15.0 | 6.0 | 86.8 | 230.3 | 10.4 | 12.0 |
| 15.2 | 6.5 | 84.0 | 207.0 | 16.8 | 20.0 |
| 16.0 | 7.7 | 79.5 | 198.5 | na | na |
| 17.2 | 1.5 | 102 | 177.6 | 16.8 | 16.5 |
| 17.1 | 0.3 | 121 | 143.9 | 19.9 | 16.3 |
| 17.5 | −2.9 | 127 | 136.4 | na | na |
| 17.9 | −1.0 | 125 | 146.1 | 87.8 | 70.2 |
| 18.4 | −6.6 | 108 | 186.2 | 76.4 | 70.7 |
| 19.0 | −0.9 | 89.0 | 223.0 | 79.8 | 89.7 |
| 19.5 | 0.8 | 82.2 | 234.9 | 76.4 | 92.9 |
| 20.0 | −0.5 | 83.9 | 239.9 | 78.2 | 93.2 |
| 20.0 | 1.1 | 88.8 | 251.8 | 77.8 | 87.6 |
| 20.6 | −4.8 | 79.5 | 309.6 | 65.7 | 82.6 |
| 21.8 | −4.1 | 97.0 | 317.5 | 70.8 | 73.0 |
| 24.2 | 3.5 | 92.0 | 301.3 | 72.9 | 79.2 |
| 27.4 | −4.3 | 94.0 | 301.8 | 92.0 | 97.9 |
| 29.9 | −6.9 | 89.5 | 303.5 | 99.4 | 111.1 |
| 31.3 | −11.2 | 82.9 | 302.7 | 124.1 | 149.7 |
| 32.9 | −6.8 | 92.6 | 321.0 | 159.0 | 171.7 |
| 34.1 | 7.5 | 100 | 331.8 | 164.9 | 164.9 |
| 31.0 | −1.7 | 97.9 | 321.3 | 162.4 | 165.9 |
| 28.9 | −6.9 | 92.4 | 318.0 | 167.3 | 175.8 |
| 26.9 | 6.1 | 132 | 292.7 | 184.9 | 140.1 |
| 24.0 | 2.9 | 139 | 230.6 | 188.9 | 135.9 |
| 19.7 | 3.1 | 168 | 247.5 | 201.5 | 119.9 |
| 18.7 | 1.1 | 200 | 245.7 | 191.6 | 95.8 |
| 19.9 | 4.5 | 264 | 267.4 | 194.2 | 73.6 |
| 22.9 | 1.2 | 289 | 225.1 | 197.3 | 68.3 |
| 24.2 | −0.8 | 237 | 131.2 | 197.3 | 83.2 |
| 26.2 | — | 226 | 129.5 | 198.1 | 87.7 |
| 28.9 | 6.3 | 285 | 102.3 | 200.2 | 70.2 |
| 33.8 | 11.1 | 332 | 109.4 | 199.1 | 60.0 |
| 36.2 | 9.8 | 341 | 122.0 | 197.6 | 57.9 |
| 43.3 | −8.9 | 312 | 144.4 | 88.9 | 28.5 |
| 52.9 | 2.5 | 308 | 118.4 | 160.9 | 52.2 |
| 68.4 | 0.4 | 293 | 119.7 | 305.2 | 104.2 |
| 78.6 | 9.2 | 281 | 111.1 | 428.9 | 152.6 |
| 89.9 | −50.6 | 243 | 107.1 | 675.3 | 277.9 |
| 94.9 | −16.7 | 234 | 70.3 | 797.3 | 340.7 |
| 104.6 | −8.5 | 235 | 71.2 | 870.7 | 370.5 |
| 107.7 | −9.7 | 233 | 79.6 | 946.7 | 406.3 |
| 109.3 | −63.8 | 251 | 84.3 | 1,043.6 | 415.8 |
| 109.1 | −31.6 | 265 | 82.9 | 1,084.8 | 409.4 |
| | −22.8 | 304 | 85.7 | 1,074.8 | 353.6 |
| | −21.4 | 327 | 86.4 | 1,159.7 | 354.6 |

| Year | Internal debt (current contos) D-3 | State foreign debt (current contos) D-4 | Foreign debt as percent of total state debt D-5 | Federal foreign debt (current contos) D-6 | State foreign debt as percent of fed. for. debt D-7 |
|---|---|---|---|---|---|
| 1888 | | | | | |
| 1889 | | 0 | | 276 | 0 |
| 1890 | | 0 | | 321 | 0 |
| 1891 | | 0 | | 484 | 0 |
| 1892 | | 0 | | 588 | 0 |
| 1893 | | 0 | | 602 | 0 |
| 1894 | | 0 | | 681 | 0 |
| 1895 | | 0 | | 862 | 0 |
| 1896 | | 0 | | 934 | 0 |
| 1897 | | 0 | | 1,079 | 0 |
| 1898 | | 0 | | 1,193 | 0 |
| 1899 | 28.3 | 59.5 | 68% | 1,247 | 5 |
| 1900 | 27.2 | 49.2 | 64 | 900 | 5 |
| 1901 | 35.6 | 44.2 | 55 | 1,105 | 4 |
| 1902 | 30.5 | 49.5 | 60 | 1,166 | 4 |
| 1903 | 30.5 | 47.7 | 61 | 1,345 | 4 |
| 1904 | 31.3 | 46.5 | 60 | 1,173 | 4 |
| 1905 | 32.6 | 33.1 | 50 | 1,250 | 3 |
| 1906 | 38.5 | 32.4 | 46 | 1,098 | 3 |
| 1907 | 38.5 | 34.4 | 47 | 1,153 | 3 |
| 1908 | 46.0 | 46.0 | 50 | 1,246 | 4 |
| 1909 | 46.0 | 53.4 | 54 | 1,284 | 4 |
| 1910 | 52.8 | 71.3 | 57 | 1,298 | 6 |
| 1911 | 57.7 | 101.0 | 63 | 1,418 | 7 |
| 1912 | 63.9 | 101.0 | 61 | 1,391 | 7 |
| 1913 | 61.4 | 101.0 | 62 | 1,564 | 6 |
| 1914 | 66.3 | 101.0 | 60 | 1,817 | 6 |
| 1915 | 65.9 | 119.0 | 64 | 2,168 | 5 |
| 1916 | 72.8 | 116.1 | 61 | 2,239 | 5 |
| 1917 | 73.1 | 128.3 | 64 | 2,021 | 6 |
| 1918 | 75.5 | 116.1 | 60 | 2,083 | 6 |
| 1919 | 78.1 | 116.1 | 60 | 1,532 | 8 |
| 1920 | 81.2 | 116.1 | 59 | 2,694 | 4 |
| 1921 | 81.2 | 116.1 | 59 | 3,924 | 3 |
| 1922 | 81.9 | 116.1 | 59 | 4,850 | 2 |
| 1923 | 84.0 | 116.1 | 58 | 5,354 | 2 |
| 1924 | 83.0 | 116.1 | 59 | 4,927 | 2 |
| 1925 | 81.5 | 116.1 | 59 | 3,849 | 3 |
| 1926 | 88.9 | — | — | 5,318 | — |
| 1927 | 157.4 | 3.5 | 2 | 5,874 | — |
| 1928 | 163.5 | 141.7 | 46 | 6,045 | 2 |
| 1929 | 222.2 | 206.8 | 48 | 5,895 | 4 |
| 1930 | 471.3 | 204.0 | 30 | 6,243 | 3 |
| 1931 | 596.3 | 201.1 | 38 | 8,916 | 2 |
| 1932 | 670.2 | 200.4 | 23 | 7,650 | 3 |
| 1933 | 746.2 | 200.5 | 21 | 8,465 | 2 |
| 1934 | 843.1 | 200.5 | 19 | 9,603 | 2 |
| 1935 | 884.3 | 200.5 | 18 | 9,297 | 2 |
| 1936 | 874.3 | 200.5 | 19 | 8,952 | 2 |
| 1937 | 959.2 | 200.5 | 17 | 11,899 | 2 |

| Debt service (current contos) DS-1 | Debt service as percent of budget DS-2 | Education (current contos) E-1 | Education as percent of budget E-2 | Força Publica (current contos) F-1 | Força Publica as percent of budget F-2 |
|---|---|---|---|---|---|
| | | 1.1 | 30% | 0.7 | 19% |
| 1.6 | 37% | 1.1 | 26 | 0.7 | 16 |
| | | 1.3 | 28 | 0.8 | 17 |
| | | 1.4 | 15 | 0.9 | 10 |
| | | 1.9 | 18 | 1.3 | 12 |
| 0.7 | 7 | 2.4 | 25 | 1.3 | 13 |
| 0.5 | 4 | 2.8 | 20 | 2.2 | 16 |
| 0.8 | 6 | 3.4 | 24 | 2.5 | 17 |
| 0.7 | 4 | 3.6 | 20 | 2.8 | 16 |
| 4.7 | 23 | 3.4 | 16 | 2.6 | 13 |
| 4.7 | 22 | 3.2 | 15 | 2.9 | 13 |
| 4.2 | 21 | 3.5 | 18 | 2.8 | 14 |
| 5.3 | 25 | 2.7 | 13 | 2.2 | 10 |
| 4.5 | 26 | 2.6 | 15 | 2.1 | 12 |
| 4.6 | 29 | 2.2 | 14 | 1.7 | 11 |
| 3.9 | 23 | 2.2 | 13 | 2.3 | 14 |
| 3.7 | 23 | 2.3 | 14 | 2.4 | 15 |
| 4.2 | 23 | 2.2 | 12 | 2.2 | 12 |
| 4.6 | 24 | 2.3 | 12 | 2.8 | 15 |
| 4.9 | 24 | 3.1 | 15 | 2.9 | 14 |
| 5.2 | 21 | 3.7 | 15 | 3.0 | 12 |
| 5.5 | 20 | 4.0 | 15 | 3.0 | 11 |
| 5.9 | 18 | 3.9 | 12 | 3.6 | 11 |
| 7.0 | 24 | 5.0 | 17 | 3.1 | 10 |
| 7.0 | 24 | 4.3 | 15 | 3.1 | 11 |
| 7.1 | 21 | 4.9 | 15 | 3.5 | 11 |
| 7.6 | 22 | 5.2 | 15 | 3.4 | 10 |
| 6.6 | 23 | 5.6 | 19 | 3.5 | 12 |
| 8.0 | 26 | 4.5 | 15 | 2.4 | 8 |
| 5.5 | 17 | 6.2 | 19 | 3.5 | 11 |
| 8.6 | 22 | 6.4 | 17 | 3.8 | 10 |
| 8.5 | 21 | 5.7 | 14 | 3.8 | 10 |
| 8.4 | 16 | 6.4 | 12 | 4.7 | 9 |
| 8.0 | 12 | 7.0 | 11 | 5.9 | 9 |
| 7.0 | 9 | 8.0 | 10 | 6.3 | 8 |
| 13.1 | 18 | 8.4 | 12 | 6.2 | 9 |
| 6.5 | 8 | 10.1 | 12 | 8.0 | 10 |
| 9.0 | 8 | 10.9 | 10 | 8.1 | 8 |
| 4.6 | 3 | 23.5 | 15 | 10.4 | 6 |
| 2.2 | 2 | 16.6 | 12 | 7.8 | 5 |
| 5.8 | 3 | 30.6 | 17 | 14.3 | 8 |
| 15.2 | 7 | 38.1 | 18 | 15.6 | 8 |
| 20.5 | 8 | 45.4 | 17 | 15.3 | 6 |
| 40.8 | 17 | 28.2 | 12 | 20.8 | 9 |
| 39.1 | 16 | 27.9 | 11 | 23.3 | 10 |
| 47.3 | 24 | 29.1 | 15 | 23.1 | 12 |
| 32.7 | 11 | 28.1 | 9 | 23.6 | 8 |
| 35.9 | 11 | 30.0 | 9 | 25.7 | 8 |
| 50.4 | 15 | 30.5 | 9 | 30.1 | 9 |
| 50.8 | 15 | 31.9 | 10 | 30.6 | 9 |

# Notes

## Chapter One

1. Sources for economic data are found in Chapter 2; population data are discussed below. A comprehensive study of the Minas economy since 1945, with some attention to the less recent past, is the excellent six-volume *Diagnóstico da economia mineira*, issued in 1968 by a research team at the Banco de Desenvolvimento de Minas Gerais. Dubbed the "prophets of catastrophe" for their rather pessimistic conclusions, the authors of this admirable diagnosis remark on the lack of data or systematic studies: "When compared with other political units at the same level of significance, the insufficiency of information about this state is flagrant" (2:5). I have relied heavily on their work throughout this introductory chapter.

Two excellent studies were also very helpful: Yves Leloup, *Les villes du Minas Gerais*, and Paul Singer's chapter on Belo Horizonte in his *Desenvolvimento econômico e evolução urbana*.

2. With some exceptions the zonal borders on my own map follow those described in the 1922 Minas, *Annuario estatistico*, Anno II, pp. 111–14, a point well within the time span of my study. To eliminate zones that were not well rooted in customary usage, I deleted the *Annuario's* arbitrarily defined "Northwest" and "Northeast" regions, but retained the East zone, which was already a booming frontier area. I enlarged the East region to include parts of the Mata: this mirrors the common historical experience of the Rio Doce Valley and conforms to recent practice. A breakdown of the zones by municípios, from 1872 to 1940, is available from the author upon request.

For a good descriptive study of the evolving subregions to 1940, see Egler, "Distribuição da população." The reasons for choosing 17 physiographic regions and for discarding the old zones as vague and analytically imprecise are discussed by Guimarães, "Divisão regional." See also map 15.1 entitled "Evolução das divisões regionais de Minas Gerais," in *Diagnóstico*, 2.

3. Secretary of Agriculture Israel Pinheiro da Silva in *Fôlha de Minas*, cited in Pereira Brazil, p. 11.

4. Leloup, *Les villes,* p. 83.

5. In 1874, Wells described a *queimada* (burning) near Cedro in Central Minas. It was several weeks before they saw blue sky again. At night, "the sky became bright with the reflection of the many fires far and near, and away to the east the bold outlines of serras were distinctly visible, illuminated by the long lines of flashing fires on their hillsides and ridges . . . which appeared as though they were lighted by innumerable flickering lamps." The conflagration ranged many miles in extent; *Three Thousand Miles Through Brazil,* 1:213.

6. For a contrary view see Emílio Willems' community study. The urban population of Cunha (near São Paulo) considered the Mineiro "a decadent element" because he "transforms cropland into pasturage, thus depopulating the município" (pp. 81–82). That Cunha was an old commercial town with a relatively impoverished hinterland may account for the negative image of Mineiro farmers there.

7. Brazil, *Recenseamento do Brazil, 1920: Agricultura,* p. xvii; and Secretary of Agriculture Israel Pinheiro, quoted by Pereira Brazil, p. 16.

8. Nelson de Senna in Minas, *Annaes da Camara,* 1919, pp. 505ff. Although the alqueire varied by subregion, Senna probably used the so-called "alqueire paulista e Sul de Minas," equivalent to 2.5 hectares, which was the standard unit for the state's real estate tax. See also Elza Coelho de Souza, pp. 47–70.

9. *Diagnóstico,* 3:5, including data indicating that the migration cycle ceased by 1960, and that the state's population may have grown 3.5 percent per year in 1960–70.

10. Nelson Coelho de Senna, ethnographer, geographer, and director of the Arquivo Público Mineiro, reached this representative view of race in *Chorographia de Minas Geraes,* p. 217, which he produced for the series "Geographia do Brazil" to commemorate the nation's independence centenary. For the whitening myth consult Skidmore, *Black into White.*

11. The precise breakdown is as follows (the 1920 census did not enumerate by race). (This revises Senna's breakdown for 1890 (*A terra mineira,* 2:76), in which he listed 46.76 percent white, 34.93 percent mestiço, and 18.31 percent black.)

|        | 1890            | 1940           |
|--------|-----------------|----------------|
| Whites | 40.60%          | 61.2%          |
| Mixed  | 38.07% (mestiços) | 19.4% (pardos) |
| Black  | 15.14%          | 19.4%          |
| Indians | 6.16%          |                |

12. Missionary activities to protect Indians from the settlers in northeast Minas are recounted by an Italian, Padre Jacinto de Palazzolo, in his memoir, *Nas selvas dos Vales Mucurí e do Rio Doce.* See also Senna's *Chorographia de Minas Geraes,* pp. 180–81, 201–10. The quote is from *O Diário de Minas,* June 25, 1901. Commenting on the recently formed Sociedade de Ethnographia e Civilização dos Indios in São Paulo, *O Diário* praised this "noble attempt" to learn about the Indian, even if no practical means to save him came of it.

13. Correia Dias, "Aspectos sociais do surto industrial de Juiz de Fora," p. 92.

14. Consult Góes Monteiro's "Esboço da política imigratória," pp. 195–216. Immigration figures are taken from Senna, *Chorographia de Minas Geraes*, pp. 203–4, and Góes Monteiro, p. 203.

15. For a concise discussion of this problem in the Mata, see Valverde, pp. 34–35. On the title-clearing problem as a barrier to immigration, see Anthouard, p. 269. In his famous essay on the interior, Virgílio de Mello Franco noted that the Brazilian fazendeiro "until recently" treated his colonos like slaves, seeing them as extensions of the chattel system (*Viagens pelo interior*, p. 73). Such attitudes helped to destroy Senator Vergueiro's parceria system in the mid-nineteenth century, and they persisted in Minas well into the next century. Also Governor Artur Bernardes, Mensagem, in Minas, *Annaes da Camara, 1920*, p. 20.

16. Bernardes, cited in note 15.

17. Frieiro, *Feijão, angu e couve*, p. 217.

18. Nelson Vianna, pp. 68–69.

19. Braga, p. 195. Belmiro's father discouraged his sons from working in Rio merchant houses, where the family had good connections, because of the yellow fever danger.

20. Alarmists said 15 percent of Brazil's entire population was afflicted by Chagas disease. In 1923 Afrânio Peixoto, an establishment public health expert and member of the elite Academy of Letters, challenged Chagas's findings and minimized them. However, in 1949 the Oswaldo Cruz Institute estimated that 204 Mineiro municipalities, or almost 65 percent of the state, were infested with barbeiros. See Ribeiro, pp. 189–212.

21. Neiva and Penna, p. 222.

22. Brazil, *Recenseamento . . . 1920*, V. 3ª *Parte, Estatísticas complementares do Censo Econômico* (Rio, 1929), and Senna, *A terra mineira*, 1:282.

23. Mário Leite, pp. 171ff.

24. Strauch, p. 54. Upon completing their famous trip through the sertão in 1912, Arthur Neiva and Belisário Penna, two public health specialists, were vividly impressed by the contrast between disease-ridden, impoverished north Goiás and the Southeast, with its zebu cattle, its prospering ranches, its well-fed population. "This region was opened up and settled almost exclusively by Mineiros" from the Triângulo and the West, they reported. Neiva and Penna, p. 223.

25. Benévolo, p. 48. For migration to Rio, consult Assis Barbosa, *Juscelino Kubitschek*, p. 155. According to the 1920 census, 44,709 Mineiros lived in the Federal District. The largest colony resided in the west, north, and northwest coffee zones of São Paulo, and in that state's capital. More than 30,000 were pioneering in Paraná, while the movement of some 1,000 to Campo Grande in Mato Grosso indicated that frontier was opening to Mineiros, as well. Thousands more could be found beyond the Minas frontiers on the Goiás, Bahia, and Espírito Santo borderlands. See Senna, *A terra mineira*, 2:103n.

26. See Silva Neves for a detailed account of the droughts and their effect on Tremendal, especially p. 19. Gaspar, a Belgian priest, reported that in every drought year great numbers of the poor left for south Minas or emigrated to São Paulo (*Dans le sertão de Minas*, p. 59).

27. Sampaio, a government engineer, observed the northern slave migration in 1879 (*O Rio do São Francisco,* p. 61). "Everyone said you could earn a lot of money in São Paulo," Esteves recalls in his *Grão Mogol,* p. 61. See also Braga, *Dias idos e vividos,* p. 56.

28. Data on agricultural conditions including wages are given in Brazil, *Aspectos da economia rural brazileira,* pp. 891–910, with the Triângulo information appearing on p. 899. For the elite's perception of migration, see the debate of Aug. 23, 1927, in Minas, *Annaes da Camara, 1927,* pp. 554–55. For migration in the 1930's, consult Graham and Buarque de Hollanda Filho, pp. 67ff.

29. Singer, pp. 221–22, 257.

30. Senna, *A terra mineira,* 2:109. The statistics are from Leloup, *Les villes,* Table 5, p. 21.

31. For more information on different types of cities and their economic bases, see Leloup, "Tipos de aglomerações e hierarquia." For the argument that cities of 10,000 and over are the only real urban environments, see especially *Diagnóstico,* 2:241. The statistics are again Leloup's, from *Les villes,* Table 5, p. 21.

32. Correia Dias, "Aspectos sociais," p. 94.

33. Menelíck de Carvalho, *A revolução de 30 e o município.*

34. Burton, 1:359.

35. See Mascarenhas, "Tentativas de desmembramento de Minas Gerais." The Mineiros were suspicious that Pernambuco and other northern provinces wanted to reduce their influence in the Imperial legislature. During the Empire, provincial rivalry was attenuated by the system of rotating officials throughout Brazil and by the Emperor's personal control over the political system. For these aspects, consult Murilo de Carvalho, "Elite and State-Building in Imperial Brazil."

36. For separatist sentiment by zone, consult the following: Nelson Vianna's *Foiceiros e vaqueiros,* pp. 161–62, for the north Minas anecdote by Antonio Augusto Veloso (*"a visão do alferes Rocha"*). Silva Neves (p. 8) blamed the Portuguese for not creating a north Minas province that by 1900 "would certainly be an opulent and prosperous state, blessed with benefits and improvements." Triângulo opinion is reported in *A Provincia de São Paulo,* March 9, 1875; articles for May 21, 1875, and April 16, 1877, said that the Sul wanted to join with São Paulo. For the scheme to unite Sul Minas with northern São Paulo in a new Provincia do Sapucaí, thus escaping domination by the Mata in Minas and by the dynamic West and South in São Paulo, see Godoy, *passim.*

37. "Preaching separatism is seditious," said *O Movimento,* the Republican Party organ, on July 2, 1891. In the broad sweep of Mineiro history, "zones rise and fall. Yesterday it was the Center, today it is the Mata."

38. Correia Dias analyzed the loss-of-substance argument in his "Estado e desenvolvimento em Minas Gerais," pp. 122ff. "Europe, like a sponge, was sucking all the substance . . . " Tiradentes said (Maxwell, p. 135). On the Empire see Iglésias, *Política econômica,* p. 209.

39. *O Movimento,* Sept. 20, 1891. Judging from the coverage of this issue in *O Movimento,* negotiations began in August and were all but dead by late October.

40. Odum and Moore, *American Regionalism*. Note their concise statement: "Regionalism provides an economy for the decentralization of political power," p. 12.

## Chapter Two

1. Analysis of Mineiro economy history for this period is almost nonexistent. See Iglésias' report in "Perspectiva" on a current team research project at the Regional Growth Center, University of Minas Gerais, and his comments on the Old Republic period.

2. Taken from Table 2.2. Contemporary estimates were not so favorable. According to the 1920 census and Brazilian statistical annuals, the value of Mineiro industrial production in 1920 was 5.7 percent of the national total, increasing to 6.7 percent in 1939. Rio Grande declined 2 percent in this period (from 11.8 to 9.8 percent), Pernambuco was stationary at 4.6 percent, and São Paulo's industrial product grew from 33 to 43.5 percent of the national total. See *Diagnóstico*, 5:12, 14.

3. This argument is stated forcefully in Minas, *Plano de recuperação econômica*, p. 26. Organized by Américo Gianetti, a leading industrialist, this 1947 study was highly critical of the state's economic performance and recommended large investments in power and transport facilities so that Minas could become more competitive.

4. Dean, pp. 193–94, and Pereira Brazil, p. 478. According to Pereira Brazil, Minas imported over 700,000 contos' worth of goods in 1936, of which two-thirds came from São Paulo, giving São Paulo a favorable trade balance with Minas of more than 100,000 contos (over $8.6 million).

5. Letter, Afonso Pena to Bernardo Mascarenhas, the textile magnate, April 22, 1890, quoted in Mascarenhas, *Bernardo Mascarenhas*, p. 225.

6. Gonçalves, *Relatorio*, p. 47.

7. The effect of abolition on the North is vividly described by Silva Neves, pp. 17–18; for the cattle industry see Silveira, pp. 907–11; and note Ferreira de Rezende's bitter account of how his coffee fazenda in the Mata was ruined, pp. 413–42. In his contemporary analysis of Paulista agriculture, João Veiga claimed (falsely) that Minas coffee production had been rendered "completely decadent," like the state of Rio de Janeiro. The Mata recovered faster and diversified more easily into dairy farming than the old coffee fazendas across the Paraíba River in the state of Rio, as Pedrosa ("A zona silenciosa," pp. 146–53) points out. Sabará and its northern hinterland suffered little because there were few slaves left by 1888, says Nielson (p. 285).

8. Furtado, pp. 152–53, and Pedrosa, p. 147.

9. Minas, Secretaria de Agricultura, *Relatório, 1894*, contains replies by municípios to a questionnaire on agricultural problems and wage rates sent out by David Campista in 1892; see p. xxi for the quote.

10. Carlos Pereira de Sá Fortes, a leading rancher, served on the Comissão Fundamental of the 1903 Congresso Agricola. His analysis of the labor problem is reprinted in *Minas Gerais*, March 22–23, 1903, p. 3. For his comments on vagrancy, see *Minas Gerais*, April 26, 1903, including information on labor legislation stalled in the federal congress. See also com-

ments of Augusto Álvares da Silva, a textile plant owner, and Sá Fortes in *Minas Gerais*, March 29, 1903, p. 4.

11. Police roundups by zone are reported in *O Diário de Minas*, Aug. 13, 1901, p. 1. The labor shortage "is due more to the lack of a law to organize labor than to a lack of people," *O Diário* commented on March 12, 1901. Camilo Prates reflected on anti-vagrant measures at the 1923 Municipal Congress (Minas, *Annaes do Congresso*, pp. 96–99) and discussed the Paulista labor contractors on pp. 101–2 and 469.

12. Prates, *A lavoura*, p. 135.

13. Wages were little used in the Mata because salaried laborers did not stay fixed to the soil, Castelo Branco reported to the 1923 Municipal Congress, Minas, *Annaes do Congresso*, p. 101. Wage data for 1910–20 by zone are in Brazil, *Aspectos*, pp. 897–910, and some data for the 1892–94 period are in Minas, Secretaria de Agricultura, *Relatório 1894*. See also Brazil, *Recenseamento geral de 1940*, tomo 3, p. 32.

14. The state commissioned Francisco Soares de Alvim Machado to study this problem in 1902. See his detailed report in four installments in the *Minas Gerais*, beginning March 9–10, 1903. Different tax collection procedures in Rio and Santos gave Sulista growers a competitive advantage (Bernardes, *Manifesto*, pp. 20–22) until 1920, when Minas signed a convention with São Paulo, diminishing the tax disparity that Mata growers had for years protested (Bernardes, Mensagem, in Minas, *Annaes da Camara, 1920*, p. 31). But the Sul was still paying less in 1927; see Jose Mariano Pinto Monteiro, "A questão do café em Minas," *O Jornal* (special supplement on Minas), Oct. 29, 1927.

15. Taunay, 9:459. "São Paulo with its huge production has glutted the market," said José Joaquim Monteiro de Andrade, a very large grower. Limits on new plantings should apply to Paulistas, not to Mineiros or the Fluminenses. Memorandum to the Commissão Fundamental, Congresso Agricola, in *Minas Gerais*, April 16, 1903, p. 3. For treasury policy, consult Peláez, "Análise econômica," pp. 40–46.

16. Commissão Fundamental, coffee theses in *Minas Gerais*, April 28, 1903, p. 1. Resolutions of the Congresso Agricola (theses 95–99) in *Minas Gerais*, May 27, 1903, p. 3; "indirect" is italicized in the original. Report of the Coffee Committee, reprinted immediately thereafter by the state government, pp. 3–5.

17. The Exchange Bank plan was modeled on the Argentine exchange bank. Nilo Peçanha suggested it at Taubaté, according to Melo Franco, *Rodrigues Alves*, 2:468, and Campista was its chief defender in the parliamentary debates.

18. For an excellent overview of the first valorization, with several references to the Minas role, see Holloway, especially pp. 72, 83–87, 110. Also, oral communication with Holloway, Dec. 1974.

19. Jacob, p. 49. He reprints the credit agreement and the statutes of cooperatives on pp. 119–25.

20. Bernardes, *Manifesto*, pp. 23–25.

21. Daniel Carvalho, *Capítulos de memórias*, pp. 175–76. Law 510 of Sept. 22, 1909, authorized the state treasury to tap surtax funds for general revenues. Receipts and disbursements of coffee support funds (for co-ops, advertising, warehousing, etc.) are shown below, in 1,000 contos (from

Lopes, p. 32, for receipts, and Minas, Secretaria das Finanças *Relatórios,* for disbursements. (The large figure for disbursements in 1909 included a 7,000 conto loan to farmers.)

| Year | Receipts | Disbursements | Year | Receipts | Disbursements |
|------|----------|---------------|------|----------|---------------|
| 1908 | 4.5 | 2.6 | 1912 | 3.6 | n.a. |
| 1909 | 4.0 | 10.0 | 1913 | 3.9 | n.a. |
| 1910 | 4.1 | 3.8 | 1914 | 2.3 | 0.4 |
| 1911 | 2.9 | 3.0 | | | |

22. Delfim Netto, p. 125, and Afrânio de Carvalho, *A actualidade mineira,* pp. 47–48.

23. Summary based on excellent overview by Peláez, "Análise econômica," pp. 66–113.

24. Antonio Carlos de Andrada, Mensagem, in Minas, *Annaes da Camara, 1927,* p. 83.

25. Congresses under the auspices of the Centro dos Lavradores Mineiros (later the Conselho) were held in June 1929, January 1931, and June 1933—all in Juiz de Fora. Oliveira Vianna praised the corporatist model of decision-making in the IMC (*Problemas,* pp. 117–8). The IMC's transformation into an interest group organ is detailed in a 32-page typewritten report, listed as Boletim 166, from the Minas Secretary of Agriculture to the Commerce Department of the Foreign Ministry (Avisos Recebidos, 1931–34, 422/2/21). See Benedicto Valladares, *Tempos idos,* pp. 71–74. Additional materials on Valladares are found in the Presidência Archive; see Interventor de Minas Gerais, Lata 3, Pasta 19, including March 1934 telegrams between Valladares and Vargas relative to the seizure.

26. Valladares, Mensagem, in Minas, *Annaes da Camara, 1937,* p. 58.

27. Silviano Brandão, "Aos Mineiros," speech of Dec. 24, 1897, in *Minas Gerais,* Jan. 1, 1898, p. 5: "Minas should be a food exporter. But now the food supply is not growing fast enough to feed the population." Export statistics in João Lyra, p. 452.

28. Luz, pp. 125ff. João Pinheiro, resumé of report to the Commissão Fundamental of Congresso Agricola, in *Minas Gerais,* April 19, 1903, p. 3. On butter, see Garden, pp. 120–25, and Senna, *Annuario, 1906,* 1:112.

29. João Lyra, pp. 16–21.

30. Correia Dias, *A imagem,* p. 94.

31. Becker, "Expansão," on changes in the interstate market; and Passos Maia, *Guapé,* pp. 170–71, for impact on the Sul.

32. Viana do Castelo, a leading merchant, at the 1923 Municipal Congress, Minas, *Annaes do congresso das municipalidades,* pp. 65–66.

33. Governor Cesário Alvim protested that the monopoly was directed against Mineiro producers and violated the law of supply and demand (telegram to the Minister of the Interior, Aug. 17, 1891, cited in *O Movimento,* Aug. 21, 1891, p. 1). See also Minas, Secretaria de Agricultura, *Relatório, 1901,* pp. 227–32.

34. Carlos de Sá Fortes, a large rancher, to the Comissão Fundamental, Congresso Agricola, in *Minas Gerais,* Jan. 15, 1903. *Correio da Manha,* April 13, 1903, p. 1, and July 26, 1905, p. 1.

35. Passos Maia, *Guapé,* pp. 173–79.

36. Padua Rezende, writing in *Jornal do Comercio,* reprinted in *Minas Gerais,* Feb. 10, 1903.

37. For Anglo's operations, see Becker, pp. 302–3, 320–21; Senna, *Chorographia de Minas Gerais,* pp. 207, 324; and Nelson Vianna, *Foiceiros,* p. 138.

38. Afrânio de Carvalho, *A actualidade mineira,* pp. 61–62. Law 8,873 of Nov. 13, 1928, authorized the plan. See also Minas, *Plano de recuperação econômica,* pp. 122–23, which called on the state to construct packing plants, perhaps in cooperation with producers. See also *Plano,* p. 25.

39. Taken from 1920 census data and the 1950 industrial census, in *Diagnóstico,* 5:14, which also contains an excellent brief overview of Mineiro industry in this period.

40. *Diagnóstico,* 5:14; Minas, *Annuario industrial, 1937,* pp. 5, 7.

41. *Diagnóstico,* 5:14; Singer, p. 249.

42. Food products, sugar milling, and textiles led the list of industrial activities in the Sul, where capitalization averaged 28 contos, or only $2,419 for each small plant. For the Mata this was 57 contos, about $4,924 per establishment. By contrast, capitalization in the Center was 197 contos, equal to $17,000 for each concern when mining activities are subtracted from the total. Minas, *Annuario industrial, 1937,* p. 258. Labor data are in Brazil, *Recenseamento, 1920,* 5:xi.

43. Francisco Mascarenhas, the textile mill owner, report to the 1903 Congresso Agricola, in *Minas Gerais,* April 9, 1903, p. 2. Afrânio de Carvalho, *A actualidade mineira,* pp. 51–52, 86–87. Stein, plant data, pp. 101–2, also pp. 116–17, 120–21, 143.

44. Wirth, pp. 76–83; Peláez, "Itabira Iron."

45. Américo Gianetti, operator of a small steel works at Rio Acima, to the congress of steel producers, Belo Horizonte, Nov. 5–7. See Silveira, pp. 83–85, and summary of the congress in *Minas Gerais,* Nov. 6, 9–10, 1925. For the role of Mineiro engineers in this industry, consult Murilo de Carvalho, "A Escola de Minas," pp. 99ff.

46. Singer (p. 255) estimated that half the population in 1950 was still integrated in the Rio and São Paulo market zones.

47. Afrânio de Carvalho, *A actualidade mineira,* p. 93.

48. Gustavo Pena's pamphlet, reprinted in *O Pharol,* Jan. 13, 1891.

49. The legislation and supporting arguments of the customs house are in Minas, Secretaria de Agricultura, *Relatório, 1895,* pp. 363–64; *1896,* pp. 429, 439; and *1897,* pp. 4, 219. See the overview by Deputy João Pandiá Calógeras on Sept. 28, 1898, in Brazil, *Annaes, 1898,* 3:551–52.

50. Sebastião Lima, president of the Associação Comercial, resolution to the 1923 Municipal Congress, Minas, *Annaes do congresso das municipalidades,* pp. 556–57. Melo Viana and other speakers at the dedication of the customs house, cited in Silveira, pp. 368–70. *O Diário de Minas,* Feb. 24, 1929, p. 1.

51. Cel. Burlemaqui, a leading merchant, memorandum to Commissão Fundamental, 1903 Congresso Agricola, in *Minas Gerais,* April 24, 1903, p. 1. Nelson Coelho de Sena, memorandum, in *ibid.* Also Minas, *Annaes do congresso das municipalidades, passim.*

52. The 1908 import list from Jacob, p. 425; 1929 imports in Afrânio de Carvalho, *A actualidade mineira*, pp. 94–95.

53. Iglésias, *Política econômica*, pp. 194–95. Pimenta, *A mata do Peçanha*, p. 196.

54. Leloup, *Les villes*, pp. 117–18, 121. Oliveira Torres, *História*, p. 1357. Statistics from Minas, *Annuario estatistico, 1921*, Anno I, p. 827; Minas, Secretaria de Agricultura, *Relatório, 1896*, p. 249; Brazil, *Anuário estatístico, 1939/40*, Ano V, p. 1356; and *1937*, Ano III, p. 365.

55. Brazil, *Anuário estatístico, 1937*, Ano III, p. 365.

56. Carlos Nunes Rabello to Afonso Pena, São João del Rei, Aug. 1, 1899, Arquivo Afonso Pena, letter 306.

57. Nelson de Senna, *A terra mineira*, 1:315.

58. Lauriano Rodriques de Andrade, report on the credit and banking situation to the 1903 Congresso Agricola, *Minas Gerais*, May 24, 1903, pp. 2–3. Teixeira da Costa, "O movimento bancário em Minas Geraes," in *O Jornal*, 1927 supplement on Minas. Daniel de Carvalho, article in *O Economista* for May 1929, reprinted in his *Estudos de economia e finanças*, p. 187.

59. Interview with Theodorico de Assis, president of the Centro dos Lavradores, in *Estado de Minas*, Dec. 14, 1933, p. 10, and with José de Magalhães Pinto, manager of the Banco da Lavoura, in *ibid.* Dec. 5, 1933, p. 3.

60. Compiled from Brazil, Banco do Brasil, *Relatório, 1937*, p. 68. According to Bank of Brazil statistics for 1945, 24 percent of the outstanding loans to agriculturalists were held in Minas, 21 percent in São Paulo. Of all loans outstanding, Mineiros held 10.8 percent, São Paulo 16.4 percent, and the Federal District—enjoying a real estate and construction boom in the late Estado Novo—46 percent. See also *Relatório, 1946*, p. 163.

61. Wells, 1:44. See also Pedrosa's comments in "A zona silenciosa," p. 141.

62. *Diagnóstico*, 3:97ff.

63. Valladão, *A campanha da princesa*, 2:411.

64. Beaumont, p. 18.

65. Azevedo, pp. 24–25. Becker, pp. 305, 309.

66. The early roads in Minas are discussed in Senna, *Chorografia de Minas Geraes*, 10:316–24. Vehicular data are in Pereira Brazil, pp. 512–13.

67. Gordilho, pp. 190ff, and Daniel de Carvalho, *Estudos e depoimentos*, pp. 114ff.

68. Daniel de Carvalho, *Estudos e depoimentos*, p. 98.

69. Pereira Brazil, pp. 511–12.

70. Quote from the Plano Geral da Viação Ferrea do Estado de Minas Geraes (Raul Soares government, 1924), cited by Silveira in *Minas Geraes em 1925*, p. 284. Triângulo trade percentages are from Pereira Brazil, pp. 294–95.

71. Pedrosa, p. 155.

## Chapter Three

1. *O Diário de Minas*, July 17, 1907, p. 1. Brazilians consider Dumont the inventor of the airplane.

2. Chronologically, Sra. Brant passed her Diamantina girlhood in the 1890's; the two men grew up before the war and moved to Belo Horizonte by the early 1920's. Her *Minha vida de menina* is available in Elizabeth Bishop's translation as *The Diary of "Helena Morley."* Cyro dos Anjos, the novelist and member of the Brazilian Academy of Letters, published his *Explorações no tempo* (*memórias*) in 1963. Carlos Drummond de Andrade's work is collected in the *Obra completa,* as organized by Afrânio Coutinho, the second edition of which I used. For a spirited literary treatment of Drummond's sense of place, consult Joaquim-Francisco Mártires Coelho, *Terra e família na poesia de Carlos Drummond de Andrade.* Pedro Nava's memoirs of his Juiz de Fora origins are compelling.

3. Anjos, pp. 190–91, 210.

4. Leloup, *Les villes,* p. 5.

5. See Harris's classic study of Rio dos Contos, a Bahian gold town north of Minas, "Minas Velhas; A Study of Urbanism in the Mountains of Eastern Brazil," pp. 29–30.

6. Stein and Stein, pp. 57–58.

7. Rebelo Horta, "Famílias governamentais de Minas Gerais," *passim.*

8. Taunay, *História do Café no Brasil,* 8.

9. Drummond, "Viagem de Sabará," p. 576.

10. Leeds, "Brazilian Careers and Social Structure."

11. Greenfield, p. 18.

12. Vasconcellos, pp. 90–91, esp. pp. 96–97.

13. Faoro, pp. 209ff.

14. After losing his first fortune in the stock market crash of 1892, Ferreira Guimarães started a textile plant in Valencia (Rio de Janeiro state) and branched out into other manufacturing activities and banking. He was also active in Espírito Santo, and bought into São João del Rei and Barbacena textile plants. In 1930, he founded the Banco de Minas Gerais, of which he was the first president. Vivaldi Moreira, in *Belo Horizonte completou 50 anos,* pp. 38–39; *Minas Gerais,* obituaries in the March 16 and 17, 1948, issues.

15. Anjos, pp. 79–80, 210.

16. Aristides Maia, "Homestead," p. 21. Other champions of reform were David Campista and Américo Werneck. On the land tax dispute, see Chapter 4; on colonization consult Goés Monteiro. Extensive commentary on the public lands issue is in Minas Gerais, Secretaria de Agricultura reports; I quoted the 1903 *Relatório,* p. 64. São Paulo also had a chaos of land titles, and this was probably true of all areas of Brazil settled after 1850.

17. Brazil, *Recenseamento geral de 1940,* 3:18.

18. Denis was impressed by the disciplined, motivated foreigners working in Paulista agriculture, in contrast to the irregular, poor-quality black field hands in Minas (*Le Brésil,* chap. 12).

19. Leloup, *Les villes,* p. 21.

20. Ferreira de Rezende, p. 412.

21. Mantua, 1:14.

22. Marques Rebelo, p. 13.

23. Miranda, p. 48.

24. Mail data in Nelson de Senna, *Annuario de Minas*, 6, tomo 1:141. São Paulo had only 445 postal agencies. Telegraph and telephone data in Senna's *A terra mineira*, 2:373–77.

25. Secretary of Agriculture Israel Pinheiro da Silva, in *Fôlha de Minas*, cited in Pereira Brasil, pp. 28–29.

26. For the press in local politics, see Diniz's lively *O Gonçalvismo em Pitangui*, p. 9.

27. Abilio Machado, "Imprensa mineira," reprinted from *O Jornal* in *Minas Gerais*, June 27, 1929, p. 10.

28. Nelson Vianna, *Foiceiros e vaqueiros*, pp. 53–56; *Minas Gerais*, Aug. 2 and 3, 1920, p. 6.

29. "Improprieties of the cinema" were discussed in the *Minas Gerais* for Aug. 3, 1913, p. 6: "The scenes of suicide, seduction, homicides, and ambushes are portrayed so vividly that the danger of imitation is immediate and inevitable." Bernardes' Mensagem of June 15, 1920, is in Minas, *Annaes da Camara, 1920*, pp. 17–18.

30. Burton, 2:105.

31. Eduardo Santos Maia, *Impressões*, p. 118.

32. Minas, *Annuario estatistico, 1921*, Anno I, pp. 421–25.

33. Outstanding among the many studies of Mineiro literature are Moog's *Uma interpretação*, chap. 6, and Martins de Oliveira's *História da literatura mineira*. The literary and social ethos of early Belo Horizonte is analyzed by Correia Dias in his *João Alphonsus* and "O movimento modernista," pp. 48ff.

34. See Correia Dias's excellent study of the modernists, who were all born around 1900, arrived in Belo at the same time, mostly studied law together, and were public functionaries; "O movimento modernista," esp. pp. 83–85.

35. Martins, *Lista geral*, and Gonçalves Maia, "Lista geral."

36. According to Pires, speaking in 1902, cited in his *Homens e factos*, p. 241. A young Paulista law student was shot by pharmacy students from Rio Grande do Sul, a group that included the Vargas brothers. José Veiga, *Ephemerides*, 2:371, and Daniel de Carvalho, *Novos estudos e depoimentos*, p. 164.

37. Cel. Ignacio Burlamaqui, commenting on one of the theses under debate at the 1903 Congresso Agricola e Industrial in Belo Horizonte *Minas Gerais*, May 8, 1903, p. 3.

38. Between 1904 and 1918, about 223 provisional licenses were requested for the first time or renewed. Several of these lawyers later obtained degrees, left for Rio or São Paulo, or abandoned the profession entirely, according to Nelson de Sena; debate of Aug. 28, 1919, in Minas, *Annaes da Camara, 1919*, pp. 701–17. The Primeiro Congresso dos Advogados e Solicitadores Provisionados is reported in *Minas Gerais*, Dec. 29–31, 1918, p. 2. In 1906 the Paulista provisionals, of whom there were about 120, fought off bills to abolish their licenses; see Manuel Casasanta, *Francisco Escobar*, pp. 85–93.

39. Melo Franco, *A alma do tempo*, p. 100. According to Pang, "The Politics of Coronelismo in Brazil," p. 102: "In terms of transportation, any town in the São Francisco Valley was closer to Belo Horizonte than to

Salvador." With its gymnasium and normal school, the Sul de Minas city of Muzambinho serviced a wide area including northern São Paulo; Mário Leite, *Paulistas e mineiros,* p. 276.

40. Augusto Franco, April 1906 editorial in *Vida Mineira,* reprinted in his *Estudos e escriptos* p. 93.

41. Afrânio de Carvalho, *A actualidade mineira,* p. 25. Correia Dias, "O movimento modernista," pp. 63–64. The congress was covered in *Minas Gerais,* Nov. 12–13, 1928, pp. 4–6.

42. The authoritative treatment of these events is from Mario de Lima's *O bom combate, passim. Minas Gerais,* Oct. 13, 1929, pp. 12–13, covered the signing and listed the Catholic organizations and notables attending at the governor's palace, where the Archbishop of Belo Horizonte presented Antonio Carlos with the cup.

43. President Bernardes and almost all of the delegates to the 1925 constitutional reform convention were unsympathetic when the religious education issue arose. Opinion then changed rapidly. Catholic political strength at the 1933 Constituent Assembly helped carry the day. See Gabaglia, pp. 172, 320–21; she neglects to mention that the campaign in Minas was critical to the national victory.

44. In addition to Dom Silvério Gomes Pimenta's *Cartas pastoraes,* see Monsenhor Alypio Odier de Oliveira, *Traços biographicos de Dom Silverio Gomes Pimenta,* and Dom Joaquim Silverio de Souza, *Vida de D. Silverio Gomes Pimenta.*

45. The role of European priests is detailed in Mario de Lima's *O bom combate.* The Belgians' experiences are related in Gaspar, esp. pp. 31 and 113. The Premonstratensians mobilized the citizens of Montes Claros to petition the Papacy for a bishopric, which was granted and installed in 1910; see Paula, p. 276. Bernardes was a French-trained Caraça graduate; French Lazarites taught Juscelino Kubitschek at the Diamantina seminary; see Assis Barbosa, *Juscelino Kubitschek,* p. 215.

46. Great Britain, Records of Leading Personalities in Brazil, Feb. 1935. PRO:FO 371/18654 3893.

47. Obituary in *Minas Gerais,* Feb. 6–7, 1928, p. 12. See the admiring sketch by Daniel de Carvalho, *Novos estudos e depoimentos,* pp. 136ff. Chalmers' many technical achievements are chronicled by Hollowood.

48. Morro Velho labor troubles are reported in an article "Morro Velho," in *Revista Industrial de Minas Geraes,* and *Correio da Manhã,* Jan. 27, 1903. The Sabará incident is related in José Veiga, *Ephemerides,* 3:286. For the Gypsies consult Dornas Filho's "Os ciganos em Minas Gerais."

49. See Weiner, "National Integration vs. Nationalism," p. 253.

*Chapter Four*

1. Concentração Conservadora, *Congresso de Montes Claros,* esp. pp. 31–39. Brito did not recount his own role in weakening the state, how, among other things, he was directing the Bank of Brazil's credit war against Minas in this campaign. Earlier, he led the famous civilista campaign of 1909–10 in Minas to fight the very tactics of bossism and forced consensus he now extolled 20 years later.

2. José, *A propaganda,* pp. 54–56.

3. Letter, Antonio Olinto dos Santos Pires to his father, Dr. Felício, Ouro Preto, Feb. 28, 1890, in Correspondência de Ruy Barbosa.

4. Estevam Oliveira, *Notas e epístolas*, p. vii. This is the most incisive contemporary analysis of Mineiro politics through the 1910 election. Oliveira was an opposition journalist from Juiz de Fora.

5. Soares, p. 84.

6. The official slate is in *O Movimento*, Jan. 3, 1891, and the historicos' opposition slate is from *A Patria Mineira*, Jan. 15, 1891.

7. Directorio do Partido Catholico do Estado de Minas Geraes, "A chapa oficial," *O Pharol*, Sept. 9, 1890, p. 2.

8. Oliveira Torres, *História de Minas Gerais*, pp. 1209–10.

9. Telegram, Bias Fortes (president of the Minas senate) et al. to Marechal Floriano Peixoto, Entre Rios, Nov. 26, 1891, in Coleção Marechal Floriano Peixoto, Caixa 1206 "1891, Cartas e telegramas."

10. On Campanha, see Valladão, 2:355–75, and Hélio Lobo, *Um varão*, pp. 103–10. For the Viçosa revolt, consult Alencar, pp. 93–109. The Viçosa rising occurred on February 7, five days *after* Governor Alvim made public his decision to resign. With the state government seemingly off balance, the rebel strategy was to remove local officials in anticipation of a complete change in state judges and municipal officers, as had already happened in every state where Floriano intervened.

11. The résumé of this convention is in *Minas Gerais*, Sept. 3, 1897, pp. 5–6, and the split is explained in *O Estado de Minas*, Oct. 6, 1897, p. 1.

12. The majority position and membership are in *O Estado de Minas*, Oct. 26, 1897, pp. 3–4. For the dissidents, consult the *Minas Gerais* for Sept. 4, pp. 6–7, and Oct. 9, p. 6. At least four of the six men elected to the PRM Executive Committee were ex-Alvinistas: Mendes Pimentel, Ildefonso Alvim, José Raimundo Teles de Menezes, and Sabino Barroso. None were from the Sul; two each came from the North, the Mata, and the Center.

13. Bressane summarized this first PRM convention in *Minas Gerais*, Dec. 24, 1897, p. 1. On the fusion Executive Committee, Vaz de Melo and Júlio Bueno Brandão represented the old PRC, Sabino Barroso, Mendes Pimentel, and Teles de Menezes the dissidents. In July 1898, Sabino and his northern coronéis defected to Silviano. Mendes Pimentel and Teles were forced out, and Teles could never get reelected to the federal delegation despite large pluralities.

14. Executive Committee bulletin of July 15, 1898, in *Minas Gerais*, July 16, 1898, p. 5. Résumé of the second PRM convention in *Minas Gerais*, Aug. 31, 1898, pp. 4–5.

15. Nunes Leal, esp. pp. 51, 109.

16. Campos Salles, *Da propaganda á presidencia*, pp. 239–40.

17. For the Executive Committee, see the brief but uneven account by Levindo Coelho, who came on in 1923 as alternate for Governor Raul Soares and became a full member in 1924 ("Depoimento," pp. 117–18). Consult Estevam de Oliveira's highly critical comments (*Notas e epístolas*, p. xxvii) and Daniel de Carvalho's *Capítulos de memórias*, p. 231.

18. The quote is from Salles's gossipy *Se não me falha a memória*, p. 122.

19. See Estevam Oliveira, *passim.*
20. *Ibid.,* p. xl.
21. Vaz de Melo, Sabino Barroso, and Júlio Bueno were the core of Silviano's original committee. Francisco Sales and Bressane joined them, as did Bias Fortes and his Mata ally and long-time companion in the state senate, Antonio Martins Ferreira da Silva. Prominant Silvianistas included Bernardo Pinto Monteiro of the Mata and Sabino Barroso of the North, as well as Francisco Alvaro Bueno de Paiva of the Sul, who joined in 1909, having been Júlio Bueno's stand-in for years. Bias and Martins were rooted in the senate, where eight-year terms and frequent reelection provided continuity while placing strong patronage and control powers in their hands. Joining Sales and Bressane in 1909 was José Monteiro Ribeiro Junqueira, a fazendeiro-banker-industrialist, who is profiled in Chapter 5.
22. Estevam de Oliveira is again the best contemporary source. See also Campello de Souza's piece and Assis Barbosa's *Juscelino Kubitschek,* p. 194. The PRM organized to fight the civilistas in September 1909. Bressane had already regained the secretariat. Sabino Barroso replaced Carlos Peixoto (Pinheiro's man) as president of the chamber, and his committee seat went to Ribeiro Junqueira, a Salista; Bernardo Pinto Monteiro came on the committee while his brother fought Peixoto in Ubá, the ousted leader's local base in the Mata.
23. For the turnover, consult Fleischer, esp. Fig. 4.1, p. 93. See also Almeida Magalhães, pp. 46–47.
24. Ata of the 1919 Convention in *Minas Gerais,* Sept. 18, 1919, pp. 3–4. Also Daniel de Carvalho, *Francisco Sales,* pp. 106–10. Sales never expected him to change the collegial format; outmaneuvered, he resigned. But Bernardes did not formally accept his resignation for almost a year, until he had purged several local bosses loyal to Sales. Américo Ferreira Lopes, who was Sales's candidate for governor in 1917, left the committee; Bressane was kept dangling until 1921; Junqueira joined Bernardes.
25. The debates over what became Additional Law 10 occurred mainly in the sessions of Aug. 22 and 23, 1919, and of Aug. 10, 1920, in Minas, *Annaes da Camara, 1919* and *1920.* Campos's eloquent statement in favor of a centralized, administrative state was reprinted in *Revista Forense,* 33 (Jan.–June, 1920):164–78. In 1925 he argued along the same lines in the federal Chamber when Bernardes pressed for a stronger central government.
26. Melo Franco, *Um estadista,* 3:1327ff, is the best account. Although he belonged to Wenceslau's wing of the PRM, Maciel was close to Bernardes and also served as Antonio Carlos's legal substitute on the Executive Committee. At 75, Maciel was considered to be beyond political ambition. Antonio Carlos did not like Brito and refused to change his substitute status on the Executive Committee to a full-time membership. Antonio Carlos apparently agreed to let Brito have a state senate seat, but then ran a Church candidate instead. Furious, Brito bolted to Washington Luís. Letter, Deputy Carneiro de Rezende to Afrânio de Melo Franco, Belo Horizonte, Aug. 21, 1929, Coleção Melo Franco, I–36, 5, BN.
27. Only 57 percent of the registered voters turned out for the presi-

dential election, in contrast to Rio Grande's 80 percent and São Paulo's 71 percent. However, the vote more than doubled over 1926 (369,768 compared with 144,750), which indicates the campaign aroused intense voter interest despite the lackluster final tally. Brazil, *Diário do Congresso,* May 24, 1930, p. 539, p. 545. State totals were 329,223 for Olegário Maciel, and 882 for Melo Viana, who did not campaign. See Brazil, *Diário do Congresso,* Aug. 14, 1930, p. 20.

28. Sir W. Seeds, Brazil, Annual Report, 1930, p. 23, in Great Britain, Public Records Office: FO 371/15067 3740.

29. The Legion's local directorates were supposed to be elected by secret ballot, but most if not all were appointed by "acclamation" and comprised the traditional local factions. The Legion simply raided the PRM's local bases. For an excellent account, see Rollim's *Ephemerides curvellanas,* pp. 292–96. Capaema's telegram and extensive reporting are in *Minas Gerais,* May 2, 1931, and *Estado de Minas,* May 3, 1931. Bernardes was prepared to adhere if he received Interior and Finance.

30. The *Estado de Minas* has excellent and extensive coverage of the August 15–18 PRM convention and the coup. For the Rio story, including Aranha's disclaimer of responsibility, see *O Jornal* for Aug. 19–25. See Hélio Silva, *O ciclo de Vargas, 1932,* pp. 86ff, and Cel. Herculano Teixeira d'Assumpção's detailed account in "Classes armadas," *Belo Horizonte completou 50 anos,* pp. 75–79. When Vargas telegramed his full support to Maciel, he was also in very close contact with Aranha and Virgílio as they ran the power play; Daniel de Carvalho, *Ensaios de crítica e de história,* pp. 139–46.

31. The exiled leaders—Bernardes, Augusto Brant, and Djamla Pinheiro Chagas, could not participate until 1934. Ovídio de Andrade, the party president, lost the federal election, and Hugo Werneck, a prominent clinician, also lost. Daniel de Carvalho and Christiano Machado, two brilliant young lawyers recruited by Bernardes in the 1920's, won their seats. So did José Carneiro de Rezende, the industrialist, and Levindo Coelho, an old Raul Soares protégé.

32. The best accounts are Benedicto Valladares, *Tempos idos e vividos,* pp. 47–52, and Afonso Arinos de Melo Franco, *A alma do tempo,* pp. 304–12. Flôres da Cunha's brother married into a Mineira family that fought the Melo Francos in local politics. Bitterly disappointed, Virgílio tried to organize a coup to install General Góes Moneiro in the presidency (Melo Franco, *A alma do tempo,* pp. 337–39).

33. Correspondence and telegrams filed in the Presidência Archive under pasta Interventor de Minas Gerais, especially the telegram of Valadares to Vargas, dated June 28, 1934, in which the Interventor requests permission to visit the Triângulo before traveling on to São Paulo and then to Rio to attend Vargas's inauguration. Vargas replied: "I accept the initiative."

34. Letter, José S. Maciel Filho to Oswaldo Aranha, Rio, [July?] 1937, in Arquivo Aranha, "Assuntos Políticos, 1935–37." In this letter Maciel relates how "Benedicto confessed yesterday that he wishes Getulio well as he would a father. Benedicto's psychology is interesting and merits a

special observation." Most of the letter concerns Valadares' key role in preparing for the 1937 coup, which Maciel, a well-informed Vargas crony, considered inevitable.

35. *Ibid.*

36. See the excellent chronology in Hélio Silva's volumes and Benedicto Valladares' *Tempos idos e vividos,* pp. 111–13.

37. For an astute evaluation of Valladares as governor, then as leader of the Partido Social Democrático (PSD) through the 1964 Revolution, see Alberto Castello Branco's column, "O chefe e o modelo do PSD de Minas," in *Jornal do Brasil,* March 29, 1973, p. 4.

38. Tarrow, pp. 7–8.

39. Consult Lemarchand and Legg, pp. 149–50; for negative aspects, see pp. 175ff.

40. Moema Siqueira, "Elites políticas," p. 179.

41. Correia Dias, "O movimento modernista," pp. 49–50.

42. Letter, Bias Fortes to Afonso Pena, Barbacena, Nov. 22, 1906, in pasta Bias Fortes, Arquivo Afonso Pena.

43. Calógeras, *Problemas de administração,* p. 225.

44. Consult Pang, "The Politics of Coronelismo in Brazil," especially chap. 7. Commercial integration of the São Francisco River Valley with the coast persuaded the coronéis to exchange warfare for the benefits of peace. Army intervention also helped.

45. Passos Maia, pp. 181, 206–8.

46. The literature is large. Consult Barbosa, *Factos e cifros,* pp. 285–307, and Lopes, *Notas sobre regimen tributario do Estado de Minas Geraes,* pp. 99–103, for an overview. Senator Carlos Alves, speech of July 10, 1894, Minas, *Annaes do Senado, 1894,* pp. 296–97; Werneck, *Reforma do systema tributario, passim;* Budget Committee report for Aug. 5, 1899, Minas, *Annaes da Camara, 1899,* pp. 317–18; David Campista, Minas, Secretaria das Finanças, *Relatorio, 1899,* pp. 22–26. The extensive debates on Bernardes' bill 746 of 1919, introducing the land tax reform, are in Minas, *Annaes da Camara, 1919.* Also, José Bernardino Alves, Minas, Secretaria das Finanças, *Relatório, 1929,* 1:87–88.

47. Anthouard, pp. 269–70.

48. The Congresso Agricola debates at Juiz de Fora in October were covered extensively in *Minas Gerais,* on Oct. 23 and 26, 1899; the Congresso dos Lavradores de Cafe da Zona de Mata, held at Categuazes on July 2, is summarized in *Diário de Minas,* July 18, 1918, and in Minas, *Annaes da Camara, 1919,* pp. 405–6. As for the voluntary system of reporting land values, it left much to be desired, said Finance Secretary David Campista. With only 117 employees to check records, the state was understaffed. And even "a very modest recalculation" would place real land values at least one-third higher than the owners declared. Minas, Secretaria das Finanças, *Relatório, 1900,* n.p.

49. Love, *Rio Grande do Sul,* p. 102.

50. Debate of Aug. 21, 1919, Minas, *Annaes da Camara, 1919,* p. 488.

51. Figures from Minas, *Finanças do Estado.*

52. A useful sketch of the Associação Commercial de Minas is in *Belo Horizonte completou 50 anos,* pp. 360–67. In 1938, Valadares forced José

de Magalhães Pinto to leave the ACM presidency for opposing his tax policies. State Chief Justice João Braulio was the first Agricultural Association president in 1909.

53. Congresso dos Funccionarios de Justiça, held in Ouro Preto, July 14, 1893, reported in José Veiga, *Ephemerides mineiras*, 3:99.

54. Partido de Lavoura e Commercio, slate for Dec. 31, 1899, in *Jornal do Povo*, Dec. 15, 1899, p. 3. Ribeiro Junqueira and Teles de Menezes belonged. José Bonifacio de Andrada was backed by the Liga da Lavoura in Barbacena for election to the state legislature in November 1898. Antonio Carlos, his brother, represented the Barbacena Liga at the August 1898 PRM convention, but his credentials were not recognized. For local accounts, consult Pontes, *História de Uberaba*, pp. 126–44; Vieira de Rezende e Silva and Vieira de Rezende, "O municipio de Cataguazes," pp. 800–801; and Dilermando Cruz, "Cartas da minha terra," part 6, in *O Pharol*, Oct. 21, 1905, p. 2.

55. J. A. Rodrigues Caldas, "A lavoura de Minas, o convenio de Taubaté," *Minas Gerais*, April 23–24, 1906, pp. 3–4.

56. Azevedo Junior, "Cartas mineiras," *Correio da Manhã*, May 27, 1905, p. 1.

57. Arquivo Afonso Pena Júnior: João Ribeiro to Afonso Pena Júnior, Juiz de Fora, July 14, 1909, letter no. 109, containing a report on bankers' opinion of Hermes. Also, João Edmundo C. Brant to Afonso Pena Junior, Diamantina, [early] 1910, letter no. 17; in talking with the coronéis, Brant heard many times *"Não se trata de Hermes, mas do Sá que vai dar o pão ao nosso povo."* And last, Aviso, Comissão das Senhoritas do Sabará to Afonso Pena Júnior, Sabará, July 27, 1910, document no. 108, for the appeal to women.

58. Leading the Minas branch of the Partido Economista was José Carlos de Moraes Sarmento, president of the Associação Comercial de Juiz de Fora. For their slate and manifesto, see *O Estado de Minas* for April 23 and 25, 1933. Both the Commercial and Agricultural Associations protested the syndicalization requirement. See *O Estado de Minas*, April 21, 1933, p. 10; and letter, João Jacques Montandon, president of the Sociedade Mineira de Agricultura, to Vargas, Belo Horizonte, June 28, 1933, Presidência Archive, pasta Interventor de Minas Gerais, lata 3.

59. Mario de Lima's excellent *O bom combate* is disappointingly weak on political aspects of the Catholic organizational drive starting in 1910. The petition figure is cited on his p. 178.

60. *A Patria Mineira*, Sept. 11, 1892, p. 2.

61. Letter, Antonio Felicio dos Santos, the Catholic journalist, to President Afonso Pena, Rio, May 27, 1909, requesting the president to intervene. Arquivo Afonso Pena.

62. Joaquim de Souza, *Vida de D. Silverio Gomes Pimenta*, pp. 297–303. It was the education issue that first prompted the hierarchy, Dom Silvério, and Furtado de Menezes to organize the Partido Regenerador, which they saw as a model for the other states; Oliveira Torres, *História de Minas Gerais*, 5:1461ff. Newspaper accounts include *O Pharol's* interview with Furtado de Menezes—"Uma questão palpitante"—for Jan. 7, 1910; *Correio do Dia* (the civilista paper), "No posto de honra," for April 26,

1910; and *O Diário de Minas* (the PRM paper), which, on Oct. 31, 1909, published the archbishop's letter to Menezes. Civilista efforts to enlist Menezes as Carvalho Brito's running mate in the state elections are cited in *O Diário de Minas*, March 6, 1910.

63. Campos do Amaral, "Os católicos e as eleições," *O Estado de Minas*, Feb. 17, 1921, p. 1.

64. Centro Popular Mineiro, *Candidaturas presidenciaes*. Also *O Diário de Minas*, Jan. 12, Feb. 20, and March 14, 1930.

65. This generalization should be tested by a systematic study of local politics statewide. See Murilo de Carvalho, "Barbacena," esp. pp. 172–77.

66. Francisco Bernardino of Juiz de Fora said he "had been unaware of the existence of these numerous and well-organized groups" but was "agreeably surprised" when they pledged to support him in the last election. Session of Dec. 7, 1906, Brazil, *Annaes, 1906*, 8:161. For paternalism, and Bernardes' attempt to co-opt labor, see Dias, pp. 119–25.

67. See Celson da Silva's master's thesis on Caeté, which was João Pinheiro's home base, "Marchas e contramarchas do mandonismo local," p. 16.

68. Salles, pp. 122–23. The falsity of this argument is shown by the prevalence of bacharéis in congress from all the other states.

69. Alice Canedo to Afonso Pena Júnior, Muriaé, Nov. 12, 1922, letter no. 127 in Arquivo Afonso Pena Júnior. Muriaé had the third largest electorate in the state, indicating, probably, that the Mata politicians counted on Canedo to deliver a large vote for the situation.

70. Carvalho Brito, editorial: "O pleito de hoje," *Correio do Dia*, Aug. 7, 1910, and Brito–Afonso Pena Júnior editorial: "Aos nossos correligionarios," in *Correio do Dia*, Aug. 10, 1910.

71. Telegram, Valladares to Vargas, Belo Horizonte, Dec. 22, 1934, in Interventor de Minas Gerais, Arquivo Presidência, lata 15.

72. Assis Barbosa, *Juscelino Kubitschek*, p. 357.

73. Mantua, *Figurões*, 2:32–45.

74. Estevam Oliveira, *Notas e epístolas*, p. xvi; Assis Barbosa, *Juscelino Kubitschek*, p. 161. For a good account of local elections, see Diniz, pp. 68ff.

75. Minas was divided into two sets of electoral districts, state and federal. District lines meandered across the customary zones, but by aggregating the registered voters by zone it is possible to assess the relative electoral power of the seven subregions. Otherwise, comparison is impossible, because the state districts rose from six to 12 in 1915, whereas the federal districts shrunk from 12 to seven in 1905. Fortunately, the total number of registered voters in each set was the same.

76. Pequeno, *Um advogado*, p. 160.

77. Botelho, *Leopoldina de outrora*, p. 43.

78. Brazil, *Diário do Congresso, supplemento*, July 1910, n.p.

79. Pequeno, *Um advogado*, pp. 387ff.

## Chapter Five

1. Assis Barbosa, *Juscelino Kubitschek*, pp. 235–36, n50.

2. Rebelo Horta, pp. 43–91.

3. Imperial elite is defined as senators or titleholders of barão or above.

It is a different kind of elite from the main one, being a combination of social and political elites. Minas ranked 11 percent behind Pernambuco, hinting at a less ossified elite.

4. Melo Franco, *Estadista*, 1:232.

5. That is, 35.5 percent, or 76 men (71 with birthplace data, five without) of 214.

6. Although the third generation (born after 1889) was more likely to take professional degrees in Minas, this group also had the largest percentage of secondary schooling out of state. Only one or two in the Minas group studied law in São Paulo after 1900.

7. Ferreira de Rezende, pp. 426–27.

8. Between 1892 and 1934 a total of ten priests served in the state legislature, six for more than one session. Francisco Xavier de Almeida Rolim, mayor of Curvelo and a canon of the Church, served from 1899 to 1930. He was the senate's Catholic spokesman and a leader of Catholic Action. Two priests were elected to the 1892 Constituinte, three to the 1934 Assembly. None were sent to the federal delegation, perhaps out of deference to the feelings of more secularized states like São Paulo and Rio Grande. Catholic lay leaders who served in the state and federal delegations, but did not hold one of our elite-defining positions, are also not enumerated here. Our elite was simply at a higher level than the bulk of priests and Catholic lay leaders in the legislature.

9. $N = 198$. Sixty-one were based politically in their birthplaces, including 14 of the 21 top regional bosses: Sabino Barroso, Bernardes, Bias Fortes, Bias Fortes Junior, Wenceslau Brás, Júlio Bueno Brandão, Carlos Chagas, Astolfo Dutra, Antonio Martins, Melo Viana, Carlos Peixoto, Ribeiro Junqueira, Francisco Sales, and Vaz de Melo; the remaining seven of the top bosses were Alvim, Antonio Carlos, Lindolfo Coelho, Olegário Maciel, Silviano Brandão, Raul Soares, and Benedito Valadares.

10. Of these, 71 were in Belo Horizonte, 17 in Juiz de Fora. The rate is the same for all (including those with no birthplace data) who were active in Belo (76) and Juiz de Fora (19), or 95 out of 214.

11. Minas professions (in percent of each adjusted state total). Note that the "Business" variable is a composite of variables 54–56, 63–65 (see Appendix A).

|  | Pernambuco | São Paulo | Minas Gerais |
|---|---|---|---|
| Industrialist | 12.6 | 27.8 | 17.8 |
| Banker | 9.1 | 18.3 | 15.0 |
| Merchant | 13.3 | 16.6 | 5.6 |
| Total | 35.0 | 62.7 | 38.4 |
| Educator | 27.3 | 21.2 | 32.2 |
| Engineer | 9.4 | 9.9 | 12.7 |
| Total | 36.7 | 31.1 | 44.9 |

12. The percentage ranking for foreign ties was São Paulo 48.1, Pernambuco 33.3, and Minas Gerais 15.7. "Foreign" is a composite of variables 16–28 (see Appendix A).

13. Significance for Minas at .004, using the chi-square test at the .05 level of significance.

14. On the composite Legislative Service variable, the states ranked as follows: Pernambuco, 66 percent; São Paulo, 57 percent; and Minas, 68 percent. In the Minas elite, 72 percent of the first generation had legislative experience, 74 percent of the second, and 63 percent of the third. "Legislative Experience" is a composite of variables 70 and 71. Minas, the smallest of our elites, had the largest federal delegation. The tri-state breakdown is, nonetheless, impressive.

15. Of Executive Committee members, 38 percent followed business careers, 62 percent did not. Among the noncommitteemen, 33 percent did, 67 percent did not. The significance is .5786. In the total Minas group, 35 percent were coded positively on the business variable. Clan ties for committeemen were 58 percent; for the others 49.5. The significance is .3408.

16. Only 16 percent of Executive Committee members held away jobs, compared to 27 percent of noncommitteemen. Stay-at-homes were thus 84 percent in contrast to 73. The significance is .0853. "Away job" is a composite of variables 29–33.

17. Twenty-three came from the first generation (55 percent), 19 from the second (45 percent). One man's birth date could not be found.

18. For the PRM in opposition, one man (5 percent) came from generation one, 14 came from generation two (64 percent), and 7 (or 32 percent) were born after 1888. This is an adjusted rate, because the birth dates of five men could not be located, itself an indicator of relative obscurity compared with the other two committees.

19. The generational breakdown for the PP is: one (5.5 percent), eight (44 percent), and nine men in the third generation (50 percent), with one individual unaccountable because of a missing birth date.

20. Administrative posts are defined as including the prefect of Belo Horizonte, chief of police, director of the state coffee institute, director of the state press, and president of the state bank. For their first elite career post, 57 Mineiros held one of these administrative jobs, and 52 were state secretaries, lieutenant governors, or governors. (The seven lieutenant governors need no explanation. Alvim and Antonio de Lima were the two governors, taking power before they held other posts in the fledgling Republic.) Another 39 entered an Executive Committee directly, without prior service in other elite status jobs. Most of these were third-generation PP men or opposition PRM politicians.

21. Obituary in *Minas Gerais*, May 15, 1946, p. 10, supplemented by other sources including Magalhães Godinho, pp. 165–66.

22. Obituary in *Minas Gerais*, Nov. 16 and 17, 1925, p. 18, filled out with other standard sources and two recent sketches in the Mineiro press: Desembargador Antônio Pedro Braga, "João Luís Alves soube honorar as tradições mineiras de cultura," *Minas Gerais*, May 27, 1970, pp. 4–5, and Bruno de Almeida Magalhães, "João Luiz Alves," *Estado de Minas*, May 30, 1970.

23. Biographical sketch in Riveira, *Pioneiros e exponentes*, pp. 182–83. His books, *Administração municipal* and *O município no Estado Novo*, were both published in 1940.

24. Honorato and Camilo each served 23 years on the Rio delegation.

Both Camilo and Antonio Gonçalves Chaves had been leading deputies at the state Constituent Assembly in 1891–92. Antonio moved to the federal senate, finally losing his seat to Vaz de Melo of the vindictive Silvianista faction in 1903. Camilo had trouble getting elected to the federal Chamber, but was allowed to "win" enough votes to join the delegation in 1904. Neither Honorato nor Camilo became leading deputies, although after 1919 Honorato served ten years on the Accounts and Pensions Committee. Note that Antonio Gonçalves Chaves appears in the Minas elite group by virtue of his state senate presidency, and João José is listed because of membership on the PP Executive Committee. For biographical sketches, see Paula, pp. 169–71, 184–87, and the standard guides, including obituaries in the *Minas Gerais*.

*Chapter Six*

1. The dynamics of presidential politics are analyzed in Love's *Rio Grande*. For the role of Minas in these national events, consult Melo Franco's three-volume biography of his father. The Army's role in the early 1890's is well covered by Schulz and Hahner.

2. Campos Salles, pp. 162, 239–40; Love, *Rio Grande*, pp. 95–96; Assis Barbosa, *Juscelino Kubitschek*, pp. 128–29.

3. Contemporary analysis by *O Estado de Minas*, June 27, 1897, p. 1.

4. Daniel Carvalho, *Capítulos de memórias*, pp. 40ff, 77–78.

5. This important address is in *Minas Gerais*, Dec. 5, 1913, pp. 3–5.

6. *Correio da Manhã*, May 7, 1903, p. 1.

7. Love, *Rio Grande*, pp. 137–38.

8. By 1970, Minas trailed São Paulo's 6.5 million registered voters by 3 million; *Jornal do Brasil*, Sept. 22, 1970, p. 3. Rio Grande was third, with 2.4 million. Registration data for 1933 are from Brazil, *Boletim eleitoral*, p. 388.

9. Melo Franco, *Estadista*, 2:473.

10. Love, *Rio Grande*, p. 176.

11. Carone, *A república velha*, 1:307–8.

12. Telegram, Governor Nestor Gomes of Espírito Santo to Afrânio de Melo Franco (leader of the Minas bancada), Vitória, April 1921, Coleção Afrânio de Melo Franco, BN I–36, 3; also Love, *Rio Grande*, p. 124.

13. Letter, Governor Bernardes to Melo Franco, Belo Horizonte, Oct. 1, 1920; letters of Nov. 7, and Nov. 22, 1920, and long telegram, Governor Rego Monteiro to Bernardes, Manaus, March 22, 1921, and another telegram of April 17, 1921—all in Coleção AMF, BN I–36, 3. State Police Chief Alfredo Sá and Col. Gabriel José Marques of the Força Pública Mineira were interventors in Amazonas. Federal Judge Alberto Diniz, a cousin of Justice Minister Afonso Pena Jr., was made Acre interventor in 1926.

14. Bernardes was not the only Mineiro concerned with foreign penetration. When Percival Farquhar received an extensive land grant in the lower Amazon in 1911, deputy João Pandiá Calógeras denounced the governor of Pará for making such a liberal concession to a foreigner. The Pará and Amazonas petroleum exploration grants to Standard Oil were particularly alarming to junior Army officers; these concessions were anulled in 1930.

15. Magalhães Drummond, "A funcção politica de Minas na politica nacional," *O Estado de Minas*, July 2, 1921, p. 1, on the balance-wheel concept, which he bolstered with quotes from Oliveira Vianna's *Populações meridionais do Brasil*. Pavão is quoted on the role of small states, significantly in his book praising Bernardes (pp. 50–51).

16. Melo Franco, *Estadista*, 2:972.

17. The one exception was Credentials, on which no Mineiro served in 1891.

18. For a brief but suggestive analysis of congressional powers in the Old Republic, consult Hudson de Abranches, esp. chap. 2, pp. 27, 31, 45. Also see James's chapter on the congress, with excellent observations on the budgetary process, pp. 73–75.

19. Telegram, Governor Olegário Maciel to Vargas, Belo Horizonte, Dec. 5, 1930, and letter, Olegário to Francisco Campos, Aug. 4, 1931, in Interventor de Minas Gerais, pasta 14. Americo Lobo in *Annaes do congresso constituinte*, I (2d rev. ed.; Rio, 1924), p. 781.

20. Based on Romeiro, a hostile critic. For the state lotteries, see Lopes, pp. 191–93. Antonio Olinto dos Santos Pires, the old Historical Republican, headed the federal lottery and was Director General of Posts and Telegraphs.

21. Pressure tactics by the Brasilianische Bank für Deutschland and by German diplomats are documented in a memorandum from Governor Silviano Brandão to the Ministry of Foreign Affairs, Dec. 13, 1901, and in a report of the State of Minas Gerais dated Oct. 25, 1902, both in Avisos recebidos, 308/3/10. Two good reports appeared in the *Minas Gerais* for March 17, 1902, p. 2, and May 9, 1903, p. 3. Having consolidated its foreign debt in 1898, Brazil could not ignore the sometimes very insistent demands of European creditors. Thus, in 1901, French pressure forced the Union to pay debt coupons on Espírito Santo's defaulted loan; *Correio da Manha*, April 2, 1903, p. 1.

22. Francisco Sá pushed hard to extend the Central northward into his native zone; Brazil, *Annaes, 1902*, 9:512–13. As Minister of Transport in 1909, Sá began linking up the Oeste de Minas with Belo Horizonte, and also consolidated three deficitary federal lines into the Rêde Mineira da Viação, which gave Minas an ocean port terminal at Angra dos Reis.

23. Duncan, pp. 67ff, 95–99.

24. Governor Silviano Brandão, Mensagem of June 15, 1899, in Minas, *Annaes da Camara, 1899;* and, for freight rate policy, Eng. Artur da Costa Guimarães, "As tarifas de transporte no Estado de Minas," in Chavantes, pp. 189–209.

25. For a brief critique of decapitalizing freight rates and the effects of featherbedding, see Calógeras, *Problemas do governo*, p. 23, and *Problemas de administração*, pp. 153–54.

26. Sir J. Tilley, Brazil. Annual Report, 1921, p. 9–10, in Great Britain, PRO:FO 371/7190 3668.

27. Quotation and analysis in Daniel de Carvalho, *Novos estudos*, pp. 134–35.

28. Address by Secretary of Finance Alcides Lins to the Associação Comercial, in *Minas Gerais*, Feb. 23, 1934, p. 7.

29. Brazil, *Annaes, 1895*, 6:64, 71, 444, 742–47; 7:622; *Annaes, 1896*, 6:479; *Annaes, 1898*, 6:474–78.

30. Especially sessions of Dec. 9 and 12, 1903, in Brazil, *Annaes, 1903*, 8:361–65, 958–59.

31. Inferred from Holloway, pp. 73–74.

32. Love, *Rio Grande*, pp. 153, 178.

*Chapter Seven*

1. This formulation follows Galtung, "A Structural Theory of Integration."

2. Melo Franco, *Estadista*, 2:1043.

3. Authorized force levels for 1892–1925 are from Minas, *Annuario estatistico*, Anno II, p. 1146. Data for the authorized strength during 1926–37 were compiled from annual *Relatórios* of the Minas Secretary of Interior, and from the Minas *Leis mineiras*. Actual force levels for specific years are in Brazil, *Anuário estatístico*, Ano V, p. 1427, and, for the late 1930's, from Minas, *Relatórios* of the Commandant, Força Pública Mineira. For most years of the Old Republic, the difference between authorized and actual force levels was the same or congruent to within 100–200 men.

4. Report of the Commandant in Minas, Secretary of the Interior, *Relatório de 1896*, pp. 6–7. The quote is from Vice-President Gama Cerqueira, speaking in the Minas Senate on July 15, 1892; Minas, *Annaes do Senado, 1892*, p. 369.

5. To Rio for the 1893 and 1910 naval revolts, and to São Paulo in 1924. For the Tiros Militares see Almeida Junior, pp. 62ff. Col. Júlio Cesar Pinto Coelho founded the Clube in November, 1898: Krüger, p. 18. It was active into the 1920's.

6. The Brazilian National Guard in 1916 had 231,044 officers in 7,778 paper brigades. Minas had 477 brigades, or nearly 20 percent. These commissions were especially important in the Northeast, being used to gain and hold the loyalty of coronéis. Pang, dissertation, pp. 41–42. For Uberaba, see Pontes, p. 133. For the Minas planters, consult *Correio da Manhã*, Feb. 18, 1904, p. 1, and Azevedo Junior, "Cartas mineiras," in *Correio da Manhã*, July 24, 1905, p. 1. Bessone comments on the importance of the guard, and on Wenceslau's desire to abolish it, pp. 244–45. For Juiz de Fora see Nava, *Baú de ossos*, pp. 191–94.

7. Minas Secretary of the Interior, *Relatório, 1913*, p. xxi. Drexler stayed on through the late 1920's. Melo Franco, *Estadista*, 2:715–16.

8. Confidential Report, W. A. Stewart to the Marques Curzon, Rio, May 30, 1923, reporting his conversation with Melo Viana, in Great Britain, PRO:FO 371/8429 3673.

9. Governor Antonio Carlos, ex-president Bernardes, gubernatorial condidate Olegário Maciel, and the state secretaries gathered for the dedication just as Minas was breaking with President Washington Luís. Account in *Minas Gerais*, Nov. 2, 1929, p. 17. Captain Luís Carlos Prestes led a large group of rebel officers through the interior of Brazil during 1924–27 to popularize revolutionary ideals; this was the famous Prestes Column.

10. Memorandum, Secretary of Finance, in Interventor de Minas Gerais, "Despesas com a Força Pública no orçamento para o Ano de 1934," dated

Dec. 27, 1933. He estimated that force increases and operations for the years 1931–33 had cost 25,513 contos over and above normal expenses, most of which the Union absorbed. Also telegram, Olegário Maciel to Vargas, Oct. 24, 1932: "As authorized by you, Minas Gerais will keep 3,000 volunteers now integrated into the Força Pública under arms, at federal expense, until December 31." Interventor de Minas Gerais, Lata 15, pasta 1.

11. Memorandum, Mr. Troutbeck to the Foreign Secretary, Rio, Oct. 6, 1933, detailing the October 2 agreement between Minas and the Union, in Great Britain, PRO:FO 371/16549 3807.

12. Valadares' hesitation in appointing Dorneles to command the militia angered Army Chief of Staff Góes Monteiro, who worried about the loyalty of the officer corps. Letter, Pantaleao Pessôa to Vargas, Feb. 2, 1934, in Hélio Silva, *O ciclo de Vargas, 1934*, pp, 246–47. Dorneles became police chief on Jan. 4, 1936, and served until Oct. 1942. The Army's full control over the Força Pública was established in Law 192 of Jan. 17, 1936.

13. McCann, p. 364.

14. Senna, *A terra mineira*, 2:270–71; the newly established garrison towns are listed on p. 169.

15. Col. Assumpção, in *Belo Horizonte completou 50 anos*, pp. 58–59, 65–68. For many years Assumpção was in charge of the Army's delicate civil-military relations in Belo Horizonte. His account is absorbing.

16. *Ibid.*, pp. 73–74.

17. Based on table "Annual number of international meetings, 1681–1919," in Union des Associations Internationaux, *Les congrès internationaux*, p. 11. Gregory's listing (*International Congresses and Conferences*) is incomplete for Brazil, but shows that Argentina was far ahead between 1889 and 1937. No inclusive listing is available for Brazilian national, state and regional congresses held during the period under study. Typical examples are taken from a file the three authors keep on these phenomna, noting especially the first example of each type.

18. In response to the Congresso Agricola da Corte, to which only Espírito Santo, Rio de Janeiro, Minas, and São Paulo were invited, the northeastern states held their own Primeiro Congresso Agricola do Norte in 1878. The first National Agricultural Congress was convened in 1901 by Campos Sales; the second in 1908 and the third in 1922 were also held in Rio.

19. "Manifesto da Grande Comissão da Exposição Permanente ao Estado de Minas," in *O Diário de Minas*, Feb. 12, 1901, p. 1.

20. Interview in 1936 by Secretary of Agriculture Israel Pinheiro, son of João Pinheiro, in *Fôlha de Minas*, cited in Pereira Brasil, *Minas na grandeza*, p. 28.

21. Sir J. Tilley, Brazil, Annual Report, 1923, in Great Britain, PRO:FO 371/9516 3692.

22. Senna, *A terra mineira*, 2:72–73; Daniel de Carvalho, *Estudos e depoimentos*, pp. 194–95. The first state statistical department was abolished for economy reasons during the coffee depression, and work on the first good state map was likewise abandoned in the late 1890's.

23. Daniel de Carvalho, *Capítulos de memórias*, p. 173.

24. The regional congresses were held at Itajubá in April 1907, at Diamantina in September, and Leopoldina in October. See the *Minas Gerais* for April 11, 1907, p. 3; Sept. 22, p. 6; and Oct. 22, p. 11. Also Assis Barbosa's brief account in *Juscelino Kubitschek*, p. 176.

25. See Pimenta's account of the Primeiro Congresso dos Municipios do Nordeste Mineira, held at Itabira on Sept. 25, 1927, in *A mata do Peçanha*, pp. 169–75.

26. For regional issues in the 1920's, see Minas, *Annaes do congresso das municipalidades*, convened by Raul Soares in June 1923.

27. Agriculture must get involved in politics to achieve results; only in São Paulo is the political leadership made up of men identified with the agrarian sector, *Correio da Manhã* editorialized while noting the Juiz de Fora congress (March 24, 1917, p. 1). See its good account of the planters' congress in the March 26 issue, p. 2.

28. The reference of course is to the Comte de Gobineau, the chief early French exponent of the theory of Nordic supremacy. This Geographical Congress (Sept. 7–15, 1919) was fully covered in the *Minas Gerais* for Sept. 8–9, 13, 15–16. President Epitácio Pessoa sponsored a conference on state boundary questions in July 1920.

29. The key issue was defining the headwaters of the Serra dos Aimores, uncertain since 1800. According to Thiers Fleming, Espírito Santo stalled at key points in the negotiations up to 1937.

30. Dom Silvério was "very proud of having secured the transfer of this territory from Vitória to the new bishopric," says Alypio Oliveira, *Traços biograficos de Dom Silverio*, p. 102. His biography also contains information on institution-building after 1889, and the Papacy's new guidelines for Latin American bishops starting with the First American Concilium, held in Rome in 1899. See also Dom Joaquim Silverio de Souza, *Vida de D. Silverio*, pp. 240–41, 251. The Aug. 1890 meeting of Brazilian bishops held in São Paulo denounced civil marriage, the separation of Church and State, and lay education in public schools.

31. Mario Lima's *O bom combate* is the standard source. After the Primeiro Congresso Católico (Jan. 1910), three more were held in Belo Horizonte (1911, 1914 and 1918). The União Popular disbanded in the early 1920's.

32. A series of eucharistic congresses was held in Bahia (1933), Belo Horizonte (1936), Recife (1938), and São Paulo (1942).

33. See Williams' excellent article on Dom Leme and the LEC, "The Politicization of the Brazilian Catholic Church."

34. For the beauty contests, see *Belo Horizonte completou 50 anos*, pp. 28–29. The year 1929 was the first time that the Rio-based Miss Brazil contest was plugged into the Miss Universe contest. The British ambassador said the 1930 judging was rigged; Sir W. Seeds, Brazil, Annual Report, 1930, in Great Britain, PRO:FO 371/15067 3749.

35. Haas, *The Uniting of Europe*. Definition on p. 16; the other citation is found on p. xxxv.

36. See the 1969 conference papers in Lindberg and Scheingold. For

my purposes, the paper by Fred M. Hayward was especially helpful: "Continuities and Discontinuities Between Studies of National and International Political Integration: Some Implications for Future Research Efforts," pp. 313–37.

*Chapter Eight*

1. This revenue base refers to the "actual budget," comprising ordinary and extraordinary revenues and income, but excluding extrabudgetary credits, which were listed separately in the annual budget reports. Unless otherwise noted, budgetary data in this chapter are from the annual *Relatórios* of the State Secretary of Finance.

2. David Campista, in Minas, Secretaria das Finanças, *Relatório, 1899*, p. 24; and Minas, *Diagnóstico*, 6:113. In 1931, Belo Horizonte supplied one-fifth of the total revenues of the state's 215 municípios; Menlíck de Carvalho, pp. 148–52.

3. Americo Wernick, in Minas, Secretaria da Agricultura, *Relatório, 1899*, p. 18; Iglésias, *Política econômica*, p. 184; Daniel de Carvalho, *Estudos de economia e finanças*, p. 174.

4. *Moody's Manual of Investments, 1930*, p. 119.

5. The Minas debt service dropped to an astounding 2 percent of the budget in 1927, and rose modestly to average 14.6 percent in the 1930–37 period. These figures are computed as a percentage of the state's actual budget, which is found in the yearly *Relatórios* of the Minas Secretary of Finance.

6. Juscelino Barbosa, "Conversão da divida externa mineira," 1910 report reprinted in his *factos e cifras*, pp. 7ff. Minas tried to pay in devalued paper francs; French creditors insisted on the equivalent in gold. In 1928 the Mineiros proposed a compromise to protect their credit rating, a few months before The Hague ruled against them on the gold clause question. See the *Minas Gerais* for July 17, 1929, p. 10, and Daniel de Carvalho's analysis in *Estudos de economia e finanças*.

7. In 1930, virtually all of the state's relatively small foreign debt— £1,775,000 and US$16,155,000—had been assumed by Antonio Carlos in 1928 and 1929. The French debt was mostly redeemed. Brazil, *Anuário estatístico*, Ano V, pp. 1424–25. Note that Minas's dollar debt was far outdistanced by Rio Grande's US$52 million and São Paulo's US$47.5 million borrowed between 1921 and 1929. For details see Bouças.

8. The source is a systematic survey of *Relatórios* of the Secretary of Finance.

9. Governor Silviano Brandão, Mensagem, June 15, 1899, in Minas, *Annaes da Camara, 1899*, especially p. 50. Sena Figueiredo in session of Aug. 18, 1894, *Annaes da Camara, 1904*, pp. 275–83.

10. Deputies from the Center and East complained that riders on bill 64 would make it impossible to fund the eastern pioneer route. Wenceslau Brás replied that the Sul must have its railroads. He reminded fellow deputies of the recent Campanha revolt, which was, he said, a protest against neglect of its vital interests by Ouro Preto. Deputies from the North also secured financing for the Bahia e Minas line under Law 64. See the debates, especially the session of July 11, 1893, in Minas, *Annaes*

*da Camara, 1893,* pp. 409–11. Belo Horizonte was not linked to Vitória via Peçanha on the eastern route until 1936.

11. Barbosa, p. 28.

12. Sena Figuerido, in Minas, *Annaes da Camara, 1904,* p. 278.

13. Minas, Secretaria de Agricultura, *Relatório, 1894,* pp. 28–30; *Relatório, 1895,* pp. 261–63.

14. Brito's amendment no. 40, discussed by the Finance Commission in report of Dec. 5, 1905, in Brazil, *Annaes, 1908,* 8:92. Carlos Wigg, report to the 1903 Congresso Agricolo, in *Minas Gerais,* May 23, 1903, p. 1. Sir Beilby Aston, Brazil, Annual Report, 1925, in Great Britain, PRO:FO 371/11118 3719, pp. 9–10. If there were other industrial credits (besides railroads) between 1898 and 1931, the Minas Finance Secretary's *Relatórios* do not list them. In 1931, 600 contos were expended on the Alcool-motor plant at Divinópolis.

15. Dispatch 165, Sir John Tilley from the British Embassy in Rio to J. Ramsay MacDonald, Secretary of State for Foreign Affairs, July 25, 1924, in Great Britain, in PRO:FO 371/9509 3689.

16. Minas Secretary of Finance Artur Bernardes, *Relatório, 1911,* pp. 20–22. Pontes, pp. 155–66.

17. Julio Bueno Brandão, Mensagem, 1914, in Minas, *Annaes da Camara, 1914,* pp. 23, 48–50; Delfim Moreira, Mensagem, 1918, *Annaes, 1918,* pp. 71–72; Bernardes, Mensagem 1921, *Annaes, 1921,* p. 44; Antonio Carlos, Mensagem, 1927, *Annaes, 1927,* p. 84.

18. Orlando de Carvalho, *Política do município,* p. 83.

19. Orlando de Carvalho is the standard source for these institutional changes in the 1930's. Municipal income after 1906 is given in Brazil, *Anuário estatístico,* Ano V, p. 1420.

20. See Romeiro's sensationalist attack, based on data for 1928, pp. 86–87. The Mineiro case was argued by Daniel de Carvalho, a rising young PRM star who defended Minas in the Chamber during the late 1920's. See his "A arrecadação federal em Minas Gerais," in *Estudos de economia e finanças,* pp. 164–72. Minas, he estimated, paid 100,000 contos in customs duties in addition to 48,000 contos collected by federal tax posts in Minas. The ratios are based on his figures.

21. Calógeras, *Problemas de administração,* p. 227.

22. Love, *Rio Grande do Sul,* p. 229, citing IBGE figures.

23. Mahar, esp. Chapter 4, "Brazilian Fiscal Federalism in Practice." The quote is on p. 144. Federal revenues and expenditures for 1912–25 are in Minas, *Annuario estatistico,* Anno II, p. 1146. Data for 1926–29 are in Brazil, *Contas do exercicio,* p. 266.

24. Federal revenues and expenditures from the actual budget are found in the statistical annuals. Total federal tax receipts from Minas were 590,-337 contos; expenditures were 338,933 contos for 1930–39.

25. Brazil Banco do Brasil, *Relatório, 1937,* p. 67.

26. Haggard's Monthly Report for June 1907, in Great Britain, PRO FO: 371/200 3816.

27. Interstate taxes ended Jan. 1, 1944, after the deadline for phasing them out (set in 1938) was extended one year. For a case study of tax policy in the Estado Novo, consult Wirth on the imposto único, a unified

petroleum tax to rationalize and expand the internal market for oil products.

28. *Correio da Manhã* for July 10, 1903, and Aug. 22, 1903.

29. Veiga, *Ephemerides*, 1:311, 393. Minas, *Annaes do Senado Mineiro, 1892*, pp. 43–46.

30. David Campista, in Minas, Secretaria das Finanças, *Relatório, 1899*, p. 27, and João Luís Alves, series in *Diário de Minas*, May 20–23, 1902; also June 4.

31. Cel. Ignacio Burlamaqui of the Associação Comercial de Minas, paper presented to the Comissão Fundamental of the 1903 Congress, in *Minas Gerais*, April 11–14, 1903, pp. 1–4. Rio de Janeiro state discussed protectionism for its industry, and Rio Grande threatened retaliation; *Correio da Manhã*, July 19, 1903. Pernambuco taxed Rio Grande's charque exports in retaliation against a tax on its rum exports; Love, *Rio Grande*, p. 114. President Afonso Pena arbitrated this dispute in 1908.

32. For a detailed analysis of the issue, with excellent commentary on the crosscurrents of congressional opinion, consult Francisco Valladares, "Questões debatidas sobre competencia tributaria." The final bill, approved by the Chamber 71 to 40 on Dec. 14, 1903, was largely the work of Arnolfo Azevedo of São Paulo. A roll call vote was taken on the second reading of this bill in October. All the major delegations voted for Azevedo's bill except Minas, and most of the Minas delegation left the hall along with Cearense deputies before the vote. For the voting, see Brazil, *Impostos interestaduaes*, pp. 411–12, 572; the key debates are included in p. 572 in the same volume.

33. Melo Franco, *Estadista*, 1:385–96, has a good account. Debates for July 25 and Aug. 17 and 18 are in Minas, *Annaes da Camara, 1904*.

34. Carlos Pereira de Sá Fortes, commenting on intermunicipal taxes at the 1903 congress, in *Minas Gerais*, April 26, 1903, p. 2.

*Conclusion*

1. For a discussion of this nineteenth-century progress model, see Weiner, "Political Integration," p. 64.

2. Williamson, "Regional Inequality," p. 5.

# Bibliography

*Unpublished Documents and Collections*

Arquivo Afonso Pena. Arquivo Afonso Pena Junior (being catalogued in 1972). Arquivo Nacional.
Arquivo Aranha. Assuntos Políticos, 1935–37.
Avisos recebidos de Minas Gerais, 1900–1934. Telegramas recebidos e expedidos, 1893–1930. Arquivo Itamaraty.
Coleção Afrânio de Melo Franco. Biblioteca Nacional.
Coleção Marechal Floriano Peixoto. Arquivo Nacional.
Correspondência de Rui Barbosa. Pastas Antonio Olinto dos Santos Pires, José Francisco Bias Fortes, and Francisco de Silviano Brandão. Casa Ruy Barbosa.
Great Britain, Foreign Office. Yearly reports from the Embassy in Rio de Janeiro, 1908–37, and selected reports, dispatches, and telegrams, 1900–1937. All in the Public Record Office, London.
Interventor de Minas Gerais. Presidência Archive. Arquivo Nacional.
Mineiridade Collection. Several hundred titles on Minas Gerais, housed separately in the Biblioteca Pública Mineira.
Obituary File. Index of obituaries appearing mainly in the *Minas Gerais,* but also from leading Belo Horizonte newspapers. Arquivo Público Mineiro.
Photo Archive. *O Estado de Minas.* Belo Horizonte.

*Newspapers*

*A Patria Mineira,* São João del Rei, 1892. Occasional issues.
*Correio da Manhã,* Rio, 1902–21. Occasional issues.
*Correio do Dia,* 1909–10. The civilista newspaper.
*O Diário de Minas,* 1898–1930. The PRM journal. Occasional issues.
*O Estado de Minas,* Ouro Preto phase, 1891–97; Belo Horizonte phase, 1921–38. Occasional issues.
*Fôlha de Minas,* 1936–38.
*O Jornal,* Rio. Special issue on Minas, Oct. 29, 1927.
*Jornal do Povo,* 1899–1900. Mendes Pimentel opposition newspaper.

*Minas Gerais,* 1892–1938. The State Gazette, open-shelf collection housed in Biblioteca Pública Mineira. Surveyed systematically.

*O Movimento,* Ouro Preto, 1888–92. Edited by João Pinheiro for the early Republican Party.

*O Pharol,* Juiz de Fora, 1891–98. Occasional issues.

*Other Sources*

"Actual imprensa periodica mineira," *Revista do Arquivo Publico Mineiro,* 3:234–36.

Alencar, Alexandre de. Fatos e vultos de Viçosa (da primeira bandeira ao ano de 1892). Belo Horizonte, 1959.

Almanach de Minas (para 1916). Juiz de Fora [1916].

Almeida Junior, Antidio, ed. "Belo Horizonte completou 50 anos . . . ; edição especial comemorativa do cinquentenário de Belo Horizonte," *Revista Social Trabalhista,* no. 59 (Dec. 12, 1947; bound volume).

Almeida Magalhães, Bruno de. Arthur Bernardes, estadista da república. Rio, 1973.

Amaral Peixoto, Alzira Vargas do. *Getúlio Vargas, meu pai.* Rio, 1960.

Amora, Paulo. Bernardes, o estadista de Minas na república. São Paulo, 1964.

Anjos, Cyro dos. Explorações no tempo (memórias). Rio, 1963.

*Annaes da Camara Mineira, see under* Minas Gerais, Annaes, Camara dos Deputados.

Annuario commercial do Estado de São Paulo para 1904, abragendo o Triangulo Mineiro. São Paulo, 1904.

Anthouard, Albert Françoise Ildefonse d', Baron. Le progrès brésilien, la participation de la France. Paris, 1911.

Assis Barbosa, Francisco de, ed. João Pinheiro: documentação sôbre a sua vida. Belo Horizonte, 1966.

———. Juscelino Kubitschek, uma revisão na política brasileira, 1. Rio, 1960.

———. "A presidência Campos Sales," *Luso-Brazilian Review,* 5, no. 1 (June 1968): 3–26.

Azevedo, Guiomar G. de. "Os primórdios do povoamento e a evolução econômica da região de Sete Lagoas, Minas Gerais," *Boletim Mineira de Geografia,* ano IV, nos. 6–7 (July 1963): 15–38.

Barbosa, Juscelino. Factos e cifras. São Paulo, 1923.

Barreto, Abilio. Bello Horizonte; memoria historica e descriptiva. 2 v. Belo Horizonte, 1936.

Barretto, Castro. Povoamento e população; política populacional brasileira. Rev. ed., 2 v. Rio, 1959.

Beaumont, H. D. Report of a Journey to the Diamond Fields of Minas Geraes and Remarks on the Province of Minas Geraes . . . London, 1899.

Becker, Bertha K. "Expansão do mercado urbano e transformação de economia pastoril," *Revista Brasileira de Geografia,* 28, no. 4 (Oct.–Dec. 1966): 297–328.

"Belo Horizonte completou 50 anos," *see* Almeida Junior.

Benévolo, Ademar. Introdução à história ferroviária do Brasil; estudo social, político e histórico. Recife, 1953.

Bernardes, Arthur da Silva. Manifesto . . . ao eleitorado mineiro. Belo Horizonte, 1918.
Bernardes, Nilo, et al. Minas Gerais, terra e povo. Pôrto Alegre, 1970.
Bessone de Oliveira Andrade, Darcy. Wenceslau; um pescador na presidência. Belo Horizonte, 1968.
Bonilla, Frank. The Failure of Elites. Cambridge, Mass., 1970.
Botelho, Luiz Eugênio. Leopoldina de outrora (historiografia). [Belo Horizonte, 1963.]
Bouças, Valentim F. História da dívida externa. 2d ed. Rio, 1950.
Braga, Belmiro. Dias idos e vividos. Rio, 1936.
Brant, Alice Dayrell. The Diary of "Helena Morley." Translated by Elizabeth Bishop. New York, 1957.
Brazil. Annaes, 1891–1928. Congresso, Camara dos Deputados.
———. Anuário estatístico do Brasil, 1908– . (Title varies; later issued by Instituto Brasileiro de Geografia e Estatística.) Directoria Geral de Estatistica.
———. Aspectos da economia rural brasileira. Ministério da Agricultura. Rio, 1922.
———. Banco do Brasil, Relatório, 1937, 1946.
———. Boletim commemorativo da exposição nacional de 1908. Directoria Geral de Estatistica. Rio, 1908.
———. Boletim eleitoral. Issues for Nov. 25, 1933, March 26, 1934, and April 3, 1935. Tribunal Superior de Justiça Eleitoral.
———. O café no segundo centenário de sua introdução no Brasil. 2 v. Instituto Nacional do Café, Departamento Nacional do Café. Rio, 1934.
———. Caixa de conversão, 1906. 2 v. Documentos Parlamentares. Paris, 1914.
———. Contas do exercicio financeiro de 1931 e relatorios da Contadoria Central da Republica. Ministério da Fazenda. Rio, 1932.
———. Diário do Congresso, 1894–1930 (for election returns).
———. Diário oficial, 1929–37.
———. Estatística das finanças do Brasil. Directoria Geral de Estatistica. Rio, 1926.
———. Estudos de desenvolvimento regional (Minas Gerais), 6. CAPES. Rio, 1958.
———. Impostos interestaduaes (1900–1911). Documentos Parlamentares. Paris, 1914.
———. Política economica. Valorização do café (1895–1906). Documentos Parlamentares. Rio, 1915.
———. Recenseamento do Brasil realizado em 1 de setembro de 1920. Directoria Geral de Estatistica. Rio, 1922–29.
———. Recenseamento geral do Brasil [1940]. Série regional. Instituto Brasileiro de Geografia e Estatística. Parte XIII, Minas Gerais. Tomo 1–3. Rio, 1950.
———. Sexo, raça e estado civil, nacionalidade, filiação, culto e analphabetismo da população recenseada em 31 de dezembro de 1890. Directoria Geral de Estatistica. Rio, 1898.
"Brazilian National Accounts—Bringing up to Date," Conjuntura Econômica, 17, no. 6 (June 1970): 49–66.
"Breve notícia histórica da Academia Mineira de Letras, Juiz de Fora

1909–1915," *Revista da Academia Mineira de Letras*, 20 (1954): 198–212.

Burton, Richard F. The Highlands of Brazil. 2 v. London, 1869.

Calógeras, João Pandiá. Problemas de administração. São Paulo, 1918.

————. Problemas do governo. São Paulo, 1928.

————. Reforma tributaria de Minas, sugestões. Belo Horizonte, 1931.

Campos, Sandoval, e Amynthas Lobo. Imprensa mineira; memoria historica. Edição commemorativo do centenario da independencia, 1822–1922. Belo Horizonte, 1922.

Campos Salles, Manuel F. de. Da propaganda á presidencia. São Paulo, 1908.

Capri, Roberto, O Estado de Minas Geraes. Belo Horizonte, 1918.

Carone, Edgard. A república nova (1930–1937). São Paulo, 1974.

————. A república velha, 2 v. São Paulo, 1970, 1971.

————. A segunda república. São Paulo, 1973.

Carvalho, Afrânio de. A actualidade mineira. Belo Horizonte, 1929.

Carvalho, Antonio de. Uma fazenda mineira; "Monographia—Estudo de uma fazenda modelo . . ." Belém, 1899.

Carvalho, Antonio Gontijo de. Vultos da republica, David Campista, Carlos Peixoto, Gastão da Cunha. Esboços biograficos. São Paulo, 1936.

Carvalho, Carlos M. D. de. Un centre économique au Brésil. L'Etat de Minas en 1908. Paris, 1908.

Carvalho, Daniel de. Capítulos de memórias. Rio, 1957.

————. De outros tempos (memórias). Rio, 1961.

————. Discursos e conferencias. Rio, 1941.

————. Ensaios de crítica e de história. Rio, 1964.

————. Estudos de economia e finanças. Rio, 1946.

————. Estudos e depoimentos. Rio, 1953.

————. Francisco Sales, um político de outros tempos. Rio, 1963.

————. Novos estudos e depoimentos. Rio, 1959.

————. Pareceres. Belo Horizonte, 1919.

Carvalho, Menelíck de. A revolução de 30 e o município. Rio, 1942.

Carvalho, Orlando M. Política do município (ensaio histórico). Rio, 1946.

————. O rio da unidade nacional, o São Francisco. São Paulo, 1937.

Carvalho, Theophilo Feu de. Comarcas e termos: Creações, suppressões, restaurações, encorporações e desmembramentos de comarcas e termos, em Minas Geraes (1709–1915). Belo Horizonte, 1922.

Carvalho Britto, Manuel Thomaz de. O civilismo em Minas. Rio, 1949.

Casasanta, Guerino. Correspondência de Bueno Brandão. Belo Horizonte, 1958.

Casasanta, Manuel. Francisco Escobar. Belo Horizonte, 1966.

Casasanta, Mário. As razões de Minas. Belo Horizonte, 1932.

Centro Popular Mineiro (Associação politica de orientação catholica). Candidaturas presidenciaes. Belo Horizonte, 1929.

Chavantes, Álcino José, org. Congresso das vias de transporte no Brazil em dezembro de 1910, Archivo dos trabalhos. Rio, 1910.

Coelho, Joaquim-Francisco. Terra e família na poesia de Carlos Drummond de Andrade. Belém, 1973.

Coelho, Levindo. "Depoimento de um velho político mineiro," *Revista Brasileira de Estudos Políticos*, 1, no. 2 (July 1959): 116–31.

Concentração Conservadora de Minas. A acção do dr. Carvalho de Britto na actual campanha da successão presidencial da Republica. Rio, 1930.
————. O Congresso de Café de Muriahé. Rio, 1929.
————. Congresso de Montes Claros. Minas Gerais, 1930.
Correia Dias, Fernando. "Aspectos sociais do surto industrial de Juiz de Fora," *Revista da Univ. Fed. de Minas Gerais*, no. 17 (Dec. 1967): 85–96.
————. "Estado e desenvolvimento em Minas Gerais," *Revista Brasileira de Estudos Políticos*, nos. 25–26 (July 1968–Jan. 1969): 111–36.
————. A imagem de Minas; ensaios de sociologia regional. Belo Horizonte, 1971.
————. João Alphonsus: tempo e modo. Belo Horizonte, 1965.
————. "O movimento modernista em Minas; uma interpretação sociológica." Ph.D. dissertation, Universidade Federal de Minas Gerais. Belo Horizonte, 1968. Published version available.
Coutinho, Afrânio, ed. Brasil e brasileiros de hoje. 2 v. Rio, 1961.
Dallari, Dalmo de Abreu. "Os estados na federação brasileira, de 1891 a 1937." Typewritten. São Paulo, 1970.
Dassin, Joan Rosalie. "The Politics of Art. Mario de Andrade and the Case of Brazilian Modernism, 1922–1945." Ph.D. dissertation, Stanford University. Stanford, Calif., 1974.
Dean, Warren. The Industrialization of São Paulo, 1880–1945. Austin, Tex., 1969.
Delfim Netto, Antonio. "O problema do café no Brasil," USP, Faculdade de ciências econômicas e administrativas, *Boletim* no. 5, Cadeira III, no. 1. São Paulo, 1959.
Denis, Pierre. Le Brésil au xxᵉ siècle. 2d ed. Paris, 1909.
Deodato, Alberto, et al. "Memória histórica, 1892–1959," *Revista da Faculdade de Direito*, 10 (Oct. 1958–March 1959), whole issue.
Diagnóstico, *see under* Minas Gerais.
Dias, Everardo. História das lutas sociais no Brasil. São Paulo, 1962.
Dias Corrêa, Oscar. Brasílio. Rio, 1968.
Diniz, Sílvio Gabriel. O Gonçalvismo em Pitanguí; história de trinta anos de domínio político. Belo Horizonte, 1969.
Dornas Filho, João. "Os ciganos em Minas Gerais," *Revista do Instituto Histórico e Geográfico de Minas Gerais*, ano III, 1948: 137–86.
Drummond de Andrade, Carlos. Obra completa. Rio, 1967.
Duncan, Julian Smith. Public and Private Operation of Railways in Brazil. New York, 1932.
Dunshee de Abranches [Moura, João]. Governos e congressos da republica dos Estados Unidos do Brazil, 1889 a 1917. 2 v. São Paulo, 1918.
Egler, Eugênia. "Distribuição da população no estado de Minas Gerais em 1940," *Revista Brasileira de Geografia*, 15, no. 1 (1953): 123–53.
Esteves, Manuel. Grão Mogol. Rio, 1961.
Faoro, Raymundo. Os donos do poder; formação do patronato político brasileiro. Rio, 1958.
Ferreira de Rezende, Francisco de Paula. Minhas recordações. Rio, 1944.
Fleischer, David Verge. "Political Recruitment in the State of Minas Gerais, Brazil (1890–1970)." Ph.D. dissertation, University of Florida. Gainesville, 1972.

Fleiuss, Max. História administrativa do Brasil. Rio, 1922.

Fleming, Thiers. Pelo Brasil unido (limites interestaduais Minas-Espirito Santo). Rio, 1948.

Franco, Augusto. Estudos e escriptos (Esboços e chronicas). Belo Horizonte, 1906.

Frey, Frederick W. The Turkish Political Elite. Cambridge, Mass., 1965.

Frieiro, Eduardo. Feijão, angu e couve, ensaio sobre a comida dos mineiros. Belo Horizonte, 1966.

————. "Notas sôbre a imprensa em Minas," Revista da Universidade de Minas Gerais, no. 12 (Jan. 1962): 64–83.

Furtado, Celso. The Economic Growth of Brazil. Berkeley, Calif., 1963.

Gabaglia, Laurita Pessôa Raja. O Cardeal Leme, 1882–1942. Rio, 1962.

Galtung, Johan. "A Structural Theory of Integration," Journal of Peace Research, no. 4 (1968): 375–95.

Garden, C. Barbacena. Rio, 1940.

Gaspar, M. M. Dans le sertão de Minas. Louvain, 1910.

Godoy, Senator Joaquim Floriano de. A Provincia do Rio Sapucahy e o journalismo da Provincia de São Paulo. São Paulo, 1888.

Góes Monteiro, Norma de. "Esboço da política imigratória e colonizadora do govêrno de Minas Gerais—1889 a 1930," Revista Brasileira de Estudos Políticos, no. 29 (July 1970): 195–216.

Gomes Pimenta, D. Silverio. Cartas pastoraes. Rio, 1921.

Gonçalves, F. de Paula Lazaro. Relatorio do director (Associação promotora de immigração em Minas). Juiz de Fora, 1888.

Gonçalves Maia, Julio Joaquim. "Lista geral. Bachareis e doutores formados pela Faculdade de Direito de São Paulo e dos lentes e diretores effectivos até 1900," Revista da Faculdade de Direito de São Paulo, 7 (1900).

Gordilho, Osvaldo. Os transportes no Brasil. Rio, 1956.

Graham, Douglas H., and Sérgio Buarque de Hollanda Filho. "Migration, Regional and Urban Growth and Development in Brazil: A Selective Analysis of the Historical Record—1872–1970," I. Instituto de Pesquisas Econômicas, Universidade de São Paulo. Mimeo. São Paulo, 1971.

Gravatá, Hélio. "Contribuição bibliografica para a história de Minas Gerais." Typewritten. Belo Horizonte, 1969.

Greenfield, Sidney M. "Differentiation, Stratification, and Mobility in Traditional Brazilian Society," Luso-Brazilian Review, 6, no. 2 (Dec. 1969): 3–21.

Gregory, Winfred, ed. International Congresses and Conferences, 1840–1937: A Union List of Their Publications Available in the Libraries of the United States and Canada. New York, 1938.

Guimarães, Alisson P. "A Cidade Industrial," Boletim Mineira de Geografia, ano I, no. 1 (July 1957): 38–54.

————. "Divisão regional do Estado de Minas Gerais," Boletim Geográfico, 1, no. 1 (July 1958): 13–29.

————. A Siderurgia em Minas Gerais. Belo Horizonte, 1962.

Haas, Ernst B. The Uniting of Europe; Political, Social, and Economic Forces, 1950–1957. London, 1958.

Hahner, June E. Civil-Military Relations in Brazil, 1889–1898. Columbia, S.C., 1969.

Harris, Marvin. "Minas Velhas; A Study of Urbanism in the Mountains of Eastern Brazil." Ph.D. dissertation, Columbia University. New York, 1953.

Holloway, Thomas Halsey. "The Brazilian Coffee Industry and the First Valorization Scheme of 1906–07." Master's thesis, University of Wisconsin. Madison, 1971.

Hollowood, Bernard. The Story of Morro Velho. London, 1955.

Hudson de Abranches, Sérgio Henrique. "O processo legislativo; conflito e conciliação na política brasileira." Master's thesis, Universidade de Brasília. Brasília, 1973.

Iglésias, Francisco. "Periodização da história de Minas Gerais," Revista Brasileira de Estudos Políticos, no. 29 (July 1970): 181–94.

————. "Perspectiva da história econômica de Minas Gerais, 1889–1930" (Projeto de pesquisa), Colloques Internationaux du C.N.R.S. no. 543. L'Histoire quantitative du Brésil de 1800 à 1930, n.p. Paris, 1973.

————. Política econômica do govêrno provincial mineiro (1835–1889), Rio, 1958.

Jacob, Rodolfo. Minas Geraes no xx° seculo. Rio, 1911.

James, Herman G. The Constitutional System of Brazil. Washington, D.C., 1923.

José, Oiliam. A abolição em Minas. Belo Horizonte, 1962.

————. Histografia mineira: esboço. Belo Horizonte, 1959.

————. A propaganda republicana em Minas. Belo Horizonte, 1960.

Krasner, Stephen D. "Manipulating International Commodity Markets: Brazilian Coffee Policy, 1906 to 1962," Public Policy, 21, no. 4 (Fall 1973): 493–523.

Krüger Corrêa Mourão, Paulo. História de Belo Horizonte, de 1897 a 1930. Belo Horizonte, 1970.

Lage, Barbosa, Oscar Vidal, Albino Esteves e Lucio d'Avila. Album do municipio de Juiz de Fora (1915). Belo Horizonte, 1915.

Lage de Resende, Maria Efigênia. "Uma interpretação sobre a fundação de Belo Horizonte," Revista Brasileira de Estudos Políticos, 39 (July 1974): 129–61.

Lago, Cel. Laurenio. Supremo Tribunal de Justiça e Supremo Tribunal Federal. Dados biograficos, 1828–1939. Rio, 1940.

Leeds, Anthony. "Brazilian Careers and Social Structure: A Case History and Model," in Dwight B. Heath and Richard N. Adams, eds., Contemporary Cultures and Societies of Latin America. New York, 1965, pp. 379–404.

Legião Liberal Mineira. Esboço de organização aprovado pela 1.ª assembléa legionaria, em 2 de Julho de 1931. Belo Horizonte, 1931.

Leite, Aureliano. São Francisco de Paulo de Ouro-Fino nas Minas Gerais. São Paulo, 1941.

Leite, Mário. Paulistas e mineiros, plantadores de cidades. São Paulo, 1961.

Leloup, Yves. "Tipos de aglomerações e hierarquia das cidades de Minas Gerais," Boletim Mineiro de Geografia, ano III, nos. 4 and 5 (July 1962): 15–28.

————. Les villes du Minas Gerais. Paris, 1970.

Lemarchand, Rene, and Keith Legg. "Political Clientelism and Development, a Preliminary Analysis," *Comparative Politics,* 4 no. 2 (Jan.1972): 149–78.

Lima, Alceu Amoroso. Voz de Minas (ensaio de sociologia regional brasileira). Rio, 1945.

Lima, João. Como vivem os homens que governaram o Brazil. Rio [1924].

Lima, José Augusto de. Augusto de Lima, seu tempo, seus ideais. Rio, 1959.

Lima, Mario de. O bom combate (subsidios para a história de 20 annos de acção social catholica em Minas). Belo Horizonte, 1929.

Lindberg, Leon N., and Stuart A. Scheingold, eds. Regional Integration, Theory and Research. Cambridge, Mass., 1971.

Lobo, Eulalia Maria Lahmeyer, et al. "Evolução dos preços e do padrão de vida no Rio de Janeiro, 1820–1930—resultados preliminares," *Revista Brasileira de Economia,* 25, no. 4 (1971): 235–65.

Lobo, Hélio. Um varão da república, Fernando Lobo; a proclamação do regime em Minas, sua consolidação no Rio de Janeiro. São Paulo, 1937.

Lopes, Américo Ferreira. Notas sobre regimen tributario do Estado de Minas Geraes. . . . Belo Horizonte, 1917.

Love, Joseph L. "An Approach to Regionalism," in Richard Graham and Peter H. Smith, eds. New Approaches to Latin American History. Austin, Tex., 1974, pp. 137–55.

———. Rio Grande do Sul and Brazilian Regionalism, 1882–1930. Stanford, Calif., 1971.

Luz, Nícia Vilela. A luta pela industrialização do Brasil (1808–1930). São Paulo, 1961.

Lyra, Augusto Tavares de. "O senado da República, 1890–1930," *Revista do Instituto de História e Geografia Brasileira,* 210 (Jan.–March 1951): 3–102.

Lyra, João. Cifras e notas (economia e finanças do Brasil). Rio, 1925.

McCann, Frank D., Jr. The Brazilian-American Alliance, 1937–1945. Princeton, N.J., 1973.

Magalhães Godinho, Vanor de. Constituintes brasileiros. Rio, 1934.

Mahar, Dennis John. "Fiscal Federalism in Brazil." Ph.D. dissertation, University of Florida. Gainesville, 1970.

Maia, Aristides de Araujo. "Homestead" (artigos publicados n'O Estado de Minas, de Ouro Preto). Rio, 1896.

Maia, Eduardo Santos. Impressões de viagem de Belmonte a Villa Jequitinhonha. Bahia, 1917.

Mantua, Simão de [pseudonym for Antonio Gomes Carmo]. Figurões vistas por dentro (estudo de psychologia social brasileira). 2 v. São Paulo, 1921.

Martins, Henrique. Lista geral dos bachareis . . . na Faculdade de Direito de Recife desde . . . 1828 até o anno de 1931. Recife, 1931.

Mascarenhas, Nelson Lage. Bernardo Mascarenhas; o surto industrial de Minas Gerais. Rio, 1954.

———. "Tentativas de desmembramento de Minas Gerais," *Revista do Instituto Histórico e Geográfico de Minas Gerais,* 5 (1958): 81–85.

Mata Machado Filho, Aires da. "Vida e política de Francisco Sales," *Revista Brasileira de Estudos Políticos,* 18 (Jan. 1965): 113–32.

Maxwell, Kenneth R. Conflicts and Conspiracies: Brazil and Portugal 1750–1808. New York and London, 1973.

Mello Franco, Virgílio Martins de. Viagens pelo interior de Minas Geraes e Goyaz. Rio, 1888.

Melo Franco, Afonso Arinos de. A alma do tempo, memórias (formação e mocidade). Rio, 1961.

———. Um estadista da república (Afrânio de Melo Franco e seu tempo). 3 v. Rio, 1955.

———. Rodrigues Alves; apogeu e declínio do presidencialismo. 2 v. Rio, 1973.

[Mendes Pimentel, Francisco.] O conflicto de 18 de novembro na Universidade de Minas Geraes; tres annos de reitorado o inquerito policial e o processo criminal. Belo Horizonte, 1931.

Menezes, Furtado de. Clero Mineiro. 2 v. Rio, 1933.

Minas Gerais. Annaes, 1891–1927. Camara dos Deputados, Congresso.

———. Annaes, 1891–94. Senado.

———. Annaes do congresso das municipalidades mineiras reunido em Bello Horizonte de 3 a 10 de junho de 1923. Belo Horizonte, 1924.

———. Annuario estatistico de Minas Geraes. Anno II (1922–25). Directoria Geral de Estatistica. Belo Horizonte, 1929.

———. Annuario estatistico de Minas Geraes, 1921. Anno I. 4 v. Serviço de Estatistica Geral. Belo Horizonte, 1925–26.

———. Annuario industrial, 1937. Directoria Geral de Estatistica. Belo Horizonte, 1938.

———. Balanço de tabellas de 1891–94 (with tables for the period 1880–81 to 1891). Contadoura do Thesouro do Estado. Ouro Preto, n.d.

———. Diagnóstico da economia mineira. 6 v. Banco de Desenvolvimento de Minas Gerais. Belo Horizonte, 1968.

———. Finanças do Estado de Minas Gerais, Período Republicano, 1890–1953. Secretaria das Finanças. Belo Horizonte, 1954.

———. Leis mineiras. Belo Horizonte, 1894– .

———. Minas e o bicentenário do café no Brasil, 1727–1927. Secretaria de Agricultura. Belo Horizonte, 1929.

———. Minas segundo o recenseamento de 1920; principaes resultos. . . . Serviço de Estatistica Geral. Belo Horizonte, 1924.

———. Plano de recuperação econômica e fomento da produção. 1, Exposição. Belo Horizonte, 1947.

———. Relatório (occasional use). Secretaria de Agricultura.

———. Relatório, 1891–1938 (systematic survey). Secretaria das Finanças.

———. Relatório (occasional use). Secretaria do Interior.

Mirando, Salm de. Rio Doce (Impressões de uma época). Rio, 1941.

Monteiro, Fernando. Figuras do Banco do Brasil. Cadernos da Associação Atlética Banco do Brasil no. 8. Rio, 1955.

Moody's Manual of Investments, 1930. v. 4. New York, 1930.

Moog, Clodomiro Vianna. Uma interpretação da literatura brasileira. Rio, 1943.

Moraes, Aurino. Minas na Allianca Liberal e na revolução. 2d ed. Belo Horizonte, 1933.

"Morro Velho," *Revista Industrial de Minas Geraes,* 5, no. 36 (Dec. 30, 1897, special issue): 156–72.

Murilo de Carvalho, José. "A composição social dos partidos políticos imperiais," *Cadernos do Departamento de Ciência Política,* no. 2 (Dec. 1974): 1–34.

———. "A Escola de Minas de Ouro Preto: Crepúsculo de uma grande obra?" Manuscript, 1976.

———. "Barbacena: a família, a política e uma hipótese," *Revista Brasileira de Estudos Políticos,* 20 (Jan. 1966): 153–93.

———. "Elite and State-Building in Imperial Brazil." Ph.D. dissertation, Stanford University. Stanford, Calif., 1974.

Nabuco, Carolina. A vida de Virgílio de Melo Franco. Rio, 1962.

Nava, Pedro. Balão cativo: memórias, 2. Rio, 1973.

———. Baú de ossos: memórias. 2d ed. Rio, 1973.

Neiva, Arthur, and Belisario Penna. "Viagem cientifica pelo norte da Bahia, sudoeste de Pernambuco e do norte a sul de Goiaz," *Memorias do Instituto Oswaldo Cruz,* 8 (1916), no. 3: 74–224.

Nielson, Lawrence James "Of Gentry, Peasants, and Slaves: Rural Society in Sabará and its Hinterland, 1780–1930." Ph.D. dissertation, University of California. Davis, 1975.

Nunes Leal, Victor. Coronelismo, enxada e voto; o município e o regime representativo no Brasil. Rio, 1948.

Odum, Howard W., and Harry Estill Moore. American Regionalism; A Cultural-Historical Approach to National Integration. New York, 1938.

Oliveira, Monsenhor Alypio Odier de. Traços biographicos de Dom Silverio Gomes Pimenta no centenário do seu nascimento; 1840–1940. São Paulo, 1940.

Oliveira, Estevam de. Notas e epístolas: páginas esparsas da campanha civilista. Juiz de Fora, 1911.

Oliveira, Martins de. Historia da literatura mineira. Belo Horizonte, 1958.

Oliveira, Paulino de. História de Juiz de Fora. 2d ed. Juiz de Fora, 1966.

Oliveira Torres, João Camilo de. A formação do federalismo no Brasil. São Paulo, 1961.

———. História de Minas Gerais, 5. Belo Horizonte, n.d.

Oliveira Vianna, F. V. Populações meridionais do Brasil. Rio, 1922.

———. Problemas de política objectiva. Rio, 1930.

Palazzolo, Jacinto de. Nas selvas dos Vale do Mucuri e do Rio Dore; como surgiu a cidade de Itambacuri fundada por Frei Serafim de Gorizia. . . . 1873–1944. 2d ed. São Paulo, 1952.

Palmério, Mário. Vila dos Confins. Rio, 1949.

Pang, Eul Soo. "The Politics of Coronelismo in Brazil: The Case of Bahia, 1889–1930." Ph.D. dissertation, University of California. Berkeley, 1970.

———. "The Revolt of the Bahian Coronéis and the Federal Intervention of 1929," *Luso-Brazilian Review,* 8, no. 2 (Dec. 1971): 3–25.

Passos Maia [Dr. Domiciano A.]. Guapé: reminiscencias. Rio, 1933.

Paula, Hermes de. Montes Claros; sua história, sua gente e seus costumes. Rio, 1957.

Pavão, Ary. Arthur Bernardes e o Brasil. Rio, 1931.

Pedrosa, Dr. Manoel Xavier de Vasconcellos. "A zona silenciosa da historiografia mineira. A zona da mata," *Revista do Instituto Histórico e Geográfico do Brasil*, 9, no. 257 (Oct.–Dec. 1962): 122–62.

Peláez, Carlos Manuel. "Análise econômica do programa brasileiro de sustenção do café—1906–1945: teoria, política e medição," *Revista Brasileira de Economia*, 25, no. 4 (Oct.–Dec. 1971): 5–211.

————. "Itabira Iron and the Export of Brazil's Iron Ore," *Revista Brasileira de Economia*, 24, no. 4 (Oct.–Dec. 1970): 157–74.

Penna, Belisario. Minas e Rio Grande do Sul, estado da doença, estado da saúde. Rio, 1918.

Pequeno, Waldemar. Um advogado aí pelos sertões, memórias. Belo Horizonte, 1966.

Pereira Brasil, Raymundo. Minas na grandeza do Brasil. Belo Horizonte, 1936.

Pereira da Silva, Gastão. Constituintes de 46; dados biográficos. Rio, 1947.

Pimenta, Dermeval José. Implantação da grande siderurgia em Minas Gerais. Belo Horizonte, 1967.

————. A mata do Peçanha, sua história e sua gente. Belo Horizonte, 1966.

Pires, Aurelio. Homens e factos do meu tempo. São Paulo, 1939.

Pontes, Hildebrando de Araujo. História de Uberaba e a civilização do Brasil Central. Uberaba, 1970.

Prates, Carlos. A lavoura e industria da Zona da Matta, Relatorio. Belo Horizonte, 1906.

Rache, Pedro. Homens de Minas. Rio, 1947.

————. Outros homens de Minas. Rio, 1948.

Rebelo, Marques [pseudonym for Eddy Dias da Cruz]. Suite n. 1. Rio, 1944.

Rebelo Horta, Cid. "Famílias governamentais de Minas Gerais," in Segundo Seminário de Estudos Mineiros, Universidade de Minas Gerais. Belo Horizonte, 1956, pp. 45–91.

"Representantes de Minas Geraes (Eleitos de 1821 a 1896). . . ." *Revista do Arquivo Publico Mineiro*, ano 1 (1896): 23–95, 397.

Ribeiro, Leonidio. Afrânio Peixoto. Rio, 1950.

Ribeiro, Marly Martinez. "Revisão constitucional de 1926," *Revista de Ciência Política*, 1, no. 4 (Oct.–Dec. 1967): 65–114.

Riveira, Bueno de, ed. Pioneiros e exponentes de Minas Gerais. Belo Horizonte, 1970–71.

Rodrigues, Lêda Boechat. Historia do Supremo Tribunal Federal. 2 v. Rio, 1965, 1968.

Rollim, Monsenhor Conego Francisco Xavier de Almeida. Ephemerides curvellanas (1706–1935), fasciculo I (janeiro, fevereiro e março). Belo Horizonte, 1937.

Romeiro, Manoel Olympio. São Paulo e Minas na economia nacional. São Paulo, 1930.

Sá, Carlos, et al. Francisco Sá; Reminiscencias biographicas. São Paulo, 1938.

Sá Pires, Gudesteu de. Historia administrativa e judiciaria de Minas Geraes; organização politica do Estado e do Municipio. Belo Horizonte, 1922.

Salles, Joaquim de. Se não me falha a memória (políticos e jornalistas do meu tempo). Rio, 1960.

Sampaio, Theodoro Fernandes. O Rio do S. Francisco, trechos de um diario de viagem e a Chapada Diamantina. . . . 1879–80. São Paulo, 1905.

Senna, Caio Nélson de. João Pinheiro da Silva; sua vida, sua obra, sua exemplo. Belo Horizonte, 1941.

Senna, Nelson Coelho de. Annuario de Minas Geraes, anno 1–6. 6 v. in 7. Belo Horizonte, 1906–18.

———. Chorographia de Minas Geraes. Geographia do Brasil, vol. 15 in series. Rio, 1922.

———. A terra mineira, 2d ed., 2 v. Belo Horizonte, 1926.

Schulz, John. "The Brazilian Army and Politics." Ph.D. dissertation, Princeton University. Princeton, N.J., 1974.

Schwartzman, Simon. "Regional Cleavages and Political Patrimonialism in Brazil." Ph.D. dissertation, University of California. Berkeley, 1973.

Silva, Celson José da. "Marchas e contramarchas do mandonismo local (Caeté-um estudo do caso)." Master's thesis, Universidade Federal de Minas Gerais. Belo Horizonte, 1972.

Silva, Hélio. O ciclo de Vargas, v. 4–9. Rio, 1966–    .

Silva, Moacir M. F. Geografia dos transportes no Brasil. Rio, 1949.

Silva, Moacir, and Magalhães Fernandes. Kilometro zero; Caminhos antigos, estradas modernas, rodovias cariocas. Irradiação rodoviária do Rio de Janeiro. Rio, 1934.

Silva Neves, Antonio da. Chorographia do município de Boa Vista do Tremendal. (Escripta especialmente para o Album Ilustrado de Minas). Belo Horizonte, 1908.

Silveira, Victor. Minas Geraes em 1925. Belo Horizonte, 1926.

Singer, Paul Israel. Desenvolvimento ecnômico e evolução urbana: análise da evolução econômica de São Paulo, Blumenau, Pôrto Alegre, Belo Horizonte e Recife. São Paulo, 1968.

Siqueira, Edmundo. Resumo histórico de "The Leopoldina Railway Company Ltd." Rio, 1938.

Siqueira, Moema Miranda de. "Elites políticas em Minas Gerais," Revista Brasileira de Estudos Políticos, no. 29 (July 1970): 173–79.

Skidmore, Thomas E. Black into White; Race and Nationality in Brazilian Thought. New York, 1974.

Soares, José de Souza. Minas-Geraes. Rio, 1931.

Souza, Maria do Carmo Campbello de. "O processo político-partidário na primeira República," in Carlos Guilherme Mota, ed., Brasil em perspectiva. Sao Paulo, 1969, pp. 163–226.

Souza, Elza Coelho de. "Distribuição das propriedades rurais no estado de Minas Gerais," Revista Brasileira de Geografia, 13, no. 1 (Jan.–March 1951): 47–70.

Souza, D. Joaquim Silverio de. Vida de D. Silverio Gomes Pimenta. São Paulo, 1927.

Stein, Stanley. The Brazilian Cotton Manufacture; Textile Enterprise in an Underdeveloped Area, 1850–1950. Cambridge, Mass., 1957.

Stein, Stanley J., and Barbara H. Stein. The Colonial Heritage of Latin America; Essays on Economic Dependence in Perspective. New York, 1970.

Strauch, Ney. A zona metalúrgica de Minas Gerais e Vale do Rio Doce. Rio, 1958.

Tarrow, Sidney G. Peasant Communism in Southern Italy. New Haven, 1967.
Taunay, Affonso d'E. História do café no Brasil. 15 v. Rio, 1939–43.
Teixeira, Edvar Nazario, ed. Album Catholico do Estado de Minas Geraes, 1918–1923. Rio, 1922.
Trinidade, Raymundo Octavio da. Velhos troncos mineiros. 3 v. São Paulo, 1955.
Union des Associations Internationaux. Les congrès internationaux de 1900 à 1919. Liste complete. Bruxelles, 1964.
Valladão, Alfredo. A campanha da princesa. 4 v. Rio, 1937–45.
Valladares, Benedicto. Política e administração. Rio, 1947.
———. Tempos idos e vividos. Memórias. Rio, 1966.
Valladares, Francisco. "Questões debatidas sobre competencia tributaria. Impostes inter-estadoaes," in Livro do Centenario da Camara dos Deputados (1826–1926), II. Rio, 1926, pp. 281–307.
Valverde, Orlando. "Estudo regional da Zona da Mata, de Minas Gerais," Revista Brasileira de Geografia, ano XX, no. 1 (Jan.–May 1958): 3–82.
Vasconcellos, Sylvio de. Mineiridade, ensaio de caracterização. Belo Horizonte, 1968.
Veiga, João Pedro da. Estudo economico e financeiro sobre o Estado de São Paulo. São Paulo, 1896.
Veiga, José Pedro Xavier da. Ephemerides mineiras, 1664–1897. 4 vols. Ouro Preto, 1926.
———. "A imprensa em Minas-Geraes, 1807–1937," Revista do Arquivo Publico Mineiro, Anno III (1898): 169–249.
Velho Sobrinho, J. F. Dicionário bio-biográfico brasileiro. 2 v. Rio, 1940.
Vianna, Nelson. Foiceiros e vaqueiros. Rio, 1956.
Vianna, Urbino de Sousa. Montes Claros; breves apontamentos historicos, geographicos e descriptivos. Belo Horizonte, 1916.
Vieira de Rezende e Silva, Arthur, and Astolpho Vieira de Rezende. "O municipio de Cataguazes, esboço historico," in Revista do Arquivo Publico Mineiro, 13 (1909): 641–1028.
Walle, Paul. Au Brésil. État de Minas Gerais. Paris, 1912.
Weiner, Myron. "National Integration vs. Nationalism: Review Article," Comparative Studies in Society and History, 15 (March 1973): 248–54.
———. "Political Integration and Political Development," The Annals, 358 (March 1965): 52–64.
Wells, James W. Exploring and Travelling Three Thousand Miles Through Brazil, from Rio de Janeiro to Maranhao. 2 v. London, 1886.
Werneck, Americo. Reforma do Systema tributario. Belo Horizonte, 1899.
Willems, Emilio. Cunha; tradição e transição em uma cultura rural do Brasil. São Paulo, 1947.
Williams, Margaret Todaro. "The Politicization of the Brazilian Catholic Church; The Catholic Electoral League," Journal of Interamerican Studies and World Affairs, 16, no. 3 (Aug. 1974): 301–25.
Williamson, Jeffrey G. "Regional Inequality and the Process of National Development: A Description of the Patterns," Economic Development and Cultural Change, 13, no. 4, part II (July 1965): 1–84.
Wirth, John D. The Politics of Brazilian Development, 1930–1954. Stanford, Calif., 1970.

# Index

Abolition, economic effect of, 34–35, 271

Academia Mineira de Letras, 84

Agricultural, Commercial, and Industrial Congress (1903), 38–39, 51, 55, 194, 271f, 274f

Agricultural Association, 122, 147

Agricultural colonies, 15f

Agriculture: productivity of, compared to São Paulo, 1, 7, 31, 32, 33 table; by zone, 4–7; basic condition of, 6–7; sharecropping system, 36–37; failure of diversification, 44–45; agricultural credit, 56–57, 275; necessity for political involvement of farm interests, 122–23, 291; fairs, 195. *See also* Coffee industry; Fazendeiros

Agriculture Minister, federal, list of titularies, 258

Agriculture Secretary, state, list of titularies, 250

Aleixo, Pedro, 80, 114, 257, 259

Alkmim, José Maria de, 179, 249

Alves, Honorato, 161ff

Alves, João José, 161–62, 163, 257

Alves, João Luís, 44, 52, 172, 221; career, 159–160; offices held, 250, 255, 257, 259

Alvim, Cesário de Faria, 99–102, 124, 136, 152f, 162, 191, 273; railroad policy, 59–60; election as governor, 101, 137; revolt against, 101–2, 188, 279; offices held, 248, 257f

Alvim, Ildefonso, 279

Amazonas State, 171

Anarchism, xv, 126

Andrada, Antonio Carlos Ribeiro de, 110ff, 116, 123, 134, 139, 160f, 196, 283; and religious instruction, 91; offices held, 110, 175, 248, 250f, 256ff, 259f; and Legion of October, 112; in PP, 114, 155; regional power base, 119; and tax reform, 121, 222; and Mineiro role in federal congress, 170

Andrada, José Bonifácio de, 179, 251, 256, 260, 283

Andrade, Mário de, 193n

Andrade Botelho, Francisco de, 157, 159

Anglo Frigorífico Co., 46, 48

Angra dos Reis (Rio de Janeiro State), 54

Anjos, Cyro dos, 66ff, 74f, 85, 276

Anti-Semitism, 95

Araguari (Triângulo), 25 table, 26

Aranha, Oswaldo, 112ff, 188n

Argentina, "congress phenomenon" in, 192, 290

Army, federal, 97, 102, 113, 186, 190; anti-militarist tradition in Minas, 189; strength of, in relation to state militias, 191–92

Assis Barbosa, Francisco de, 110n, 141, 181

Associação Commercial, Industrial e Rural (Uberaba), 83